HASHTAG ACTIVISM
INTERROGATED AND EMBODIED

HASHTAG ACTIVISM INTERROGATED AND EMBODIED

Case Studies on Social Justice Movements

EDITED BY
MELISSA AMES AND KRISTI MCDUFFIE

UTAH STATE UNIVERSITY PRESS
Logan

© 2023 by University Press of Colorado

Published by Utah State University Press
An imprint of University Press of Colorado
1624 Market Street, Suite 226
PMB 39883
Denver, Colorado 80202-1559

All rights reserved

   The University Press of Colorado is a proud member of the Association of University Presses.

The University Press of Colorado is a cooperative publishing enterprise supported, in part, by Adams State University, Colorado State University, Fort Lewis College, Metropolitan State University of Denver, University of Alaska Fairbanks, University of Colorado, University of Denver, University of Northern Colorado, University of Wyoming, Utah State University, and Western Colorado University.

ISBN: 978-1-64642-440-5 (hardcover)
ISBN: 978-1-64642-317-0 (paperback)
ISBN: 978-1-64642-318-7 (ebook)
https://doi.org/10.7330/9781646423187

Library of Congress Cataloging-in-Publication Data
Names: Ames, Melissa, 1978– editor. | McDuffie, Kristi, 1981– editor.
Title: Hashtag activism interrogated and embodied : case studies on social justice movements / edited by Melissa Ames and Kristi McDuffie.
Description: Logan : Utah State University Press, [2023] | Includes bibliographical references and index.
Identifiers: LCCN 2022040066 (print) | LCCN 2022040067 (ebook) | ISBN 9781646424405 (hardcover) | ISBN 9781646423170 (paperback) | ISBN 9781646423187 (epub)
Subjects: LCSH: Hashtags (Metadata)—Case studies. | Social media and society—Case studies. | Social justice—Case studies. | Social movements—Case studies.
Classification: LCC P302.37 .H37 2023 (print) | LCC P302.37 (ebook) | DDC 361.201/4—dc23/eng/20221123
LC record available at https://lccn.loc.gov/2022040066
LC ebook record available at https://lccn.loc.gov/2022040067

Cover photographer credits (left to right). Top: Kalea Morgan; Rene Bernal; Stephanie Valencia. Middle: Li-An Lim; Clay Banks; Jeppe Mønster. Bottom: Joseph Chan; Gayatri Malhotra; Jannes Van den wouwer. All photographs from Unsplash.com.

To the hashtag activists who work tirelessly to bring visibility to victims of injustice.

CONTENTS

Foreword: The Significance of Hashtag Activism in This Political Moment
   André Brock   ix

Acknowledgments   xiii

Introduction: Redefining Hashtag Activism
   Melissa Ames and Kristi McDuffie   3

SECTION I: INTERSECTIONS BETWEEN ONLINE AND EMBODIED ACTIVISM

1. Networked Intervention and the Emergence of #BostonHelp
   Megan McIntyre   21

2. Sticky Hashtags: The Role of Emotions and Affect in Hashtag Activism
   Salma Kalim   38

3. Affecting Digital Activism: Comparative Study of Tweets from the March for Our Lives Rallies and Women's Marches
   Melissa Ames and Kristi McDuffie   52

SECTION II: (RE)EXAMINING SOCIETAL NARRATIVES THROUGH HASHTAG ACTIVISM

4. #iLookLikeAnEngineer: Women Reclaiming STEM through Hashtag Activism
   Holly M. Wells   75

5. The Ideograph and the #Pussyhat: Multimodal Rhetorics of Brevity in the Women's March
   Sarah Riddick   100

6. Imagi(ni)ng Radicalism in the Context of Indian Student Activism: The Discursivity of Hashtags and Memes
   Avishek Ray and Neha Gupta   119

SECTION III: FAN CULTURE AND DIGITAL ACTIVISM

7. Wake Up Mr. West: Kanye West, the Sunken Place, and the Rhetoric of Black Twitter
   Kyesha Jennings   139

8. Lexa Deserved Better: How One Character's Death Sparked a Revolution and Changed Media Representation for the LGBTQ+ Community
   Erin B. Waggoner   158

9. Constructing Digital Diasporic Spaces and Reframing Black Masculinity through *Insecure*'s #LawrenceHive
   Robert Barry Jr.   175

SECTION IV: INTERRUPTIONS AND INTERPRETATIONS OF DIGITAL ACTIVISM

10. Meme Warfare and Fake Hashtag Activism: 4chan's Alt-right Trolling Culture
    Jeffrey J. Hall   193

11. A Rhetoric of Zaniness: Trolling, the Alt-right, and Pepe the Frog
    Sean Milligan   210

12. Who's the #FakeHistorian? The Rhetoric of #FakeHistory among Conservative (Counter)Publics on Twitter
    Anonymous   227

13. Digital Matters: Twitter Reacts and Hashtivist Narratives
    Gabriel I. Green and Morgan K. Johnson   246

    Conclusion: Capturing a Moving Target: Ethical Research Practices for Hashtag Activism
    Elizabeth Buchanan, Rosemary Clark-Parsons, Stephanie Vie, William I. Wolff, and Kristi McDuffie   260

    Index   285
    About the Authors   291

FOREWORD

The Significance of Hashtag Activism in this Political Moment

André Brock

I've been thinking about hashtags for a long time, even if I've never published on them specifically. I once wrote offhandedly—as I tend to do—that hashtags should be understood as a signifier, as a sign, and as the signified: "marking as it does the concept to be signified, the cultural context within which the tweet should be understood, and the 'call' awaiting a response" (Brock 2012, 537). I wrote these words before Trayvon Martin's murder at the hands of George Zimmerman and the associated social media posts of celebrities and entertainers wearing hoodies to show solidarity; before the iconic Instagram photos of protests in Ferguson and the rise of Black Lives Matter as an organization and an online movement. While I was aware of this nascent Black social media activism, at the time I saw it only as an expansion of earlier digital mediations like Black bloggers' efforts to promote organizing around injustices, such as the lynch mob charges against the six boys in Jena, Louisiana, or the jailing of young Shaquanda Cotton for "insubordination" to her teacher.

I have, however, paid attention to how online activism has been argued for and against over the last half decade. From the earliest online insults about keyboard warriors to the more modern social justice warriors, digital libidinal practices in support of activism have rarely been understood as effective or practical. These critiques rested on digital dualist perspectives that (1) digital practitioners should always and only be rational and logical rather than emotional and (2) online activities are distinct and separate from offline life. One of the most infamous critiques, issued by Malcolm Gladwell (2010), was that only activists with "boots on the ground" were *real* activists. Somehow, the lowering of barriers to information and access to advanced computational tools didn't translate to expanded understandings of what activism could be.

This collection rebukes, rebuts, and brilliantly inquires into the possibilities of computational activism. The authors within illuminate the hashtag's digital capture of rhetorical exigency around sociopolitical and sociocultural moments and patterns of engagement around issues vital to the participants. I particularly appreciate this collection's attention to anti-activism hashtags but also to the libidinal pleasures of fandom hashtag movements. Across these studies, the researchers reveal that these online activist movements can be understood as intersectional thanks to the hashtag's collation and elevation of diverse voices not limited by geography, time, or community of practice, lending a new valence to the concept of intersectionality.

I first became aware of the racial valences of hashtag activism by encountering Tara L. Conley's (then a Columbia PhD student) website of the same name in 2013. Dr. Conley built the website in response to Twitter practices she observed following the brutal murder of Renisha McBride by a Detroit homeowner when seeking help after a car crash. She published on the concept in *Feminist Media Studies*, exploring how hashtags worked to counteract the slow media coverage and response to this tragedy thanks to advocacy efforts by individuals and organizations like Color of Change, which garnered support with the #RememberRenisha hashtag (Conley 2014). Similarly, Sherri Williams (2015) expanded the concept of Black feminist hashtag activism, noting that the 1968 Kerner Commission's finding that mainstream media failed to show the complexities and realities of Black life has been ameliorated by Black feminist use of social media to cover Black women's issues.

These articles and several others build upon my research on Black Twitter to ground their analyses of the hashtag. It wasn't until 2020, in *Distributed Blackness: African American Cybercultures*, that I revisited and expanded on my claim of triple signifier for the quotidian electronic discourse convention of the hashtag. For the hashtag *is* quotidian now; it was not when I started researching Twitter in 2009. As part of our everyday communicative practice, hashtags have become the province of influencers, of political campaigns, of brands, and specifically of activist organizations and movements. By naming them as quotidian, I do not mean to understate their importance, no more than I would say that a crosswalk is a banal part of crossing a busy thoroughfare. For hashtags provide a similar function: they orient us to a phenomenon worth paying attention to.

My original conceptualization of the hashtag specifically referred to Black Twitter and Black discursive identity. But meaning making is a human activity, and the strategies I argued for as Black digital discourses can apply to others' usage of it as well. So, in addition to my original arguments for hashtags as a triple signifier, I have gradually theorized hashtag use—particularly for activist movements—from a libidinal economic perspective. By this I mean that hashtags, through their call and response affordance, collate and expand upon the visceral, cathartic energies of everyday digital practitioners. While a celebrity endorsement may grow a particular hashtag's audience, it is the participation and libidinal investment of mundane social media users that propel these peculiar phrases. Their engagement—through hashtagged posts, quote tweets including the hashtags, and even likes and shares/retweets—is the crucial libidinal element for hashtag activism, as it marks an informational collectivity (if not consensus) determined to exercise their will through digital participation and performance. They do so in a way that goes far beyond the sentence-level affect of emoticons, in the process nearly approximating the reach of viral memes or videos while providing a moral vector seeking to make the world a better place. While this libidinal economy can be expressed for ill, such as by QAnon and other far-right radicals, the use of the quotidian hashtag as an element for social change can be appreciated for good as well. The chapters to follow do a most excellent job of showing just how crucial the research on these online movements is to understand our past, our present, and our future.

REFERENCES

Brock, André. 2012. "From the Blackhand Side: Twitter as a Cultural Conversation." *Journal of Broadcasting and Electronic Media* 56 (4): 529–549.

Brock, André. 2020. *Distributed Blackness: African American Cybercultures.* New York: New York University Press.

Conley, Tara L. 2014. "From #RenishaMcBride to #RememberRenisha: Locating Our Stories and Finding Justice." *Feminist Media Studies* 14 (6): 1111–1113.

Gladwell, Malcolm. 2010. "Small Change: Why the Revolution Will Not Be Tweeted." *New Yorker,* September 27. https://www.newyorker.com/magazine/2010/10/04/small-change-malcolm-gladwell.

Williams, Sherri. 2015. "Digital Defense: Black Feminists Resist Violence with Hashtag Activism." *Feminist Media Studies* 15 (2): 341–344.

ACKNOWLEDGMENTS

First, we would like to acknowledge the creative and courageous work being done by individuals who are fighting for social justice every day through hashtag activism. We hope that this collection highlights and exemplifies this vital work. Next, we are excited that the University Press of Colorado / Utah State University Press is publishing this collection on hashtag activism. As digital writing scholars, we are invested in cross-disciplinary dialogue about the ways twenty-first-century technology and communication practices impact our everyday lived existences and the larger cultural systems we all navigate through. We would like to thank Rachael Levay who enthusiastically championed this manuscript and the entire editorial team who helped see it through to publication. Special thanks to Elizabeth Matresse, Meg Cole, and Suzanne Valentine as well for their editorial work on this manuscript. And, of course, we extend our thanks to the authors who contributed to this volume. Their unique case studies highlight not only the many ways activism is enacted in digital spaces but also the diverse ways scholars from various fields analyze the impact of this ever-evolving online engagement. Finally, we would each like to individually acknowledge friends, family, and colleagues for their support as we pursued this project. We are only as strong as our support systems, and we are fortunate to have such excellent ones in place.

FROM MELISSA

I would like to thank Eastern Illinois University for its support and the English department specifically. I work alongside incredible, talented, thoughtful colleagues and for a terrific supervisor, our department chair, Angela Vietto, who supports our efforts to be both engaged scholars and teachers. Particular thanks to the colleagues who collaborate regularly with me on teaching and service tasks or who chat with me about scholarly projects I attempt to accomplish between the two: Randall Beebe, Donna Binns, Melissa Caldwell, Tim Engles, Terri Fredrick, Jeannie Ludlow, Elizabeth Tacke, Tim Taylor, Chris Wixson, and Marjorie Worthington.

Second, as much of the collection explores the ways identity and community are formed in both offline and online spaces, I would like to thank my many friends and communities outside of work—from the friends I still retain from childhood, teenage jobs, graduate school, and early teaching posts to the ones I've made as I've taken on my various motherhood-inspired identities (e.g., PTA Rockstar, Dance Mom). Being that this book was edited and sent off to press during the height of a global pandemic, the ways online technology and communication can strengthen relationships were never more apparent to me. So, for all those individuals who logged on for Facebook Messenger cocktail hours, Zoom game nights, online book clubs, and Facetime catch-up sessions: thank you for proving that friendships can endure time, distance, and even quarantine.

Third, I would like to thank my family, especially my daughters, McKinley and Madison, who often have to coax me away from my office computer to take breaks from work. I hope the social justice work being done today makes your future world a better place. And I hope your generation is able to fix anything mine or the ones before it damaged.

And last but not least, I would like to thank my co-editor, Kristi McDuffie. I am forever grateful that our personal and professional paths crossed at EIU. I wouldn't be the person or scholar I am today without your influence in my life. In terms of the latter, I credit you with my shift into the field of composition and rhetoric, as well as my interest in multimodal composition, digital activism, and research methodology. I am glad you came up with the idea to study tweets from the Women's March in 2017, the study that would start us down the path to this collection. I've enjoyed our years of collaborating on various projects, traveling to academic conferences, working alongside each other at our local coffee shop, and talking shop while socializing and raising our children together. I look forward to the future projects and adventures we will take on in the years to come.

FROM KRISTI

My largest thank you for this project goes to my co-editor and the best friend I never expected to make in my adult life, Melissa Ames. Although I have long since been dedicated to social justice and enamored with technology, it is Melissa who lights a fire under me to publish. I spend most of my working hours on writing program administration and the rest of my waking hours on PTA activities, but you ask a busy woman how to get stuff done and Melissa will make it happen.

I am also grateful to my supportive family. My husband listens to my stories and complaints and cooks dinner every night. My mother is a godsend who raised me to be an ambitious woman and now watches my children more than I do. And to those children—much of this work is inspired by you. I am desperate for a society that will view you as more than Black men and me as more than their white mom. I long for a past that didn't whitewash my Mexican heritage out of my family culture. I hope for a future that truly embodies intersectionality and individuality and have faith that our networked practices will be a major thoroughfare that will drive, reveal, and complicate that journey.

HASHTAG ACTIVISM
INTERROGATED AND EMBODIED

Introduction
REDEFINING HASHTAG ACTIVISM

Melissa Ames and Kristi McDuffie

In early 2020, it seemed as though the COVID-19 pandemic was the biggest emergency facing the United States. By late March, most states had their residents on stay-at-home orders and millions of people were navigating their new circumstances, such as working from home, working in unsafe conditions, or not working at all. But as the summer months approached, many Americans were drawing attention to another ongoing threat. News outlets and social media reported (yet again) on a number of unthinkable killings of African Americans, many at the hands of law enforcement. In February 2020, Ahmaud Arbery was shot down by white men in Georgia while running. In March 2020, Breonna Taylor was shot in Louisville by police officers when they entered her home on a warrant in the middle of the night. In May 2020, George Floyd was killed in Minneapolis when a police officer kneeled on his neck for over eight minutes. By early June, the Black Lives Matter movement—both its Twitter movement #BlackLivesMatter and in-person marches and gatherings—resurged into the largest social justice movement in US history (Buchanan, Bui, and Patel 2020). Tens of millions of people protested the killing of George Floyd, including half a million in 550 places on June 6 alone (2020). In the months since, both violence against African Americans and demonstrations in response to it have continued across the US, with protests in cities like Kenosha, Wisconsin, and Portland, Oregon, erupting in even more violence. This social justice activism has made inroads in a variety of ways, but its long-term outcomes remain to be determined. What is clear, however, is that the accomplishments and visibility of Black Lives Matter are largely possible through #BlackLivesMatter hashtag activism. Since 2013, #BlackLivesMatter has been tweeted more than 30 million times, with a primary focus on police killings of Black Americans (Anderson et al. 2018). By leveraging the affordances of the networked hashtags, activists quickly raised awareness about problematic deaths of African

Americans across the US and drew attention to systematic racism in law enforcement. This hashtag movement has been pivotal in raising awareness about the dangerous racism people of color face every day and in organizing activists to demand change.

In this collection on hashtag activism, contributors investigate the affordances of hashtag activism across different social justice movements and using various methods. Our overall purpose is to demonstrate how hashtag activism has influenced and will continue to shape contemporary social change. Authors in this collection emerge from a variety of disciplines to explore questions of identity, affect, visual rhetoric, language, and more and situate these inquiries within academic areas such as digital rhetoric, feminist theory, internet research ethics, and more. In addition to covering a range of hashtag movements and theoretical frameworks, this collection utilizes a variety of research methods. Many chapters present in-depth cases studies of qualitative hashtag data, while others research hashtags through more theoretical lenses. Ultimately, this collection contributes more than a dozen original investigations into the potentials and pitfalls of hashtag activism as it intersects with people's material lives. An overall outcome of these chapters is an expanded conceptualization of hashtag activism that goes beyond the functional definition of a searchable tag that collects social media posts naming the same social justice movement. This collection defines hashtag activism as inclusive of established social justice movements such as racial and gender equality movements, but it also includes social networked movements that bring attention to other non-normative identities, spaces, and topics where users advocate for social change. Furthermore, this collection establishes anti-activism as an important part of research into hashtag activism. Anti-activism includes a variety of trolling, appropriation, discrediting, and other techniques that disrupt and derail social justice activism. Numerous chapters in this collection demonstrate how anti-activist movements use digital technologies and rhetorical techniques to intervene in social justice goals. By covering these different aspects of hashtag activism, this collection demonstrates the range and power of digital movements in the recent past and reveals implications for the near future.

(SCHOLARLY) LIKES, RETWEETS, AND MENTIONS: ENTERING THE DIALOGUE ON DIGITAL ACTIVISM

While much scholarship has interrogated the affordances and nuances of activism mediated by technology, this collection is focused on hashtag activism as a particular technique, tool, and rhetorical strategy of social justice work. Hashtag activism emerges from the more general digital activism, which is "an organized public effort, making collective claim(s) on a target authority(s), in which civic initiators or supporters use digital media" (Edwards, Howard, and Joyce 2013). Hashtag activism specifically leverages hashtags to engage in social justice work. The hashtag—literally a metadata tag that labels and sorts digital content (Losh 2020, 2)—has been both digitally and rhetorically monumental in shaping contemporary activist landscapes. Hashtag activism usually occurs through Twitter and refers to the use of repeating and circulating hashtags for the purposes of protest, community organizing, and creating social change.

One major area of focus in contemporary scholarship has been on hashtag feminism. Kitsy Dixon (2014) was one of the first scholars to popularize hashtag feminism when she identified the term and discussed the benefits and risks of digital activists identifying themselves as feminists online. Rosemary Clark (2016) applied the term to a movement when she analyzed the ways hashtag feminism becomes a collective movement through the case study of #WhyIStayed (789). Clark found that hashtag feminism, "in its form, content, and production process, empowers its users to take control of the sociocultural narratives associated with their identities and subjective experiences" (798). The way Twitter users can become empowered and take control of problematic narratives has continued to be a common theme in hashtag activism scholarship. In a later study, Clark-Parsons (2019) continued her work on hashtag feminism by investigating user perspectives on #MeToo. She examined how digital activists perform on social media to create social change while simultaneously trying to maintain enough privacy to keep themselves safe.

Research on racial and ethnic identity in social media is also widespread. Before the term *hashtag activism* was coined, scholars were studying Black Twitter, which refers to the community of African Americans using Twitter to connect on issues ranging from politics to TV shows. André Brock (2012) described how Twitter functioned as a cultural outlet for Black Twitter users given Twitter's digital affordances, discursive support for performativity, and connectivity supported by hashtags. These conversations have migrated into targeted investigations of particular hashtags and social movements. Nora Gross (2017), for example, analyzed the way Black youth utilized the #IfTheyGunnedMeDown hashtag to problematize the photos media outlets use of young Black victims of police violence. Sarah J. Jackson (2016) studied the Black

Lives Matter movement within the context of the historical Black Civil Rights movement and argued that #BlackLivesMatter is taking advantage of its networked tools to make intersectional social justice goals more visible, such as insisting on space at white-dominated political rallies and protesting police presence at Pride events.

Yet other studies have considered additional aspects of marginalized identities. Tanja Dreher and colleagues (2016), for example, considered two Indigenous campaigns in Australia, #IdleNoMore and #sosblakaustralia, and determined that while the social media environment enabled more Indigenous voices to be heard, that did not necessarily translate into political bodies listening to the voices and taking them into consideration when making policy. Benjamin W. Mann (2018) examined representations of disabilities in his study of #CripTheVote. Mann argued that social justice movement terminology relies on historical understandings of embodiment and needs to be reassessed for inclusivity for people with different abilities. #CripTheVote was a hashtag movement that aimed to bring more awareness to disability-related issues in American politics, and Mann outlined the ways users leveraged the hashtag to center disability issues within campaigns and to make people with disabilities feel represented and included.

In an example of hashtag activists protesting hegemonic rule in valuing their identities, Sara Liao (2019) studied #IAmGay on Weibo in China as the hashtag responded to a governmental shutdown on homosexual content and found that the hashtag lent itself to storytelling posts through personal narratives. The censorship was soon removed, but the hashtag increased solidarity among LGBTQ groups and with heterosexual users as well and showed how collective action was created. Roughly a quarter of the posts were deleted (2326), probably by the users themselves, demonstrating again that hashtag activism is not without risks, particularly in such a regulated environment. While numerous contributors in this collection have taken up identity issues in hashtag activism, identity formation and performance are not the primary focus, which reflects both the diverse use of hashtag activism in this contemporary moment and our focus on expanding the definition of hashtag activism.

Chapters in this collection utilize and build upon several approaches to and methodologies for studying hashtag activism, beginning with rhetorical studies. An example of foundational work in this area includes Gross's (2017) investigation of #IfTheyGunnedMeDown, which utilizes visual rhetoric to examine Black youth responses. The hashtag emerged after the shooting of Michael Brown and refers to the idea that the media often show unflattering images of Black victims rather than wholesome images. Gross employed a double-consciousness framework to showcase the rhetorical prowess of hashtag activists and noted the limitations placed on users because of the Twitter template. Aqdas Malik and colleagues (2018) also examined the role of visual rhetoric in hashtag activism when they studied a large sample of #iLookLikeAnEngineer tweets to understand the different ways users engage audiences (through text, images, and URLs). They also looked at who participates in the hashtag campaign (whom they call actors) and found that these various facets support the campaign in its success. Rhetoric is a strong theme in our collection, given both the disciplinary backgrounds of many of our contributors as well as the affordances of viewing hashtag activism for the rhetorical strategies utilized by Twitter users and the rhetorical effects on Twitter audiences.

Affect theory is another productive lens through which to consider hashtag activism. For example, Corrina Laughlin (2020) applied affect theory to hashtag activism when she studied Christian female bloggers and the #AmplifyWomen hashtag through an affective public framework. Social media facilitates evangelical women today in rearticulating what it means to be Christian and to rearticulate traditional notions of white patriarchy. Multiple chapters in this collection consider how hashtag activist movements are shaped by affect, including the ways affect circulates through digital publics and the way affective communities are built through online networks (Gong 2014; Dean 2015; Paasonen 2015). These studies add to existing scholarship, such as Sanjay Sharma's (2013) study of Blacktags (racialized hashtags), which connected identity to affect by arguing that racialized identities are discursively constructed by using the hashtags. Affect is one of the main themes addressed in this collection, particularly as theorized through Sara Ahmed's (2014) *The Cultural Politics of Emotion* and Zizi Papacharissi's (2015) *Affective Publics: Sentiment, Technology, and Politics*. These texts, along with the studies described above, set a foundation for the hashtag activism cases in this collection that show how affect functions in depth in particular contemporary hashtag movements.

While the research described so far focuses on issues of identity, representation, and activism, other scholars have examined the material effects of hashtag activism. Sky Croeser and Tim Highfield (2014), for example, analyzed how Twitter was used during the Occupy Oakland movement to understand how much of the movement was place-based and what connections existed between other locations of the Occupy movement. Like many of our contributors in this collection, Croeser and Highfield (2014) found an intricate relationship between online communication and physical places, where users leveraged both spaces for their social justice goals. Carrie A. Rentschler (2017) also demonstrated the ways hashtag activism can have a positive, material effect on people's lives through her study of bystander intervention. Rentschler examined #YouOkSis and #BystanderIntervention for the ways activists raised awareness about street harassment and performed affective witnessing. While online activism is not without risk, it is safer than confronting harassers in person and also reframes the narrative away from punishment and toward a politics of care (578). Rentschler's work thus connects hashtag responses to offline experiences and showcases themes that flow through this collection, including feminist interventions in problematic narratives and the role of affect in creating online collective communities.

Digital activism scholarship has also focused on the question of whether Twitter truly builds community, imagined or otherwise (Chen 2011; Gruzd, Wellman, and Takhteyev 2011). Many of the chapters presented here delve into this debate, some doing so to push the boundaries in terms of what communities and actions are included and excluded in conceptualizations and definitions of activism. For example, those studying fan activism follow in the steps of previous studies such as Apryl Williams and Vanessa Gonlin's (2017) inquiry into Black Twitter's engagement of *How to Get Away with Murder*. Williams and Gonlin conducted a discursive analysis of television viewers' comments on race and gender and argued that these second screening practices enabled a productive technocultural discourse on a shared cultural history of Black womanhood. In a different study, Erin B. Waggoner (2018) analyzed fan hashtag activism responding to a trend of lesbian character deaths on television, which activists called the Bury Your Gays trope. Studying fan responses on Twitter and Tumblr through a communitarian ethics lens, Waggoner showcased how viewers used online platforms to critique LGBTQ media representation. Multiple chapters in this collection take up fan activism specifically and explore the affordances of hashtags as they interact with other media.

While much scholarship about digital activism is focused on activism for equality and justice, there is less scholarship on organized negative online activity related to or opposed to social justice. In this collection, we refer to the negative activity that seeks to interrupt positivity and intervene in social justice as anti-activism. This kind of anti-activism can take on different forms in digital spaces. One common practice for anti-activists is co-opting existing hashtags in an attempt to disrupt dialogue and progress toward social justice. For example, following the debut of Gillette's "The Best a Man Can Be" 2019 Super Bowl commercial, those opposed to the corporation's commentary on toxic masculinity employed Gillette's own hashtag to draw attention to problematic gender norms. Anti-activists also produce their own movements and hashtags. For example, during the COVID-19 health crisis, numerous protests unfolded across the United States to criticize the government's role in legislating public health. While those supporting national and global social distancing practices were circulating tweets with #StayAtHome, groups critical of such mandates tweeted out their own hashtags. One example was #OperationGridlock, a hashtag tied to one of the first COVID-19-related protests to occur in the United States—one that resulted in thousands of citizens on the stairs and streets surrounding Michigan's state capitol building. The most common way anti-hashtag activism occurs is through the rise of counter-hashtags, which serve as foils to specific movements—for example, #AllLivesMatter as a response to #BlackLivesMatter, #NotAllMen as a response to #YesAllWomen, and so forth.

Although there remains a need for additional research in the area of anti-activism, an example of this in existing scholarship is Karen Lumsden and Heather Morgan's (2017) study of victim blaming and silencing strategies employed online. They argued that the advice commonly given to victims of online abuse (i.e., the "do not feed the trolls") perpetuates the sexism and sexual abuse at play in these exchanges. In a different study, Erika M. Sparby (2017) analyzed the ways in- and out-groups within 4chan's /b/ board (notoriously known for aggressive trolling behavior) drew upon their understanding of the site's ethos and collective identity to navigate offensive comments. Her study detailed how two transwomen engaged in the 4chan community with differing levels of success, given the ways they each identified with the community. The final section of this collection draws attention to anti-activist hashtag movements and strategies such as these. By researching problematic digital networking practices that directly engage with and derail digital activism, these chapters expand traditional definitions of hashtag activism beyond its typical association only with progressive causes.

The trends in hashtag activism scholarship outlined in this introduction—while not exhaustive—set the stage for the chapters included in this collection. Different contributors take up various research questions, such as how affect contributes to the efficacy of hashtag activism and how anti-activists leverage networks to spread problematic messages. Authors emerge from a range of disciplines and utilize a variety of methodologies to interrogate the life span and trajectories of specific hashtag campaigns, study rhetorical strategies engaged by online communities, analyze how hashtags are employed for particular purposes, and consider how digital interactions carry over into external spaces and are embodied by participants and spectators alike. Delving into hashtag activism in a variety of forms (tweets, memes, personal narratives) and spaces (Twitter, Facebook, in-person protests), these studies reveal the strategies used by participants to question and construct online and offline identities (and imagined and actualized communities) in order to resist and reclaim societal narratives. They also showcase the complicated ways hashtag activism intersects with consumer culture, popular culture, and celebrity culture. This collection, then, makes a unique contribution to scholarship in digital rhetoric and networked technologies given its breadth and depth of original case studies on hashtag activism. By placing these diverse case studies into conversation with one another, this collection argues for broader inclusion in what is considered hashtag activism. These chapters demonstrate how digital fan tweets, co-opted hashtags, anti-activist political discourse, and media outlet practices all work in tandem with practices such as hashtag feminism and Black Twitter to shape today's social justice movements online. Furthermore, investigations into these practices are happening in an era of constantly evolving ethical concerns. These chapters are produced in an ethical framework that attempts to balance researcher goals and social media users' rights, and the editors were informed by practices recommended through the Ethical Guidelines published by the Association of Internet Researchers (franzke et al. 2020). To highlight the numerous factors influencing decisions scholars make when conducting hashtag activism research, this text contributes a novel conversation dedicated to ethics in a hashtag activist framework to round out and conclude this collection.

EXPANDING HASHTAG ACTIVISM: THE CASE STUDIES AND ORGANIZATION OF THIS COLLECTION

The organization of this collection is designed to support this argument about what defines hashtag activism. The collection is divided into four sections to emphasize different contributions of hashtag activism and build a coherent conversation. The first section, "Intersections between Online and Embodied Activism," considers how hashtag campaigns interact with offline movements, such as how in-person and online protestors created an imagined community in #MarchForOurLives. Together, these chapters analyze the various rhetorical strategies hashtag activists use to accomplish their social justice goals and engage their particular communities. The case studies presented here showcase some of the affective elements that can be employed in social commentary, such as visual play and personal narratives.

In chapter 1, "Networked Intervention and the Emergence of #BostonHelp," Megan McIntyre presents a qualitative analysis of one of the hashtags that emerged in the aftermath of the 2013 Boston Marathon bombing. Because of the location of the blasts and the large numbers of tourists and runners visiting downtown Boston for the marathon, thousands of people were cut off from their belongings, accommodations, and transportation. #BostonHelp was born from conversations online about how to help runners and spectators stranded downtown. McIntyre's analysis reveals two emphases in these tweets: specific, material offers to help stranded people and instances of boundary work, the promotional and definitional behaviors that seek to maintain the hashtag's focus on specific material offers. She argues that these two sets of interventions—both a form of digital activism—are dependent on one another for their relevance and success.

Next, chapter 2 studies a particular aspect of successful digital activism campaigns: the generation and circulation of affect. In "Sticky Hashtags: The Role of Emotions and Affect in Hashtag Activism," Salma Kalim studies the formation of an affective digital public that rose in response to the brutal rape and murder of a seven-year-old girl, Zainab, in the city of Kasur, Pakistan. Kalim theorizes digital texts (hashtags, images, tweets) as sites of emotionality where subjects, objects, and their past histories come into play, leading to the chain of signification. Building on the work of Sara Ahmed (2014), this chapter uses notions of stickiness, blockage, and binding to complicate our understanding of the role of emotions and affect in hashtag activism and argues for tracking hashtags as they circulate and interact with other signs, objects, and events instead of treating them as a fixed repository of feelings and emotions.

Continuing to grapple with the role emotion plays in both online and offline protests, chapter 3 investigates hashtag movements facilitating and supporting the 2017 Women's Marches (which followed the presidential inauguration of Donald Trump) and the 2018 March for Our Lives rallies (which followed the school shooting at Marjory Stoneman Douglas High School in Parkland, Florida), examining the role affect played in their larger activism goals. Through qualitative analysis of thousands of tweets, Melissa Ames and Kristi McDuffie present a comparative study that identifies the most effective rhetorical strategies within the two datasets, attending to recurring affective devices (e.g., personal narrative, imagined communities) and considering their implications for digital rhetoric.

The second section, "(Re)Examining Societal Narratives through Hashtag Activism," takes on traditionally recognized aspects of digital activism where authors interrogate hashtag movements that challenge dominant norms concerning gender, race, and social status. Analyzing a variety of hashtagged dialogue and the ways they intersect with various digital spaces, these chapters reveal how digital activists respond to a variety of cultural issues, such as societal stereotypes and systemic oppression. For example, in chapter 4, "#iLookLikeAnEngineer: Women Reclaiming STEM through Hashtag Activism," Holly M. Wells studies the visual rhetoric of engineers through an analysis of the #iLookLikeAnEngineer social media campaign, which was launched in 2015 as a response to sexism directed at female engineers, and a dataset of photographs collected through the algorithm of Google's Image Search feature. This chapter explores the visual strategies employed by the hashtag activists and considers how both sets of images work to reinforce and reject problematic gender stereotypes that impact women's access to, and success within, STEM fields.

Sarah Riddick continues this focus on the visual rhetoric at play in hashtag activism campaigns in "The Ideograph and the #Pussyhat: Multimodal Rhetorics of Brevity in the Women's March." Chapter 5 focuses specifically on brevity as a multimodal rhetorical strategy and presents a case study analyzing the ways it functions in the Pussyhat Project, a grassroots movement that contributed substantially to the 2017 Women's March on Washington. Riddick argues that the project's rhetorical use of brevity—including and beyond the hashtag "#Pussyhat"—played an essential role in the march's rapid international success and continues to play a role in its ongoing influence. Chapter 6 studies memes (and other digital text) associated with three hashtags—#Hokkolorob, #HandsOffJU, and #SaveJNU—that feature dissenting student politics in contemporary Indian university spaces. Avishek Ray and Neha Gupta study the eliticization of certain universities and the processes through which certain "imagined communities" are framed as radical in these digital dialogues. This study questions how these hashtags enable imaginations of university spaces and attends to how certain kinds of political participation are encouraged/discouraged and which voices are amplified/effaced.

The third section, "Fan Culture and Digital Activism," moves into newer territory by exploring how hashtag activism is affecting other forms of media. The chapters in this section showcase digital activism sparked by popular culture, such as reactions to celebrities and media representation. These case studies highlight how fans use digital tools to protest or support cultural conversation surrounding, or depictions of, race, masculinity, and sexuality. In chapter 7, "Wake Up Mr. West: Kanye West, the Sunken Place, and the Rhetoric of Black Twitter," Kyesha Jennings studies reactions to rap artist Kanye West's public comment that "slavery was a choice." In particular, this chapter studies humorous memes that circulated on Twitter under the satirical hashtag #IfSlaveryWasAChoice. Jennings presents a rhetorical analysis of these tweets that reveals how Black Twitter users employ African American vernacular, creativity, shared in-jokes, and catchphrases through memetic media to offer a viral clap-back that falls within the cultural traditions of signifyin' and that participate in a contemporary form of social activism.

Chapters 8 and 9 turn to activist campaigns tied to television fandom. In "Lexa Deserved Better: How One Character's Death Sparked a Revolution and Changed Media Representation for the LGBTQ+ Community," Erin B. Waggoner studies the #LGBTFansDeserveBetter campaign wherein fans of *The 100* criticized the murder of a queer character, Lexa, who was killed in a common trope called Bury Your Gays. Through a queer theoretical and technological determinist lens, this case study examines how fans used social media to fight for better media representation. Robert Barry Jr. turns to digital conversations concerning media representations of Black masculinity in his chapter, "Constructing Digital Diasporic Spaces and Reframing Black Masculinity through *Insecure*'s #LawrenceHive." Through a case study of fan tweets produced by viewers of HBO's *Insecure* (2016–2018), specifically the hashtag #LawrenceHive, this chapter demonstrates the ways fan engagement can be viewed as a form of activism. In this instance, Barry argues that viewer interactions on social media allowed for therapeutic conversations about Blackness in general and Black masculinity in particular.

The fourth section, "Interruptions and Interpretations of Digital Activism," continues arguing for broader considerations of what counts as activism by including anti-activism efforts that use hashtags to shape—and sometimes derail—social justice movements. These include infiltrating activist dialogues (e.g., to shift conversations and interfere with social justice goals) and framing social justice movements (e.g., strategically curating Twitter narratives to cater to or influence specific communities). In chapter 10, "Meme Warfare and Fake Hashtag Activism: 4chan's Alt-right Trolling Culture," Jeffrey J. Hall presents a case study of 4chan /pol/ threads in 2017 and 2018, analyzing the trolling culture found on this popular anonymous bulletin board associated with the so-called alt-right. Through a combination of online ethnography and qualitative interviews with 4chan, this chapter explores the cultural context in which users engage in meme warfare and the variety of motivations that drive users to fabricate or co-opt hashtag activist campaigns.

Moving from the co-option of campaign to the co-option of cultural figures, chapter 11 studies Pepe the Frog's transformation into a political icon during the 2016 presidential campaign, arguing that it is one of the more blatant examples of the way zaniness has permeated contemporary American culture, particularly in online discourse. Using the framework of zaniness, Sean Milligan analyzes the rhetorical uses of Pepe the Frog memes by the alt-right. Turning to the use of the hashtag #FakeHistory following a 2018 Twitter fight between Dinesh D'Souza, a far right-wing provocateur, and Princeton historian Kevin Kruse over the political history of the Civil Rights movement, chapter 12 delves into another example of what could be called anti-hashtag activism. Anonymous analyzes D'Souza's use of this hashtag to frame universities and the media as partisan and unreliable. Their chapter ultimately argues that #FakeHistory contributes to the cohesion of the alt-right as a powerful counter-public in current political activism and threatens to deepen partisan fault lines around questions of education and expertise.

Chapter 13, "Digital Matters: Twitter Reacts and Hashtivist Narratives," looks at how media curations such as listicles can disrupt or distort digital activism. Gabriel I. Green and Morgan K. Johnson examine the Twitter Reacts genre of media content, in this case online articles that purport to represent the dialogue unfolding within the #BlackLivesMatter movement. They trace the ways these Twitter curations synthesize and circulate digital discourses while also producing new narratives. Together, the chapters in this section stress the complicated multi-directional conversations unfolding within and around hashtag activism.

Fittingly for a collection that features a variety of research methods employed by academics from diverse disciplinary backgrounds, this book closes by addressing the challenges and benefits of studying digital activism as it relates to responsible and ethical research practices. Internet scholars continue to grapple with complicated questions concerning how to ethically conduct research on/within online communities, including how to weigh the benefits of studying important sociocultural digital engagement against the need to protect the participants who inhabit those spaces. The conclusion, "Capturing a Moving Target: Ethical Research Practices for Hashtag Activism," presents a conversation about internet research ethics by four scholars who engage in and study such work. This final piece is forward-looking in that the participants reflect on the practices included in this collection and also recommend best practices for other researchers.

In sum, this collection takes up a number of investigative questions, beginning with, how do we define hashtag activism? Many questions related to social justice in analog and other digital environments have been extended to this rhetorical situation wherein activism has been mediated by hashtags, presenting us with the question, how does this networked mediation affect digital rhetoric? How does it impact, alter, expand, and otherwise limit activism? How does intersectionality work (or not work) through hashtags? How do partisan arguments unfold? How are some voices privileged over others? What is it about the particular platforms, interfaces, and infrastructures that facilitate or intervene in these movements? How do hashtags expand visibility to underprivileged voices and increase access to social justice movements? What are the material affordances (and consequences) of hashtag activism? Not all of these questions will be thoroughly answered, and we aim to inspire our readers to take up this work in new and varying ways. While these chapters have much to offer, there are certainly many areas that remain to be studied. For example, most of our authors take a rhetorical or textual analysis approach to studying their qualitative data. This leaves much room for hashtag activism to be studied from a big data standpoint or a deeper standpoint, such as ethnography and participant interviews. Next, while we have also taken up issues of anti-activism—the use of hashtags for nefarious purposes like trolling—there is much more to be studied about the ways anti-activists co-opt hashtags to take control of a conversation (e.g., #YesAllMen, #BlueLivesMatter) and use online activity to create harm, like doxxing, that has not been largely taken up in this collection.

Finally, we have entered into internet research ethics conversations, in large part through the collective voices in the final chapter; as a collection, we have largely followed the advice offered by Amy Bruckman (2002) about disguising data. Given the difficulty in obtaining consent for online data (Hudson and Bruckman 2004) and given the way our authors are basing their arguments on numerous pieces of textual data, we find that this approach adheres to current best practices in internet research ethics. Yet because these standards are constantly evolving and will continue to evolve, we argue that our collection represents but a moment in time in this decades-long conversation. As editors and authors, we will certainly continue to develop our own thinking and practices in the coming years, and we encourage fellow scholars to take up these questions as well.

REFERENCES

Ahmed, Sara. 2014. *The Cultural Politics of Emotion*. 2nd edition. New York: Routledge.
Anderson, Monica, Skye Toor, Kenneth Olmstead, Lee Rainie, and Aaron Smith. 2018. "An Analysis of #BlackLivesMatter and Other Twitter Hashtags Related to Political or Social Issues. Part 2 of Report Titled, Activism in the Social Media Age." Pew Research Center. https://www.pewresearch.org/internet/2018/07/11/an-analysis-of-blacklivesmatter-and-othertwitter-hashtags-related-to-political-or-social-issues/.
Brock, André. 2012. "From the Blackhand Side: Twitter as a Cultural Conversation." *Journal of Broadcasting and Electronic Media* 56 (4) (December): 529–549.
Bruckman, Amy. 2002. "Studying the Amateur Artist: A Perspective on Disguising Data Collected in Human Subjects Research on the Internet." *Ethics and Information Technology* 4: 217–231.
Buchanan, Larry, Quoctrung Bui, and Jugal K. Patel. 2020. "Black Lives Matter May Be the Largest Movement in U.S. History." *New York Times*, July 3. https://www.nytimes.com/interactive/2020/07/03/us/george-floyd-protests-crowd-size.html.
Chen, Gina Masullo. 2011. "Tweet This: A Uses and Gratifications Perspective on How Active Twitter Use Gratifies a Need to Connect with Others." *Computers in Human Behavior* 27 (2) (March): 755–762.
Clark, Rosemary. 2016. "'Hope in a Hashtag': The Discursive Activism of #WhyIStayed." *Feminist Media Studies* 16 (5) (February): 788–804. https://doi.org/10.1080/14680777.2016.1138235.
Clark-Parsons, Rosemary. 2019. "'I SEE YOU, I BELIEVE YOU, I STAND WITH YOU': #MeToo and the Performance of Networked Feminist Visibility." *Feminist Media Studies* 21 (3): 362–380. https://doi.org/10.1080/14680777.2019.1628797.
Croeser, Sky, and Tim Highfield. 2014. "Occupy Oakland and #oo: Uses of Twitter within the Occupy Movement." *First Monday* 19 (3) (March). https://firstmonday.org/article/view/4827/3846.
Dean, Jodi. 2015. "Affect and Drive." In *Networked Affect*, edited by Ken Hillis, Susanna Paasonen, and Michael Petit, 89–100. Cambridge, MA: MIT Press.
Dixon, Kitsy. 2014. "Feminist Online Identity: Analyzing the Presence of Hashtag Feminism." *Journal of Arts and Humanities* 3 (7): 34–40.
Dreher, Tanja, Kerry McCallum, and Lisa Waller. 2016. "Indigenous Voices and Mediatized Policy-making in the Digital Age." *Information, Communication and Society* 19 (1) (October): 23–39. https://doi.org/10.1080/1369118X.2015.1093534.
Edwards, Frank, Philip N. Howard, and Mary Joyce. 2013. "Digital Activism and Non-Violent Conflict." Digital Activism Research Project, November 22. https://philhoward.org/digital-activism-and-non-violent-conflict/.
franzke, aline shakti, Anja Bechmann, Michael Zimme, Charles M. Ess, and the Association of Internet Researchers. 2020. "Internet Research: Ethical Guidelines 3.0." https://aoir.org/reports/ethics3.pdf.
Gong, Rachel. 2014. "Indignation, Inspiration, and Interaction on the Internet: Emotion Work Online in the Anti-trafficking Movement." *Journal of Technology in Human Services* 33 (1): 87–103. https://doi.org/10.1080/15228835.2014.998988.
Gross, Nora. 2017. "#IfTheyGunnedMeDown: The Double Consciousness of Black Youth in Response to Oppressive Media." *Souls* 19 (4): 416–437. https://doi.org/10.1080/10999949.2018.1441587.
Gruzd, Anatoliy, Barry Wellman, and Yury Takhteyev. 2011. "Imagining Twitter as an Imagined Community." *American Behavioral Scientist* 55 (10) (July): 1294–1318. https://doi.org/10.1177%2F0002764211409378.
Hudson, James M., and Amy Bruckman. 2004. "'Go Away': Participant Objections to Being Studied and the Ethics of Chatroom Research." *Information Society* 20 (2): 127–139. https://doi.org/10.1080/01972240490423030.

Jackson, Sarah J. 2016. "(Re)Imagining Intersectional Democracy from Black Feminism to Hashtag Activism." *Women's Studies in Communication* 39 (4): 375–379.

Laughlin, Corrina. 2020. "#AmplifyWomen: The Emergence of an Evangelical Feminist Public on Social Media." *Feminist Media Studies* 21 (5): 1–15. https://doi.org/10.1080/14680777.2020.1711794.

Liao, Sara. 2019. "'#IAmGay# What about You'? Storytelling, Discursive Politics, and the Affective Dimension of Social Media Activism against Censorship in China." *International Journal of Communication* 13: 2314–2333.

Losh, Elizabeth. 2020. *hashtag: Object Lessons*. New York: Bloomsbury.

Lumsden, Karen, and Heather Morgan. 2017. "Media Framing of Trolling and Online Abuse: Silencing Strategies, Symbolic Violence, and Victim Blaming." *Feminist Media Studies* 17 (6): 926–940. https://doi.org/10.1080/14680777.2017.1316755.

Malik, Aqdas, Aditya Johri, Rajat Handa, Habib Karbasian, and Hemant Purohit. 2018. "How Social Media Supports Hashtag Activism through Multivocality: A Case Study of #ILookLikeanEngineer." *First Monday* 23 (11). https://doi.org/10.5210/fm.v23i11.9181.

Mann, Benjamin W. 2018. "Rhetoric of Online Disability Activism: #CripTheVote and Civic Participation." *Communication Culture and Critique* 11: 604–621.

Paasonen, Susanna. 2015. "A Midsummer's Bonfire: Affective Intensities of Online Debate." In *Networked Affect*, edited by Ken Hillis, Susanna Paasonen, and Michael Petit, 27–42. Cambridge, MA: MIT Press.

Papacharissi, Zizi. 2015. *Affective Publics: Sentiment, Technology, and Politics*. Oxford: Oxford University Press.

Rentschler, Carrie A. 2017. "Bystander Intervention, Feminist Hashtag Activism, and the Anti-carceral Politics of Care." *Feminist Media Studies* 17 (4): 565–584. https://doi.org/10.1080/14680777.2017.1326556.

Sharma, Sanjay. 2013. "Black Twitter? Racial Hashtags, Networks and Contagion." *New Formations* 78: 46–64. https://muse.jhu.edu/article/522093.

Sparby, Erika M. 2017. "Digital Social Media and Aggression: Memetic Rhetoric in 4chan's Collective Identity." *Computers and Composition* 45 (September): 85–97. https://doi.org/10.1016/j.compcom.2017.06.006.

Waggoner, Erin B. 2018. "Bury Your Gays and Social Media Fan Response: Television, LGBTQ Representation, and Communitarian Ethics." *Journal of Homosexuality* 65 (13): 1877–1891. https://doi.org/10.1080/00918369.2017.1391015.

Williams, Apryl, and Vanessa Gonlin. 2017. "I Got All My Sisters with Me (on Black Twitter): Second Screening of How to Get Away with Murder as a Discourse on Black Womanhood." *Information, Communication and Society* 20 (7): 984–1004. https://doi.org/10.1080/1369118X.2017.1303077.

SECTION I

Intersections between Online and Embodied Activism

1
NETWORKED INTERVENTION AND THE EMERGENCE OF #BOSTONHELP

Megan McIntyre

The annual Boston Marathon is the world's oldest marathon. Inaugurated in 1897, the marathon is part of numerous events on "Patriots Day," a uniquely Massachusetts holiday created to commemorate the American Revolution Battles of Lexington and Concord. Race day 2013 began like most others: the weather was cool and blustery, and the course was daunting; wheelchair runners left the line first, followed by the elite women's group and finally, at 10 a.m. EST, the elite men's group. Four hours and nine minutes into the race, long after the elite competitors had completed the course, two bombs, built in pressure cookers and stashed in trash cans near the finish line, exploded. The blasts killed 3 spectators and injured 264 others. In the aftermath of the bombing, Boston became a crime scene: police cordoned off most of downtown, closed down public transportation, and began searching for evidence of the perpetrators.

INTRODUCTION: ACTIVISM AND AGENCY IN #BOSTONHELP

This chapter offers a qualitative analysis of one of the hashtags that emerged in the aftermath of the bombing: #BostonHelp. Because of the location of the blasts and the large numbers of tourists and runners visiting downtown Boston for the marathon, thousands of people were cut off from their belongings, accommodations, and transportation. #BostonHelp was born from conversations online about how to help runners and spectators stranded downtown. An analysis of the tweets using the #BostonHelp tag reveals two emphases: specific, material offers to help stranded people and instances of boundary work, the promotional and definitional behaviors that seek to maintain the hashtag's focus on specific material offers. Both sets of activities (the offers of support and the boundary work) represent a kind of digital activism.

https://doi.org/10.7330/9781646423187.c001

Much of #BostonHelp is dedicated to actively intervening in the chaotic aftermath of the bombing by offering concrete support; this support is shared—and made efficacious—by a decentralized network of Twitter users. This online activist work was a uniquely immediate way of distributing help to those in most need and/or cut off from more traditional support networks. The boundary work enlarges the network and maintains its focus on one specific kind of support; it too is a kind of activism, as it raises awareness and directs attention to the network of #BostonHelp. This boundary work is largely rhetorical, but it enables the more tangibly material interventions supported by the hashtag. These two sets of interventions are dependent on one another for their relevance and success. The dependent nature of these actions reveals something about our conceptions of rhetorical agency, namely, that rhetorical agency itself operates dependently, as humans and nonhumans act alongside one another in pursuit of a common goal. In short, the emergence and efficacy of #BostonHelp suggests that both agency and activism are produced by networks full of humans and nonhumans acting together.

It might be useful to begin, then, by defining the two terms that frame the work of this chapter: agency and activism. Following Jane Bennett (2016, 155), this chapter views agency as the "capacity to make a difference in the world without knowing quite what you are doing." Neither perfect knowledge nor clear intention is necessary to act agentively, though both knowledge and intention might be present. Agency of this kind is also the product of a network of actors (human, nonhuman, plant, animal, or technology) united by common cause or circumstance. Put simply, agency is the ability to function within a network to have an impact on the world.

Agency, then, is part of my definition for activism: working to have an impact. (The Oxford English Dictionary defines activism as "using vigorous campaigning to bring about political or social change.") Intentionality matters, but it does not map perfectly onto outcome. In digital environments, activism is the ability to have an impact on causes or circumstances that matter to us using the tools (tweets, hashtags, direct messages, and more) afforded to us by the platforms with which we engage.

Malcolm Gladwell (2010) has famously opined the shortcomings of such digital activism. In digital environments, Gladwell argues, real activism has been replaced by slacktivism, which relies only on weak social ties (42). The problem with an activist movement based on weak social ties, he says, is that such ties break easily and render any social movement impotent to enact substantial, sustainable change. I return to Gladwell here, despite all the excellent work done to challenge and complicate his view and definition of slacktivism (Jones 2015; Seelig 2018; Vie 2014), because much contemporary scholarship (Croeser and Highfield 2014; Skoric et al. 2016) on slacktivism still works to answer the binary he articulates between "real-world" and digitally mediated activism. Perhaps Gladwell's (2010) argument persists, in part, because there is a small kernel of truth here, not in Gladwell's oversimplified articulation of online activism but in his attention to how "weak ties" might complicate activist work. The Arab Spring offers some cautions for those touting the power of digital activism, as once promising revolutions proved largely ineffectual in the medium term (Bayat 2017; Brown 2013; Taub 2016).

Gladwell's theory of slacktivism, though, represents a deficit model of online activist work. A more productive model might be the one articulated by Liza Potts (2013): for Potts, social media responses to natural and human-made disasters might best be understood as successful, networked interventions by diffuse participants. Activism, then, requires gathering data, curating audiences and information, producing new ways of understanding and disseminating knowledge, and mobilizing necessary participants. The "shortened existence" of these types of communities owes itself not to any lack of tools but rather to a clarity of purpose (8). Longevity and durability are not of primary concern for these types of networks; in fact, such ties might be counterproductive if they limit the recruitment and boundary work displayed by responsive networks like #BostonHelp. Instead, "especially in the case of disaster," Potts notes, "people use technology to connect, complete a task, and get out" (112).

As Potts (2013) also notes, social media lowers the barrier for participation and therefore requires less commitment and motivation. Certainly, these ties are easier to break when confronted with consequences (Hindman 2009; Morozov 2011), but these ties are also easier to forge (Dennis 2019; Marichal 2013; Morozov 2011; Potts 2013); and in cases where movements are best served by immediacy rather than longevity, far-reaching networks with weak social ties can quickly solve real-world problems. In their discussion of *los indigados* and the Occupy movements, for example, W. Lance Bennett and Alexandra Sergerberg (2012, 742) argue that "more personalized, digitally mediated collective action formations have frequently . . . scaled up more quickly [than non-digital activism]; and have been flexible in tracking moving political targets." Though they acknowledge that such organizations may also fall apart more quickly, the efficacy of these networks depends on their breadth, speed, and flexibility rather than their longevity. This is the case with #BostonHelp, where users relied on the power of the hashtag as an organizing feature, the building desire for action in the face of terrorism, and the kindness of strangers to do good.

Activism can be about causing sweeping social and/or political changes, but activism can also be about making a positive change and finding local ways of addressing social problems. Gladwell's critique of digital activism is that it does not have a real-world effect and that awareness is not enough. But for some problems, timely material support aided and amplified by attention from others interested in the network's goals is enough to solve a big, if short-lived, problem. This chapter focuses on just this kind of activism. The qualitative analysis of #BostonHelp reveals a network sustained by rhetorical work and able to have a significant impact; in other words, through an analysis of the #BostonHelp network, I argue that the most effective digital activism is that which leverages rhetorical *and* material interventions in support of specific goals.

LITERATURE REVIEW: CAUSAL AGENCY IN RHETORICAL THEORY

Like long-standing conceptions of activism, traditional notions of causal agency force us to oversimplify both rhetorical work and the agents and networks involved in that work. Despite postmodern and post-human turns in philosophy and increased attention to technological objects within rhetorical studies, in rhetorical theories of agency, humans remain the primary object of our discussions of agency and the primary or sole possessors of agentive capacities (Cooper 2011; Gorzelsky 2009). From Aristotle to Burke (1969), rhetoric has long relied on a human rhetor to exert or perform agency, to persuade or move the audience to action.

Some theorists of rhetoric have, of course, worked to complicate a humanist, individualistic rhetorical tradition while continuing to emphasize the value of the human rhetor (Bizzell 1996; Cooper 2011; Foss 2006; London Feminist Salon Collective 2004; Miller 2007). Patricia Bizzell, for example, in her address to the 1996 Rhetoric Society of America Conference, offers a definition of rhetorical agency that accounts for the fractured subjectivity of the postmodern subject. She contends that through revisiting our disciplinary history, especially Lloyd Bitzer and Edwin Black's 1971 report, *The Prospect of Rhetoric*, we can envision rhetorical agency as something available even to subjects fully constituted by discourse (Bizzell 1996). Bizzell argues that the postmodern subject derives agency from the convergence of social and historical forces that constitute structures of power and from an awareness of these forces; s/he knowingly acts within, among, and against the forces that constitute her subjectivity.

This attention to more complex notions of agency also extends to new materialists (Alaimo and Hekman 2008; Braidotti 2013; Coole and Frost 2010; Dolphijn and van der Tuin 2012; Grusin 2015). Jane Bennett (2010, 55), for example, argues that agency is "power flowing across multiple bodies." Similar to the notions of "distributed agency" and "networked intentionality" present in Bruno Latour's Actor Network Theory (1993, 261), for new materialists, agency becomes not a feature of any single actor in the network but a product of the confluence of multiple actors (who might be human or nonhuman) at a particular kairotic moment. For example, Karen Barad (2007, 214) defines agency not as an *attribute* of someone or something but rather as a *process* of cause and effect in "enactment." The autonomous human of Enlightenment models of agency is replaced by an actor completely engaged in a formative set of relationships with others. Autonomy, individual purposefulness, and freedom are displaced by dependence and shared purpose. The flexible and fluctuating nature of the networks imagined by new materialists reveals an expanded notion of agency and cause: no longer does the human actor stand alone as the agent of change; s/he is now joined in the position by a multitude of other actors. Further, s/he is shaped by these nonhuman actors as much as s/he shapes them, and within his/her relationships with these other actants (human and nonhuman), agency is produced (van der Tuin 2014; Flatschart 2017). The ability to act or create change (what we understand as agency) is not, then, the product of either the human or the nonhuman members of the network but of the relationship among the actors. This deeply dependent, networked view of agency mirrors notions of interrelationship and dependence from Native American tribes like the Lakota (Grant 2017). For the Lakota, communication, ontology, spirituality, and agency are built on the concept of "all my relations": communities operate in connected ways where "the relations are reciprocal, each one affecting the other as elements retain their individuality" (72). Individuality persists, but the "relations matter more" (73). Relationality and agency extend to nonhumans as well; as Grant argues, "nonhuman beings . . . have agency because they have always had agency; reciprocity with them is a given" (80). Only those (human or nonhuman) deeply embedded in and dependent on the network have access to effectual action and causal power; the more enmeshed an actor becomes, the sturdier it becomes. It is this sturdiness born of innumerable ties on which digital agency and activism rely.

In an environment mediated by digital technologies (computers, smart phones), platforms (Twitter), language markers (hashtags), and constraints (the 140-character limit, threaded replies), networked visions of agency/activism allow for a fuller account of the process that produces #BostonHelp. Autonomous agents simply cannot account for the confluence of people, materiality, and platforms that produce this complex network. The members of the #BostonHelp network are able to have an effect only because they are connected to one another and moving toward the same goal. Likewise, activism is the intentional performance of agency in furtherance of a particular goal with a specific social impact. Here, the intention—articulated by members of the #BostonHelp network—is to provide shelter, food, power, and other material support to those stranded in downtown Boston by the bombing, something that can only be accomplished when all members of the network are present and productive.

METHODOLOGY

The group of tweets analyzed for this project was gathered approximately fifteen hours after the creation of the hashtag. First, I used Twitter's basic search function to find individual tweets bearing the tag. Once I discovered such a tweet, I clicked on the hashtag to take me to a Twitter-generated webpage dedicated to the hashtag. In 2013, this hashtag-specific page organized tweets into a few categories: "Top," "All," and "People You Follow." I utilized the "All" category to access all tweets sent using #BostonHelp from the instantiation of the tag to the time of the search.

This search yielded nearly 2,000 tweets; 1,177 tweets were sent in the first three hours of the tag. I coded only tweets from the first three hours for two reasons: first, if, as the data suggest, the primary object of the hashtag (after promoting its own existence) was to offer material support to displaced persons (mostly food, lodging, and charging stations), then the hours before dark were the most important. After sunset, which happened around 7:30 p.m. EST on April 15, 2013, these offers were less likely to provide needed support because Google's People Finder, local news stations' websites, and other more mainstream outlets had begun to host such offers and most users likely assumed that stranded individuals had already found help or would find help through one of the more mainstream sources. Second, perhaps owing to the logic outlined above, traffic on the #BostonHelp hashtag dropped off sharply by 8:00 p.m. EST.

Following a grounded theory approach, my codes emerged from my initial examination of the data. Originally, I worked with eight categories: hashtag promotion, self-promotion, policing, material support, emotional support, advice, information/resources, and other. After a preliminary pass through the tweets, I combined advice and information/resources into a single "Information and Resources" category because the content of tweets in those two categories was fairly similar; I also combined policing (defining the purpose of the tag in original tweets and responses to other users) and hashtag promotion into the category "Boundary Work" because it was sometimes difficult to distinguish between policing and promoting behaviors. In addition, I eliminated the "Self-Promotion" category as only two tweets fit within that category. Instead, these two tweets are now classified as part of the "Other" category, which represents tweets that either did not fit into one of the other four categories or whose purpose was difficult to identify. See table 1.1 for additional information regarding these categories.

FINDINGS: #BOSTONHELP AND THE LIFE OF AN AGENTIVE NETWORK

An analysis of the 1,177 tweets sent in the first three hours after the hashtag was established (at 4:18 p.m. EST on April 15, 2013) suggests that both rhetorical acts and material goods are necessary to the successful creation of an activist network. The emergence of this particular network offers proof that rhetorical and material resources depend on one another for the creation of agentive acts. As noted in the literature, the kind of agency advanced by this analysis has three key features: (1) actors are dependent on one another, (2) actors are shaped by one another, and (3) connections create strength, reach, and durability. In what follows, I review my qualitative analysis of the collected data (1,177 tweets spanning from 4:18 p.m. EST to 7:18 p.m. EST on the day of the bombing). Table 1.1 lists the coding categories and their relative frequency in the first three hours after the hashtag was established.

The coded tweets fall into five main categories: emotional support, information and resources, material support, boundary work, and other. The network begins with an offer of material support (@fellinline's initial offer of his guest room, tweeted at 4:18 p.m.). This first offer is followed by a bit of boundary work: users—exemplified by @mollfrey—reached

Table 1.1. Definitions, examples, and frequency of codes

Category	Description	Example	Number of Tweets	Percentage of Total
Emotional Support	Offered emotional/ spiritual support and/ or cathartic displays	@BergenerLaw: "Our thoughts are with Boston following today's tragic events. #BostonHelp"	55	4.7
Information and Resources	Provided additional information about the bombing, police activity, and the like or links to other useful resources	@HampCC: "Find who you're missing through Google's Person Finder: google.org #bostonhelp #bostonmarathon"	115	9.8
Material Support	Offered access to or requested lodging, food, transportation, and similar items for displaced runners and other tourists	@fellinline: "If you need a place to crash/water/etc. I am in the south end near back bay. message me. #bostonhelp"	396	33.6
Boundary Work	Policed content, defined the purpose of the hashtag, and/or encouraged others to read the content of the tag	@mollfrey: "@BostonTweet Can a hashtag—maybe #bostonhelp—be promoted for offers of aid and housing for those displaced/stranded?"	537	45.6
Other	Did not fall into one of the other categories or did not have a clear purpose	@EstefanyMMusic: "Helping my hometown! #BostonHelp"	74	6.3

out to others on Twitter who were offering food, shelter, transportation, and other resources and suggested they use the tag. Users also tweeted to popular Boston-based accounts, encouraging them to let their followers know about the hashtag. This work is particularly vital in creating an agentive network: if connections produce strength, durability, and reach, then tweets that create additional connections strengthen the network and create more opportunities to have an impact.

Meanwhile, some users, especially once the hashtag began to appear among the trending tags and in news stories about the digital responses to the bombing, used the tag to offer emotional support as well. These emotionally based messages, however, are a relatively small portion of the network and are isolated mainly to a thirty-minute period after the tag began to trend. Emotional support, then, represents the smallest coded category of tweets, with only 4.7 percent of tweets coded as emotional support. These tweets included offers of "thoughts and prayers," inspirational memes, and other well-wishes or articulations of grief (see figure 1.1).

> 12h
> My heart aches for #Boston #Praying4Him #marathonhell #senseless #bostonmarathon #**bostonhelp**

Figure 1.1. Example of a tweet coded as emotional support

> 14h
> How to talk to children about tragedy. bit.ly/10YoBnB #mrrogers #**bostonhelp**

Figure 1.2. Example of a tweet coded as information sharing

Offers of emotional support proliferated on other hashtags, especially the generic #BostonMarathon tag, which transitioned from a race-related tag sharing information about the marathon and its history to a catch-all tag for information about the status of affected runners and, later, about the progression of the investigation into the bombing and its perpetrators. In the #BostonHelp network, however, these passive offers of thoughts and prayers represent only a small fraction of the activity during the height of the hashtag's usage. I attribute this discrepancy, at least in part, to the active boundary work undertaken by members of the #BostonHelp network. The specific, clearly articulated activist focus of the network combined with consistent reminders of the hashtag's goals encouraged Twitter users to use #BostonHelp only to offer material support to those stranded or to point people to other sources offering such material support. Such offers, while certainly rhetorical, are not agentive in the way boundary work tweets were. Emotional support tweets do not do much to expand reach; nor do they further the material goals of the #BostonHelp network.

Information sharing, another rhetorical intervention into the network, also represents a remarkably small portion of the tweets in #BostonHelp. As with emotional support above, information sharing proliferated across race-associated tags in the hours and days after the explosions. Users offered links to resources (see figure 1.2) on how to talk to children about terrorism, as well as links to news stories about developments in the investigation of the bombings. As with emotional support tweets, these information-sharing tweets neither expand nor support the material goals of the network. Rather, the small number of such tweets is further evidence of the health and agentive/activist character of the #BostonHelp network. @mollfrey's initial tweet defining

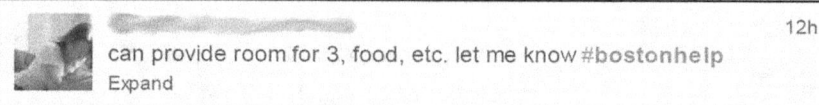

Figure 1.3. Example 1 of a tweet coded as material support

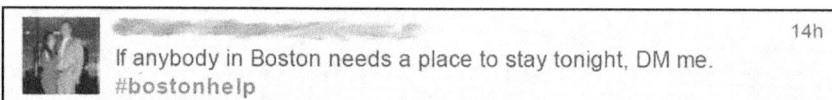

Figure 1.4. Example 2 of a tweet coded as material support

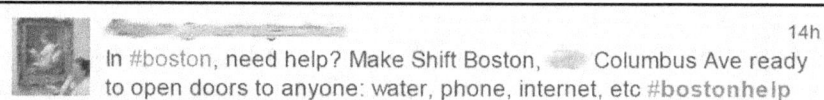

Figure 1.5. Example 3 of a tweet coded as material support

the purpose of the network and other users' subsequent boundary work seems to have encouraged posters in #BostonHelp to focus their tweets on specific offers of shelter, food, charging stations, and transportation.

These specific offers make up the second largest portion of #BostonHelp tweets. Nearly one third of all tweets bearing the hashtag offer or connect readers to offers of housing, food, transportation, or other material support for those separated from their belongings by the ongoing police investigations of the bombing site and the hunt for perpetrators (see figures 1.3, 1.4, 1.5).

The largest group of tweets, though, attends to the rhetorical work of maintaining an agentive/activist network. Boundary work accounts for more than 45 percent of the total tweets in the first three hours of #BostonHelp's existence. Some of these tweets define the goals of the hashtag (see figure 1.6); others reach out to Boston-based accounts with large follower counts or to accounts tweeting about how to help to suggest #BostonHelp as a place to offer help (see figure 1.7, for example). Some do both simultaneously, as seen in figure 1.8.

Some tweets—which I characterize as "policing"—specifically encourage or discourage particular kinds of behavior related to the hashtag. For example, in figure 1.9, @EnriquetaT encourages a user to also add their tweet to a Google Doc of offers started and shared by a local news outlet. Policing behaviors also include recommendations about what not to do (see figure 1.10): @lissbourgoine also recommends behavior concerning

Networked Intervention and the Emergence of #BostonHelp 31

12h
If you have anything immediate to offer Boston folks/visitors— food, shelter, clothing, WiFi, a ride— use hashtag #bostonhelp on Twitter.

Figure 1.6. Example 1 of a tweet coded as boundary work

14h
@NotifyBoston Please help spread word about #bostonhelp hashtag and google.org/personfinder/2...

Figure 1.7. Example 2 of a tweet coded as boundary work

15h
@BostonTweet Can a hashtag -- maybe #bostonhelp -- be promoted for offers of aid and housing for those displaced/stranded?

Figure 1.8. Example 3 of a tweet coded as boundary work

12h
_____, here is the google doc to ensure your tweet is seen by those in need. #BostonHelp goo.gl/TQFxj

Figure 1.9. Example 1 of a tweet coded as boundary work/policing

11h
while you should def check out #bostonhelp, don't open the google doc unless you're looking for somewhere to stay- doc overloaded w/ viewers

Figure 1.10. Example 2 of a tweet coded as boundary work/policing

the associated Google Doc, noting that the document could be overloaded by onlookers and therefore not accessible to those who most need it.

As table 1.1 notes, data from 4:18 p.m. (when the first tweet was sent) to 7:18 p.m. suggest that the vast majority of the nearly 1,200 tweets served just two purposes: "Material Support" (tweets including offers of tangible goods and spaces) and "Boundary Work" (tweets that reinforce the material purpose of the tag and/or encourage others to use the tag to mark these kinds of offers). These account for 79.2 percent of the tweets bearing the #BostonHelp hashtag. Offers of nonmaterial support (represented above by the "Information and Resources" and

"Emotional Support" categories) make up only 14.5 percent of the collected tweets.

The prevalence of tweets coded as material support might be most easily attributed to the boundary work, the policing and promoting behaviors, exhibited by members of the #BostonHelp community that specifically defined appropriate content for tweets bearing the tag. Of the numerous users exhibiting this kind of policing and promoting behavior, as noted earlier, the first and potentially most influential is @mollfrey. Of the fourteen tweets @mollfrey sent bearing the #BostonHelp tag in the three hours under consideration here, thirteen are coded as either material support or boundary work. In the first three hours, in fact, @mollfrey attempted to connect with three highly visible Boston-focused Twitter feeds: she tweeted directly (by including their username in the text of her tweet) to @BostonMarathon (the official Twitter feed for the race), which boasts more than 65,000 followers; @BostonTweet (a feed focused on, to quote their Twitter bio, "loving life in Boston and things to do of value in the city"), which has more than 97,000 followers; and @watertowntab (which tweets news about the Watertown township), with its 2,500 followers. These three accounts share two features important to the work of the #BostonHelp network: first, they are local, and their followers are likely to be local as well. For material offers to be useful to stranded runners, those offering the help must be close enough to interact physically with those in need. Followers of these accounts are likely to fit that criterion. Second, each of these accounts represents a fairly large, already established network of users. The followers of these accounts are united by their interest in local Boston issues but are otherwise a diverse lot, ranging from local news personalities to small business owners to students. The tweets directed to these three accounts, viewed in the larger context of boundary work, demonstrate concerted attempts to draw on established local networks to extend the reach of the hashtag-based community.

This rhetorical boundary work is necessary to create the most opportunities to offer material support, the second most common function of tweets in the #BostonHelp network in the first three hours of its existence. #BostonHelp's material support took two main forms. First, many users tweeted directly to those in need. The first tweet to bear the hashtag, sent by @fellinline at 4:18 p.m., is an example of such a direct offer. Similar messages populate the first three hours. @ElPelonTaqueria, the official Twitter feed for a Mexican restaurant near Fenway Park, sent a similar message at 5:07 p.m.: "open wifi, place to charge cell, or just don't want to be alone, food and drinks, pay only if you can #bostonhelp." That one tweet was retweeted—copied word for word and sent to a progressively larger network of Twitter users—1,264 times. This large number of retweets brought this one message and the #BostonHelp network into contact with an ever expanding group of users and potential contributors. Offers of material support also took the form of direct links to websites containing the list of available hosts and runners in need. The primary Google Doc, created and archived by the *Boston Globe*, boasted nearly 6,000 unique offers for shelter and transportation by the time they stopped accepting submissions two days after the explosions.

The balance of tweets, weighted as it is toward boundary work and offers of material support, has two important implications. First, acts that might be considered wholly (or at least largely) rhetorical are a vital part of the network. Of my five coding categories, two are rhetorical: boundary work and offers of emotional support lack an overt material component (though they certainly rely on invisible material elements, including the technological objects necessary to participate on Twitter). The boundary work in particular represents an important rhetorical intervention: if we examine the network created by the #BostonHelp hashtag over time, we see that the incidences of tweets meant to offer emotional support—a purpose not supported by the promotional work of some members of the network—tapers off quickly as users begin to understand the purpose of the group as material and not emotional. Still, this seemingly nonmaterial boundary work is vital to the efficacy of the offers for material support. That is, the rhetorical work of policing and promoting the hashtag allows the network to expand and reach additional displaced runners and material supporters.

It is not just a general kind of agency at work here, however; it is activism. And not just activism, broadly conceived, but exactly the kind of digital activism that Gladwell (2010) critiqued. In particular, the rhetorical work that enabled others to discover the offers of help hosted on and connected to by hashtag is precisely the kind of clicktivism that Gladwell argues is ineffectual. In this case, however, the work of those who structured, shared, and policed content on the tag helped create and protect a network that did specific, necessary work in the aftermath of disaster. #BostonHelp represents the kind of digital activism that leverages a network of users, connected only by the weak social ties of Twitter and exigence of a tragic disaster. Yet despite Gladwell's warnings, this network coheres, at least long enough to find beds and food and phones and community for hundreds of temporary Boston residents experiencing what was surely among the most tragic and terrifying days of their lives.

The network represented by #BostonHelp is a rhetorical and a material one; the rhetorical presence of the tweets and the organizing feature of the hashtag are necessary conduits to access the material support desperately needed by those stranded in downtown Boston in the aftermath of the bombings. The rhetorical work of policing and promoting the hashtag allows the network to expand and reach additional displaced runners and material supporters. This is, at its core, rhetorical agency in action. It does not, however, look like the rhetorical agency of old: there are human actors here, certainly, but they act among and alongside nonhuman actors in networks. @mollfrey is a key actor; she participates in agency. But she does so as a member of a network of computers, platforms, people, and places. The agency produced by this network affects runners, Twitter users, journalists, and other humans; but it also affects apartments, restaurants, and Twitter itself.

Future work on social media activism in the aftermath of disasters might refocus on the many acts of everyday Twitter users. Work has been done to understand how social media operates as an organizing or help resource (Ewing and McIntyre 2018; McNely and Rivers 2014) and how organizations might craft experiences to best enable responsiveness (Castillo 2016; Potts 2013), but less work considers the interplay among activism, agency, intention, and kindness that, I have argued, underlay acts of engagement like those seen in #BostonHelp. Such work, especially if it examines particular networks that emerge in response to external events or exigence, might well expand the coding taxonomy I have developed for this project to capture more specifically the ethical dimensions of such networks.

CONCLUSION

The acts of kindness—the fruit of digital activism by members of the network—that emerged under the #BostonHelp hashtag represent a kind of gift economy and a set of networked relationships that are not adequately represented in our traditional notions of individual human agency. This agency is more dependent than previous theories of agency allow. #BostonHelp is a tangible example of an agentive network, composed of humans and nonhumans that depended on one another to provide needed services to displaced runners. This network also demonstrates the inextricability of rhetorical and material means: the function of this dependent network of connected entities relied quite heavily on the rhetorical policing and promoting behavior that characterized nearly half of the coded tweets. This rhetorical work, however, depended on external material conditions (the horrifying events of the day), network technologies (a material-semiotic actor composed of physical interfaces and linguistic code), and physical goods (the beds, goods, and power cords that figure so heavily in the tweets offering material support).

This study affirms the rhetorical work necessary to create and maintain ties within agentive networks. Just as the promotional and policing work enabled the #BostonHelp network to reach an ever expanding set of possible participants, so it is for agentive networks more generally. Rhetorical work sustains and enlarges digital activist networks, so both scholars of digital activism and activists themselves would do well to identify the kinds of rhetorical work successful networks employ and explore how rhetorical framing, policing, promotion, and outreach function to support material impacts.

Efficacious agency and activism require networks of humans and nonhumans; they require interventions that are both material and rhetorical, sometimes simultaneously. This is not, however, some new state of affairs. Rather, digital activist networks like #BostonHelp reveal a longstanding set of affairs: we have always needed (human and nonhuman) others in order to have an impact on the world. Agency requires nonhumans as much as it requires humans, and the most effective social media activism crafts material, rhetorical, and material-rhetorical interventions.

REFERENCES

Alaimo, Stacey, and Susan J. Hekman, eds. 2008. *Material Feminisms*. Bloomington: Indiana University Press.

Barad, Karen. 2007. *Meeting the Universe Halfway: Quantum Physics and the Entanglement of Matter and Meaning*. Durham, NC: Duke University Press.

Bayat, Asef. 2017. *Revolution without Revolutionaries: Making Sense of the Arab Spring*. Redwood City, CA: Stanford University Press.

Bennett, Jane. 2010. "A Vitalist Stopover on the Way to a New Materialism." In *New Materialisms: Ontology, Agency, and Politics*, edited by Diana Coole and Samantha Frost, 47–69. Durham, NC: Duke University Press.

Bennett, Jane. 2016. *The Enchantment of Modern Life*. Princeton, NJ: Princeton University Press.

Bennett, W. Lance, and Alexandra Sergerberg. 2012. "The Logic of Connective Action." *Information, Communication and Society* 15 (5): 739–768. http://dx.doi.org/10.1080/1369118X.2012.670661.

Bizzell, Patricia. 1996. "The Prospect of Rhetorical Agency." In *Making and Unmaking the Prospects for Rhetoric: Selected Papers from the 1996 Rhetoric Society of America Conference*, edited by Theresa Enos and Richard McNabb, 37–42. New York: Routledge.

Braidotti, Rosi. 2013. *The Posthuman*. Malden, MA: Polity.

Brown, Nathan. 2013. "Tracking the 'Arab Spring': Egypt's Failed Transition." *Journal of Democracy* 24 (4): 45–58.

Burke, Kenneth. 1969. *A Grammar of Motives*. Berkeley: University of California Press.

Castillo, Carlos. 2016. *Big Crisis Data: Social Media in Disasters and Time-Critical Situations.* New York: Cambridge University Press.

Coole, Diana, and Samantha Frost, eds. 2010. *New Materialisms: Ontology, Agency, and Politics.* Durham, NC: Duke University Press.

Cooper, Marilyn. 2011. "Rhetorical Agency as Emergent and Enacted." *College Composition and Communication* 62 (3): 420–449.

Croeser, Sky, and Tim Highfield. 2014. "Occupy Oakland and #oo: Uses of Twitter within the Occupy Movement." *First Monday* 19 (3). http://dx.doi.org/10.5210/fm.v19i3.4827.

Dennis, James. 2019. *Beyond Slacktivism: Political Participation on Social Media.* London: Palgrave MacMillan.

Dolphijn, Rick, and Iris van der Tuin, eds. 2012. *New Materialism: Interviews and Cartographies.* Ann Arbor, MI: Open Humanities Publishing.

Ewing, Laura A., and Megan M. McIntyre. 2018. "An Intercultural Analysis of Social Media Use in Disaster Response." In *Citizenship and Advocacy in Technical Communication: Scholarly and Pedagogical Perspectives,* edited by Godwin Y. Agboka and Natalie Matveeva, 111–136. New York: Routledge.

Flatschart, Elmar. 2017. "Feminist Standpoints and Critical Realism: The Contested Materiality of Difference in Intersectionality and New Materialism." *Journal of Critical Realism* 16 (3): 284–302.

Foss, Sonja K. 2006. "Rhetorical Criticism as Synecdoche for Agency." *Rhetoric Review* 25 (4): 375–379.

Gladwell, Malcolm. 2010. "Small Change." *New Yorker* 86 (30): 42.

Gorzelsky, Gwen. 2009. "Working Boundaries: From Student Resistance to Student Agency." *College Composition and Communication* 61 (1): 64–84.

Grant, David M. 2017. "Writing Wakan: The Lakota Pipe as Rhetorical Object." *College Composition and Communication* 69 (1): 61–86.

Grusin, Richard, ed. 2015. *The Nonhuman Turn.* Minneapolis: University of Minnesota Press.

Hindman, Matthew. 2009. *The Myth of Digital Democracy.* Princeton, NJ: Princeton University Press.

Jones, Cat. 2015. "Slacktivism and the Social Benefits of Social Video: Sharing a Video to 'Help' a Cause." *First Monday* 20 (5). http://dx.doi.org/10.5210/fm.v20i5.5855.

Latour, Bruno. 1993. *We Have Never Been Modern.* Cambridge, MA: Harvard University Press.

London Feminist Salon Collective. 2004. "The Problematization of Agency in Postmodern Theory: As Feminist Educational Researchers, Where Do We Go from Here?" *Gender and Education* 16 (1): 25–33.

Marichal, Jose. 2013. "Political Facebook Groups: Micro-Activism and the Digital Front Stage." *First Monday* 18 (12). http://dx.doi.org/10.5210/fm.v18i12.4653.

McNely, Brian, and Nathaniel Rivers. 2014. "All of the Things: Engaging Complex Assemblages in Communication Design." In *SIGDOC '14: Proceedings of the 32nd Annual International Conference on Design of Communication,* edited by Dave L. Jones and Brian McNely, 1–10. New York: ACM Press.

Miller, Carolyn R. 2007. "What Can Automation Tell Us about Agency?" *Rhetoric Society Quarterly* 37 (2) (Spring): 137–157.

Morozov, Evgeny. 2011. *The Net Delusion: The Dark Side of Internet Freedom.* New York: Public Affairs.

Potts, Liza. 2013. *Social Media in Disaster Response: How Experience Architects Can Build for Participation.* New York: Routledge.

Seelig, Michelle I. 2018. "Social Activism: Engaging Millennials in Social Causes." *First Monday* 23 (2). http://dx.doi.org/10.5210/fm.v23i2.8125.

Skoric, Marko M., Qinfeng Zhu, Debbie Goh, and Natalie Pang. 2016. "Social Media and Citizen Engagement: A Meta-Analytic Review." *New Media and Society* 18 (9): 1817–1839. https://doi.org/10.1177/1461444815616221.

Taub, Amanda. 2016. "The Unsexy Truth about Why the Arab Spring Failed." *Vox*, January 27. https://www.vox.com/2016/1/27/10845114/arab-spring-failure.

van der Tuin, Iris. 2014. "Diffraction as a Methodology for Feminist Onto-Epistemology: On Encountering Chantal Chawaf and Posthuman Interpellation." *Parallax* 20 (3): 231–244.

Vie, Stephanie. 2014. "In Defense of 'Slacktivism': The Human Rights Campaign Facebook Logo as Digital Activism." *First Monday* 19 (4). http://dx.doi.org/10.5210/fm.v19i4.4961.

2
STICKY HASHTAGS
The Role of Emotions and Affect in Hashtag Activism

Salma Kalim

Note: The material pertaining to sexual violence contained in this chapter may be disturbing to some readers.

Over the past few years, there has been increasing interest in the study of digital publics within and beyond the field of rhetoric and composition. Although there is significant scholarship documenting and theorizing the formation of online affective communities that advocate anti-racism (McVey and Woods 2016; De Choudhury et al. 2016), gender equality (Stenberg 2018; Clark 2016; Larson 2018), disaster response (Potts 2013), and political protest (Penney and Dadas 2014), the focus of existing work has largely been on the West and the Middle East; hence, the digital landscape of South Asia in general and of Pakistan in particular remains relatively less explored. In Pakistan, with over 45 million internet users, social media platforms are facilitating the construction and dissemination of democratized ground-up discourses (Kalim and Janjua 2018). This study brings attention to the changing and shifting dynamics of digital activism in the South Asian region. It documents and theorizes the affective digital publics that emerged in response to the brutal rape and murder of a seven-year-old girl, Zainab, in Pakistan by looking at the rhetorical work of Twitter users that happened following her case.

Hashtags remain central to the study of digital activism. Drawing on tweets with the hashtag #JusticeForZainab, I investigate how the emotionality or affective value of hashtags increases during circulation. Building on Sara Ahmed's (2015) argument of accumulation of affect due to circulation, I explore how the hashtag #JusticeForZainab became sticky and saturated with affect during circulation over a period of ten months. Drawing on selected tweets from a corpus of those with the hashtag #JusticeForZainab, I map out the range of emotions (shame, grief, anger, and pride) as they stick to the hashtag #JusticeForZainab and theorize stickiness as a paradoxical situation, as it involves both binding effect and blockage. Building on this idea of how affect is generated through (1) repetition, (2) contact with other signs, and (3) contact with past histories, I see digital platforms such as Twitter as affective sites where subjects, objects, and their past histories come into play, leading to the chain of signification. This study, hence, argues for more critical inquiries into the complex role of emotions and affect in hashtag activism.

THE CASE OF #JUSTICEFORZAINAB

On January 5, 2018, seven-year-old Zainab Amin went missing near her home. Four days later, her body was found in a heap of trash, brutally tortured, raped, and murdered. Pictures of her body went viral on social media. Due to the speedy circulation of pictures and news of the rape and murder of a child on social media, the event triggered a series of nationwide protests with the slogan #JusticeForZainab. During this troubling time, the hashtag #JusticeForZainab had been also widely used by activists, politicians, and celebrities to raise awareness against the case of social injustice in the country.

In the wake of the Zainab case, actress and activist Nadia Jamil took to Twitter to share her personal childhood sexual abuse experiences. Following Jamil, many other celebrities and social media users also shared their testimonies about child/sexual abuse experiences, which was seen as a significant move in a conservative Muslim society. This online activism (which took place on various social media platforms following the Zainab case) was also underscored by coverage by both local and international media outlets. Many compared the trending of the hashtag #JusticeForZainab with #MeToo. As Faria Akram (2018) contends, "It was #MeToo that sparked an international movement to end sexual assault and harassment. As we grieve, we also hope that #JusticeforZainab ignites a similar passion for Pakistan."

The Zainab case, hence, can be considered a watershed moment in the history of Pakistan in terms of the use of digital tools for writing for social change. This study describes the rhetorical activity of Twitter users in the context of the Zainab case to illustrate the growing use of Twitter for social advocacy in a South Asian context. Furthermore, I focus on how hashtags both facilitate and constrain public writing for a social cause by investigating the complex role of emotions and affect in hashtag activism. Drawing on a corpus of tweets that contain the hashtag #JusticeForZainab over a period of ten months, I argue that while the hashtag #JusticeForZainab brought due attention to the event and generated important conversations about breaking the taboo of child abuse in the country, the intensity of the shared anger of the moment also diverted attention away from the important conversations initiated by the hashtag itself. Investigating these complexities of hashtag activism can help us understand the complex role of emotions and affect in digital activism.

EMOTIONS AND AFFECT IN HASHTAG ACTIVISM

Emotions and affect remain central to the study of digital publics and counter-publics. Contemporary rhetoric and communication scholars have re-theorized the role of emotions and affect in the formation of online communities within the last decade (Edwards and Lang 2018; Nash 2013; Papacharissi 2015; Pritchard 2016). For example, communication scholar Zizi Papacharissi (2015) uses the term *affective publics* to describe networked publics that have been mobilized, connected or disconnected through expressions of sentiments, feelings, and emotions. She insists that "technologies network us" but that it is primarily our stories with affect that connect us with unknown and remote publics to discuss relevant issues, topics, or events. These "structures of feelings," she argues, open up and sustain discursive spaces where stories can be told, disruption and interventions can be made, and hence underrepresented viewpoints can be amplified (130–131).

Theorizing hashtags as "curious rhetorical things" with complex, ever-changing rhetorical life, Dustin Edwards and Heather Lang (2018, 120, 117) also underline the role of affect in the rhetorical life of the hashtag #YesAllWomen by asking "what sticks (and doesn't stick) to the rhetorical becoming of #YesAllWomen?" They maintain that some elements are blocked or prevented from sticking to the tag #YesAllWomen, such as issues concerning racial inequalities due to heavy focus on gender inequality. Citing Ahmed (2015, 91), Edwards and Lang (2018) remind us that "what sticks 'shows us' where the object has traveled through what it has gathered onto its surface." They argue for "more energy" to be invested in "exploring *how* the circulation of a hashtag comes to matter" (118, original emphasis).

Many digital rhetoric scholars have underlined the impact of hyperpublicity due to increased affective intensity or emotionality of online communication. For instance, building on case studies of hashtag activism of #BringBackOurGirls and #Kony2012, Caroline Dadas (2017, 23–24) contends that although these hashtags have been successful in bringing attention to cases of injustice and oppression, the increased attention also led to the oversimplification and backgrounding of the role of various complex social, political, historical, and economic factors that led to these injustices in the first place. Dadas argues for more critical awareness about how increased attention can bring concealment in hashtag activism.

This chapter draws on this emerging scholarship on hashtag activism that acknowledges the potential as well as constraints of using digital platforms for social and political advocacy. As a digital rhetoric scholar, I'm interested in exploring how sticky hashtags amplify the voice of an affective community bonded through shared emotions of shame, anger, or pride yet also lead to the blockage or stopping of movement. While Dadas uses the notion of concealment to illustrate this concept of backgrounding, I use Ahmed's notion of stickiness to underscore how hashtags both facilitate and constrain public advocacy for any social and political cause.

THE NOTION OF STICKINESS: A PARADOXICAL SITUATION

Focusing on the role of emotion in the cultural and political spheres, Ahmed (2015) laid out her model of emotions in *Cultural Politics of Emotion*. Affect, she argues, "does not reside in an object or sign, but is an effect of the circulation between objects and signs" (45). According to Ahmed's view of emotions, when signs get repeated, they accumulate an affective value and generate an affect. Furthermore, "The more signs circulate, the more affective they become" (45). Signs also become sticky due to past and present histories of association. As Ahmed explains, "A sticky surface is one that will incorporate other elements into the surface such that the surface of a sticky object is in a dynamic process of re-surfacing . . . But the stickiness of that surface *still tells us a history of the object that is not dependent on the endurance of the quality of stickiness*: what sticks 'shows us' where the object has travelled through what it has gathered onto its surface, gatherings that become a part of the object, and call into question its integrity as an object" (91, original emphasis).

Since sticky things incorporate other elements during circulation, Ahmed insists that we need to focus on how emotions circulate; how they stick, slide, or move between bodies; and how they generate meanings. Ahmed (2015, 91) also reminds us to consider stickiness as a paradoxical situation: "When a sign or object becomes sticky it can function to 'block' the movement (of other things or signs) and it can function to bind (other things or signs) together." This binding effect of a sign is also a blockage, as it stops signs from moving or acquiring new value. This notion of stickiness helps us understand and relate blockages with binding effect: first, it shows us how a sticky tag can hold things together, leading to the formation of an affective community based on shared feelings of shame, grief, regret, or pride; and second, it also directs our attention to how stickiness involves blockages as things stop moving. I consider the notion of stickiness helpful in thinking about how the affective economy of hashtags increases during circulation and how it leads to both binding effect and blockages when used by the public for social and political advocacy. I consider Ahmed's framework useful for exploring the role of emotion and affect in digital publics, as it opposes the idea of exploration of texts as fixed repositories of feelings and asks us to track or follow emotions as they interact with other signs, objects, and events. This idea of tracking emotions, I argue, can be helpful in theorizing digital publics. Following Ahmed (14), I argue that it is important to consider how emotions circulate, move, and stick as "we move, stick and slide with them." In other words, I'm interested in exploring not only how emotions move and circulate with the hashtags but also how we move with sticky hashtags.

Ahmed's theory also opposes the distinction between affect and emotions and, hence, asks us to appreciate the continuity of various aspects or dimensions of feelings—such as sensations, thoughts, feelings, and judgments—without making distinctions. Following Ahmed's view of emotions and affect, this study considers emotions to be messy experiences and avoids making sharper distinctions among various forms of emotions and affects. The following section further discusses the methodology adopted for the study.

METHOD AND METHODOLOGY

To collect my tweets studied in this chapter, I searched tweets with the hashtag #JusticeForZainab using the Twitter advanced search engine, which generated over 2,000 tweets within the time frame of January to October 2018. I transferred the data to an Excel sheet and coded data according to themes emerging in the data, such as showing solidarity with the victim, expressing grief and sorrow, demanding the arrest of the rapist, critiquing rape culture, sharing personal testimonies, and so on. During my second round of coding the data, I paid more attention to moving and shifting emotions as users responded to the hashtag #JusticeForZainab and recorded my data according to emotions such as grief, shame, anger, and pride. While categorizing tweets, I was aware of the fact that these categories of emotions, which I listed as writing shame, grief, anger or pride, were nevertheless fluid and blurry. Since multiple affective states were articulated in each tweet, it was not possible to neatly categorize or label every tweet under a single heading; hence, I tried to focus more on the rhetorical function of each tweet: Does it generate a shared feeling of shame, grief, hate, or anger? Does it align subjects, bodies, or events with other bodies, subjects, or events? To acknowledge this complex role of emotions in hashtag activism, I deployed the notion of stickiness to explore how the stickiness of the hashtag #JusticeForZainab generates an affective community, how stickiness has a binding effect, and how it leads to the blockage of ideas. In my reading of these tweets, I paid attention to the offline context and drew a time line of events starting from January 4, 2018 (when Zainab was reported missing), until October 17 (when the rapist was hanged), which helped me contextualize the data in relation to the subsequent development of the Zainab case.

Following the recommendations of the Association of Internet Researchers (Markham and Buchanan 2012) for ethical decision-making, I only collected data from public accounts and also concealed users' identity by blurring their names and profile pictures. I did, however, include the real names of celebrities because their accounts and tweets are public, and these tweets are widely circulated and quoted in both local and international media.

WRITING NATIONAL SHAME

Shame, Ahmed (2015, 107) explains, is an affective cost of not following the scripts of normativity, as "we feel shame because we have failed to approximate 'an ideal' that has been given to us." With an average rate of twelve cases per day, child abuse has always been "Pakistan's Hidden Shame" (Shah 2014). However, the graphic pictures of the dead body of another child dumped on garbage exposed and uncovered what was hidden and concealed under what Ahmed (2015) calls skin or cloth. As seen in figure 2.1, users share the collective shame in response to the event.

How do these declarations of shame bring the public into existence as an affective community? To acknowledge wrongdoing, Ahmed (2015, 72) contends, means "to enter into shame; the 'we' is shamed by its recognition that it has committed 'acts and omissions.'" Hence, users using the hashtag #JusticeForZainab also enter into the shared shame by recognizing their failure to protect another child from the horror of child sexual abuse. Since it is this relation of having an ideal that allows

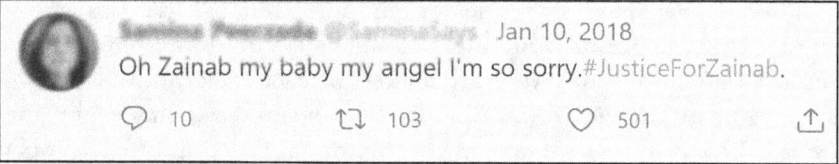

Figure 2.1. Example of a tweet writing national shame

Figure 2.2. Example of a tweet writing national shame

"I" and "we" to be aligned, tweets that state "I am sorry" can be read as "we are sorry" and vice versa (see figure 2.2). These performative utterances, hence, generate an affective community united through shared feelings of shame, grief, and sorrow.

Since feelings are crucial to the forming of surface, walls, or borders, what separates us from others also connects us to others. Many users employed the tag #JusticeForZainab to express their shared disgust. By naming this shared emotion of disgust, these users are bound together through the shared condemnation of the event of child abuse of an innocent girl. As Ahmed (2015, 94) explains, " 'That's disgusting!' generates more than simply a subject and an object; it also generates a community of those who are bound together through the shared condemnation of a disgusting object or event. A community of witnesses is generated whose apparent shared distance from an event or object that has been named as disgusting is achieved through the repetition of the word 'disgust.' " These emotions of shame, disgust, and grief as articulated by users intensified the affective value of the hashtag #JusticeForZainab. Signs also become sticky due to histories of association; in the case of #JusticeForZainab, the affective value of the hashtag has been shaped by past histories of associations. Pakistan, ranked as the sixth most dangerous country in the world for women, has numerous victims of sexual abuse; so the public's shared feelings about the Zainab case were also shaped by memories of other sexual abuse cases in Pakistan.

The stickiness of the hashtag also increases due to contact between signs. For example, some tweets demonstrate how the contact with other bodies, events, and signs makes the tag stickier. Consider this tweet, which contained the following warning: "when you seek to silence the feminists in your community, know you are making it easier for predators to destroy lives."

This tweet invokes memories of the histories of oppression faced by feminists in the region, recognizing that in Pakistan, feminists are delegitimized by the state as well as by the patriarchal social structure as Western propaganda that makes it "easier for predators to destroy lives" of women. The message in this particular tweet was amplified by the inclusion of a string of hashtags mirroring the pattern of #JusticeForZainab (e.g., #JusticeForNaila, #JusticeForKhadija, #JusticeForShazia), referring to many known and unknown victims of sexual abuse in Pakistan. One of these hashtags included the name of Mukhrara Bibi, a survivor of gang rape—one of the most gruesome cases of rape in Pakistan, which attracted a great deal of international and local media attention. This connection with other sexual abuse victims intensifies the emotional appeal of the tag #JusticeForZainab. This accumulation of affect due to contact with past memories reminds us that histories stay alive, even though sometimes they are (or are not) consciously remembered. Here we also see how emotions open up future possibilities as the user asks the public to think about how and what can be done to secure justice for women.

The data contained many other references to past events of child abuse cases in the country (such as the famous child abuse scandal in 2014 when hundreds of videotapes showing children performing forced sex acts were found in the same city: Kasur, Pakistan). This frequent contact with past memories of shame, pain, and grief led to the accumulation of affect, intensifying the stickiness of the hashtag. Here, emotions can be theorized as performative, as they invoke the past association as well as generate new meanings. Soon, the hashtag #JusticeForZainab also had contact with contemporary social justice movements of gender equality, as the tag #MeToo soon started trending in Pakistan alongside the hashtag #JusticeForZainab.

The above-mentioned tweets demonstrate how the hashtag #JusticeForZainab served as an invitation tool and allowed users to reflect back on their childhood experiences of sexual abuse. The tweets also bring attention to the taboo of child sexual abuse in the country, as the events of such abuse are rarely reported due to fear of shame and dishonor in the society. Another example is Pakistani model and event manager Frieha Altaf reflecting on how her family remained silent when she was abused at the age of six (figure 2.3). Due to her family's silence, she internalized shame and only realized later as an adult that "shame is keeping SILENT." The addition of the hashtags #MeToo, #ChildAbuse, and #HowToStopChildAbuse not only increased the stickiness of the tag #JusticeForZainab but also broadened the scope of the latter's hashtag activism.

BLOCKAGE: FROM ANGER TO NATIONAL PRIDE

How can stickiness stop things from moving? Ahmed reminds us to ask "what sticks" because when signs become sticky, they turn into sites of tension. According to Ahmed, stickiness is a paradoxical situation and involves both fluidity and fixity: when there is fluidity, signs keep on moving; but when there is fixity, things stop moving. So how did stickiness in the case of #JusticeForZainab clog the hashtag's movement? During the circulation of the hashtag #JusticeForZainab (both within and outside the digital networks), the rhetoric "hang him publicly" got stuck to the hashtag as many demanded the public hanging of the rapist. The following tweets demonstrate how the intensity of shared anger of the moment can block or clog activism for social change.

Figure 2.3. Example of contact with other signs, subjects, and events

Many Twitter users asked others to support the idea of hanging the rapist by retweeting the tweet. Soon many users, one after another, reinforced the idea of publicly hanging the rapist. This shared anger of the moment as expressed in these tweets (figure 2.4 and figure 2.5) illustrates how things stop moving due to blockage. In other words, this continuing appeal of violent action is a testimony to how the power of shared anger can limit the horizon of the social movement. Many scholars and analysts argued that the growing demand for the public hanging of the rapist was problematic. For instance, Abira Ashfaq (2018) explains that "public execution only kills the rapist, not the problem," and only shows a cynical preference for violence as a desperate solution to child abuse. Rather than retributive, public hanging resembles revenge killing, normalizes violence, and can cause more damage than repair.

This blockage of the social movement due to the intensity of the shared anger aptly demonstrates how hyper-publicity often leads to the foregrounding of some immediate solution and backgrounding

Sticky Hashtags   47

Figure 2.4. Example of writing national anger

Figure 2.5. Example of writing national anger

of the real cause. As Dadas (2017) contends, "attention brings concealment" because things are relegated to the background in an effort to sustain attention in a certain direction. Hence, in the case of #JusticeForZainab, we see how the rhetoric "hang him publicly" diverted the public's attention away from the important social, cultural, political, and economic issues behind an extremely high rate of child abuse in Pakistan. In other words, various important concerns and issues raised by the activists and other users—breaking the taboo of child abuse, exposing the rape culture and victim blaming, educating children about good and bad touching, and more—were backgrounded to sustain attention in a certain direction.

Another reason why the shared emotion of anger and its rhetoric—hang him publicly—in the case of hashtag activism is problematic is because it undermines the spirit of the social cause of #JusticeForZainab—that is, breaking the taboo of child abuse. An editorial titled "Justice for Zainab?" (2018) shed light on the impact of growing calls for a public hanging following the Zainab case: "A not insignificant number of rapes are carried out by family members or those known to the victims. Thus in the midst of stop-start efforts to teach children what constitutes (in)appropriate touching by an adult combined with the onslaught of twenty-four-seven media—there is the real risk that minors may be afraid to speak out for fear that they will be the ones actively tightening the hangman's noose." Hence, we see that while these intensified emotions, as Papacharissi (2019, 2) insists, can be a powerful force because they can drive a movement forward, amplify the voice of a community, and disrupt the status quo, they can also "entrap publics in a state of . . . a lot of intensity" without actual movement forward.

Expressing national shame, Ahmed (2015, 109) contends, demonstrates that subjects are ideal subjects and "have the ideals that made such shame shameful in the first place." In other words, bad feelings are only temporary, as shame can be reworked to reproduce the nation as an ideal. On October 17, 2018, when Zainab's rapist was hanged by the police, the hashtag #JusticeForZainab resurfaced on Twitter as the public celebrated the restoration of the lost national ideal by declaring victory with claims of "we did it." The shared emotion of shame expressed earlier in the form of "we are sorry" was restored and recovered by hanging one rapist. This celebratory utterance of "we did it" oversimplifies and obfuscates the full cause behind the circulation of the tag #JusticeForZainab.

CONCLUSION

This chapter explored the role of emotion and affect in the formation of an affective community around #JusticeForZainab that emerged in response to the rape and murder of a seven-year-old girl, Zainab, in Pakistan in 2018. Drawing on Ahmed's (2015) notion of stickiness, Dadas's (2017) theorization of how attention brings concealment, and Papacharissi's (2015) notion of affective publics, I analyzed the intersections of affect and digital public studies. Drawing on a corpus of tweets using the hashtag #JusticeForZainab over a period of ten months, I showed how affect is not already present in hashtags but rather is generated through (1) repetition and circulation of the hashtag within digital networks; (2) contact with other sticky signs (such as #MeToo and #StopChildAbuse in this case); and (3) contact with past histories, events, and subjects (such as Mukhtar Bibi's gang-rape case and Kasur's child abuse scandal in Pakistan) and national and global discourses of victim blaming, rape culture, shame, and sexual harassment. I hence see digital platforms such as Twitter as affective sites where subjects, objects, and past histories lead to a chain of signification. In my analysis of tweets, I also highlighted the performative nature of emotions, as they do work by giving orientations or directions toward others (the rapist, patriarchy, society). Emotions viewed in this manner are not psychological states but rather are social and cultural practices.

While I focused on the case of hashtag activism in a South Asian community, I investigated a complex working of emotions and affect in hashtag activism that has implications for affect and digital public studies. Because the emotionality of hashtags is generated not only by the present event of social or political injustice but also by past and present histories of association, I argue for tracking hashtags forward as they circulate and interact with other signs (such as images, videos, or hashtags) and backward as they invoke past histories of social and political injustices. This approach of tracking hashtags forward and backward opposes the approach of treating hashtags such as #BlackLivesMatter as a fixed depository of emotions or seeing hashtags as a mere reaction to a present event of injustice and asks researchers to pay attention to how hashtags accumulate affect when they circulate within and outside the digital networks. This understanding affirms Laurie E. Gries's (2015) call to pay attention to the rhetorical becoming of circulating signs or images in the digital age. Framing "tracing" as a way of examining how things (ideas, texts, images) circulate, materialize, interact with other entities, and trigger change (94), Gries (xix) argues for reconfiguring theories of rhetoric and public to account for dynamic, distributed, and emerging aspects of digital discourse. Building on Gries's call to trace the rhetorical becoming of things, I argue for tracking hashtags both forward and backward to acknowledge the dynamic, distributed, and emerging nature of digital texts. This approach of tracking hashtags helps us understand why hashtags are so powerful, dynamic, and influential.

Another important implication of this study is the notion of blockage. I deployed Ahmed's notion of stickiness to illustrate the complex processes of binding and blockage. I demonstrated how the sticky hashtag #JusticeForZainab had a binding effect, as it generated an affective community united through emotions of shame, grief, sorrow, and anger and initiated important, meaningful, and powerful conversations about breaking the taboo of child abuse and disrupting the notion of shame concerning sexual abuse in a conservative South Asian community that has long silenced conversations about sexuality, abuse, and women's bodies. I also showed how the intensity of shared anger directed attention toward one direction at the cost of others. In other words, various issues raised by activists and other users such as breaking the taboo of child abuse, exposing rape culture and victim blaming, educating children about good and bad touching, and more were backgrounded to sustain attention on hanging one rapist. This pattern affirms Dadas's (2017) claim that there is a backgrounding of certain factors in social media activism to retain attention in another direction. In other words, while the emotionality of the hashtag #JusticeForZainab outlined new possibilities for future action, the increased stickiness of the hashtag also led to the blockage of the movement of many emancipatory discourses. There is a growing need to act, teach, and write as responsible social media users and activists when advocating for any social or political cause on digital platforms such as Twitter by considering the real cause or motive behind a hashtag and rethinking social, political, and economic factors behind the injustice. As the case of #JusticeForZainab demonstrates, the stickiness of the hashtag amplified the voice of the community yet simultaneously diverted attention away from important social, cultural, political, and economic factors behind an extremely high rate of child abuse in Pakistan. Therefore, there is a need to adopt a more critical rhetorical approach to hashtag activism that acknowledges both the potential and the constraints of this form of social justice protest.

REFERENCES

Ahmed, Sara. 2015. *The Cultural Politics of Emotion.* New York: Routledge.

Akram, Faria. 2018. "Patriarchy and Rape Culture Create Blame Game Instead of #JusticeforZainab." *Brown Girl Magazine,* January 12. https://www.browngirlmagazine.com/2018/01/justiceforzainab-the-internet-continues-to-play-the-blame-game/.

Ashfaq, Abira. 20018. "Public Execution Only Kills the Rapist, Not the Problem." *Express Tribune* (Pakistan), February 21. https://blogs.tribune.com.pk/story/64121/public-execution-only-kills-the-rapist-not-the-problem/.

Clark, Rosemary. 2016. "'Hope in a Hashtag': The Discursive Activism of #WhyIStayed." *Feminist Media Studies* 16 (5): 788–804.

Dadas, Caroline. 2017. "Hashtag Activism: The Promise and Risk of 'Attention.'" In *Social Writing/Social Media: Publics, Presentations, and Pedagogies,* edited by Douglas M. Walls and Stephanie Vie, 17–36. Boulder: University Press of Colorado.

De Choudhury, Munmun, Shagun Jhaver, Benjamin Sugar, and Ingmar Weber. 2016. "Social Media Participation in an Activist Movement for Racial Equality." In *Proceedings of the International AAAI Conference on Web and Social Media* 10 (1): 92–101. International AAAI Conference on Weblogs and Social Media. https://www.ncbi.nlm.nih.gov/pmc/articles/PMC5565729/.

Edwards, Dustin, and Heather Lang. 2018. "Entanglements That Matter." In *Circulation, Writing, and Rhetoric,* edited by Laurie Gries and Collin Gifford Brooke, 118–134. Boulder: University Press of Colorado.

Gries, Laurie. 2015. *Still Life with Rhetoric: A New Materialist Approach for Visual Rhetorics.* Boulder: University Press of Colorado.

"Justice for Zainab?" 2018. Editorial. *Daily Times,* October 20. https://dailytimes.com.pk/312206/justice-for-zainab-8/.

Kalim, Salma, and Fauzia Janjua. 2018. "#WeAreUnited, Cyber-Nationalism during Times of a National Crisis: The Case of a Terrorist Attack on a School in Pakistan." *Discourse and Communication* 13 (1): 68–94. https://doi.org/10.1177/1750481318771448.

Larson, Kyle. 2018. "Remonstrative Agitation as Feminist Counterpublic Rhetoric." *Peitho* 20 (20): 261–298. http://peitho.cwshrc.org/remonstrative-agitation-as-feminist-counterpublic-rhetoric/.

Markham, Annette N., and Elizabeth Buchanan. 2012. "Ethical Decision-making and Internet Research: Recommendations from the AoIR Ethics Working Committee (Version 2.0)." *AoIR,* December. http://www.aoir.org/reports/ethics2.pdf.

McVey, James Alexander, and Heather Suzanne Woods. 2016. "Anti-Racist Activism and the Transformational Principles of Hashtag Publics: From #HandsUpDontShoot to

#PantsUpDontLoot." *Present Tense* 5 (3): 1–9. http://www.presenttensejournal.org/volume-5/anti-racist-activism-and-the-transformational-principles-of-hashtag-publics-from-handsupdontshoot-to-pantsupdontloot/.

Nash, Jennifer. 2013. "Practicing Love: Black Feminism, Love-Politics, and Post-Intersectionality." *Meridians* 11 (2): 1–24.

Papacharissi, Zizi. 2015. *Affective Publics: Sentiment, Technology, and Politics.* New York: Oxford University Press.

Papacharissi, Zizi. 2019. "Forget Messiahs." *Social Media + Society* 5 (3): 1–3. https://doi.org/10.1177/2056305119849710.

Penney, Joel, and Caroline Dadas. 2014. "(Re)Tweeting in the Service of Protest: Digital Composition and Circulation in the Occupy Wall Street Movement." *New Media and Society* 16 (1): 74–90.

Potts, Liza. 2013. *Social Media in Disaster Response.* New York: Routledge.

Pritchard, Eric Darnell. 2016. *Fashioning Lives: Black Queers and the Politics of Literacy.* Carbondale: Southern Illinois University Press.

Shah, Bina. 2014. "Pakistan's Hidden Shame." *Feministan*, September 1. https://thefeministani.com/2014/09/01/pakistans-hidden-shame/.

Stenberg, Shari. 2018. "'Tweet Me Your First Assaults': Writing Shame and the Rhetorical Work of #NotOkay." *Rhetoric Society Quarterly* 48 (2): 119–138.

3
AFFECTING DIGITAL ACTIVISM
Comparative Study of Tweets from the March for Our Lives Rallies and Women's Marches

Melissa Ames and Kristi McDuffie

Political activism, enabled and amplified by digital technology, rose steadily in the US during the early decades of the twenty-first century. For example, the Black Lives Matter movement, one of the era's most influential and continuous social justice movements, broke record numbers of participation in on-the-ground protests. Following the deaths of George Floyd and Breonna Taylor in 2020, weeks of protesting erupted across the country, with protests taking place in more than 40 percent of US counties. Data analytics estimate that 15 million to 26 million people participated in the US demonstrations during the month of June, with a half million attending events on June 6 alone (Buchanan, Bui, and Patel 2020). Larry Buchanan, Quoctrung Bui, and Jugal K. Patel (2020) suggest that this record participation may reflect "a country that is more conditioned to protesting," noting that "the adversarial stance that the Trump administration has taken on issues like guns, climate change, and immigration has led to more protests than under any presidency since the Cold War." Polling from the Kaiser Family Foundation confirms the upswing in political activism during this time period, with 20 percent of Americans reporting that they had participated in a protest during the Trump administration—19 percent of whom claimed to be new to protesting (2020). While the 2020 Black Lives Matter protests are situated at the end of Trump's presidency, the next two largest protests from this time period occurred during the beginning and the middle of his time in office. This chapter focuses on this large activist trend by studying the hashtag activism related to these two in-person events: the Women's March and March for Our Lives ("These Are the Four" 2018).

On January 21, 2017, more than 3 million women participated in the Women's March throughout the US, one day after President Donald Trump's inauguration. There were half a million marchers

https://doi.org/10.7330/9781646423187.c003

in Washington, DC, more than doubling the projected attendance of 200,000 (Politi 2017). Along with this historic march emerged a robust digital movement. There were 11.5 million tweets on January 21 alone, rivaling the 12 million tweets from the previous day's inauguration (Cohen 2017).[1] Just over a year later, thousands gathered again[2]—this time to protest gun violence at March for Our Lives protests spread across the US and abroad. Accompanying the in-person march were 4 million tweets, which were part of the 11.6 million tweets under this hashtag that amassed in February 2018. The #MarchForOurLives hashtag movement emerged in response to the school shooting at Marjory Stoneman Douglas High School in Parkland, Florida, on February 28 (Deng 2018). Emotion played a vital role in these protest movements, and this chapter investigates the role of affect in the hashtag movements that facilitated and supported these in-person protests. Through qualitative analysis of thousands of tweets, this comparative study identifies the most effective rhetorical strategies in #WhyIMarch (one of the most utilized hashtags during the 2017 Women's March) and #MarchForOurLives, identifying affective devices that were similar in the two datasets (e.g., personal narratives, evocations of imagined communities,[3] first-person pronouns), as well as ones that differed (e.g., dedications, humor, juxtaposition, second-person pronouns). After discussing the most prominent rhetorical strategies leveraging affect for social change and their implications for hashtag activism, we conclude by offering suggestions for how future digital writing might leverage affect to mobilize online protests accompanying in-person movements.

LITERATURE REVIEW

This chapter contributes to several ongoing conversations related to hashtag activism, including discussions on the interactions between online and offline movements and the role of affect in hashtag activism and hashtag feminism in particular. Much existing scholarship on digital activism emerged from inquiries about how online movements facilitated in-person protests, such as Paolo Gerbaudo's (2012) study of the 2011 political uprisings in Egypt and the Occupy Wall Street movement; Gerbaudo argued that social media resonates with the social justice movements taking place on the ground. Also studying the Occupy Wall Street movement, Sky Croeser and Tim Highfield (2014) attended to the ways geographically specific posts (in this case #oo for Occupy Oakland) were linked to tweets from protests unfolding in other cities and contributed to a collective digital movement. Like the Women's

Marches and the March for Our Lives Rallies addressed in this chapter, Coeser and Highfield found that while the occupy protests were organized around public spaces, the physical and online parts of the movement were interwoven.

In terms of the studies presented here, many tweets include geographic-specific hashtags that announce their physical locations while also including the large umbrella hashtags (#WhyIMarch, #March ForOurLives, #WomensMarch) that connect the protests occurring simultaneously across the globe. In addition to those protesting on the ground in different physical spaces, users unable to join a physical space were able to participate virtually through the shared "digital" space the hashtags provide. Being that the majority of the Women's Marches and March for Our Lives rallies were pre-planned, pre-approved events (often with permits to meet on public grounds), as opposed to protests that were purposely designed to be disruptive presences in public spaces, Twitter did not need to provide this function. Regardless, such studies clearly indicate that the digital conversations unfolding under such hashtags can have a utilitarian function as well as the more general function of connecting "geographically dispersed but politically linked physical spaces" (Croeser and Highfield 2014). (For more on this, see chapter 1, this volume.) In terms of tweets that used a place-specific variation of a larger hashtag movement, Croeser and Highfield also found that they showcased the identity of the local movement as well as "the complex relationship between local manifestations" and broader movements. They question the assumption that "place-based activism is always more authentic, inclusive, and meaningful than online communications," and the studies in this chapter are indeed as inclusive and meaningful as in-person protests.

This chapter builds on these conversations connecting the physical and the digital by adding the affective component. Affect and digital activism have usually been addressed through hashtag feminism. Kitsy Dixon (2014), for example, studied the role of emotion when social media users identified as feminists online. Although such identifications contain risks, Dixon found that personal narratives and emotion were leveraged to form online communities (36). Similarly, Shenila Khoja-Moolji (2015) studied the affect in terms of the creation of intimate publics through hashtag feminism. Although not specifically focusing on hashtag activism, Rachel Gong (2014) also found that affect was vital in digital activism within the online anti-trafficking movement. Through interviews with activists, Gong identified that emotion was created through storytelling and motivational moments and helped construct collective identity, inspire action, and facilitate solidarity between activists and non-activist supporters (88). This important role of affect in creating digital communities (Gruzd, Wellman, and Takhteyev 2011) is confirmed in our study, and we detail the digital rhetorical strategies protestors use to create these affective outcomes.

METHODS

To facilitate our investigation into affect and hashtag activism, we examined a sample of tweets from #WhyIMarch and #MarchForOurLives for their affective rhetorical strategies and what those strategies imply for hashtag activism. This inquiry was driven by these research questions:

1. What were the most common rhetorical strategies used in the two Women's March tweet samples, and how did these strategies leverage affect to create social change?
2. What do these findings imply about the way hashtag activists can employ affect to accomplish their goals, especially in relation to an in-person movement?

To address these questions, we collected more than 200,000 #WhyIMarch tweets from the day of the Women's March through NodeXL and coded a sample of 2,600 of those through the online software program Dedoose. We collected more than 100,000 #MarchForOurLives tweets from the day of the rallies and coded a sample of 2,000 of those through Dedoose. We coded the tweets using a grounded theory approach (Corbin and Strauss 2008) where our coding categories emerged from the data themselves. Given our focus on rhetorical strategies of hashtag activism related to affect, we also looked for themes related to that focus. Although the coding process initially resulted in almost 100 different codes, we ultimately narrowed down our codes into four primary categories: Feminist Themes, Rhetorical Strategies, Emotion, and Media Included. Given our research questions in this chapter, we will focus our discussion on the primary Rhetorical Strategies used and the effects of the Emotion in the tweets.

FINDINGS: RHETORICAL STRATEGIES THAT RESONATED IN BOTH MARCHES

Through our data analysis, we determined that the rhetorical strategies that best utilized affect to address social change were personal narratives and the use of first-person plural pronouns.

Personal Narratives

Considering the prevalence of personal narratives in prior hashtag feminism and the narrative logic of #WhyIMarch tweets, there were not as many personal narratives in the Women's March tweets as we had expected, but the ones present were effective at raising awareness of the issues and leveraging emotion to create social change. The narratives in our dataset ranged from stories of the user's experiences that day at the march (e.g., "On way to #WomensMarchBoston when guy tells train conductor to run over any protesters. #WhyIMarch"; "a man just yelled 'Men own the world. You can't change anything.' to a crowd of women on their way to the March") to stories of past experiences illustrating why she was protesting.[4] Users recounted instances of sexism ("WhyIMarch because I told a guy yesterday that I work at a software company and he asked if I was an accountant"), gender discrimination ("Because a male doctor once refused to give me birth control because I wasn't married"), and sexual assault ("#WhyIMarch bc a guy thought he could grab my neck while dancing"). In addition to such stories that explain the user's motivation for participating, many users listed specific people by name or more generally stated that they were marching for their sons, daughters, mothers, or others.

#MarchForOurLives tweets show uses of personal narratives aligning with the practices found in the #WomensMarch tweets. For example, while #MarchForOurLives did not use the #WhyIMarch hashtag as frequently, users nonetheless identified the reasons they were marching in quick personal narratives. For example, one tweet included a photo of someone holding a sign that reads "I'm a teacher, not a sharpshooter," which identifies both their profession and their reason for marching. Also similar to Women's March tweets, #MarchForOurLives included narratives of people at the march. One user wrote, "The school kids walking behind me are discussing the best ways to hide from bullets. THIS HAS TO END."

In addition to educators and students, one of the larger groups providing personal narratives was veterans. A number of users identified themselves as veterans who had experience with military-grade weapons and expressed support for gun control (e.g., "I served in three different deployments. My weapon was an M-16. I've seen the damage it can do to the body. The same damage the AR-15 does. I'm a Veteran & I'm for a ban on assault rifles"). Finally, personal narratives were used as a counternarrative as well. One user wrote, "Speaking from personal experience, the criminals who robbed me at gunpoint didn't get their gun legally . . . and no law, or ban would have stopped them. I on the other hand, would have been safer had I been concealed carrying that day." This last example shows that users who did not support the march also leveraged affect to be persuasive.

First-Person Plural Pronouns

Of the numerous rhetorical strategies we identified in the tweets from both studies, one of the most direct strategies that utilized affect was the use of first-person plural pronouns. The pronoun "we" implies a multiplicity of subjects that, together, impact the rhetorical uptake of the tweet and build affective community among users in some cases and reinforce an us-versus-them binary in others.

There were five main ways authors utilized first-person plural in the Women's March dataset. As the majority of the tweets reported participation and described the marches, one of the primary uses of first person was to create an imagined audience for the protests (e.g., "This is what it looks like when we show up"). The next common use of first-person plural was to refer to women as the subject of the march ("to defy anyone who would seek to diminish our worth"). First-person plural was also often used to denote American citizenship: a variation of "we the people" appeared as a phrase or hashtag in multiple tweets (e.g., "this administration needs to know we are watching, and 'we' are the people"), as did other statements wherein the focus on US citizens is relatively obvious, such as in references to the president (e.g., "Because our country elected a person who bragged about sexual assault"). "We/our" was also used to suggest that the author's imagined audience shared the same political ideology, implying that the reader would be a Democrat or liberal (e.g., "This is what the #SnowFlakeArmy looks like"). Finally, some tweets used first-person plural in a broad sense to represent people and humanity in general (e.g., "so our future knows we are better than this shit").

The use of first person in the #MarchForOurLives tweets aligned with these practices to some extent but also exposed a major difference between the two hashtags. First person aligned with the first study when "we" was used to denote humanity (e.g., "We are on this Earth to support one another"), to mark citizenship (e.g., We as Americans or global supporters), to claim membership in particular groups with something at stake in gun violence or school shootings (e.g., Black community members, educators, students), to announce partisanship or political ideologies (e.g., We as Democrat/liberal), and to imply shared values (e.g., support for gun control, support for the second amendment). However, unlike the Women's March tweets, "we/us/ our" was often used to mark one's age group (and direct addresses utilizing second person were most commonly aimed at youth versus older generations as imagined communities). While most often these addresses were done in supportive ways (e.g., "So inspiring yet tragic that our children have to tell us that enough is enough. But we have your backs"), this practice was at times divisive (e.g., "The adults failed us, it's time we fight and change"). Since the March for Our Lives dataset was trafficked heavily by those critical of the march, the hashtag was often co-opted; therefore, these pronouns were also used to highlight political divides and differences of opinion on the second amendment (e.g., "What a joke this #MarchForOurLives is. Kids have been co-opted to push liberal gun control narrative. No matter how much you chant and march we aren't giving you #2A. We will not have children dictate the Constitution").

The examples in this section show that #WhyIMarch and #MarchForOurLives tweets, as two recent in-person marches with considerable accompanying digital protest movements, use personal narratives and first-person pronouns to leverage affect to create social change. Next, we consider areas where the marches did not align as well.

RHETORICAL STRATEGIES THAT DIVERGED BETWEEN MARCHES

Several rhetorical strategies that appeared in the Women's March data were not as prominent in the March for Our Lives data, including what we call Dedications. Dedications refer to tweets where users explain that they are marching for a person or persons, such as a child or an elder, and emerge as a natural response to the #WhyIMarch prompt. An example is a tweet dedicated to a recently deceased grandmother that gives the grandmother's name along with two images: a picture of a typed dedication to her grandmother and a picture of a backpack with a WhyIMarch pin and a memorial flyer. Dedications were not as common in #MarchForOurLives tweets, but they contained powerful appeals to emotion when they appeared. In one sample tweet, a user posted side-by-side photos of two friends who died during the mass shooting at the Pulse nightclub: "I'm not able to march today but these are my friends who were killed at Pulse and shot down in the street. Thank you for marching."

Humor was also a prominent rhetorical strategy found in the #WhyIMarch tweets that did not surface regularly in the #MarchForOurLives tweets. Much of the humor in the #WhyIMarch tweets appeared in the

Figure 3.1. Examples of humor as a rhetorical strategy in #WhyIMarch tweets

photographs of signs. Users posted photos of signs they were carrying or that they saw, and some humorous signs were tweeted without added commentary or with only hashtags as extra commentary (e.g., "#supercallousfascistracistextrabraggadosiosis ATROCIOUS"). As figure 3.1 demonstrates, users utilized humor rhetorically through a variety of visual means. The leftmost image uses a combination of pun and illustration to simultaneously mock Trump and warn him against stripping citizens of their rights with the play on "hell to pay/toupee." The center image includes a posed shot of a woman in pink pussy hat taking a drink from a coffee cup, but it transforms the picture with a caption incorporating the oft-used phrase "tears of patriarchy." Finally, the rightmost image uses the combination of the sign holder's biblical costuming along with "you shall not pass" wording to produce commentary on the anti-abortion legislation supported by conservatives.

While both protests stemmed from serious issues—ones that prompted millions to march in the streets—the tone of the tweets differed considerably. The Women's March tweets were predominantly positive (and sprinkled with fear and anger) while the March for Our Lives tweets were more balanced between fear and anger (and sprinkled with hope and optimism). The grave circumstances that prompted the latter likely account for these tonal differences and the decreased presence of humor in the March for Our Lives tweets. The absence of humor in this dataset is noteworthy being that research has established that Twitter as a platform privileges humorous posts (Holton and Lewis 2011), making it unsurprising when it surfaces as a strategy for hashtag activism.

A prominent rhetorical strategy that appeared in the #MarchForOur Lives dataset but not as much in #WhyIMarch tweets was the use of juxtaposition. While juxtaposition is better known for being a literary device, we use it here to capture the ways teacher activists conveyed the problematic nature of their roles in our new societal norm of school violence. In this first example, "I'm a teacher, not a sharpshooter," the teacher is presented in direct contrast to the military term *sharpshooter*. This juxtaposition appears over and over again: teachers need funding not firearms, often combined with other literary strategies such as rhyming and alliteration. Books instead of bullets, for example, is catchy, brief, and gut-wrenching all at once. These activist slogans operate on an affective level and are simultaneously witty, sobering, and memorable.

A second strategy that was more prevalent in the March for Our Lives tweets was the use of second-person pronouns. Typically used for direct addresses, second person worked quite differently than the first person of #WhyIMarch, which helped create collective affect. Second-person pronouns in #MarchForOurLives tweets were more likely to express division and negative affect. For example, "you" was used as a direct address to protestors, including teenage participants (e.g., "If you teens want to protest, I suggest you go to school to learn"). "You" was also used to address citizens who use the second amendment to justify not supporting gun reform (e.g., "Gun rights people need to ask themselves: do you love the AR-15 more than you love kids"). And often "you" was used to target politicians (e.g., #ThoughtsAndPrayers to any policymakers who do not support #GunControl. You'll be voted out soon), most commonly Republicans (e.g., GOP are you listening? While your electorate dies, the young demand you govern for them, not the NRA [National Rifle Association]). While there were tweets coded for positive affect and second person (most often direct addresses from adults to youth), second person was often used to demonstrate division between groups based on age, issue, and political party.

If a goal of hashtag activism is to raise awareness about social injustices, the March for Our Lives tweets were more successful in this regard. Many Women's March tweets provided a laundry list of social issues users were concerned about. Again, this may be due to the #WhyIMarch prompt that evokes such responses. The result, however, was that few tweets provided much information about individual issues or instances of injustice. The March for Our Lives tweets contain more posts that provide information about gun legislation and links to information on gun violence and mass shootings. For example, some users compared gun violence in the US to that in other countries (e.g., "Gun control laws in Japan and Australia have prevented mass shootings like those in Parkland while still allowing citizens to own firearms. We need to implement those laws in the US"). Other tweets provide statistics on the impact gun violence has on specific communities (e.g., "Black Men are 13 times more likely than white men to be shot and killed with guns"). One such tweet captured a powerful visual tactic to commemorate the many mass shootings that motivated people to march. The protest sign in this post is titled "Mass Shootings since 2000 in U.S." and then in small print lists thirty-two different instances and the resulting deaths, ending with the common phrase "Never Again!" This strategy reminds viewers of the other mass shootings that are relevant to the march and also leverages affect to persuade viewers of the importance of the march and its issues.

The use of the background information through links and other digital tools that was more prominent in #MarchForOurLives tweets demonstrates a productive use of digital activism according to Caroline Dadas (2017). Dadas (2017, 18–19) argues that hashtag activism often oversimplifies the issues represented by a hashtag, given the limited features of social networking sites and the rapid way both tweets and issues circulate online. She suggests that hashtag movements need to maintain the backgrounds and contexts of their issues to accurately represent those issues and that retweeting informational posts and linking to reputable news stories can help honor the original intentionality of the movement (19, 32). The narrower scope of #MarchForOurLives tweets (about gun violence and school shootings) compared to #WhyIMarch (about feminist issues and politics more generally) likely explains the more sophisticated use of background information and linking in #MarchForOurLives tweets and demonstrates that narrower issues make for more effective hashtag campaigns. The other rhetorical strategies discussed in this section, dedications and humor, likewise diverged in the samples given the different rhetorical situations of the marches, yet both suggest productive ways of arresting viewers and leveraging affect to create social change.

DISCUSSION: THE EFFECT OF AFFECTIVE RHETORICAL STRATEGIES

While many tweets in the sample leveraged emotion, three particular outcomes emerged from the rhetorical strategies discussed above related to affect: calls to action, expressions of vicarious affect, and evocations of imagined communities. This focus builds off previous research that considers social media's role in triggering, intensifying, and/or circulating affect (Paasonen 2015, 31). Susanna Paasonen (2015,

30) argues that "social media users are largely driven by a search for intensity—a desire for some kind of affective jolt, for something to capture one's attention." The previous discussion demonstrated the ways these strategies effectively garner attention by employing such "affective jolts." The following discussion, however, sheds more light on their results: the affective capital that is accumulated and exchanged as these emotive tweets are posted and consumed.

Calls to Action

The #WhyIMarch tweets contain a dominant focus on emotion; for example, a number of users explicitly name an emotion, such as hope or pride, and these emotions are overwhelmingly positive, like love, pride, gratitude, inspiration, and hope. While references to positive emotions emerge in #MarchForOurLives, they are accompanied by many tweets that note or express anger (directed at various persons and issues). In #WhyIMarch tweets, these calls to action invite readers to join the march (e.g., "#wmwyhm crowd gathering. Still time to join us") or to join feminist causes (e.g., "this is the time to roll up our sleeves, to be courageous, to be radical. We must make resistance our lifestyles"). These motivational posts served multiple roles: some were expressing and encouraging enthusiasm (e.g., "Hate will never make America great. Let's keep protesting, organizing, and advocating"), some were celebratory and encouraging ("Be loud as fuck today, but be safe. You're all beautiful"), and others were encouraging about the potential impact of the march (e.g., "Together we fight for equity. Let's send a message to our new govt on their 1st day"). Some calls to action invoked girl power and resistance. Posts were punctuated with rallying cries like "join the resistance," "come together," and "let's do this." One of the most popular (and recurrent) battle cries was an allusion to Beyoncé's politically charged 2016 album *Lemonade*, which appeared in multiple posts under the #WomensMarch hashtag: "okay ladies, let's get in formation."

In #MarchForOurLives, the calls to action largely stemmed from the vicarious tweets, which will be discussed in the next section. Many of the supportive words expressed disappointment at not being able to attend the march ("Wish I was at #MarchForOurLives I am with you guys"; "I can't be at the march today, but I'm proud of everyone marching. You are changing the world"). A smaller number of tweets were more straightforward pronouncements of excitement ("#MarchForOurLives is happening here. I got my sign, my boots, my water and my attitude").

Compared to the #WomensMarch tweets, the #MarchForOurLives tweets were more indicting. There were more direct challenges issued in the tweets, such as in the example "We're here. Are you?" and more direct partisan callouts ("Reminding people to #VoteBlue at #MarchForOurLives").

Vicarious Affect

As noted, our data suggest that #WhyIMarch tweets overwhelmingly conveyed positive emotion. Posts from marchers and non-attendees alike referenced the positive affect and energy the march and accompanying tweets conveyed. Participants referenced being emotionally uplifted by the crowds in person (e.g., "feeling the energy sisters!! Downtown is lit!!"; "Today feminist energy is tangible"), while those following the march on Twitter made similar claims (e.g., "To everyone marching today, you are what HOPE looks like! Resist Everyday!"; "Yes! Seeing all the pictures & video so far is giving me more hope than the fear & disgust I was feeling all week"). Many users expressed gratitude to the marchers ("So intensely proud of everyone marching. Thank you: we are making a difference. Xo"); more still used phrasing that noted that they were participating in the march vicariously with phrases like "with you all virtually" and "wish I could be at the Women's March today. I stand with you all every step of the way."

Vicarious participation was also present in #MarchForOurLives tweets, with users noting positive affect gained from it: "I have chills watching #MarchForOurLives. This is only the beginning. Change is coming." As with the previous study, posts also reflected the inclusiveness of such digital participation (e.g., "I have severe anxiety and can't participate. Just know I support all of you"). These posts reveal the extended dialogue and engagement with the protest happening beyond the actual march sites: "Eating breakfast with my kids. Talking to them about the #MarchForOurLives movement and all of the students, teachers, parents, and politicians who are marching for a better future for our children. I can't march today but I can plant a seed in the minds of my littles." This example also contains layered affect meaning with its reference to children.

Overall, the virtual and vicarious tweets were one of the most productive engagements of hashtag activism in both movements in this study. Users posted from the march and to marchers, and both ultimately participated in creating the vicarious affect and supported each other and the issues surrounding the marches.

Collective Affect

In addition to tweets that labeled users' own emotions, solicited emotion in others, and claimed to experience another's emotion, there were tweets that erased any separation between self and other. These tweets projected the author's feelings onto a crowd or community. While Women's March posts occasionally reference shared negative affect, such as the "soul crushing" election of Trump, more often tweets express shared positive affect. One example of these collective tweets involved proclamations of shared love (e.g., "Anger got us started, love will keep us going"). Some of the tweets convey the mood of the crowd (e.g., "Passion, strength & unity here in DC. Great movement and inspiration"), while others assign an emotion to a group. For example, the tweet "We raise feminists. Proud, loud, strong, angry, and indignant" associates feminism generally with these named emotions. Statements like these can be problematic because they are presumptuous. Nonetheless, these examples have the same outcome of portraying a group—whether march participants or feminists overall—as a collective affective community.

One way users in our dataset invoked an affective imagined community was by referencing Hillary Clinton's campaign slogan, "Stronger Together." Another strategy was through references to sisterhood. One tweet, for example, reads, "We're here with 1000s of our friends." This post, too, has multiple layers in that it uses first-person plural to invoke collective affect while also addressing a hyperbolic 1,000 fellow marchers as friends. Even though this community is not real in most senses of the word, it conveys a powerful sense of solidarity and support that is one of the best outcomes of the march and its digital companion protest. The fact that many marchers truly felt this sense of community is evident throughout the dataset and perhaps captured best by the photograph in our dataset in which lyrics from John Lennon's protest song "Imagine" float above a crowd of pink hats.

Similarly, the March for Our Lives tweets both describe and assign feelings of imagined community and shared affect. Users labeled the collective mood of the crowd (e.g., "The energy here in the streets is amazing. Students are going to change the world") and projected feelings onto participants (e.g., "To the young folks for whom #MarchForOurLives is their first protest, the warmth you're feeling as you stare at your fellow demonstrators is the warmth of solidarity, of democracy in action, of having a voice. Let this first taste make you an addict"). While the feelings surrounding the imagined community created by marchers (be they physical or virtual participants) were overwhelmingly positive, the motivations for marching time and time again pointed to the collective affect of fear (e.g., "It's really messed up that our youth have to march just to let everyone know they want to just be able to grow up in a world without fear of being killed or hurt in school, the mall, clubs . . . etc. keep marching & never stop").

As noted earlier, since the focus on gun control (expanded more generally into second amendment rights for some) brought both proponents and opponents to the #MarchForOurLives dialogue, the posts as a whole tended to avoid overgeneralizing claims about participants using the hashtag. However, in terms of marchers themselves, some perspectives were more predominant, and assumed to be shared, more than others. Take, for example, this tweet: "As a teacher who is ABSOLUTELY against arming teachers and does fear a school shooting taking place at my school, as a US citizen who, one day, want[s] to be proud of how we, the US, do not have to fear gun violence . . . I wish I could join the march today." The dialogue unfolding under this hashtag does largely imply shared beliefs about gun control among students and educators, which is not necessarily the case. This post in particular references one particular measure being enacted to deter school shootings: allowing educators to carry firearms.

FRAMING THE FUTURE: GENERATIONAL POSTS AND THE VISUAL RHETORIC OF CHILDREN

Overall, the shared rhetorical strategy we found to be the most effective at leveraging affect for social change (often in the ways discussed above) was the generational focus. Users engaged dedications, personal narratives, photographs, and more to draw attention to past and future social progress. While occasionally the historical tweets expressed frustration, like a tweet from the Women's March noting slow feminist progress ("I can't believe we still have to protest this shit"), others embraced the spirit of ongoing social activism, such as these tweets: "My mother marched in the 60s. It would be a disservice to her memory and everything she taught me if I didn't do it now" (from the Women's March) and "Older man to his wife: 'I can put you on my shoulders to see. It'll be like Woodstock all over again'" (from March for Our Lives). The majority of tweets utilizing this rhetorical affective strategy referenced the past as a source of inspiration and motivation, such as literal and figurative mothers who laid a foundation for future generations of women to succeed in the case of the Women's March and past tragedies that detailed the need for gun reform in the case of the March for Our

Lives. Within both datasets, the future-orientated posts often focused on children as a source of hope and motivation that may inspire investment and action among readers. From dedications to declarations, from the heartwarming to the heart-wrenching, these posts were among the most successful at leveraging affect to inspire social change.

The generational focus often emerged in our samples through photographs of children. Photographs have routinely been "mobilized by citizens as resources for public argument," but the circulation of pictures within hashtag activism has an extra affectively charged dimension (Finnegan 2015, 124). Researchers have attended to the rhetorical ways images of children have been used to frame conflicts and to prompt social change. For example, Karen Wells (2007, 55) studied pictures of Iraqi children featured in British newspapers during the 2003 war and argues that "images of children are particularly potent resources for constructing narratives about the motivations and outcomes of" conflicts. Similarly, Erica Burman (1994, 240), studying the use of children in framing disaster narratives, argues that they come to represent the shape of the evolving future. In Western culture more generally, children have come to represent purity and goodness (Lutz and Collins 1993; Holland 1992); they are used as symbols to depict "innocence and playfulness and hope for the future" (Wells 2007, 55). Images of children are thus emotionally loaded and can be used rhetorically as powerful pathos-ridden aids in arguing for social justice issues.

The use of imagery of children in activist campaigns also connects to the imagined community affective result. Harry Hendrick (1997, 51) explains, "Just as the nation is often imagined as the family and talked about in familial metaphors (the mother land), the fate of the child, a role that is central to the production of family, is collapsed into the fate of the nation . . . The innocence of the child, its exclusion from political calculus, and its universal appeal to adults' duty of care makes it a useful symbol." More recently, Wells (2007, 60) echoed this belief that children play a strong role in fashioning an imagined community when she said that a child, in representing the potential for redemption and progress, can be a "potent resource for constructing narratives about collective futures and, in particular, the future of the nation." In our samples of march tweets, we find numerous text-only references to children that effectively employed many of the above-mentioned narratives, such as directly naming children as the motivating factor in participating in the Women's March (e.g., "B/c I want to be able to look my future children in the eye & tell them, 'Your mom was there, and she did everything she could' ") or referencing fallen youth to explain one's dedication to

Affecting Digital Activism   67

Figure 3.2. Examples of Women's March tweets utilizing children for affective purposes

fighting for gun control (e.g., "B/c my oldest daughter was the same age as the Sandy Hook first graders when that shooting happened. It's burned deeply on my heart their senseless deaths should have been enough to change legislation. 4 them & for every victim of gun violence we #MarchForOurLives"). However, we find that the numerous examples of children in photographs were even more effective in leveraging emotion to create multiple rhetorical effects, from leveraging pathos to creating imagined community.

In #WhyIMarch tweets, children were strategically captured in various stages of the protest with signs that reinforced their symbolic roles: coloring messages about love, holding up signs calling for unity, being named as the face of a revolution (see figure 3.2). Other choices in photographs posted under this hashtag by virtual participants carry additional social commentary. Consider the lower right-hand photograph of the young girl dressed up in a pink ballerina tutu and butterfly wings. The purposeful juxtaposition of the feminist phrase "the future is female" against what one might consider a stereotypically girlish play outfit can be read as critiquing the erroneous belief that one cannot embrace femininity and feminism simultaneously. While many users simply included photographs of their own children to underscore their

Figure 3.3. Examples of March for Our Lives tweets using images of children

#WhyIMarch response, the photographs they posted often contain additional layers of meaning. Take, for example, the upper right photo in figure 3.2. The protest sign is a picture frame with the hashtag written across the bottom. A young child reaches out from within that window, reinforcing the unspoken message that the protest is needed to rescue the younger generation from the potential dangers of inaction.

This presence of children in #MarchForOurLives worked on similar affective registers. Many users discussed the march in generational terms (e.g., "overwhelmed with emotions as I watch my daughter's generation take the reins"; "I marched with my parents for stricter gun control when I was in high school in the early 1980s. Excited to join my daughter marching today"). As with the Women's March, visuals of children were used for affective purposes. The first image in figure 3.3 features a young girl with a caption reading "my little activist," showing that children are associated with hope for the future. The second image again showcases the message that children must be protected with a child and an "Am I Next" poster, along with a "She can NOT be next" textual response. In the third image it is actually the absence of children that relays this message. This chilling photograph reveals 14,000 empty children's shoes lining the lawn in front of the US Capitol. As the tweet explains, these shoes represent the lives of children lost to gun violence.

In both the #WhyIMarch and #MarchForOurLives datasets, photos of and allusions to children displayed considerable emotion from both march and digital participants and encouraged viewers to vicariously participate in these motions. Furthermore, these tweets invited viewers to see themselves as responsible for our nation's children and to participate collectively in an imagined community. In this way, Twitter users, activists, and viewers alike are encouraged to participate affectively and work collectively to enact social change.

A TALE OF TWO MARCHES: IMPLICATIONS AND OPPORTUNITIES

Our analysis of the Women's Marches and March for Our Lives rallies demonstrates specific rhetorical strategies that were effective in leveraging affect to inspire social change. For example, the uses of personal narratives and visual imagery of children were rhetorical techniques that hashtag activists showcased to create collective responsibility for the social justice issues prioritized in these marches. Despite these effective strategies, however, we ultimately question the overall impact of these hashtags in furthering the particular missions of these marches, primarily because the hashtags were tied to specific events. To be clear, these hashtags were not limited because of their connection to place-based activism, as our analysis shows that the affective strategies employed successfully joined the physical and virtual aspects of these marches. In fact, digital activism was vital for increasing access to the marches, facilitating various affects, and increasing the imagined communities related to these issues. Rather, these hashtag movements were limited by their temporal restraints because the marches had a limited time frame (mostly one day). Twitter's ephemerality is always a challenge when it comes to hashtag activism—even the most successful social justice hashtags have a relatively short shelf life and eventually run their course. But the Women's March hashtags had a shorter shelf life than most. The vast majority of the posts associated with this hashtag occurred within twenty-four hours of the march, with most of the rest coming in days after. While this short life span may suggest that hashtag campaigns tied to in-person events are ineffective, there are ways to extend the impact of the hashtag activism. March for Our Lives tweets, for example, lasted longer because they addressed gun control as an issue in addition to the march itself. Users thus included hashtags related to second amendment rights discussions such as #2A and gun reform activism like #NeverAgain and #BooksNotBullets, to specific school shootings like #Parkland and #MSDstrong, to other hashtag movements like #BlackLivesMatter and #TakeAKnee, and to other protest rhetoric such as #RiseUp and #ThisIsWhatDemocracyLooksLike. By engaging in these various issues, hashtag activists made connections between #MarchForOurLives and other hashtag movements and increased the opportunity for the hashtag's staying power.

As a feminist hashtag movement, the Women's March could have engaged in similar strategies, such as connecting the #WhyIMarch hashtag to existing hashtag movements to increase their visibility and interaction with digital activists. Our dataset revealed that #WhyIMarch tweets posted during the 2017 Women's March indicate that this strategy was rarely utilized. For example, #EveryDaySexism was used twice, #BlackGirlMagic appeared six times, #YesAllWomen appeared eight times, and #HeForShe appeared eleven times. These are strikingly low numbers considering the thousands of #WhyIMarch tweets, and we saw no evidence of hashtag connections to successful pre-2017 movements like #WhyIStayed.

Future research might take up this question of increasing the effectiveness of hashtag movements that accompany in-person protests. Visual network analysis could be particularly effective at tracing the relationships between hashtags in order to make suggestions for increasing the visibility and circulation of hashtag protests. Other suggestions for future research include more in-depth studies on the findings included in this chapter, such as the rhetorical strategy of including visual images of children and of using humor to inspire social change. While previous scholarship has attended to the role of personal narratives in creating collective affect, for example, less attention has been paid to the ways hashtag activists invoke humor and satire to create social change. Whether it's humor or tragedy or anger, it is certain that affect will continue to play a prominent role in hashtag activism for a variety of future protests.

NOTES

1. Researcher Nick Ruest (2017) puts the tweet volume at 14 million.
2. Crowd size was estimated at 200,000 in Washington, DC, for the March for Our Lives rally, although organizers estimated attendance at 800,000. More than 800 sister marches occurred globally on this day as well. https://www.cbsnews.com/news/march-for-our-lives-crowd-size-estimated-200000-people-attended-d-c-march/.
3. In discussing imagined communities and audience throughout this chapter, we are drawing on Arjun Appadurai's (1996) notion of "imagined worlds" (3) and "virtual neighborhood" (195), which he theorized as the digital equivalent to Benedict Anderson's (1983) original conceptualization of imagined communities. Appadurai's argument that the people are able to visualize and internalize an interconnectedness within the world as never before is demonstrated well through the ways tweets are circulated, consumed, and utilized in the work of the imagination.
4. To adhere to best practices in internet research ethics, we protect Twitter users' identities by disguising names, usernames, and faces in our examples (Bruckman 2002).

REFERENCES

Anderson, Benedict. 1983. *Imagined Communities: Reflections on the Origins and Spread of Nationalism.* New York: Verso.

Appadurai, Arjun. 1996. *Modernity at Large: Cultural Dimensions of Globalization.* Minneapolis: University of Minnesota Press.

Bruckman, Amy. 2002. "Studying the Amateur Artist: A Perspective on Disguising Data Collected in Human Subjects Research on the Internet." *Ethics and Information Technology* 4: 217–231.

Buchanan, Larry, Quoctrung Bui, and Jugal K. Patel. 2020. "Black Lives Matter May Be the Largest Movement in U.S. History." *New York Times*, July 3. https://www.nytimes.com/interactive/2020/07/03/us/george-floyd-protests-crowd-size.html?auth=link-dismiss-google1tap.

Burman, Erica. 1994. "Innocents Abroad: Western Fantasies of Childhood and the Iconography of Disaster." *Disasters* 18 (3): 238–253.

Cohen, David. 2017. "Twitter: 12 Million Inauguration Tweets Friday, 11.5 Million Women." *Adweek.com*, January 23. http://www.adweek.com/digital/twitter-12-million-inauguration-tweets-friday-11-5-million-womens-march-tweets-saturday/.

Corbin, Juliet, and Anselm Strauss. 2008. *Basics of Qualitative Research*. 3rd ed. Los Angeles: Sage.

Croeser, Sky, and Tim Highfield. 2014. "Occupy Oakland and #oo: Uses of Twitter within the Occupy Movement." *First Monday* 19 (3). http://dx.doi.org/10.5210/fm.v19i3.4827.

Dadas, Caroline. 2017. "Hashtag Activism: The Promise and Risk of 'Attention.'" In *Social Writing/Social Media: Publics, Presentations, and Pedagogies*, edited by Douglas M. Walls and Stephanie Vie, 17–36. Fort Collins, CO: WAC Clearinghouse. https://wac.colostate.edu/books/perspectives/social/.

Deng, Olivia. 2018. "March for Our Lives Was Born on Social Media." *Brandwatch.com*, March 30. https://www.brandwatch.com/blog/march-for-our-lives-social-media/.

Dixon, Kitsy. 2014. "Feminist Online Identity: Analyzing the Presence of Hashtag Feminism." *Journal of Arts and Humanities* 3 (7): 34–40.

Finnegan, Cara. 2015. *Making Photography Matter: A Viewer's History from the Civil War to the Great Depression*. Urbana: University of Illinois Press.

Gerbaudo, Paolo. 2012. *Tweets and the Streets: Social Media and Contemporary Activism*. New York: Pluto Press.

Gong, Rachel. 2014. "Indignation, Inspiration, and Interaction on the Internet: Emotion Work Online in the Anti-trafficking Movement." *Journal of Technology in Human Services* 33 (1): 87–103.

Gruzd, Anatoliy, Barry Wellman, and Yury Takhteyev. 2011. "Imagining Twitter as an Imagined Community." *American Behavioral Scientist* 55 (10): 1294–1318.

Hendrick, Harry. 1997. "Constructions and Reconstructions of British Childhood: An Interpretative Survey, 1800 to the Present." In *Constructing and Reconstructing Childhood: Contemporary Issues in the Sociological Study of Childhood*, edited by Allison James and Alan Prout, 34–62. Washington, DC: Falmer.

Holland, Patricia. 1992. *What Is a Child? Popular Images of Childhood*. London: Virago.

Holton, Avery, and Seth C. Lewis. 2011. "Journalists, Social Media, and the Use of Humor on Twitter." *Electronic Journal of Communication* 21: 1–21.

Khoja-Moolji, Shenila. 2015. "Becoming an 'Intimate Publics': Exploring the Affective Intensities of Hashtag Feminism." *Feminist Media Studies* 15 (2): 347–350. doi:10.1080/14680777.2015.1008747.

Lutz, Catherine A., and Jane L. Collins. 1993. *Reading National Geographic*. Chicago: University of Chicago Press.

Paasonen, Susanna. 2015. "A Midsummer's Bonfire: Affective Intensities of Online Debate." In *Networked Affect*, edited by Ken Hillis, Susanna Paasonen, and Michael Petit, 27–42. Cambridge, MA: MIT Press.

Politi, Daniel. 2017. "Women's March on Washington Beats Expectations: Half a Million Descend on Mall." *Slate.com*, January 21. http://www.slate.com/blogs/the_slatest/2017/01/21/women_s_march_on_washington_beats_expectations_half_a_million_descend_on.html.

Ruest, Nick. 2017. "Exploring #WomensMarch." *Medium.com*, February 10. https://medium.com/on-archivy/exploring-womensmarch-dcc30221101c.

"These Are the Four Largest Protests since Trump Was Inaugurated." 2018. *Washington Post*, May 31. https://www.washingtonpost.com/news/monkey-cage/wp/2018/05/31/these-are-the-four-largest-protests-since-trump-was-inaugurated/?mc_cid=14731c9979&mc_eid=d6c3ec1ce4&utm_term=.d71d0d7b31b7.

Wells, Karen. 2007. "Narratives of Liberation and Narratives of Innocent Suffering: The Rhetorical Uses of Images of Iraqi Children in the British Press." *Visual Communications* 6 (1): 55–71.

SECTION II

(Re)Examining Societal Narratives through Hashtag Activism

4
#ILOOKLIKEANENGINEER
Women Reclaiming STEM through Hashtag Activism

Holly M. Wells

On August 1, 2015, Isis Anchalee Wenger wrote a blog post on *The Coffeelicious* (part of *Medium.com*) that detailed her experiences of sexism following participation in her employer's ad campaign in which she and three colleagues were photographed for recruiting posters for the engineering company.[1] A man had posted a photograph of Wenger to Facebook (see figure 4.1) and questioned whether Wenger could actually be an engineer because she did not "look like an engineer" (Wenger 2015). Comments followed confirming this doubt that engineering is a career choice for attractive or average-looking women and questioning Wenger's employer, OneLogic, for using her image to attract *male* applicants. From that experience emerged the hashtag #iLookLikeAnEngineer, which Wenger coined with her *Medium* blog post and which went viral within days—producing over 75,000 tweets as of August 13, 2015, from other engineers (mainly women) who wanted the world to know how diverse the profession really is (Bates 2015). Wenger (2015) said, "Do you feel passionately about helping spread awareness and increase tech diversity? Do you not fit the 'cookie-cutter mold' of what people believe engineers 'should look like?' If you answered **yes** to any of these questions I invite you to help spread the word and help us redefine 'what an engineer should look like.' **#iLookLikeAnEngineer**."

Through a two-part study analyzing images collected from Google Images and the viral #iLookLikeAnEngineer movement, I review the rhetoric about engineers attending to two research questions: what are our stereotypes about engineers as evidenced in popular images about engineers, and what do we learn about them from the text and visuals facilitated through the hashtag intervening in those stereotypical narratives? In this chapter I first demonstrate that images of engineers reinforce stereotypes about who can be an engineer and risk leaving girls and young women without role models, imagining that only men

Figure 4.1. Facebook post of Wenger featured in a promotional poster for OneLogic alongside sexist comments

can become engineers. Further, these stereotypes can also encourage boys and men to continue to treat women as "outsiders" when women attempt to enter the various fields of engineering. I then show that this hashtag intervenes in this problematic cultural script and makes space for more socially just representations of engineers.

Using a method developed from components of Gunther Kress and Theo van Leeuwen's (1996) concept of "social semiotics of visual design" and Cara Finnegan's (2001) notion of "naturalistic enthymeme," this study compares visual arguments from a set of Google Image search results for "engineer" and "engineer stereotypes" to those from a series of images from the hashtag campaign #iLookLikeAnEngineer. The findings reveal that images tagged with #iLookLikeAnEngineer feature (primarily) women whose expressions, clothing, work settings, and races do not conform to the visual stereotypes evident in the Google Image results. For example, stereotypes about engineers portray them as nerdy, awkward, and unattractive (predominantly white or Asian) males dressed in shirts and ties with pocket protectors; the examined sample of engineers featured in the social media campaign, however, shows them to be much more diverse, featuring mostly women (both white women and Women of Color) who appear to be average to attractive, socially competent, and smartly or casually dressed (with nary a pocket protector in sight). This chapter concludes by considering the value of comparing stereotypes about engineers to lived realities, arguing that the #iLookLikeAnEngineer hashtag contributes to the discussion of how stereotypes about women in STEM, as well as the lack of visible role models of women in such fields, keep women from success in STEM professions. I suggest that by providing role models for a new generation of women, digital activism campaigns such as #iLookLikeAnEngineer may help pull more girls and young women into STEM fields and, by extension, encourage employers to hire and welcome more women.

LITERATURE REVIEW

Several recent studies have focused on connections between traditional feminist activism and hashtag feminism. Caitlin Gunn (2015) equates cyber-feminism (including hashtag feminism) with second-wave feminism's "personal is political" concept; Tracy L. M. Kennedy (2007) argues that although the feminist discourse in blogging, for example, is more democratized and inclusive than the second wave allowed for, white feminists are still not completely accepting of an online intersectional feminism. However, Rosemary Clark (2014), Tanya Horeck (2014), and Michelle Rodino-Colocino (2014) argue that hashtag feminism does unsettle and disrupt sites of oppression. As Clark (2014, 1109) puts it, "Hashtag feminism has unleashed a multiplicity of voices that demand recognition of differences across intersections of gender, sexuality, race, and class, so that more effective coalition building might occur."

Not all scholars agree that hashtag activism is always positive. For example, Shenila Khoja-Moolji (2015) argues that hashtag feminism can sometimes oversimplify or conflate the problems being discussed and ignore or flatten nuanced layers of responsibility of the actors involved. In her essay on the #BringBackOurGirls campaign, she argues for feminist participation "supplemented by attention to the broader principles and politics that feminism has inaugurated" (349). Similarly, a study of images connected to the #Ferguson hashtag that arose following the shooting of an unarmed Black man, Michael Brown, and the protests that took place in Ferguson, Missouri, reveals this lack of nuance. Holly Cowart, Lynsey Saunders, and Ginger Blackstone (2016, 7–8) found that mainstream news media developed a narrative of whites as passive or non-interacting and Blacks as in action or interacting. They also found that the images used by news media in their Twitter feeds rarely depicted protesters and police in the same shot, reflecting the existing divide between races and social groups in society, in which these "divided forces [were] working against each other" (7). These studies of hashtag activism suggest that in some cases, it brings invisible voices and faces to the foreground, but the online platform for activism has not necessarily been the democratizing force once imagined by scholars of the 1990s and early 2000s.

The #iLookLikeAnEngineer campaign offers a unique opportunity to study both the hashtag feminism disrupting the oppressive discourse around sexism in STEM and the visual narrative of that campaign: how engineers look is part of the hashtag itself. Visual representations of women in online spaces are sorely lacking in general; a recent Pew Research study found that on Facebook, men appear in photos twice as often as women do (Hughes et al. 2019). As discussed in the methodology section, representation of female engineers is likely even worse, judging by the results of a Google Images search. This study contrasts stereotypes about engineers against the coalition building at work in the #iLookLikeAnEngineer campaign to illustrate how the campaign works to disrupt these existing narratives in favor of a more inclusive, intersectional image of engineering as a field. In so doing, it emphasizes the importance of the formation of a narrative around women in engineering, which helps normalize engineering as a career choice for females.

STEREOTYPES AND IMAGES OF ENGINEERS

Stereotypes of engineers abound in our culture—on television, in movies, in books and comics, and on social media. Brandon Buckhalt of the website thecreativeengineer.com (n.d.) lists numerous engineer stereotypes held by adults:

- "Engineers have no soft skills. They are introverted and difficult to work with."
- "Engineers are geeks" with pocket protectors.
- "Engineers must love math."
- "Engineers aren't creative people."
- "Engineering is a male-dominated profession."
- "Engineering school is difficult."

Stereotypes held by children, on the other hand, seem to reflect some misunderstandings about what engineers actually do. According to a study by Meredith Knight and Christine Cunningham (2004, 4), 44 percent of boys in grades 3–5 and 41 percent of boys in grades 9–12 believe an engineer "builds," and 33 percent of boys in grades 6–8 believe an engineer "fixes."[2] Eighteen percent of girls in grades 6–8 think an engineer "drives (trains)" (4). This combination of negative and/or inaccurate stereotypes about engineering probably has much to do with the field's failure to attract girls, particularly in middle and high school (Shapiro et al. 2015).

PART I: DETERMINING EXISTING STEREOTYPES ABOUT ENGINEERS IN GOOGLE IMAGES

As noted earlier, the methodology I use to analyze images for visual argument is based in the work of Kress and van Leeuwen (1996, 2006) and Finnegan (2001). Kress and van Leeuwen's *Reading Images* (2006, 114) supplies a "visual grammar" for examining both the interactions between subjects in an image and interactions between image and viewer, or, as the authors put it, "represented participants" and "interactive participants." Finnegan's (2001) concept of a "naturalistic enthymeme" helps explain how an image, once accepted as "naturalistic" (i.e., as representing a possible reality, not a fictional one), can be broken down into the visual equivalent of a verbal argument. If we accept that rhetorical arguments rely on the enthymeme (with the understanding that the enthymeme is a syllogism with propositions that are probabilities or signs), it is then possible to examine an image for rhetorical syllogisms, or enthymemes, that put into words the propositions that are likely at work in an image. However, to make a case for these propositions, we must rely on cultural endoxa (the beliefs of a consensus of the wisest people in a given culture or society), with the caveat that the enthymeme in a given image can never be "proven" or "disproven," only that it can be said to be "likely."

Before examining images associated with the #iLookLikeAnEngineer campaign, I wanted to determine what some of the most pervasive visual stereotypes are about engineers, to give me a starting point for comparison. According to Net Market Share (2019), Google is still the leader in search engines by a large margin, so I began my search for visuals there. To determine whether Google Images's search algorithm produces images that reinforce the verbal stereotypes about engineers mentioned earlier, I performed a keyword search in Google Images using the search term *engineer*. According to a large study of clickstream data published by software company Moz (Fishkin 2017), the average Google search session lasts under one minute, with 3 percent of clicks going to images. A study from Advanced Web Ranking (2014, 25) found that more than 67 percent of search engine users' clicks go to the first five results listings and more than 71 percent of clicks occur on the first page of results, leaving only 5.59 percent for pages 2 and 3. As such, it seemed logical to collect the first two pages of image results, since research suggest it is unlikely that many users go beyond the first two pages when searching for an image of an "engineer." This resulted in a dataset of sixty-eight images. I then performed an analysis to tally gender, uniforms/clothing, setting, and any visual stereotypes pertaining to engineers. The results follow.

Table 4.1. Overview of key findings from Google Image analysis of search for engineers

Number of images:	68
Gender (n = 87)	M: 72 (83%) | F: 15 (17%)
Race (n = 87)	White: 79 (91%) | People of Color: 8 (9%)
Uniform/clothing (n = 87)	Hard hats: 74 (85%) | button-down shirts: 82 (94%) | coveralls or uniform jacket/trousers: 12 (14%) | suit jackets/suits: 17 (20%) | safety vests: 11 (13%)
Contextualization (n = 68)	Outdoors: 31 (46%) | indoors: 23 (34%) | no context: 11 (16%) | unsure: 3 (4%) (only 6 women outdoors)

As evident in table 4.1, the search aligned with the previously discussed stereotypes, with the vast majority of the photos featuring white men in professional (or profession-specific) attire working in outdoor settings. Some additional observations were noted, such as the fact that hard hats are worn, oddly, even by the subjects indoors; blue is the dominant color in almost every image; many subjects are carrying large rolls of paper (suggesting blueprints); and people featured working indoors are mostly working alone. Not pictured are the types of engineers whose jobs have little or nothing to do with outdoor structures or hard hats, such as software engineers, electrical engineers (who work predominantly in computer-aided design [CAD] settings), biomedical engineers (who complete the majority of their work tasks in labs), and audio engineers (who log hours in front of both mixing boards and computers), not to mention materials, chemical, electrical, marine, nuclear, computer, and petroleum engineers—all of whom have diverse work settings (some that look no different from traditional office environments and many that do not require a hard hat).

In addition, the majority of the photographs appear staged and artificial, likely because Google's search algorithms find mostly stock photography, which may have implications about the way engineering companies themselves conform to existing stereotypes. These limited representations of engineers reflect the cultural stereotypes the #iLookLikeAnEngineer campaign aimed to counter.

PART II: A LOOK AT #ILOOKLIKEANENGINEER PARTICIPANTS: FIGHTING STEREOTYPES ON TWITTER

As discussed earlier, Wenger's #iLookLikeAnEngineer hashtag took Twitter by storm in August 2015 and is still appearing in Twitter results as of this writing. Wenger's experiences of sexism began before her

Figure 4.2. OneLogic poster campaign as seen in the subway, 2015

Table 4.2. Sample responses to Wegner's Facebook post

I can believe that *everyone on an engineering team is smart* and possibly creative, but hilarious is harder to achieve.
There's [sic] clearly some *comedians in the marketing department* . . . if you catch my drift.
If their intention is to attract more women then it would have been a better [sic] to choose a picture with a warm, friendly smile rather than a *sexy smirk*.
This is some weird haphazard branding. I think they want to appeal to women, but are probably just *appealing to dudes*. Perhaps that's the intention all along. But I'm curious *people with brains find this quote remotely plausible* and *if women in particular buy this image of what a female software engineer looks like*. Idk. Weird.

company's poster campaign, in which she and three other employees were featured (see figure 4.2). In her blog post, she discusses a time when a male colleague threw dollar bills at her at the office and a time when she received lewd text messages from a salaried engineer, noting that he wanted her to "be friends with benefits" (Wenger 2015). In her letter on *The Coffeelicious*, she decries the so-called playful/harmless behavior, arguing that it "fosters an unconscious lack of sensitivity towards those who do not fit a certain mold" in the engineering industry (2015). "Lack of sensitivity" is a euphemistic way of describing some of the Facebook reactions to Wegner's photo in her company's poster. Wenger recounts some of the more stereotypical comments she received (see table 4.2) (2015, emphasis added).

From these few comments, we can assume the following cultural endoxa and enthymemes:

1. Attractive women are not engineers. Therefore, anyone who depicts engineers as attractive women is trying to be funny or is stupid.
2. Showing an attractive woman is a way to get male attention. Therefore, this ad is just trying to appeal to males.

3. Women are more attracted to women with warm, friendly smiles than with sexy smirks. Therefore, women would not find this ad appealing.

4. Engineers are smart. Some engineers may even be creative. But they are not funny. Therefore, this ad is wrong.

If the commenters were trying to scare women away from engineering as a potential career, they certainly have given it a good try. The comments reflect the "male gaze." For example, the comment that suggests that the original intention of the ad was to "appeal to dudes" subverts the friendly, welcoming message the company seemed to be trying to send and turns it into a message that is "all about the men."[3]

As a result of these responses to the marketing campaign, Wenger suggested that engineers take to Twitter to change the image of engineering. Her initial post asked readers "to help spread the word and help us redefine 'what an engineer *should* look like' #iLookLikeAnEngineer" (2015, emphasis added).

And tweet they did—in droves; one source put the total at more than 75,000 in the first few days (Bates 2015). The campaign circulated beyond average Twitter users, appearing in tweets from corporate entities such as Microsoft, Tesla, and Caterpillar and mainstream media outlets such as the *New York Times* and *Fortune* (Malik et al. 2018, 5). The next section examines a selection of posts using the #iLookLikeAnEngineer hashtag, analyzing them by first determining naturalism and then determining possible visual and verbal enthymemes.

DETERMINING VISUAL ARGUMENTS IN #ILOOKLIKEANENGINEER IMAGES ON TWITTER

Because many of the hashtagged posts featured images only, I employed a visual analysis method I developed for reading enthymemes from images. The coding categories examined, borrowed from Kress and van Leeuwen's tests of image modality (1996, 2006), included horizontal and vertical angles, gender, uniform/clothing, vectors/interactions (gaze), expression (smiling, neutral, frowning), size of frame (close shot, long shot), and social distance (personal, public), with the additional category of inclusion of the hashtag sign (#). In instances when text was included in a post, it was also included in the analysis.

This study uses Kress and van Leeuwen's (1996, 2006) "grammar of visual design" to study photos accompanying the #iLookLikeAnEngineer hashtag. While previous studies have applied their theories and tests on image modality to analyze informal portraiture (snapshots) and selfies (e.g., Zappavigna 2016; Frosh 2015; Wetzstein 2017; Georgakopoulou

2016), to my knowledge, this is the first project to employ it to study a collection of such photographs from Twitter specifically. Analyzing informal portraits posted for digital activism through this framework allows us the opportunity to acknowledge that whereas informal/self-photographers may not be intentionally sending certain messages with their visuals, these messages nonetheless come through and are read and interpreted using our cultural endoxa.

To analyze the hashtag campaign years after Wenger's initial call to action, I analyzed fifty tweets with images from a single day in October 2017. Some previous Twitter studies have been case studies composed of a small set of tweets, but others have examined large corpuses (for example, Rosemary Clark's [2016] study of the #WhyIStayed hashtag involved a corpus of 2,522 tweets, and Aqdas Malik and colleagues' [2018] study of #iLookLikeAnEngineer analyzed 19,492 original tweets and 89,650 retweets); importantly, these larger studies examined the verbal aspects of the message, not the visual components. In Clark's (2016, 6) case, for instance, she used the Annenberg Twitter API (Twitter's Application Programming Interface), which "randomly select[s] and archive[s] approximately 1 percent of all public tweets." Searching this type of data using a simple keyword search in Microsoft Word or Excel quickly yields quantifiable results that can then be analyzed for themes and categories. Malik and colleagues (2018) used software (Latent Dirichlet Allocation and Gephi) to identify textual themes and analyze for tweet popularity. Because visual analysis, as featured in this study, must be done manually and cannot be aided by software, the process usually requires a much smaller sample and should, as such, not be considered generalizable.

During the collection process, tweets with images that contained collages were eliminated due to poor image quality, as were tweets with images that were too blurry to be coded. When a tweet was excluded from the dataset for either of these reasons, the next tweet in reverse chronological order was selected to maintain the desired total of fifty tweets. Some Twitter users tweeted a pair of images—one more business-like, the other more of a "personal-life" photo—and these remained in the dataset and were analyzed as follows. Gender was counted only once for the post (because it was a single engineer), as was use of the hashtag, but clothing/uniform, horizontal/vertical angles, gaze, expression, frame size, and social distance were counted twice—once for each photo. Race was also tracked throughout all posts to determine whether stereotypes about engineering, computer science, and race were reproduced among the Twitter community using the hashtag. However, coding for race is of questionable accuracy in any project involving visuals, due in part to the own-race bias or "other-race effect" (ORE) (see, e.g., Malpass and Kravitz 1969; Shepherd, Deregowski, and Ellis 1974). Human beings tend to remember the faces of unfamiliar individuals of their own race better than they do unfamiliar faces of other races. Therefore, the general terms "white" and "Person of Color" (or POC) are used to distinguish broad categories of race, visually estimated by the author, and do not necessarily represent how each individual identifies.

RESULTS AND DISCUSSION

Out of the fifty tweets studied, which included fifty-four images, 122 different people were represented. Of those, 115 (94%) were female and 7 (6%) were male. This finding is not surprising. Although Wenger's original call to action was broad in scope (asking for participation from any individual who felt they did not fit the stereotypical image of an engineer), it stemmed from an instance of sexism directed at her as a woman in the field. As is often seen in hashtag feminism, the sharing of an incidence of hashtag activism results in "large numbers of comments and retweets" that "consist of numerous [related] personal stories and appear in temporal order" (Yang 2016, 14), resulting in a larger narrative coming to life.

Clothing and Uniforms

Coding for clothing offered the opportunity to gauge how these engineers wished to perform the role of an "engineer" through their choice of clothing, whether in work or private settings. The percentages are as follows: 80 percent were in street or business clothing, 5 percent in uniform or safety clothing, and 15 percent Other or Unknown (because clothing was cropped out). The vast majority of participants wore street clothing or standard business attire, such as suits or shirts and ties. Three individuals wore either some kind of uniform or a safety vest over normal clothes, so these were coded as Uniform or Safety. Finally, some women had cropped their photos so close that clothing was not visible. It is clear from this sample that the stereotype of engineers in hard hats and uniforms or coveralls is largely unfounded and that these engineers, at least, wear "normal" clothing to work. The photographs also reveal that clothing did not always align with the stereotypical masculine culture of the profession. That is, women were featured in clothing that could be classified as stereotypically feminine. If "all women love fashion" is a commonplace assumption in our culture, then these

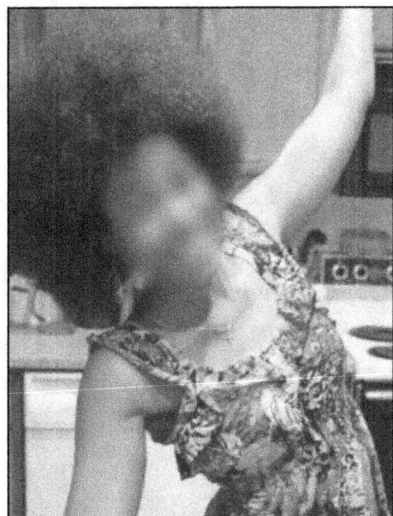

Figure 4.3. Photo featuring woman in "feminine" attire

Figure 4.4. Example of photo at eye level with the viewer, with the subject smiling and making eye contact

photos help dispel any notion that an engineering career means putting our pretty clothes away or performing in traditionally masculine ways. Figure 4.3 features a participant dressed in what might be considered a traditionally feminine outfit. Not unimportant, featuring her natural hair also suggests a critique of traditional femininity that has long been associated with whiteness.

Visual Angles

Horizontal angle (Kress and van Leeuwen 1996) conveys the vantage point from which the viewer "stands" in relation to the subject: does the viewer look up at, into the eyes of, or down on the subject? Determining this angle indicates whether the photograph presents a narrative reading that suggests a subject may feel a superior, equal, or inferior relationship with the subject. The majority of photos (59%) were taken from an eye-level vantage point, although 35 percent were taken from above eye level; this seems to indicate photos that were taken by the subject, either using her own arm or a selfie stick (see figure 4.4 for an example). A very few (6%) were taken from an angle below eye level. The analysis of horizontal angle indicates that these hashtag activism posts convey a feeling of equality with viewers that welcomes viewers into the world of engineering rather than helping maintain its image as an inaccessible profession only for white males. The subjects are not looking down on their viewers, implying that they are somehow at society's pinnacle; rather, the narrative they produce is that they are just like the rest of us.

When evaluating photographs, the vertical angle (Kress and van Leeuwen 1996) describes the way the observer surveys the scene: from directly in front of the subjects—implying involvement with them, as though they can look back—or from an oblique angle that puts the observer outside the happenings in the scene. In this selection of photos, 89 percent were composed from a direct vertical angle and only 11 percent from an oblique angle. The direct angles in these portraits convey to viewers that these (mainly) women *see* their followers and viewers—indeed, with their direct eye contact, they are even *inviting* viewers into the conversation about gender in engineering. Facing their viewers head-on, they can almost reach out and shake hands, welcoming us to the team, even showing us what they do. To be clear, the focus here—and throughout—is the narrative these photos provide. What cannot be deduced, obviously, is the poster's intent. While professional photographers and directors may strategically use particular angles to establish power dynamics, we cannot assume that these laypersons either are aware of such strategies or are purposefully employing them in their posts.

Taken together, the analysis of visual angles in the engineers' tweeted photos produces the narrative that engineering is for people of all backgrounds and is welcoming, especially for women. "Look at me," these photos seem to say. "I'm a woman, and I'm an engineer. Come and find out more."

Gaze

Gaze is another category that helps discern viewer involvement. The demand gaze (Kress and van Leeuwen 1996) draws the viewer in, "demanding" that he or she meet the subject's eye. The offer gaze covers every other type of gaze that does not involve eye contact between subject and viewer (1996). In these images, demand gaze occurred 94 percent of the time. Where offer gaze was observed, the photos tended to be candids in which the subject assumedly did not know she was being photographed. Consider the example in figure 4.5: the subject on the left meets the viewer's gaze, and her smile draws the viewer in; in contrast, the subject on the right, who seems to have been photographed during a meeting, leaves the viewer outside the conversation looking in. The predominant use of the "demanding" gaze seems to align with the purpose of hashtag activism: to arrest, to engage, to draw

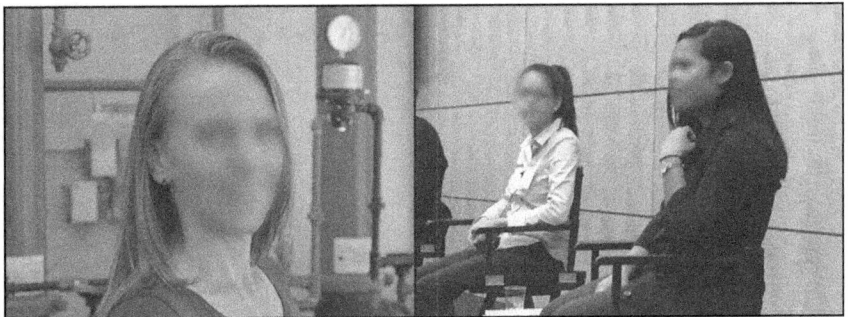

Figure 4.5. Side-by-side comparison of demand and offer gazes featured in posts

attention to the social critique featured in the movement. However, the high number of photos using this gaze may also be a by-product of current selfie culture, which finds users employing this gaze regularly (and perhaps not always intentionally).

Expression

Expression is yet another way of suggesting involvement between subject and viewer. Smiles are engaging; research suggests that people who are popular with their peers (have high sociometric status) smile more than others (Cashdan 1998). A large study of 66,000 social media profile photos on Twitter found that smiling is highly positively correlated with the personality trait of conscientiousness (Liu et al. 2021). A Google search for "personality traits of engineers" quickly demonstrates that "conscientious" is one of the top results.

This engagement with smiles is developed in humans from the earliest months: social smiles show up in infants during their third month, and at the same time, they begin to react by becoming sober at the sight of impassive expressions (Ekman and Oster 1979). Although studies have supported the stereotype that females smile more than males, a meta-analysis of those studies found that males smile more when they are unaware of being observed (still less than females, but the increase in smiling was statistically significant) (LaFrance, Hecht, and Levy Paluck 2003). As it turns out, 96 percent of subjects in this sample smiled in their photos, and just 4 percent wore neutral expressions—mainly those subjects who were not posing for a photograph. Figure 4.6 illustrates the contrast between a smiling expression and a more serious one. The subject on the left smiles in her photo, conveying high sociometric status and conscientiousness. In contrast, the subject on the right wears a

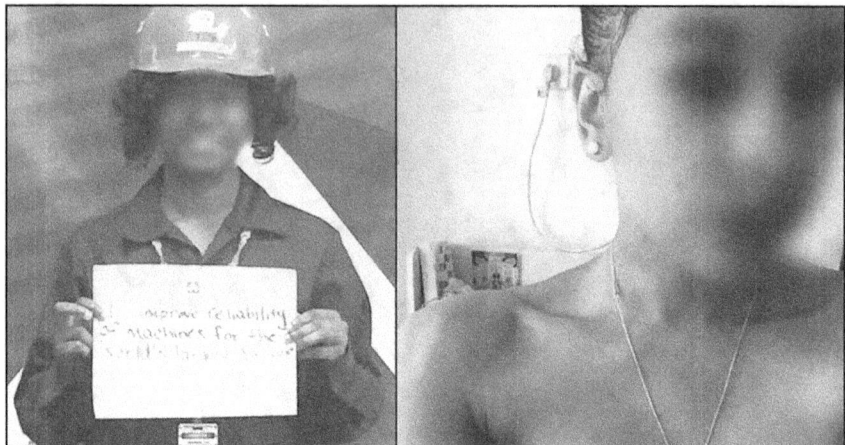

Figure 4.6. Contrasting photographs of participant expressions

more neutral expression—not quite a frown, but far from a smile. The latter could be read as the activist wanting to be taken more seriously or wanting the photo to reflect the seriousness of the issue the movement is addressing. Still further, the expression could be read as a protest on even a different level, as a direct reaction (and resistance) to the common sexist comment "you'd be prettier if you just smiled more."

Since the vast majority of subjects smiled in their portraits, research would suggest that this increased the likelihood of positive reception. This choice may not have been purposefully aligned with such a goal. In fact, the dominance of smiling participants may simply reflect that even when engaging in social activism, people tend to—consciously or not—present themselves in the most attractive way possible.

Sample Analyses

To illustrate how this methodology aids in understanding the collective argument made by images connected with the #iLooklikeAnEngineer hashtag, it is helpful to see how individual posts were read through all these lenses. Figure 4.7 and table 4.3 illustrate a sample analysis of one particular #iLookLikeAnEngineer post attending to visual enthymemes that can be inferred from the image.

As evidenced in the above analysis across categories, this selected image effectively pushes back against the stereotypes of engineers as male, awkward, introverted, and unfashionable. The participant looks like a woman we might meet in the grocery checkout line or see enjoying

#iLookLikeAnEngineer 89

Table 4.3. Analysis of woman posing with #iLookLikeAnEngineer poster

Horizontal and vertical angles	H = eye level; V = direct
Gender	G = female
Race	R = Person of Color
Uniform/clothing	U/C = street clothes
Vectors/interactions	V/I = demand gaze
Expression	E = smiling
Inclusion of hashtag sign	# = yes, with additional explanatory text
Size of frame	SF = close-up
Social distance	SD = close social
Observations	Young, attractive woman with an Indian first name, smiling, wearing a pink top, looking directly at the viewer from a stance that appears to be in front of the viewer at a close social distance, holding an #iLookLikeAnEngineer sign
Assumed premises (based on cultural endoxa)	People who use this hashtag are engineers who are trying to promote an image of diversity in the field. Pink is associated with femininity.
Inferences	Engineers can be pretty females who dress in a feminine way and are friendly and approachable. Not all engineers are awkward, nerdy, introverted white males with no social skills.

Figure 4.7. Woman with #iLookLikeAnEngineer poster

an after-work beer with friends. The argument this image offers is that we should also expect to see people like her at engineering team meetings and project postmortems. Consider this second example from the campaign (see figure 4.8). This tweet self-consciously fights stereotypes about women in engineering, both visually and verbally. As of October 2019, the tweet had 896 "likes" and 403 retweets, indicating a high level of engagement with this post.

An analysis of potential visual enthymemes that can be inferred from this image is found in table 4.4. The photo's caption reinforces the argument her visual makes by verbalizing what the photo argues: "I'm female, wear pink and I'm pregnant." In essence, she is saying, "When you look at me, you probably imagine a different career choice based

Figure 4.8. Image of pregnant woman participating in campaign

Table 4.4. Tests of naturalism for photograph of pregnant woman

Horizontal and vertical angles	H = slightly above eye level; V = oblique
Gender	G = female
Race	R = Person of Color
Uniform/clothing	U/C = street clothes
Vectors/interactions	V/I = demand gaze
Expression	E = smiling
Inclusion of hashtag sign	# = yes, with additional explanatory text
Size of frame	SF = medium
Social distance	SD = close social
Observations	A pregnant, Asian-appearing woman wearing a pink dress stands before a window. Another person is presenting her with a chocolate cake. A bouquet of pink flowers stands on a table in front of her. She smiles at the photographer.
Assumed premises (based on cultural endoxa)	Women who wear pink dresses are girly and feminine. Women who like pink flowers are feminine. Women often like chocolate. Pregnant women like sweets. Software engineers are usually men. Men do not like feminine things. Men are not known to be particularly partial to chocolate.
Inferences	Engineering is not solely a career for men and masculine women. Stereotypically feminine women also work as engineers. Therefore, it is acceptable to be both "girly" and an engineer.

on my looks. But you would be wrong because I'm a software engineer." Thus, the text and image work together to argue that so-called feminine women do work in the field of engineering.

One final example may be helpful. In another post, the user places herself in an outdoor construction site scene where we might expect to see a male engineer, wearing what we might expect a male engineer to be wearing. With her long hair worn loose and topped by a hard hat, she defies viewers to categorize engineering as a male-only profession. The tweet further draws attention to potential gender barriers and assumptions with the text "I finished college as a single mom and now I am a Transportation Engineer Supervisor!!!"

Some of the choices in this photograph may be functional, in support of the activism goal. For example, the choice to have her portrait shot from the far social distance is likely an attempt to include the workplace setting in the photo. Other details infer that this potentially was a photograph taken particularly for use in this campaign. Her smile and stance allow us to assume that she has posed for the picture (for one reason or another), making evident that this is not a candid shot of her at work.

An analysis of potential visual enthymemes that can be inferred from this image is included in table 4.5. As mentioned in the analysis of the previous photo, engagement with the tweets is an important indicator of how well the overall message is reaching the public. In the case of this tweet, the user received five retweets and twenty-one "likes," which are significantly smaller numbers than the previous example received. It is impossible to know why this was the case; it may be due to something non-content related, such as time of day the tweet posted (8:48 p.m. for the one with fewer likes vs. 5:14 p.m. for the one with more likes). There is a chance, however, that content-specific elements impacted reception and circulation. For example, the vast majority of the posts using this hashtag featured women, presumably to counter the gender stereotypes concerning the profession. It may be that this practice—when adopted by the masses—was not as attention-grabbing. Figure 4.8 may suggest that people were more engaged with posts that explicitly drew attention to gender stereotypes by featuring (and arguably embracing) things not typically associated with engineers (e.g., pink, pregnancy, and chocolate cake).

Let us return to the discussion of narrative in the #iLookLikeAnEngineer campaign. The results of this analysis suggest a visual narrative that engineering is for women as well as for men, that engineering welcomes a diverse community of workers, and that an engineering career does not require one to look or dress blandly or to be antisocial

Table 4.5. Analysis of woman posed outdoors at civil engineering worksite

Horizontal and vertical angles	H = above eye level; V = slightly oblique
Gender	G = female
Race	R = white (likely)
Uniform/clothing	U/C = safety vest and hard hat over street clothes
Vectors/interactions	V/I = demand gaze (but difficult to be sure because of sunglasses)
Expression	E = smiling
Inclusion of hashtag sign	# = yes, with additional explanatory text; she also tags @SWEtalk (Society of Women Engineers)
Size of frame	SF = long shot
Social distance	SD = far social
Observations	A woman wearing what could be considered the stereotypical uniform of an engineer poses outdoors in a civil engineering setting. Her caption states that she "finished college as a single mom" and is now a supervisor. She is dressed comfortably in skinny jeans and a blue top and has medium-long hair.
Assumed premises (based on cultural endoxa)	Being a single mother is a challenge. Engineering is a difficult major. Women are rare in civil engineering. It is even rarer to see women as supervisors in a male-dominated field. Women prefer indoor jobs.
Inferences	It is possible for a woman to be not only a civil engineer but a supervisor. Some women enjoy working outdoors. It is possible for a single mother to finish college in a difficult program like engineering.

or unattractive. Recall, adults' stereotypes about engineers included the following: Engineers have no soft skills. They are introverted people who are difficult to work with and who love math. Engineers are geeks with pocket protectors who are not creative. Engineering is a male-dominated profession. Engineering school is difficult. A review of the fifty tweets chosen for this analysis quickly debunks many of these stereotypes. For example, nearly every engineer pictured wore a smile, and the majority of them were broad, genuine-looking smiles. It is impossible to know whether any of the engineers are introverted; however, they all manage to look approachable enough in their photos. Not one of them looks stereotypically geeky or wears a pocket protector, although quite a few wear glasses. And in their actual tweets, many of them describe (and sometimes picture) hobbies they have and projects they have taken on at work, so they clearly are creative.

However, not every stereotype can be debunked through this campaign, such as the commonly held belief that "engineering school is difficult." We do, however, know from cultural endoxa that "engineering comprises a great deal of difficult science and mathematics training" and that "men are [supposedly] better at science and math than women." With these commonplaces, it is easy to see how one arrives at the (faulty) premise that "women cannot do well as engineers because they are not as good at difficult science and mathematics as men" and therefore at the conclusion that "women should not be engineers." The fact that so many women *are* engineers is visually illustrated by the hashtag campaign, thus negating the false conclusion that women should not be engineers, a conclusion based on faulty premises. However, as mentioned, the images do not support or negate the stereotype of engineering school as difficult; they simply suggest that women could succeed in engineering programs even if they are difficult.

The overarching message from these images, taken together, is that women of all races, ages, sizes, and styles work in engineering fields. Similarly, Malik and colleagues (2018, 1), who studied 19,492 #iLookLikeAnEngineer tweets and 89,650 retweets, argue that "multivocality" was the key to the campaign's success: they refer to it as a "new form of digital polyphonic narrative," supported by the platform of social media. It is precisely because of the campaign's diversity that it succeeds.

Occasionally, however, the #iLookLikeAnEngineer hashtag was, and is, co-opted by people and entities outside the originally intended participants (women): for example, 7 of the 122 pictured engineers were male. (Tech giant Intel seemed to encourage men to post; a broader review of the hashtag beyond these fifty tweets reveals quite a few more of men from Intel holding the same blue hashtag sign as the ones in the photos analyzed.) Further, a casual review of more recent (August 2019) usage of the hashtag suggests that it was then used primarily (though not entirely) by corporations. This suggests that it may be useful to study the "shelf life" of such hashtag activism, paying particular attention to what happens to the hashtags after interest in the movement itself dies down—do corporations and other entities pick them up, seeing possibilities for marketing? It would be interesting to know whether this form of co-opting a social movement works well for a corporate entity—does it build the corporation's ethos, or do social media denizens see it as a cynical marketing move? Future studies of hashtag activism could address these questions.

We also know that engineering is broadly defined by these Twitter users, encompassing coding as well as traditional engineering (e.g., electrical, mechanical, civil). Many of the women identified themselves as software engineers and "coders." This finding alone helps dispel the

Table 4.6. Breakdown of features of #iLookLikeAnEngineer sample

Genders (n = 122)	M: 7 (6%) | F: 115 (94%)
Races (n = 110)	White: 80 (72.7%) | POC: 30 (27.3%)
Uniforms/clothing (n = 110)	Hard hats: 1 (0.9%) | button-down shirts: 15 (13.6%) | coveralls or uniform jacket/trousers: 2 (1.8%) | suit jackets/suits: 15 (13.6%)[5] | safety vests: 1 (0.9%)
Contextualization (n = 50)	Outdoors: 6 (12%) | Indoors: 43 (86%) | No context: 0 | Unsure: 1 (2%)

stereotype of the coder as a greasy male basement dweller, unaware of the passing of hours and days as he sits glued to his three monitors, coding away.[4]

A breakdown of the fifty-image #iLookLikeAnEngineer sample by genders, races, uniforms/clothing, and contextualization yields the following results (see table 4.6).

CONCLUSION: CONTEMPLATING AND COMPARING RHETORICS ABOUT ENGINEERS

A comparison of the results from the two datasets is telling. The Google Image results depict an engineer who is overwhelmingly male and white, wears a hard hat and button-down shirt, and (where visual context is given) works outdoors (see table 4.7).[6]

In stark contrast with the Google Images results, the engineers who used the #iLookLikeAnEngineer hashtag were, of course, mostly female. More important for this comparison, they wore almost *no* hard hats, very few button-down shirts (in fact, most wore soft, colorful tops or even T-shirts), almost no coveralls or uniforms, very few suits, and almost no safety vests; and they were primarily pictured indoors. Although 73 percent of them were white, a much greater percentage of this group than of the Google group consisted of People of Color (27%).

The findings of this two-part study align well with the originally stated purpose of the #iLookLikeAnEngineer hashtag campaign: to illustrate that engineering is a career for women, too, not just men. However, the reality is that engineering, as a broad career field, appears closer to Google Images's search results than to the hashtag campaign, at least as regards gender. According to the US Census Bureau, just 15 percent of the engineering workforce was female in 2019 (Martinez and Christnacht 2021), which seems to align with the stereotypes predominant in the Google Images search for engineer. The purpose of the #iLookLikeAnEngineer campaign was primarily to offer a counterpoint to the visual argument

Table 4.7. Visual elements of Google Images engineers vs. Twitter's #iLookLikeAnEngineer images

Image Element	Google Image Sample (68 images, 87 people)	#iLookLikeAnEngineer Sample (50 images, 122 people)
Genders[7]	M: 83% | F: 17%	M: 6% | F: 94%
Hard hats	85%	0.9%
Button-down shirts	94%	14%
Coveralls/uniforms	14%	1.8%
Suits/suit jackets	20%	14%
Safety vests	13%	0.9%
Outdoors	46%	12%
Indoors	34%	86%
White/Caucasian	90%	73%
People of Color	0.9%	27%

and stereotypes of engineering as an all-male enterprise by showing both men and women that engineering is a career for women. But another consequence of the campaign is that the hashtag users also helped diversify the image of engineering by incorporating images of People of Color, particularly women. As a result, we have a visual narrative of the diversity of the broad field of engineering as white and nonwhite, male and female, indoors and outdoors, nerdy and average, young and old, well-dressed and casual. In other words, was this hashtag campaign an "accurate" representation of what the broad field of engineering looks like? In a word, no, but that never seemed to be the goal; rather, Isis Anchalee Wenger and other participants in the campaign aimed to represent the invisible faces of engineering: those who are female—Women of Color and white women—of varying age and attractiveness and presentation of femininity, doing the varied and diverse work of engineering. In that goal, the campaign has been a success.

How will seeing diverse images of women in engineering affect the interests of the average young girl in her middle school or high school years? It is not within the scope of the present project to answer that question, but it is reasonable to guess that seeing almost nothing but white males in hard hats, carrying blueprints, is not going to appeal to the average teenage girl. Studies bear this out. Sapna Cheryan, John Oliver Siy, Marissa Vichayapai, Benjamin Drury, and Saenam Kim (2011, 661) found, after two studies, that "STEM role models who projected stereotypes of the field interfered with women's beliefs that they would be successful in STEM fields"; further, these role models need to be *non-stereotypical*—that is, "average-looking," not "geeky." Lola B. Smith (2000, 15) recommends amending the stereotypes of STEM professionals away from the negative—people who are "cold" and "non-nurturing"—toward an image of the work as having "social and nurturing aspects."

According to the American Association of University Women's analysis of US Census Bureau data from 2011 (Hill 2013), the engineering workforce in the US at that time was 88 percent male and 12 percent female. Of those 12 percent, 8 percent were white women. Asian and Pacific Islander women made up just 2 percent,; Black women, 1 percent; Hispanic women, 1 percent; and American Indian and Alaska Native women just 0.04 percent (2013). And although more women than ever are going to college—more women than men, in fact—just 20 percent of undergraduate computer science and engineering degrees are awarded to women, with only 6 percent awarded to Women of Color (Society for Women in Engineering 2019). In addition, women in the broader science and engineering fields are far more likely than men to cite family needs as their reason for working only part-time (1,327,000 vs. 293,000 respondents) or not at all (913,000 vs. 169,000) (2017). Further, Nadya A. Fouad (2014) found that nearly 40 percent of women with engineering degrees drop out once they get to the workplace. As Fouad stated in a presentation at the American Psychological Association Convention in 2014, "It's the climate, stupid" (quoted in St. Fleur 2014). What this means in everyday life is that not enough women are getting their college education in engineering and computer science, and when they do, many are not using it. With STEM needs at a high level in the United States, this country cannot afford to have some of its best and brightest minds sidelined by sexism or family expectations.

As to the question of whether hashtag activism can help effect change in the engineering fields, perhaps the next collection of data the NSF publishes will provide some clues. Currently, researchers disagree on whether hashtag activism results in positive change. Some feel this type of activism "represent[s] fleeting moments of awareness, quickly replaced by the customary innocuousness of social media pleasantries" (Bonilla and Rosa 2015, 10); others argue that "participation in forms of digital activism prove[s] transformative in unpredictable ways," such as being "inherently aggregative" (10)—over time, as more and more instances of injustice employ a hashtag, the narrative widens, deepens, and becomes a written history of social justice activism.

Perhaps most important, the #iLookLikeAnEngineer hashtag campaign, which continues to draw participation on various social media (albeit not in nearly the numbers it did in 2015), provides a visual narrative and record for current and future engineers that the field is open to all—particularly, that it is open to women. This visual record may be useful in combatting both individual instances of sexism, such as in an individual workplace or engineering classroom, and broader, more institutionalized forms of sexism, such as when an entire program discriminates against women applicants. For engineering does not simply have a problem with recruitment of women; it has a deep and long-standing problem of male sexism in the field, a sexism that comes from K–12 teachers, parents, professors, hiring committees, colleagues, and gender socialization more generally. The visual narrative of women actively participating in engineering as a career is useful not just in recruiting more women to the field but also in proving that sexist attitudes about women and engineering are outdated and need to change. This hashtag unites women around the world in a collective activism for the betterment of engineering and engineers everywhere, suggesting that such hashtag activism work can productively counter problematic stereotypes and help craft more egalitarian cultural scripts.

NOTES

1. At the bottom of her post she states, "I give permission for press to use the material from this post" (Wenger 2015).
2. Girls' results were also high for "builds" and "fixes," but not as high as the boys' results.
3. For further discussion of the male gaze, see Mulvey (1975).
4. The excellent webcomic "xkdc" (xkcd.com) contains many that explore stereotypes and take society to task for sexism against women in mathematics, engineering, the sciences, and computer programming. See references.
5. All but three of the suit wearers appeared in a shot with an older, tall white man and all his female employees.
6. The Google Image data were collected two years after the campaign was originally launched, so it is impossible to know if there might have been more similarity between the two datasets had these images been collected when the campaign was more active.
7. Because the main purpose for the hashtag was to increase visibility of the females in engineering, this is not an apples-to-apples comparison.

REFERENCES

Advanced Web Ranking. 2014. *Google Organic CTR Study*. https://www.advancedwebranking.com/blog/google-organic-ctr/.

Bates, Laura. 2015. "#ILookLikeAnEngineer—How One Woman Turned the Tables on Sexism in Her Industry." *The Guardian*, August 13.

Bonilla, Yarimar, and Jonathan Rosa. 2015. "#Ferguson: Digital Protest, Hashtag Ethnography, and the Racial Politics of Social Media in the United States." *American Ethnologist* 42 (1): 4–17. https://doi.org/10.1111/amet.12112.

Buckhalt, Brandon. n.d. "A Few Common Myths about Engineers." *Creative Engineer.* https://www.thecreativeengineer.com/a-few-engineering-myths/.

Cashdan, Elizabeth. 1998. "Smile, Speech, and Body Posture: How Women and Men Display Sociometric Status and Power." *Journal of Nonverbal Behavior* 22 (4): 209–228.

Cheryan, Sapna, John Oliver Siy, Marissa Vichayapai, Benjamin Drury, and Saenam Kim. 2011. "Do Female and Male Role Models Who Embody STEM Stereotypes Hinder Women's Anticipated Success in STEM?" *Social Psychological and Personality Science* 2 (6): 656–664.

Clark, Rosemary. 2016. "'Hope in a Hashtag': The Discursive Activism of #WhyIStayed." *Feminist Media Studies.* doi: 10.1080/14680777.2016.1138235.

Cowart, Holly, Lynsey Saunders, and Ginger Blackstone. 2016. "Picture a Protest: Analyzing Media Images Tweeted from Ferguson." *Social Media + Society* (October–December): 1–9.

Ekman, Paul, and Harriet Oster. 1979. "Facial Expressions of Emotion." *Annual Review of Psychology* 30: 527–554.

Finnegan, Cara. 2001. "The Naturalistic Enthymeme and Visual Argument: Photographic Representation in the 'Skull Controversy.'" *Argumentation and Advocacy* 37 (3): 133–149.

Fishkin, Rand. 2017. "The State of Searcher Behavior Revealed through 23 Remarkable Statistics." *Moz.com.* https://moz.com/blog/state-of-searcher-behavior-revealed.

Fouad, Nadya A. 2014. "Leaning in, But Getting Pushed Back (and Out)." Paper presented at the American Psychological Association 2014 Annual Convention, Washington, DC. August 7–10. https://www.apa.org/news/press/releases/2014/08/pushed-back.pdf.

Frosh, Paul. 2015. "The Gestural Image: The Selfie, Photography Theory, and Kinesthetic Sociability." *International Journal of Communication* 9: 1607–1628.

Georgakopoulou, Alexandra. 2016. "From Narrating the Self to Posting Self(ies): A Small Stories Approach to Selfies." *Open Linguistics* 2: 300–317. doi: 10.1515/opli-2016-0014.

Gunn, Caitlin. 2015. "Hashtagging from the Margins: Women of Color Engaged in Feminist Consciousness-raising on Twitter." In *Women of Color and Social Media Multitasking: Blogs, Timelines, Feeds, and Community*, edited by Keisha Edwards Tassie and Sonja M. Brown Givens, 21–34. London: Lexington Books.

Hill, Catherine. 2013. "Three Reasons the Wage Gap Hurts Women in STEM." American Association of University Women, April 5. https://empowering710.rssing.com/chan-42594765/latest-article3.php.

Horeck, Tanya. 2014. "#AskThicke: 'Blurred Lines,' Rape Culture, and the Feminist Hashtag Takeover." *Feminist Media Studies* 14 (6): 1105–1107. doi: 10.1080/14680777.2014.975450.

Hughes, Adam, Onyi Lam, Stefan Wojcik, and Brin Broderick. 2019. "Men Appear Twice as Often as Women in News Photos on Facebook." Pew Research Center. https://www.pewresearch.org/journalism/2019/05/23/men-appear-twice-as-often-as-women-in-news-photos-on-facebook/.

Kennedy, Tracy L. M. 2007. "The Personal Is Political: Feminist Blogging and Virtual Consciousness-Raising." *Scholar and Feminist Online* 5 (2). https://sfonline.barnard.edu/blogs/kennedy_01.htm.

Khoja-Moolji, Shenila. 2015. "Becoming an 'Intimate Publics': Exploring the Affective Intensities of Hashtag Feminism." *Feminist Media Studies* 15 (2): 347–350.

Knight, Meredith, and Christine Cunningham. 2004. "Draw an Engineer Test (DAET): Development of a Tool to Investigate Students' Ideas about Engineers and Engineering." *American Society for Engineering Education (ASEE) Annual Conference Proceedings*, 1–11. http://engineering.nyu.edu/gk12/amps-cbri/pdf/Draw%20an%20Engineer%20Test%20(DAET)%20-%20Development%20of%20a%20Tool%20to%20Investigate%20Students%E2%80%99%20Ideas%20about%20Engineers%20and%20Engineering.pdf.

Kress, Gunther, and Theo van Leeuwen. 1996. *Reading Images: The Grammar of Visual Design.* New York: Routledge.

Kress, Gunther, and Theo van Leeuwen. 2006. *Reading Images: The Grammar of Visual Design*. 2nd ed. New York: Routledge.

LaFrance, Marianne, Marvin A. Hecht, and Elizabeth Levy Paluck. 2003. "The Contingent Smile: A Meta-analysis of Sex Differences in Smiling." *Psychological Bulletin* 129 (2): 305–334.

Liu, Leqi, Daniel Preotiuc-Pietro, Zahra Riahi Samani, Mohsen E. Moghaddam, and Lyle Ungar. 2021. "Analyzing Personality through Social Media Profile Picture Choice." *Proceedings of the International AAAI Conference on Web and Social Media* 10 (1): 211–220. https://ojs.aaai.org/index.php/ICWSM/article/view/14738.

Malik, Aqdas, Aditya Johri, Rajat Handa, Habib Karbasian, and Hemant Purohit. 2018. "How Social Media Supports Hashtag Activism through Multivocality: A Case Study of #ILookLikeAnEngineer." *First Monday* 23, no. 11 (November): 1–9.

Malpass, Roy S., and Jerome Kravitz. 1969. "Recognition for Faces of Own- and Other-race Faces." *Journal of Personality and Social Psychology* 13 (4): 330–334. doi: 10.1037/h0028434.

Martinez, Anthony, and Cheridan Christnacht. 2021. *Women Are Nearly Half of US Workforce but Only 27% of STEM Workers*. US Census Bureau. https://www.census.gov/library/stories/2021/01/women-making-gains-in-stem-occupations-but-still-underrepresented.html.

Mulvey, Laura. 1975. "Visual Pleasure and Narrative Cinema." In *Feminism and Film Theory*, edited by Constance Penley, 57–68. New York: Routledge.

Munroe, Randall. *Xkcd: A Webcomic of Romance, Sarcasm, Math, and Language*. xkcd.com.

Net Market Share. 2019. *Search Engine Market Share*. https://netmarketshare.com/.

Rodino-Colocino, Michelle. 2014. "#YesAllWomen: Intersectional Mobilization against Sexual Assault Is Radical (Again)." *Feminist Media Studies* 14 (6): 1113–1115. doi: 10.1080/14680777.2014.975475.

Shapiro, Mary, Diane Grossman, Suzanne Carter, Karyn Martin, Patricia Deyton, and Diane Hammer. 2015. "Middle School Girls and the 'Leaky Pipeline' to Leadership: An Examination of How Socialized Gendered Roles Influences the College and Career Aspirations of Girls Is Shared as Well as the Role of Middle Level Professionals in Disrupting the Influence of Social Gendered Messages and Stigmas." *Middle School Journal* 46 (5): 3–13.

Shepherd, John W., Jan B. Deregowski, and Haydn D. Ellis. 1974. "A Cross-cultural Study of Recognition Memory for Faces." *International Journal of Psychology* 9 (3): 205–212. https://doi.org/10.1080/00207597408247104.

Smith, Lola B. 2000. "The Socialization of Females with Regard to a Technology-Related Career: Recommendations for Change." *Meridian: A Middle School Computer Technologies Journal* 3 (2): 2–30.

Society for Women in Engineering. 2019. *SWE Research Update: Women in Engineering by the Numbers*. SWE.org. https://alltogether.swe.org/2019/11/swe-research-update-women-in-engineering-by-the-numbers-nov-2019/.

St. Fleur, Nicholas. 2014. "Many Women Leave Engineering, Blame the Work Culture." *NPR All Tech Considered*. https://www.npr.org/sections/alltechconsidered/2014/08/12/339638726/many-women-leave-engineering-blame-the-work-culture.

Wenger, Isis Anchalee. 2015. "You May Have Seen My Face on BART." *The Coffeelicious*. https://medium.com/the-coffeelicious/you-may-have-seen-my-face-on-bart-8b95610o3eof.

Wetzstein, Irmgard. 2017. "The Visual Discourse of Protest Movements on Twitter: The Case of Hong Kong 2014." *Media and Communication* 5 (4): 26–36. doi: 10.17645/mac.v5i4.1020.

Yang, Guobin. 2016. "Narrative Agency in Hashtag Activism: The Case of #BlackLivesMatter." *Media and Communication* 4 (4): 13–17.

Zappavigna, Michele. 2016. "Social Media Photography: Construing Subjectivity in Instagram Images." *Visual Communication* 15 (3): 271–292. doi: 10.1177/1470357216643220.

5

THE IDEOGRAPH AND THE #PUSSYHAT
Multimodal Rhetorics of Brevity in the Women's March

Sarah Riddick

Although brevity has long been promoted as an integral feature of good style and persuasive communication, discussions over time suggest a somewhat narrow view of brevity. Long ago, Longinus (1890, III.4) cautioned that "bulk, when hollow and affected, is always objectionable, whether in material bodies or in writings"; but approaches to brevity have tended to focus on the latter, which I argue reflects the broader modal tension that has historically run through our approaches to rhetoric and writing. Given the field's long-standing dedication to discursive, alphanumeric writing (Murray 2009, 3), it is unsurprising that discussions of brevity often center around such texts. Yet, as others have shown, rhetoric and writing have always featured multimodality; thus, the aforementioned modal tension should be investigated and challenged (Kress 2010; Palmeri 2012; Alexander and Rhodes 2014; Ball and Charlton 2016). This chapter, through a case study of how brevity facilitates hashtag activism, joins this effort.

Composed of an octothorpe (#) plus a word or phrase that together create a concise, circulating communicative unit, the hashtag appears to be the contemporary paradigm of brevity as a style and strategy. Hashtag activist campaigns such as #BlackLivesMatter, #MeToo, and many more demonstrate how apt hashtags inspire and sustain activism and social movements, thus leading to lasting, widespread change. Because hashtags are brief alphanumeric texts, we may, as with brevity, be inclined to attend predominantly to hashtag activism's discursive elements. However, as others show (e.g., Jackson and Welles 2015; Kuo 2018; Hill 2018) and as I illustrate in this chapter, hashtag activism's rhetorical strategies and effects extend further, and our examinations should too. This chapter attends to brevity's inherent yet often overlooked multimodality, which I argue can help us better understand the multimodal persuasiveness of hashtags and hashtag activism.

Through a discussion of brevity's role in the composition of hashtags, including for hashtag activism, I recover brevity's affective, material, and temporal qualities. I argue that these qualities also underlie brevity's ability to positively affect a text's persuasiveness because they increase the likelihood of mass audience uptake and circulation. Next, I show how brevity's multimodal style affects online social movements by analyzing the Pussyhat Project, a grassroots movement that contributed substantially to the peaceful protest against Donald Trump's presidency on the day following his inauguration. This protest, known as the 2017 Women's March on Washington, experienced incredible turnout in Washington, DC, and in sister marches around the world, largely thanks to the Pussyhat Project. I argue that the Pussyhat Project's strategic use of brevity in its various texts—including and beyond the hashtag #Pussyhat—played an essential role in the marches' rapid, ongoing international success because these texts collectively create an *ideograph*, or a brief communicative unit whose use metonymically signals a larger ideology (McGee 1980). Arguably, hashtags exemplify ideographs today. As hashtags like #BlackLivesMatter and #MeToo illustrate, "the hashtag must be able to simplify complex messages into a compact phrase that is both culturally resonant and widely understood" and is thus widely circulated (Kuo 2018, 496). Indeed, hashtags fit well the original conception of ideographs, which is grounded in linguistic communication (McGee 1980). Yet, others have begun expanding this boundary to include other types of texts (Edwards and Winkler 1997; Gries 2015; Ballard 2016).

In this case study, I further push this boundary to show how multiple (types of) texts can collectively comprise a multimodal ideograph. By attending to the way brevity functions in the Pussyhat Project's four-pronged approach—through its name, web materials, hashtag, and namesake hat—I showcase how its collective components create a multimodal ideograph that continues to encourage audience uptake and sustain the project's influence. This chapter closes by analyzing select #Pussyhat tweets to highlight the ways hashtag activism can strategically employ brevity to aim for and achieve sizable, sustained audience participation.

BREVITY OVER TIME

Social media supports an array of activist endeavors, such as fundraising (Pressgrove, McKeever, and Jang 2017), responding to natural disasters (Potts 2013), organizing events (Theocharis et al. 2015), and, of course, dissenting (Dadas 2017). Indeed, hashtag activism illustrates one of the most notable rhetorical successes that can arise from social media's ability to organize individuals into networked publics and counter-publics (Leung and Lee 2014; Jackson and Welles 2015; Kuo 2018; Rosenbaum 2018).

In part, the rise of these digital publics and the success of their activism are owed to the media that supports them. According to Tony D. Sampson (2012, 32), social media taps into "the biological desire to be surrounded by friends—to increase the size of the crowd—and seize on the generative processes of the subsequent excitable social imitation to anticipate and produce novel extensions of unconscious consumption." This shared affective energy coupled with a structure that efficiently organizes it, then, leads to rhetorically "viral" events that are characterized by their widespread circulation and audience engagement—a primary outcome that hashtag activism strives to achieve. Zizi Papacharissi (2015, 316) also argues for the link between social media virality and affect, suggesting that networked publics' activity on social media shows the transformation of raw affective energy into affective power. Key to this affective power are social media's features. For instance, as danah boyd and colleagues (2010, 1) point out, the retweet "contributes to a conversational ecology in which conversations are composed of a public interplay of voices that give rise to an emotional sense of shared conversational context." Indeed, features such as the mention (i.e., tagging another user in a post by typing the "@" symbol and their [user]name), the retweet, and the hashtag facilitate the sharing of this context and the possibility for its seemingly limitless expansion.

Social media may offer structural support, but it is the users who comprise, lead, and sustain these networked publics. To mobilize participants through hashtag activism, users must have a keen understanding of social media's rhetorical conditions. For instance, Twitter is a favored venue for hashtag activism, but this venue has distinct textual constraints—namely, word count. Consequently, users need to effectively and creatively employ brevity, such as shortening URLs and creating their own truncated expressions (boyd, Golder, and Lotan 2010, 2). Prior to recent updates, initial tweets were more restricted in word count, and retweets even more so (Perez 2018, 2019). Thus, users would compose tweets with future retweets' word count in mind, making choices that would support widespread circulation while also giving other users enough characters with which to comfortably respond (Dadas 2017, 21).

The composition of hashtags exemplifies the strategic use of brevity on social media. In general, effective hashtags must function as shorthand for a larger message, carry that message forward through mass circulation, and preserve the fundamental meaning of that message through an indefinite period of recomposition and circulation. In other words, an effective hashtag is one whose composition lends itself to mass circulation and to what Jim Ridolfo and Dànielle Nicole DeVoss (2009) call "rhetorical velocity," or "the strategic theorizing for how a text might be recomposed (and why it might be recomposed) by third parties, and how this recomposing may be useful or not to the short- or long-term rhetorical objectives of the rhetorician." Caroline Dadas (2017, 32) argues that one must compose a hashtag with rhetorical velocity in mind, including the recomposition that can occur along the way. A hashtag should be intuitive and straightforward enough to increase the likelihood of mass audience uptake. Such a hashtag is likely to be concise, which limits the possibility for typos or other alterations (e.g., adding or changing articles, pluralizing) and increases the possibility for a central, networked conversation. Moreover, in a space like Twitter, a concise hashtag gives participants more characters with which to compose alongside the hashtag.

In essence, to increase audience uptake and circulation, social media users should employ brevity well—a strategy that appears throughout rhetoric and composition's history. For instance, Aristotle (1954, III.X) advocates for the persuasiveness of "lively and taking sayings." Although there are many ways to express an idea, Aristotle says, "the more briefly and antithetically such sayings can be expressed, the more taking they are, for antithesis impresses the new idea more firmly and brevity more quickly" (III.XI). This high valuation of brevity persists over time. Throughout his 1869 handbook for writing teachers, for instance, Simon Kerl (1869, 211) repeatedly designates brevity as one of the best choices a writer can make, advising "write what is true, what is worth communicating, what the occasion requires or makes proper, and nothing else." Similar to Aristotle's (1954, III.X) "lively and taking sayings," Kerl (1869, 382–384) encourages writers to produce "vividness," which "discards all encumbrance of expression, and selects only what is most sufficient, most obvious, or most striking."

In addition to and preceding hashtags, sound bites epitomize brevity's persuasive "vividness" today. Megan Foley (2012, 615–616) explains, "Given the limited space of the news broadcast, newsmakers elevated brevity into a stylistic virtue," particularly through sound bites. Foley (614) observes that contemporary oratory suggests an increasing emphasis on writing to produce sound bites, which has created anxiety that the art of political oratory is in decline; in response, Foley counters that this "textual condensation intensifies audiences' attachment to public speech." She continues, "Sound bites are remarks marked not only by their length, but by their lure," and their persuasiveness is owed largely to the latter, to "their readiness for uptake" (615). Creating such textual condensations is perhaps an art in itself, and a critical component is necessarily brevity.

Here, note the relationship of brevity to circulation. Sound bites' conciseness *and* vividness give them a distinct "readiness for uptake" and circulation (Foley 2012, 614). In this context, uptake and circulation lie primarily in the news media's hands; they circulate the sound bite through frequent broadcasts or discussions. Hashtags have a similar—if not more potent—conciseness and vividness; but their uptake, circulation, and (often) composition depend primarily on the audience. Along these lines, we can see the significance of brevity's temporal qualities. Besides being concise, a persuasive brief text is one whose composition encourages immediate, widespread, and ongoing circulation. By defining brevity in this way, we can look beyond alphanumeric texts and consider other types of brief texts whose conciseness and vividness encourage audience uptake and circulation. For instance, Guobin Yang (2016, 15) suggests that part of the success of hashtag activism campaigns like #BlackLivesMatter is owed to the "skillful invention" users demonstrate in response to medial constraints, including (re)composing and/or circulating several types of texts. Although Yang does not explicitly name brevity or multimodality, we can infer their influential roles and relationship to one another: "Part of the artistry of a collective hashtag narrative derives from its versatility of expressive forms. Besides the common practices of tweeting and retweeting, the posting itself takes different forms. There are photographs, jokes, slogans, curses, and cartoons. There are links to news, videos, music, and songs. In the middle of these personalized but artful story-telling [*sic*], a protest narrative is created and carried forward" (16). Indeed, brief content in the form of images, videos, gifs, and more persuade us (Edwards and Winkler 1997; Gries 2015; Ballard 2016), and we should update our conceptions of brevity to improve our understanding of this influence.

A view like Russel Hirst's (2007) can help take us in a more multimodal direction. Hirst (2007, 312, emphasis added) writes that style "incorporates, even more profoundly than its sister rhetorical arts, an art of omission, of shunning away cascades of words, *patterns, images,* devices, letters, and *marks* of all kinds—and of leaving rhetorically effective gaps throughout one's prose." We can glean from this an opportunity to extend our view of brevity to include more of the texts around us. In fact, the invitation to build these approaches is already there. Recall Longinus's (1890, III.IV, emphasis added) point that "bulk, when hollow and affected, is always objectionable, whether *in material bodies* or in writings." Although it makes sense that historically, rhetoric and composition's approach to brevity has tended to focus on the latter, maintaining this approach would fail to account for brief texts that veer away from these characteristics.

I argue that the tendency to focus on brevity's use in discursive, alphanumeric texts is a reflection of the broader tension surrounding our engagement with multimodality. The term *multimodal* is relatively new but increasingly popular, its nuances still being discovered (Lauer 2009, 237). Descriptions of multimodal texts tend to situate them as different from alphanumeric texts (e.g., Sheridan, Ridolfo, and Michel 2005, 809–811; Anderson et al. 2006, 59; Carpenter 2014, 70), which might suggest the latter is monomodal. Yet, as Cheryl E. Ball and Colin Charlton (2016, 43) point out, "there is no such thing as a monomodal text." For example, we can recognize the multimodality of "the traditional first-year-composition research essay" if we attend to not just "its linguistic mode" but also "its visual and spatial arrangement on the page" (43). In effect, then, multimodality seems to run into the inverse problem of brevity: we tend to restrict brevity as a style to discursive, alphanumeric texts and communication, whereas we tend to use *multimodal* to represent everything else or to describe texts that combine the features of a traditional print text with other, often digital features.

Joddy Murray (2009) also challenges this division between multimodal and monomodal texts (162), calling our attention to what he argues is the misunderstood relationship between the discursive and the non-discursive (8–9). This chapter builds on Murray's theory of "non-discursive symbolization," which "accounts for the many other ways humans use symbols to create meaning—methods wholly outside the realm of traditional, word-based, discursive text" (12)—and considers the role brevity plays in symbolization. Murray argues that non-discursive communication necessitates "a willingness by the author and by the audience to construct their own meaning (or not)" (52). Like Murray, I also want to draw attention to the space between discursive and nondiscursive rhetoric, as well as the potential meaning making and communication that can emerge from that space. Further, I argue that the brevity employed in hashtag activism has the potential to better amplify and circulate both. To illustrate this idea, I examine the Pussyhat

Project's various texts: its web materials, name, hat, and hashtag. These texts are intentionally brief and open enough to invite varied appropriation, interpretation, and circulation. As I will show, brevity is a key style and strategy for this movement, evidenced not only by words but also by images, materials, time, and space.

THE PUSSYHAT PROJECT'S MULTIMODAL BREVITY

"The more we are seen, the more we are heard," state Pussyhat Project founders Krista Suh and Jayna Zweiman (2017). Indeed, the project's success depends on its ability to recruit as many participants as possible and to motivate those participants to promote the project through their engagement. Thus, the project is wise in its web design to consistently (a) provide information in a concise and clear manner and (b) direct audience members to take action. With a white background and minimal sans-serif black text, each page prominently displays the project's name at the top, followed by a horizontal menu with eight items: "Get Involved," "Donate," "Blog," "Patterns," "Hat Tracker," "Register Your Hat," "Locations," and "Info and Contact" (see figure 5.1). In different ways, each page points to direct actions the audience can take. Together, they illustrate the movement's substantial credibility, sincere goodwill, and sizable community engagement; they engage the audience through emotional and logical appeals; and they provide the tools needed to participate (Suh and Zweiman 2017). Most important, the website never wastes the audience's time. The goal is to transform the audience into participants, and the website's straightforward, action-oriented design provides multifaceted motivation for the audience to do its part.

Most of the project's crucial information is formatted as an image to encourage mass circulation, online or offline. For instance, the website's first page presents a printable image with twenty-eight ways to participate, key information about the project, and more (see figure 5.2). This PDF is impressive in terms of the amount of information it presents in a single graphic without being overwhelming. On a standard printer page, the PDF explains that "knitters, crocheters and sewers of all levels" can make these hats; when and where marchers should convene for the 2017 march; and how "everyone can" support the movement, even if they will not be making a hat or marching.

Overall, this infographic is inviting rather than daunting or off-putting. On one level, the infographic encourages readers to consume an array of information by employing brief stylistics, such as concise and clear sentence structure. Direct commands like "enclose," "take,"

The Ideograph and the #Pussyhat   107

Figure 5.1. "Homepage" for Pussyhat Project

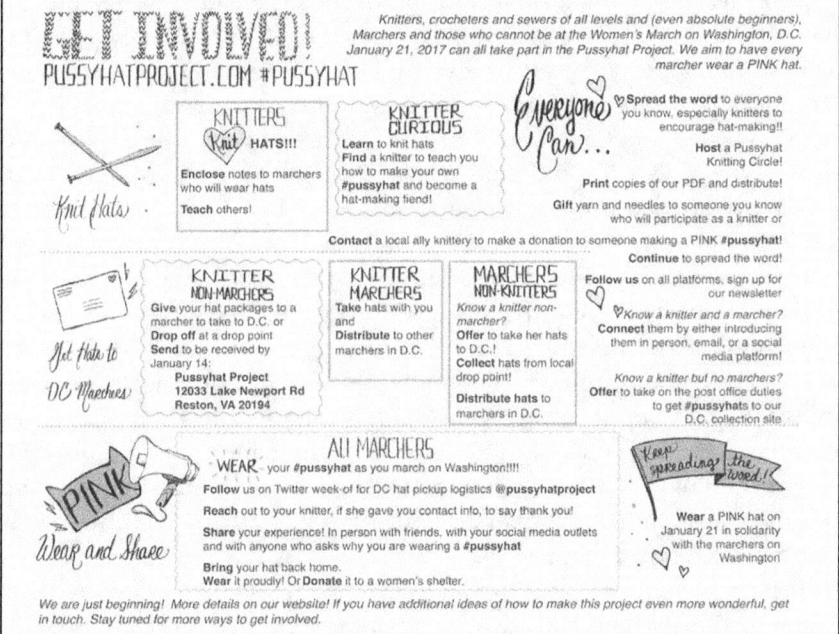

Figure 5.2. "Get Involved!" infographic, Pussyhat Project

"offer," "connect," and "send" frequently appear, transforming aspects of the movement into direct actions. Of the infographic's forty-two sentences, thirty-three begin with direct commands, and each verb at the beginning of the sentence is emboldened. In addition to creating hats and gifting them to marchers, audience members can also "**gift** yarn and needles" to hat makers, "**host** a Pussyhat knitting circle," "**collect**" and "**distribute** hats" after they arrive at local post offices and "drop points," and "**enclose** notes to marchers" (see figure 5.2). These commands convey the ease and importance of participating, encouraging the audience to read the text and learn about the movement. In addition, it is important to note a material element of brevity at play: that the infographic's succinct presentation fits on one shareable, online image or one printable, offline flyer, which encourages the audience to participate through circulation. The project uses this strategy throughout the website, such as in the customizable notes hat makers can send to marchers, as well as posters marchers can print (Suh and Zweiman 2017).

Shareability and succinctness are critical to the Pussyhat Project because it depends first and foremost on viral participation. Gaining participation for this project is challenging because it requires participants to go a step further than many movements or organizations do. Supporting the Pussyhat Project primarily means creating or obtaining a handmade product. This support requires more effort than, say, writing a check or making a sign. Participation here requires multiple materials, considerably more time, and perhaps even the acquisition of a new skill set. Given the general difficulty of moving an online reader to do more than visit the website, the aims of the Pussyhat Project are ambitious. Consequently, the project is wise to make its digital materials succinct and shareable in offline and online contexts.

Again, for the Pussyhat Project, time is of the essence. Whereas many initiatives ultimately aim to earn a profit or a dedicated following that can sustain them over time, the Pussyhat Project was initially defined, in a sense, by its nonprofit urgency and ephemerality. Although most businesses, organizations, projects, movements, and so forth benefit from mass circulation in terms of publicity, such circulation is especially critical for the Pussyhat Project; the project's success depends largely on the number of audience members it can recruit to create, distribute, and don pussyhats on a specific day. Thus, the Pussyhat Project's strategies prioritize communal, widespread recruitment of audience members. Many of the PDF's commands, for instance, revolve around publicity, asking readers eight times to do something along the lines of "spreading the word" (see figure 5.2). Likewise, the website heavily promotes the short, intuitive hashtag #Pussyhat to encourage the creation of a large dialogical network. In the PDF the hashtag #Pussyhat appears five times, encouraging the audience to "follow us on Twitter week-of for DC hat logistics @pussyhatproject" (see figure 5.2).

These strategies paid off in immediate, international audience uptake. Yet the project has also had considerable cultural staying power. Across the marches for the third annual Women's March on January 19, 2019, pussyhats appeared prominently in the crowds and in social media posts. Whereas the project's web materials played a critical role in the project's initial uptake, the Pussyhat Project continues to enjoy an impressive amount of "positive appropriation" because of its signature brief texts (Ridolfo and DeVoss 2009): the hashtag #Pussyhat and the pussyhat itself.

In general, hashtags are an impressive demonstration of brevity's persuasiveness. Like sound bites, hashtags are composed with uptake and circulation in mind but with far fewer characters at their disposal. In this sense, hashtags exemplify the textual condensation to which Foley (2012, 614) points, especially given their ability to operate metonymically. For instance, although the hashtag #MeToo may be too vague for comprehension without context, its context is so widely recognized and understood that it now serves as cultural shorthand for broader arguments against sexual harassment and sexual assault. Prominent activist hashtags communicate their broader meanings so well, in fact, that they regularly circulate offline. Yet when hashtags appear offline, they tend to do so as themselves: hashtags written on offline materials (e.g., a shirt with a hashtag printed on it). The Pussyhat Project goes a significant step further. Its hashtag is inextricably linked to the material counterpart it names. This counterpart—the pussyhat—is a unique physical item designed to be worn as a visual, material, non-discursive sign of protest, which many people continue to circulate and comprehend long after the initial Women's March.

To persuade its audience of this significance, the project explains that creating a pussyhat is "a practical thing to do" and a "POWERFUL" one in five ways: "Numbers," "Pink," "Individuals within Large Groups," "the Handmade," and "Pussy" (Suh and Zweiman 2017). Through this series of justifications, the page illustrates well the project's characteristic juxtaposition of the playful and the meaningful. "Power of Pussy," for instance, is an alarming and disarming headline that reminds its readers that "pussy" is a "derogatory" and "loaded" term used against women—as exemplified by Trump's "grab 'em by the pussy" statement that grounds the project—and the project founders "want to reclaim the term as a means of empowerment" (2017).

Indeed, naming the hats that define this movement *pussyhat* is empowering in multiple ways. First, it is a cheeky transformation of the cutesy term *pussycat* that sexualizes and objectifies women. Although the

Figure 5.3. Cropped photo of a pussyhat. WikiMedia Commons (2018).

pussy element may seem too vulgar for such mainstream prominence, the full term *pussyhat* is yoked to the already acceptable term *pussycat*, which highlights the hypocrisy one faces if they seek to censor it. That said, *pussy* is meant to be front and center in this movement, which is one reason the hats are pink (see figure 5.3). Pink is closely associated with female genitalia, so the "sea of pink hats" sends a strong visual message that supporters of the movement want to protect their bodies from invasive legislation and sexist treatment (Suh and Zweiman 2017). This color choice also makes sense because "pink is considered a very female color representing caring, compassion, and love—all qualities that have been derided as weak but are actually STRONG" (2017). Here, the project seeks to reclaim pink just as it seeks to reclaim the word *pussy*. It acknowledges the ways the color is used against women, but it also repositions the color as a positive symbol of the qualities—"caring, compassion, and love"—that underpin the movement and its participants.

However, perhaps brevity works against the pussyhat in its attempt to symbolize the larger movement(s) it stood in for. While these hats can be read as holding the various productive critiques mentioned above, the pussyhat has also been criticized for the ways it is not, in fact, a one-size-fits-all symbol embraced by all activists. Since its inception, the pussyhat—like the Women's March—has been criticized for being insufficiently intersectional and thus exclusionary and potentially harmful to the communities it aims to uplift (Deer 2017; Kai 2017; Shenton 2019). Many argue that "the pink pussyhat excludes and is offensive to transgender women and gender nonbinary people who don't have typical female genitalia and to women of color because their genitals are more likely to be brown than pink" (Shamus 2018). These critiques eventually prompted a clarifying statement from Zweiman (2018) a few days before the second Women's March.

Critiques against the pussyhat's design notwithstanding, it is evident that the various components of the Pussyhat Project—its name, its hat, its hashtag, its web materials—congeal to produce meanings that are taken up or resisted by those who engage with it, as updates to the hat illustrate. Some have revised its design to be "more inclusive," such as Jasmin Knitmore's "sweet peach hat" (Knitmore quoted in Jagannathan 2018); others have remixed the design for other activist purposes (McClurg 2017). Overall, the various parts of the movement work together in ways that mirror the hybridity of multimodal texts, "interacting in individually incomplete or incoherent ways that, when taken as a whole, become articulate" (Murray 2009, 169). The collapsing of these various elements (the knitted attire, the digital space, the Twitter-friendly phrase) creates a shorthand wherein the pussyhat stands for each and all of these things. I argue that the project's ultimate brevity contributes to the pussyhat's circulation and function as a multimodal ideograph.

In 1980, Michael Calvin McGee introduced the *ideograph*, or "an ordinary language-term found in political discourse" (15). Ideographs are concise containers for complex cultural concepts. As such, they function in different communities as shorthand summaries of broader, divergent ideologies (6). McGee explains that people are "conditioned" to understand and accept the meaning of these "one-term sums of an orientation," but not everyone does; thus, an ideograph's communal circulation involves "uniting" those who accept their meaning and "separating" them from those who reject it (7–8). In short, brevity is integral to ideographs.

McGee defines the ideograph in linguistic terms, but its actual function and effects can be found in other types of texts as well. For example, Janis L. Edwards and Carol K. Winkler (1997, 297) use the Iwo Jima image, which "has become a discourse fragment that multiple publics appropriate for diverse purposes," as evident through the many political cartoons that parody or satirize it. Another example, argues Laurie E. Gries (2015, 220), is the Obama Hope image, "for by the time Obama began his first term, it had become so widely and highly visible that it could easily function as a visual ideograph in many political cartoons to satirize Obama's administration and US Americans' responding sentiment." Tom Ballard (2016) further extends the scope of ideographs in his call for the inclusion of video ideographs, as well as the inclusion of ideographs that are based in culture rather than politics. Ballard points out that if "ideographs are about communicating a separate message by re-appropriating material from the original" (16), such as through satire and parody, culturally

Figure 5.4. Photo of MAGA hat. From Bradshaw (2019).

based parody videos can qualify as ideographs as much as political cartoons. (For more on ideographs, see chapter 11.) In either case, they meet the basic criteria of being "cultural icons" or at least reasonably "valuable artifacts" related to something with "long ideological staying power" (14). Indeed, shared among these cases is the ideograph's mass recognition *and* interpretive and ideological nuance (Edwards and Winkler 1997, 304–305).

I argue that the pussyhat is a multimodal ideograph that communicates commitment to and rejection of different ideologies, namely, commitment to feminist ideologies and rejection of misogynist and patriarchal ideologies. It "contains concrete images and themes that invoke ill-defined ideological concepts (e.g., women's rights)" (Ballard 2016, 15), as seen in the tension between (a) the hat's overarching commitment to feminism and (b) critiques that the hat signals a lack of inclusivity (Zweiman 2018). We might also say it "imitate[s] elements of the original precisely" if we consider the relationship of the pussyhat to the "MAGA hat" (Ballard 2016, 15). Throughout Trump's campaign, he wore a red baseball cap that bore in white stitching his campaign slogan, "Make America Great Again" (see figure 5.4). This hat quickly reached international iconic status in appearance and in name, and it continues its controversial circulation among supporters. Although there is not time here to unpack the significance of the MAGA hat, we can draw an important connection between it and the pussyhat. Parody videos and political cartoons are ideographs because they appropriate fundamental components of an original text while also incorporating rhetorical and compositional elements that create or play into ideological nuance; so, too, does the pussyhat if we consider how its form mimics the MAGA hat while also significantly altering and challenging it, including through the infusion of its own ideologies. The MAGA hat is a mass-produced, commercialized, and conventionally styled campaign product for a presidential candidate. In protest of this candidate's election to office, a grassroots group designed and recruited international audience support for the creation and circulation of a handmade hat that symbolizes their dissent.

Both hats serve as visual stand-ins for much more complicated ideologies, and both designs gesture toward the ideologies that underpin them. Through a straightforward, machine-stitched slogan on a standard red baseball cap, the MAGA hat's design evokes patriotism, nationalism, and capitalism (Budds 2016; Stribley 2019). Likewise but with distinct cleverness and creativity, every element of the pussyhat's design—its name, its production, its style—communicates its dissenting message. The pussyhat reappropriates polemical phrases from our cultural lexicon—"pussycat" and "pussy"—and transforms their meaning through the new term *pussyhat* and its material counterpart. As a visual metonym, the pussyhat points to Trump's statement "grab 'em by the pussy" and presents an argument in protest of it and him specifically but also of the much larger, ongoing cultural history of such actions and abuses. People wore and still wear the pussyhat in protest, and the collective effect creates an overwhelming image of resistance to Trump, to the sea of MAGA hats that emerged during the campaign, and to the ideologies fueling the support for both.

The Pussyhat Project exemplifies how hashtag activism can strategically employ brevity to aim for and achieve sizable, sustained audience participation, evidenced by tweets that document the uptake of the task of hand-making materials: "You'd be happy to hear that I haven't knit in ages but I started a #Pussyhat tonight"; "This week I learned to knit so I could make myself a #Pussyhat"; "Of course my neighbour, who hardly knits, has a ball of hot pink yarn in her stash and plans to knit a hat in a day and a half. #Pussyhat"; "My hands are not in great shape right now, but I had to make at least one. Just off the needles. It will go to Denver #Pussyhat"; "My #Pussyhat from a mom of 4, who doesn't have the time to knit. But she did"; "I did it! Despite not being very proficient in crochet I made a #Pussyhat."

Moreover, these tweets show the audience's eagerness to labor for others: "I sent 2 to Portland. This one will stay right here in KS. #Pussyhat"; "It took me almost 15 hours to knit a #Pussyhat, but I did it and my friend is gonna wear it in the DC march!"; "If anyone near the Knoxville TN area heading to DC for the march needs a #Pussyhat let me know. I can make you one and give it to you."

Tweets also show efforts to mobilize more audience members to perform this labor: "No time to make both? Here are free knit/crochet patterns for a #messybun / #Pussyhat hybrid"; "One day left. You can totally make another #Pussyhat (or your first!) for the #womensmarch. I can help if you need it. Don't be shy!"; "In solidarity w/ @PussyhatProject we made this @knitting pattern free til the @womensmarch. #Pussyhat"; "If you want a #Pussyhat and don't have time to knit one (or can't, like me), here's a fast and easy alternative."

In general, the tweets illustrate the project's widespread uptake by this point, such as tweets from participating cities around the world and tweets depicting participants' pilgrimage to the DC march. These tweets tend to include photos of actual pussyhats, which encourage uptake by showcasing the enthusiastic uptake of other audience members. The photos show the range of approaches to producing pussyhats and the different finished products, which conveys the task's accessibility; they also often show the hat being worn, usually by a person smiling at the camera, which creates a more real sense of the community prospective participants are joining.

The above tweets all include #Pussyhat, which points to the hashtag's significant role in the project's uptake. #Pussyhat names—and thus publicizes—its project, and it does so as a brief noun, fitting easily into various sentence structures. Likewise, the pussyhat's brief, accessible design in terms of production and everyday use, combined with the message it conveys, contributes to its ongoing rhetorical velocity. Indeed, following the 2017 Women's March, the pussyhat continues circulating widely as a hashtag, term, image, and object in political contexts and popular culture (Soo Hoo 2017). On social media, the image and hashtag circulate, though often without one another. For instance, 2018 Women's March tweets frequently only employed #WomensMarch hashtags but showed images of pussyhats to promote the march or showed pussyhats worn en masse by 2018 participants. Since the first Women's March, proponents and opponents have continued to circulate the pussyhat, particularly in ideographic manners that signal broader political and cultural conversations (Garber 2018). For instance, a March 2019 tweet reads: "When #childabuse wears a #Pussyhat. There must surely be a special corner in Hell for parents who use their children as living ideological voodoo dolls. Let your kids be kids. #Whaleoil #auspol #feminism #FeminismIsCancer." Embedded in the tweet is a political cartoon, which features a pregnant person wearing a pussyhat and explaining to their physician, "I'm here to find out if I'm having a male predator or a female victim."

From its creation to its culmination, every element of the project is designed to foster ongoing audience uptake and circulation. Notably, these elements are distinctly brief in style, as its name, web materials, hashtag, and hat illustrate. Through the visual, verbal, material, and spatial use of brevity, the Pussyhat Project in name, image, and explanation makes a series of appeals that—when coupled with many easy ways to lend support—affect and motivate its audience to take action, which they continue to do years later.

CONCLUSION

In this chapter I examined the multimodal qualities of brevity as a rhetorical strategy and compositional style, which provides a necessary update to the predominantly discursive, alphanumeric approach to brevity that tends to appear. To show how these qualities appear in brief texts today, I examined how multimodal brevity is a defining feature of the Pussyhat Project's texts: I discussed how the Pussyhat Project employed a concise and clear writing style and created succinct and easily shareable materials to encourage mass audience uptake for the initial Women's March on Washington, and I demonstrated how its hashtag and its hat contribute to its ongoing influence.

Ultimately, a more comprehensive approach to brevity can help us attend to the multimodal persuasiveness of hashtag activism, which strategically employs brevity to garner mass audience uptake and engagement. Such success is especially striking when we consider how choice constantly overwhelms audiences. Citing Richard Lanham's concept of the "attention economy," Hirst (2007, 314–315) avers that "human attention is now the scarce commodity, and style that rightly, effectively engages and directs human attention is more important than ever before. *Brevitas* is a flood-gate key for holding back, and draining off, the seas of information." We must develop better strategies for understanding the influence of the brief texts that capture our attention. We can begin, I suggest, by recovering brevity's multimodal qualities. As the Pussyhat Project demonstrates, broadening our parameters for brevity to encompass its multimodal qualities can help us better appreciate its value today.

REFERENCES

Alexander, Jonathan, and Jacqueline Rhodes. 2014. *On Multimodality: New Media in Composition Studies*. Urbana, IL: National Council of Teachers of English.

Anderson, Daniel, Anthony Atkins, Cheryl Ball, Krista Homicz Millar, Cynthia Selfe, and Richard Selfe. 2006. "Integrating Multimodality into Composition Curricula: Survey Methodology and Results from a CCCC Research Grant." *Composition Studies* 34 (2): 59–84.

Aristotle. 1954. In *Rhetoric*. Translated by W. Rhys Roberts. http://classics.mit.edu/Aristotle/rhetoric.html.

Ball, Cheryl E., and Colin Charlton. 2016. "All Writing Is Multimodal." In *Naming What We Know: Threshold Concepts of Writing Studies*, edited by Linda Adler-Kassner and Elizabeth Wardle, 42–43. Boulder: University Press of Colorado.

Ballard, Tom. 2016. "YouTube Video Parodies and the Video Ideograph." *Rocky Mountain Review* 70 (1): 10–22.

boyd, danah, Scott Golder, and Gilad Lotan. 2010. "Tweet, Tweet, Retweet: Conversational Aspects of Retweeting on Twitter." January 6. *HICSS-43*. Kauai: Institute of Electrical and Electronics Engineers.

Bradshaw, R. Nial. 2019. "180903-dsc_1063." *Flickr*, September 3. https://creativecommons.org/licenses/by/4.0/.

Budds, Diana. 2016. "The Worst Design of 2016 Was Also the Most Effective." December 16. *Fast Company*. https://www.fastcompany.com/3066599/the-worst-design-of-2016-was-also-the-most-effective.

Carpenter, Russell. 2014. "Negotiating the Spaces of Design in Multimodal Composition." *Computers and Composition* 33: 68–79.

Dadas, Caroline. 2017. "Hashtag Activism: The Promise and Risk of 'Attention.'" In *Social Writing/Social Media: Publics, Presentations, and Pedagogies*, edited by Douglas M. Walls and Stephanie Vie, 17–36. Fort Collins, CO: WAC Clearinghouse.

Derr, Holly. 2017. "Pink Flag: What Message Do 'Pussy Hats' Really Send?" *Bitch Media*, January 17. https://www.bitchmedia.org/article/pink-flag-what-message-do-pussy-hats-really-send.

Edwards, Janis L., and Carol K. Winkler. 1997. "Representative Form and the Visual Ideograph: The Iwo Jima Image in Editorial Cartoons." *Quarterly Journal of Speech* 83: 289–310.

Foley, Megan. 2012. "Sound Bites: Rethinking the Circulation of Speech from Fragment to Fetish." *Rhetoric and Public Affairs* 15 (4): 613–622.

Garber, Megan. 2018. "*Roseanne* vs. the 'Nasty Woman.'" *The Atlantic*, March 23. https://www.theatlantic.com/entertainment/archive/2018/03/roseanne-reboot-review/556316/.

"Get Involved!" 2017. *Pussyhat Project*. https://www.pussyhatproject.com/print.

Gries, Laurie E. 2015. *Still Life with Rhetoric: A New Materialist Approach for Visual Rhetorics*. Boulder: University Press of Colorado.

Hill, Marc Lamont. 2018. "'Thank You, Black Twitter': State Violence, Digital Counterpublics, and Pedagogies of Resistance." *Urban Education* 53 (2): 286–302.

Hirst, Russel. 2007. "Virtues and Vices of Omission." *Technical Communication* 54 (4) (2007): 308–318.

Jackson, Sarah J., and Brooke Foucault Welles. 2015. "Hijacking #MYNYPD: Social Media Dissent and Networked Counterpublics." *Journal of Communication* 65 (6): 932–952.

Jagannathan, Meera. 2018. "The Case against Pussyhats, Ahead of This Year's Women's March." *MarketWatch*, January 12. https://www.marketwatch.com/story/the-case-against-pussyhats-ahead-of-this-years-womens-march-2018-01-12-0883824.

Kai, Maiysha. 2017. "Ain't I a Woman: Marching Forward—What Now?" *The Root*, January 24. https://www.theroot.com/ain-t-i-a-woman-marching-forward-what-now-1791562448.

Kerl, Simon. 1869. *Elements of Composition and Rhetoric: Practical, Concise, and Comprehensive*. New York: Ivison, Blakeman, Taylor.

Kress, Gunther. 2010. *Multimodality: A Social Semiotic Approach to Contemporary Communication.* New York: Routledge.

Kuo, Rachel. 2018. "Racial Justice Activist Hashtags: Counterpublics and Discourse Circulation." *New Media and Society* 20 (2): 495–514.

Lauer, Claire. 2009. "Contending with Terms: 'Multimodal' and 'Multimedia' in the Academic and Public Spheres." *Computers and Composition* 26 (4): 225–239.

Leung, Dennis, and Francis Lee. 2014. "Cultivating an Active Online Counterpublic: Examining Usage and Political Impact of Internet Alternative Media." *International Journal of Press/Politics* 19 (3): 340–359.

Longinus. 1890. In *On the Sublime*. Translated by H. L. Havell. London: Macmillan.

McClurg, Lesley. 2017. "Pussy Hat Inspires Protest 'Resistor Hat' for Science March." *KQED*, April 3. https://www.kqed.org/science/1518249/pussyhat-inspires-protest-beanie-for-science-march.

McGee, Michael Calvin. 1980. "The 'Ideograph': A Link between Rhetoric and Ideology." *Quarterly Journal of Speech* 66 (1): 1–16.

Murray, Joddy. 2009. *Non-discursive Rhetoric: Image and Affect in Multimodal Composition.* New York: SUNY Press.

Palmeri, Jason. 2012. *Remixing Composition: A History of Multimodal Writing Pedagogy.* Carbondale: Southern Illinois University Press.

Papacharissi, Zizi. 2015. "Affective Publics and Structures of Storytelling: Sentiment, Events, and Mediality." *Information, Communication, and Society* 19 (3): 307–324. doi: 10.1080/1369118X.2015.1109697.

Perez, Sarah. 2018. "Twitter's Doubling of Character Count from 140 to 280 Had Little Impact on Length of Tweets." *Tech Crunch*. https://techcrunch.com/2018/10/30/twitters-doubling-of-character-count-from-140-to-280-had-little-impact-on-length-of-tweets/.

Perez, Sarah. 2019. "Twitter Gives Retweets an Upgrade." *Tech Crunch*. https://techcrunch.com/2019/05/06/twitter-gives-retweets-an-upgrade/.

Potts, Liza. 2013. *Social Media in Disaster Response: How Experience Architects Can Build for Participation.* New York: Routledge.

Pressgrove, Geah, Brooke Weberling McKeever, and S. Mo Jang. 2017. "What Is Contagious? Exploring Why Content Goes Viral on Twitter: A Case Study of the ALS Ice Bucket Challenge." *International Journal of Nonprofit and Voluntary Sector Marketing* 23 (1): 1–8.

Ridolfo, Jim, and Dànielle Nicole DeVoss. 2009. *Composing for Recomposition: Rhetorical Velocity and Delivery.* https://kairos.technorhetoric.net/13.2/topoi/ridolfo_devoss/intro.html.

Rosenbaum, Judith E. 2018. *Constructing Digital Cultures: Tweets, Trends, Race, and Gender.* London: Lexington Books.

Sampson, Tony D. 2012. *Virality: Contagion Theory in the Age of Networks.* Minneapolis: University of Minnesota Press.

Shamus, Kristen Jordan. 2018. "Pink Pussyhats: The Reason Feminists Are Ditching Them." *Detroit Free Press.* https://www.freep.com/story/news/2018/01/10/pink-pussyhats-feminists-hats-womens-march/1013630001/.

Shenton, Jamie E. 2019. "The Pussyhat's Identity Crisis." *Sapiens*, January 17. https://www.sapiens.org/biology/pussyhat-identity-crisis/.

Sheridan, David M., Jim Ridolfo, and Anthony J. Michel. 2005. "The Available Means of Persuasion: Mapping a Theory and Pedagogy of Multimodal Public Rhetoric." *JAC* 25 (4): 803–844. http://www.jstor.org/stable/20866716.

Soo Hoo, Fawnia. 2017. "The Costumes in Marvel's New Teen Superhero Series 'Runaways' Include Pink Pussy Hats and Feminist Slogan T-shirts." *Fashionista*. https://fashionista.com/2017/11/marvel-hulu-runaways-costume-design.

Stribley, Robert A. 2019. "The MAGA Hat Rorschach Test." *Medium*. https://medium.com/s/story/the-maga-hat-rorschach-test-41f466364cfc.

Suh, Krista, and Jayna Zweiman. 2017. *Pussyhat Project.* https://www.pussyhatproject.com/.
Theocharis, Yannis, Will Lowe, Jan van Deth, and Garma Garcia-Albacete. 2015. "Using Twitter to Mobilize Protest Action: Online Mobilization Patterns and Action Repertoires in the Occupy Wall Street, Indignados, and Aganaktismenoi Movements." *Information, Communication and Society* 18 (2): 202–220.
"Transcript: Donald Trump's Taped Comments about Women." 2016. *New York Times.* https://www.nytimes.com/2016/10/08/us/donald-trump-tape-transcript.html.
Yang, Guobin. 2016. "Commentary: Narrative Agency in Hashtag Activism, the Case of #BlackLivesMatter." *Media and Communication* 4 (4): 13–17.
Zweiman, Jayna. 2018. "The Project of Pussyhat." *Pussyhat Project.* https://www.pussyhatproject.com/blog/2018/1/14/the-project-of-pussyhat.

6
IMAGI(NI)NG RADICALISM IN THE CONTEXT OF INDIAN STUDENT ACTIVISM
The Discursivity of Hashtags and Memes

Avishek Ray and Neha Gupta

Protests such as those in Tehran following the 2009 Iranian elections, the Arab Spring, the Occupy movements, the 2012 Nirbhaya protests in Delhi, and others have featured social media platforms as the locus of political mobilizations. In the era of new media, the proliferation of dissent on the internet has impacted the political landscape; in particular, Web 2.0 technologies are harnessed more frequently to optimize oppositional politics. Hashtags in particular have globally fueled the vortex of the politics of dissent. In this chapter, we focus on three hashtags—#Hokkolorob, #HandsOffJU, and #SaveJNU—that illustrate dissenting student politics in contemporary Indian university spaces. #Hokkolorob emerged from a particular case of student molestation at Jadavpur University (JU) (Kolkata) in 2014, #HandsOffJU as a reaction to the change in that university's undergrad student acceptance procedure in 2018, and #SaveJNU from student unrest directed at the supposed bureaucratic takeover of Jawaharlal Nehru University (JNU) (Delhi) in 2017 in the wake of (what the state perceived as) a rise in anti-national sentiment.[1]

We examine the hashtags and tagged memes to critique (1) the eliticalization of certain universities framed as intellectual institutions with concentrated power, privilege, influence, and increased social status and (2) the enclavist values eliticization evokes by separating people associated with universities from the larger population. We examine how certain universities are construed as epitomes of progressive values, wherein certain "imagined communities" (Anderson 2006)—the JU-ites and the JNU-ites, for example—become the referent for radical identity. For instance, the Calcutta Medical College (CMC, Kolkata) protests demanding appropriate hostel facilities, though unfolding simultaneously with

https://doi.org/10.7330/9781646423187.c006

#HandsOffJU, barely merited any social media attention.[2] The way these three hashtags have articulated the radical identity of certain universities is reflective of the implicit politics of identity differentiation within academic spaces. This differentiation deems the CMC as a less radical political outfit; therefore, its protests are less worthy of media attention. Similarly, the 2018 protests for the hike in fellowship for the research scholars of India[3]—though it had a significant social media presence—was not deemed radical enough. Arguably, this was because it did not stem from a university preconceived as radical. It simply did not capture public attention the way the movements under discussion in this chapter did. The hashtag in use, #HikeStudentFellowship, did not privilege one radical identity over another.

As we progress through this chapter, we will systematically unpack the discursive articulation of dissent on social media that emanates from urban institutions deemed to be radical and highlight the elite-enclavist referentiality configured within social media activism. That is, we will examine the rhetorical practices related to student activism that ultimately reinforce the university-as-elite identity construct. This expression of protest as a "sphericule" (Gitlin 1998) becomes amplified and legitimatized through social media circuits and therefore becomes emblematic of all iconoclasm. This study considers the way digital activism, unwittingly or not, participates in reinforcing or rejecting cultural narratives—in this instance, those about academic spaces. This chapter considers how the discursivity of the hashtags and memes reinforces certain registers of radicalism that emanate from the (perceived) uber-liberal urban universities.

QUESTIONING AND THEORIZING TRUTH CLAIMS

This chapter operates under the assumption that specific online practices often align with more general schemata that reinforce offline practices, as well as perceptions of people and places. That is, our heuristic truth claims (or beliefs) are, in fact, manifestations of how we (re)construct our (selective) reality. This (re)construction of reality happens in both online and offline spaces and informs our understanding of and engagement with the realities we then re-present. Further, our contextual deployment of those re-presented categories in turn (re)configures and (re)contextualizes the categories (or claims/beliefs) in question (Hacking 1999). These articulations again fashion how we think about and deploy the reconfigured categories. For the purpose of this study, this means that such articulations (in the form of social media posts) impact attitudes concerning the universities under analysis. That is, we find that they reinforce the purportedly radical identity the students of the university inherit.

In this chapter, we examine the ways these social media posts provide a narrative of/for the "radical" student body, attending to the "dramatic performativity" (Clark 2016) of dissent and radicalism and how it defines and "brings into existence" the community itself (Bourdieu 1984, 479). The goal here is not to determine what constitutes radicalism or who constitutes the ideal dissenter. We are interested in probing how radicalism as a concept is articulated through the three hashtags in question. In particular, we examine the matrix within which the imaginative articulation of dissent and radicalism unfolds in the context of these three hashtags.

From here, we engage in discourse analysis of the social media posts relating to the protests, critically examining the cultural appropriation of the ethos of elitism in these select threads and posts. If narration, as Homi K. Bhabha (1990) posits, can function as a metaphor of the nation, our goal here is to demonstrate how the "dissenters"—as an "imagined community" (Anderson 2006)—territorialize certain elite educational spaces. We find Benedict Anderson's notion of imagined communities particularly instrumental in making sense of the "sphericules" within which these student movements operate (Gitlin 1998, 170). Our intention is not to draw an analogy between the student bodies and the nation-state; rather, we are trying to underline this aspect of imagination. Anderson (2006, 49) posits that "the members of even the smallest nation will never know most of their fellow-members, meet them or even hear of them, yet in the minds of each lives the image of their communion." Applying this line of thought to the student bodies under study, we find that the dissenting students of certain universities have an inclination for communion—some imagined connection—with their counterparts from *only* certain universities and not some others. JU-ites from Kolkata, for example, solidarized with JNU-ites from Delhi during the JNU protests, while students from IIT Delhi—which was closer geographically to the JNU campus—were rather indifferent to their plight. Similarly, when the Indian Institutes of Technology (IITs) and Indian Institute of Science (IISCs) spearheaded the 2018 countrywide protests concerning the research fellowship hike, the JU-ites and JNU-ites, though in support of the hike, did not present this support as visibly. As publicly funded top-tier technology schools, the IITs have competitive screening and are relatively expensive to attend; therefore, in actuality, they are no less elitist than JU or JNU (if elitism is seen as tied to selectivity and cost). Yet the two groupings differ when it comes to perceptions or demonstrations of radicalism; when it comes to participation in dissent/protest, the JU-ites and JNU-ites, as imagined communities, are more inclined to join in solidarity to speak out against perceived injustice.

To illustrate, let us turn to perceptions of the digital activists connected to #Hokkolorob. Supriya Chaudhuri (2019, 45), professor emerita at Jadavpur University, provides an "insider" perspective through her affiliation with JU, arguing that given "the many upheavals in the Indian higher education landscape over the past few years, [Hokkolorob] needs to be understood in the context of a crisis that affects both the public university and the Indian polity." Chaudhuri's claim that #Hokkolorob occupies a unique space in this moment in which the public university is faced with this neo-liberal turn suggests that she is willing to accept the expression of dissent of a particular subjectivity as the emblem of all radicalism. That is, the expression of dissent "brings into existence" the categorization of the university as radical; participation in this protest places the university and its students into this radical sphericule. Notwithstanding social media's role in fostering public spheres, scholars have often pointed to how the chaotic-fragmented, self-cocooned (instead of dialogic) discourses on digital platforms lead to balkanization: the formation of parallel communities, isolated groups, with competing and often extremist viewpoints that are at odds with the purportedly democratic and liberatory principles of the internet. In light of these schisms, this chapter examines how the rhetoric of the dissenting student unfolds within the ambit of a digitally networked, netizen-enhanced identity politics and often characterizes a particular sphericule.

Turning to a different hashtag activism campaign, let us illustrate this with an example. A meme (see figure 6.1) that circulated on Facebook during the JNU protests was related to the administrative changes (or bureaucratic takeover) at the university. In this image, the lawn mower is shaped like a tank and is marked "state machinery." As a clearly labeled metaphor for state machinery, it is presumably mowing the heads of the dissenting students that comprise the "lawn" lining the bottom portion of the illustration. Among the heads, only three are clearly visible. Further, the protruding heads are labeled with the abbreviations of three Indian universities: University of Hyderabad, JU, and JNU. The meme's symbolism is rather explicit. This meme clearly recalls the iconic Tiananmen Square image (Widener 1989): a solitary man standing fearlessly in front of a column of tanks in the face of the Chinese military

Figure 6.1. Tank meme (origin unknown)

crackdown at Tiananmen Square in 1989. Digital media often recycles contents from other (older) media, in this case the original artwork by Pawel Kuczynski,[4] with the intent of re-purposing it. Jay David Bolter and Richard Grusin (1999) term this "remediation." This theory explains that new visual media gain cultural significance by referencing and refashioning older media. Likewise, the reference in this meme—the iconic Tiananmen Square image—remediates the registers of dissent and iconoclasm the original image embodies, attaching them to the student protests. Student hashtag activism can sometimes take on an ideological role, advancing debates about the larger issues of political existence. As Pramod K. Nayar (2019, 30) posits, "Protests in a neoliberal higher education context in India are instantiations of a larger debate about the nature of democracy, and about the nature of the 'public' across the country itself." We are arguing that this ideological role seems to be achieved only by those protests that come out of urban-elite pedagogic spaces. Meanwhile, the caption, placed at the base of the meme, reads "keu jege aache bole / karo chokheaaj ghum nei" [in Bangla, this translates as "Because some are awake(ned), some can't rest in peace today"]. Again, only three heads protrude, which is to suggest that only the three urban-elite institutions dare to stand out. Thus, these institutions have been imagined to be (figuratively) "awake(ned)." This is illustrative of the curious triangulation of radicalism, dissent, and elitism, which has ramifications for how certain student protests are articulated.

THE HASHTAG AS SPHERICULES

The study in this chapter has two goals. The first is to establish that dissenting students from urban, elite, deemed-to-be-radical university spaces, in their social media movements, often deploy language—especially in the usage of hashtags and memes—that services identity differentiation, which draws strength from the purportedly radical status of certain universities. This fragmentation and subsequent elevation of the dissenter's identity is reinforced through social media echo chambers. The second aim is to argue that engendering this identity and radical-ness can be claimed by only some and not others; anyone outside the periphery of this urban-elite-university-sphericule is another/outsider to be engaged with suspiciously or sympathetically and not as an equal. The manner in which the protest manifests and is articulated is then a marker of elite culture. Thus, the study will establish that a symbiotic relationship exists between radical university culture and elite culture. From here, we seek to understand: how do the three hashtags in question enable new imaginations and articulations of belonging and political partisanship? What imaginations of the university—as both a concept and a pedagogic outfit—do they furnish and reinforce? Which voices are amplified and which voices effaced in these examples of hashtag activism?

Far from assessing the impact, virality, or efficacy of these hashtags, this study looks into how they serve as conduits for conveying "a privileged position in the communicative exchange (from the viewpoint of circulation)" (Hall 1980, 118). Assessing the impact of these social media movements would require methodologies that seldom measure impact conclusively or account for a specific impact. Such a goal is not useful to this study because the hashtag, in general, is not necessarily an outcome-driven instrument. The function of the hashtag, rather, is to link and add momentum to meandering ideas on specific discourses and, at best, to serve as a coupling apparatus coalescing divergent ideas under one rubric. What we are looking at here is the discursive event that underpins the imagination of the university as an enclavist space and the articulation of the radical student identity.

This study provides a discursive analysis of the posts tagged with the three hashtags on Facebook—the most popular social media platform in India—and the identity politics they endorse. These three hashtags evoke preferred readings that reinforce/legitimize perceptions about the radical-ness (or lack thereof) of the universities they stem from. With this awareness we unpack the discursive codes embedded in the Facebook posts that use these hashtags to opine on the events associated with the movements. This ethnographic approach draws from posts available in the authors' Facebook networks.[5] Facebook is a platform and not a search engine, and as such a login is necessary to access Facebook posts. However, the arguments made in this chapter are not based solely on the analysis of posts from our own feeds or those of our "friends"; rather, they come from the corpus of results that searching each hashtag yields within the accessible pages of Facebook networks as a whole. As such, analysis also stems from posts made on public Facebook pages outside our personal networks. It is significant to highlight this because the results are susceptible to some element of convenience and subjectivity. Eli Pariser (2011) attributes this to the "filter bubble." Algorithms that allow for extreme customization on the internet control and limit the information users can access, creating personalized universes of information. Facebook, for instance, organizes users' news feeds, prioritizing news and posts that it believes align with their preexisting beliefs and interests. It privileges links the user is likely to click on. The search results on Facebook are organized similarly; links and posts shared by friends will appear first, so what is familiar is prioritized. Despite these limitations, we chose Facebook as the platform for this study because it is the most popular social media in use (Kwatra 2018).

Our analysis is limited to the ways these posts depict the JNU-ite and the JU-ite as radical in order to problematize these narratives. Our search for these three hashtags on Facebook led to a number of posts, memes, and comment threads that we discuss below. Memes in particular are significant to the discussion because their multimodal nature provides an additional layer of commentary that can be studied alongside the hashtags. The visual rhetoric of the meme adds to the specificity of the discursive encoding—encoding that generates public affect only within specific echo chambers. Memes acquire cultural signification in strategic and/or noteworthy ways. Consider, for instance, what happened when posts with the hashtag #MeToo were filtered out from the Chinese social media site Weibo. Users started posting with the hashtag #RiceBunny and with emojis and memes of rice bowls and bunny heads instead. Out loud, rice bunny is pronounced "mi tu," so users eluded censorship (Zeng 2018) while producing discursive meanings to participate in #MeToo.

#HOKKOLOROB AND THE CLAIMS TO TRUTH

As noted earlier, the Hokkolorob movement was initiated to protest against the alleged molestation of a female student at JU in 2014 (Dey

Figure 6.2. Talk to the hand meme (Hokkolorob 2014)

2020). As the movement gained momentum, the state machinery intervened. On the night of September 17, 2014, the protesting students were assaulted by the state police (Indo-Asian News Service 2014). Thereafter, the movement changed course, and the original goal of demanding a probe into the student molestation was forgotten. The movement evolved into a demand for an inquiry into the police atrocities and the resignation of Vice Chancellor Abhijit Chakraborty.

With that background in mind, we turn to the meme shown in figure 6.2 as an example of how the rhetoric of the dissenting students on social media functioned to bracket them as exalted individuals. This meme was posted on the Facebook page of the Hokkolorob movement. Text has been imposed on the "talk to the hand" meme, which reads "we are here for the truth [and] not for the page likes." A single animal, the lemur, embodies the monolithic JU identity—the emancipated liberal—and demands access to the truth. Here, the original talk to the hand meme has been repurposed to serve the discursive function of laying claim to the "truth" by a specific subjectivity. The truth thus sought, however, remains unspecified and can range from the identity of the molester to the identity of the perpetrator of the police atrocities to the vice chancellor's resignation to an abstract ideal truism. The disavowal of page likes—one of the indices of the popularity of a Facebook page—is invoked to underscore the sincerity of their commitment. However, there is a contradiction here. Clearly, the movement sought amplification through social media. Garnering page likes therefore has to be a goal because it is a tangible indicator of the increasing traction of the movement. After all, digital activism requires attention and circulation to fulfill its goals. The dismissal of page likes can be read, then, as a general disregard for others from outside the university, spectators, whose support the creators of the page arguably should seek.

Regardless of whether this makes sense from a social activism perspective (in terms of a goal of gaining supporters), Hokkolorob's stated disregard for page likes in the text of the meme is reinforced by the implied phrase "talk to the hand" portrayed in the meme's visual component. This idiom is arguably invoked to delegitimize and express frustration with the opposition, and it claims authority for the JU-ites' subjectivity. This implied authority, or superiority, status is further revealed through the haughty facial expression affixed to the lemur. So, what does this meme suggest about those posting or circulating it? Or, more accurately, what messages does it then attach to those posting or circulating it? The text's demand for the truth suggests a sense of entitlement, purportedly reserved for the students of the elite-urban university. It is also illustrative of the JU-ites' aspiration—we highlight the question of agency here—to advance a certain narrative as true, based on *their* acceptance of it as truthful. This practice is problematic because it suggests the alignment of specific subjectivities with truth claims and knowledge-power coupling(s). This fractionation legitimizes the rhetoric of territorialized elite educational spaces by refusing to dissipate into a larger we-subject. However, in this case, the movement itself emerges from a fragmented subjectivity—that of a territorially imagined pedagogical space—which the meme reiterates by invoking an exclusive claim to the truth. To put it simply, the meme makes clear an us-versus-them binary wherein only the "us" (the elite university student body) is framed as knowledgeable and/or deserving of the truth.

#HANDSOFFJU AND THE INSIDER/OUTSIDER DICHOTOMY

The reinforcement of these narratives about the radical nature of elite universities can be seen in memes circulating in support of another movement. As discussed earlier, the proposed change by the government of West Bengal to the undergraduate student acceptance procedure at Jadavpur University (a state university) sparked the #HandsOffJU movement in 2018. The new system wanted to use external personnel—official mediators from outside the university space—to conduct entrance examinations (believing this would produce a more fair/neutral evaluation). Later, the university's revised acceptance policy sought to scrap the entrance examination altogether and instead to screen students based on their performance on standardized secondary school exit exams.[6] There was an outcry against both the inclusion of external personnel and the decision to weight the scores of the moribund board examination in the entrance process.[7] The board examination—a national-/state-level public examination—was not considered rigorous enough to assess future JU-ites. In addition, those against the new policy felt that allowing an outside evaluator to participate in the screening process would negatively impact the university's academic integrity.[8] Both arguments take on an elitist edge, all but stating that their university exams and personnel are better than any other measure/resource that could be used.

Critiques of these policies took various forms, including memes, and were circulated online among students. The example seen in figure 6.3 utilizes the image from a popular meme, the distracted boyfriend, superimposing text that frames the reform as frivolous infatuation with an outsider of whom the JU-ite was suspicious. The original stock image, photographed by Antonio Guillemin in 2015, has launched a thousand memes since January 2017; in this instance, it has been repurposed to articulate students' outrage at the changing university policies. The triangulated figures in this meme are labeled "Byartho's corrupt methods," "JU Administration," and "Fair entrance examinations." *Byartho* is a Bangla word that means useless and is used here as a noun to designate the useless external, the outsider, the bureaucratic ombudsman. These words are superimposed on the image of the "other woman" who distracts the eponymous boyfriend. The meme's visual uses antiquated gender imagery—the sensuous other woman in blazing red, the adulterous male, and the figure of the girl next door—to tell the tale of the imagined contamination of the university (due to these new policies). The seductive figure of the other woman can be read as symbolizing the corruption in the imagined idyllic and untainted elite university space. In this rendition, the university's administration (labeled on and represented by the sole male figure in the frame) is portrayed as an adulterous masculine figure. Arguably, this is because attributes of masculinity in the patriarchal discourse align with the imagined power dynamics the students want to address.

There are therefore two complimentary metaphors at play. The primary metaphor of adultery is apt here because the students feel cheated by the administration and threatened by an outsider whose induction has disturbed their status quo. The new acceptance procedure takes the form of the other woman, a corrupting allurement. The girlfriend in the meme, the quintessential innocent girl next door, in this narrative

Figure 6.3. Distracted boyfriend meme (Basu 2018)

becomes the loyal students being cast aside for the other/outsider, the non-JU-ite. There is a second point of identification for the students here and hence a secondary metaphor at work. The students can be read as more than just the betrayed girlfriend of the boyfriend but also—extending this metaphor to the family level—as the abandoned children of a wayward father figure. This metaphor, operating within the register of patriarchy, associates the university with the masculine patriarch who abandons the students/children for an "other" outside the institution/family.

It is in this discursive context—of the innocent we and the treacherous other—that the adoption of the popular distracted boyfriend meme by the #HandsOffJU movement can be understood. While this meme, like the talk to the hand one before it, certainly showcases the us/them, insider/outsider messaging at play, the notion of the JU-ite as radical is harder to unpack here. Although it is tempting to conclude that the students who want no change to their system can be read as taking a more conservative than radical stance, we argue that their rhetoric continues to connect them with elitism and superiority in a way that suggests that their actions, their protest, their radicalism are in the right (and that they are the right type of radical). In this way, the university is read as either "too radical," perhaps as too irresponsible in their move for change, or as instrumenting too drastic a change, making it impossible to be radical in any positive way. All of these readings reveal that the referentiality configured within the meme uses an agreed-upon image of othering: that of the outsider, posited in a contentious position against the insider. This othering underpins the rhetoric that emerges from the #HandsOffJU movement, naturalizing the categories of us and them in its discourse, and is a subtle (or not so subtle) reinforcement of the elevated (collective) self.

To further elucidate this othering, let us move away from memes and consider a text-only post associated with the #HandsOffJU movement: Rimi B. Chatterjee's Facebook post on July 6, 2018. The above analyzed meme and this post were circulated on the same day. Chatterjee teaches in the Department of English at Jadavpur University (JUDE). The post speaks in the register of we and them, the familiar and the unfamiliar, the insider and the outsider, the ethical worker and the bureaucratic ombudsman, and services the same elitist scruples that manifest in the narratives of student protesters. This language reinforces the radical identity of the elite educational space: "*We*, the faculty of the department, always prided *ourselves* on how it was very difficult to cheat in the test, since the only 'text' that could prepare you to give a correct answer (for a given value of 'correct') was life itself" (Chatterjee 2018, emphasis added). The post then goes on to prompt a mock JUDE essay exam question paper, the syllabus for which, Chatterjee proposes, is life itself. Any examination is necessarily evaluative and privileges certain skills over others. Because the syllabi here is life (not texts), we contend that it is a kind of life—with a certain cultural grooming—that is being prioritized. In this scheme, students with lives *different* from the JU-ites'—and therefore bereft of that "cultural capital" (Bourdieu 1984)—stand disadvantaged.

The rare comment in this Facebook thread that does not celebrate the post reads: "I thought people stopped asking questions of this kind . . . but they don't look like questions adhering to judge any particular quality in a person (in this case English) . . . hence [it's a] flawed way of selection." This comment prompted the following response: "This is not an evaluation of what one knows nor is it one of what one thinks. It's an evaluation of //how// one thinks, //how// one formulates and expresses their thoughts, whether an individual's //process// of thinking is one that is suited to the way one will be required to, as a student of the discipline." This attests to the fact that the exam prioritizes skills, and there are realities more disposed to the acquisition of those skills. The necessary contention about the efficacy of the entrance examination and the inclusion of the external is ignored in this discussion. The rhetoric of imagined elitism, whereby no external exam/criteria could be better than the traditional internal entrance examination, converges with the identity politics that underlies the articulation of dissent here.

#SAVEJNU: TITLES OF CULTURAL NOBILITY

We now turn to one final example to see how elitism surfaces in yet another university-related activism campaign. The hashtag #SaveJNU encompasses all the narratives of dissent that have emerged from this prodigious urban university since 2016, when it was first used to protest the arrest of three students, including JNUSU (Jawaharlal Nehru University Student Union) president Kanhaiya Kumar, following the allegation that they had voiced "anti-India" slogans (Chattarji 2019). The hashtag documents not only this original protest but also the subsequent ones that have become associated with this pedagogical space. Within these is a subset of posts that emerged to critique the apparent bureaucratic takeover of the university. These posts highlight dissent in the university space and the elitist ethos that is immanent in such discussions. The post below by a JNU faculty member, for example, talks about a system of compulsory attendance that was imposed in the university in early 2018. This system prescribed compulsory daily classroom attendance for all undergraduate and post-graduate students, required teachers to mark attendance for bachelors and masters students, and expected even doctoral scholars to sign registers kept in the offices of their respective schools. The students refused to comply with this system, and teachers also resisted the move by the administration. Consider this lengthy post reflecting on this shift in the context of the university's longer (less restricted) history:

> The answer, once again, is obvious. Privatising a public university requires that its very character be changed completely. JNU was created as a research university in 1970, and has always maintained a very *special* character. It has provided *a very high standard* of higher education to students from different regions of India, belonging to any social or economic strata, at minimal cost. The decades following its creation saw at least two kinds of developments in the university. One was a very *high quality* of research output, both of the faculty and of young researchers. This also helped in creating many generations of teachers who are presently employed in colleges and universities in India and abroad. The other was an organic emergence of an *extraordinary* university culture that synthesised the intellectual and the political—enabling students not only to find their feet as scholars, but also [to] *articulate their selfhood as citizens.* Students in JNU have historically debated everything from American imperialism, the many failures of the Indian state, to what the university itself ought to be. (G. 2018, emphasis added)

This post highlights the key ideas that have been iterated in emancipatory narrative(s) more generally, such as that of the radical student and teacher. In terms of the specific policy under critique, it expresses fears that the decision will undermine the university's purported excellence (one perhaps indebted to said radical students and teachers). This narrative features the trope of the differentiated dissenter common among our collected data; it functions to lay claims to the elite status of this specific type of university. In the rhetorical exchanges that construct the dissenter in this post, what is lost is a serious engagement with the actual proposed changes to the current system. Any attempt at reform is couched in the language of coercion, is considered to be an assault on the exceptional academic tradition of the university, and is perceived to be anti-academic/university. Consider the phrase "articulate their selfhood as citizens." It indicates the fractionation that is symptomatic of an education system that reproduces cultural hierarchies. This articulation of a self-engendered subjectivity reflects a preserve of elite culture that is propagated through the very pedagogical structure this culture fosters. This elevated selfhood is a manifestation of academic capital, which is a product of the cultural transmission by the family and the school (Bourdieu 1984). The cultural capital of the university, what Arunima G. (2018) calls a "very special character," renders the JNU-ites as exalted students, (better) capable of "articulat[ing] their selfhood as citizens." The point therefore is to understand how certain dissenting academic communities "convince themselves that they are speaking not just for themselves, but in the name of a higher instance that has to be defined and brought into existence" (Bourdieu 2014, 44). Significant here is the description of the student. The teacher as a knowledge dispenser, bestowing this exalted status on her students, is illustrative of this. This depiction of the student in effect creates a rupture or bolsters one that already exists, excluding and including students within the bounds of university elitism. A potential impact is that those conjured into this subjectivity then align with their beliefs and actions accordingly, whether consciously or not. In this context, recall the JU-ites' entitlement to the truth (demanded through the "talk to the hand" meme analyzed earlier) and apparent beliefs that they could (and should) designate what counts as truth.

The posts we have retrieved here as examples suggest how the idea of "legitimate academia" is constructed and curated. This idea operates within the intersection of the radical-urban-elite triad. Access to the titles of cultural nobility deems that members of legitimate academia are qualified to practice dissent because the titular nobility then validates their dissent. One thing the social media frenzy over these examples of activism has failed to acknowledge is how even "liberal" acts of dissent—by claiming titular nobility—feed into the structural inequities encoded in the academe. Here, the rhetoric of dissent, we argue, steers public affect more toward the nobility of the "clan" of dissenters than toward the issue itself. The tendency to glorify those possessing elite cultural capital validates the rhetoric they convey. In this particular example, auto-legitimization is set up between the cultural capital acquired from certain universities and the dissenting cultures that emanate from them. Thus, the university as the vehicle of dissent and the dissent that emanates from there become the emblem of elitism, thereby looping the radical university with the ethos of elitism. Therefore, the universities associated with dissent (and that have served as voices of dissent) are seen as more appropriate for and natural participants in digital activism.

Narratives in general, and those present within hashtag activism specifically, do not intrinsically make sense in or by themselves. They accrue meaning within their particular contexts. In unpacking narratives, we therefore have to make sense of the references they invoke. The referent invokes a system of allied references against which certain narratives accrue meaning. Consider the purposed meme alluding to the 1989 Tiananmen Square photograph or the gender normativity in the distracted boyfriend meme; they constitute nodes of referentiality and therefore contain a potent discourse: imaginative articulation involving implicit manipulation by, for, and against certain "imagined communities." In the case of #Hokkolorob, the discursive articulation of dissent is seamlessly synced with the JU-ite as the emblem of radical student(s). The hashtag itself thus renders possible the convergence of a web of references through a single prism and narrativizes those references into a self-referential discourse. The claims to radical pedagogy, in the discursive practices we have discussed, reflect the ways a "system of shared social dispositions and cognitive structures . . . generates perceptions, appreciations and actions" (Bourdieu 1984, 279). This study suggests that there are layers of meaning—sometimes both productive and problematic at once—that can occur in digital activism, as posts invoke imagined communities invested in the same issues and construct narratives about those that may reside on either side of an issue. Future scholarship would benefit from not only tracking the issues raised in hashtag activism campaigns or the strategies used to craft and circulate messages but also by investigating the ways such posts reflect and reinforce existing narratives about (who has the right to be) the protestor.

NOTES

1. This was anti-national in the statist gaze. In 2016, some JNU students protested against the 2013 hanging of Afzal Guru, convicted for the 2001 terror attacks on the Indian Parliament. Certain media outlets perceived their sloganeering at the organized protest as anti-national, which was later reiterated in the statist idioms.
2. The second-, third-, fourth-, and fifth-year students at Calcutta Medical College, Kolkata, mounted a protest in June 2018, demanding that the hostel allotment procedure be made transparent after they failed to get desired hostel rooms while the new hostel facilities were allocated to the first-year students.
3. A Facebook group, Hike in Research Fellowship 2018, was created to mobilize research scholars from leading institutions—including the IITs (Indian Institutes of Technology), NITs (National Institutes of Technology), IISc Bangalore, and others—to demand an 80 percent increase in fellowship amounts awarded by the Ministry of Human Resource Development, Government of India. The increase was due in 2018.
4. The original image (without the touchups) was created by Pawel Kuczynski and is hosted on his website: http://www.pictorem.com/profile/Pawel.Kuczynski.
5. We selected pertinent posts from among those available to us. Though this method is highly subjective, it does not detract from the merit of the arguments pertaining to this specific dataset, especially when all the posts seem to hint at what Hall (1980, 118) has referred to as the "privileged position in the communicative exchange." However, in this selection process, some perspectives are likely not represented, as we were not able to engage with posts that were inaccessible due to the way social media curates content.
6. Students in India at the end of the tenth and twelfth grades appear for a public examination, referred to as the board examination. The scores achieved on the examination conducted at the end of the twelfth grade are important because they weigh in the screening for university admission. Some universities may decide to conduct an entrance examination to screen students—as was the practice in some departments of Jadavpur University until recently—and not consider the board examination score.
7. The issue was heavily debated in the media, since it involved an urban-elite institution. For example, see the *Times of India* report titled "JU Professors Threaten Admission Boycott over 'External' Hand" (Times News Network 2018).
8. The entrance examinations were not the standard undergraduate acceptance procedure; rather, they were only conducted by specific departments.

REFERENCES

Anderson, Benedict. 2006. *Imagined Communities: Reflections on the Origin and Spread of Nationalism.* New York: Verso.

Basu, B. 2018. [Facebook update]. Facebook, July 6. https://www.facebook.com/barshana.basu/posts/1695553303873678.

Bhabha, Homi K. 1990. *Nation and Narration.* New York: Routledge.

Bolter, Jay David, and Richard Grusin. 1999. *Remediation: Understanding New Media.* Cambridge, MA: MIT Press.

Bourdieu, Pierre. 1984. *Distinction: A Social Critique of the Judgement of Taste.* Translated by Richard Nice. Cambridge, MA: Harvard University Press.

Bourdieu, Pierre. 2014. *On the State: Lectures at the College de France 1989–1992.* Cambridge, UK: Polity Press.

Chattarji, Subarno. 2019. "Student Protests, Media and the University in India." *Postcolonial Studies* 22 (1): 79–94. doi: 10.1080/13688790.2019.1568170.

Chatterjee, Rimi B. 2018. "I have been a paper setter for the controversial Jadavpur University English Admission Test." [Facebook update]. Facebook, July 6. https://www.facebook.com/rimi.b.chatterjee/posts/10155734972457201.

Chaudhuri, Supriya. 2019. "On Making Noise: Hokkolorob and Its Place in Indian Student Movements." *Postcolonial Studies* 22 (1): 44–58.

Clark, Rosemary. 2016 "'Hope in a Hashtag': The Discursive Activism of #WhyIStayed." *Feminist Media Studies* 16 (5): 788–804. doi: 10.1080/14680777.2016.1138235.

Dey, Sreyoshi. 2020. "Let There Be Clamor: Exploring the Emergence of a New Public Sphere in India and Use of Social Media as an Instrument of Activism." *Journal of Communication Inquiry* 44 (1): 48–68.

Don. 2017. "Distracted Boyfriend." Knowyourmeme, August 22. https://knowyourmeme.com/memes/distracted-boyfriend.

G., Arunima. 2018. "The Battle for JNU's Soul." *The Wire*, December 25. https://thewire.in/education/the-battle-for-jnu-soul.

Gitlin, Todd. 1998. "Public Sphere or Public Sphericules?" In *Media, Ritual, and Identity*, edited by Tamar Liebes and James Curran, 168–174. New York: Routledge.

Hacking, Ian. 1999. *The Social Construction of What*. Cambridge, MA: Harvard University Press.

Hall, Stuart. 1980. "Encoding/Decoding." In *Culture, Media, Language: Working Papers in Cultural Studies, 1972–79*, edited by Stuart Hall, Dorothy Hobson, Andrew Lowe, and Paul Willis, 117–127. New York: Routledge.

Hokkolorob. 2014. [Facebook update]. Facebook, December 11. https://www.facebook.com/hokkolorob2013/photos/a.1531664473712260/1559131764298864/?type=3&theater.

Indo-Asian News Service. 2014. "JU Police Lathicharge: West Bengal Governor Extends 'Moral Support' to Protesters." Firstpost, September 21. https://www.firstpost.com/india/ju-police-lathicharge-west-bengal-governor-extends-moral-support-to-protesters-1722631.html.

Kuczynski, Pawel. 2014. *Perfect Garden*. http://www.pictorem.com/profile/Pawel.Kuczynski.

Kwatra, Nikita. 2018. "Why Instagram Has Become the Next Facebook." Livemint, August 27. https://www.livemint.com/Companies/MAEImnLVCnNqCntNtk31AJ/Why-Instagram-has-become-the-next-Facebook.html.

Nayar, Pramod K. 2019. "Public Protest, Public Pedagogy and the Publicness of the Public University." *Postcolonial Studies* 22 (1): 30–43. doi: 10.1080/13688790.2019.1568167.

Pariser, Eli. 2011. *The Filter Bubble: What the Internet Is Hiding from You*. New York: Penguin.

Times News Network. 2018. "JU Professors Threaten Admission Boycott over 'External' Hand." *Times of India*, July 3. https://timesofindia.indiatimes.com/city/kolkata/ju-professors-threaten-admission-boycott-over-external-hand/articleshow/64834511.cms.

Widener, Jeff. 1989. "Tiananmen Square." http://www.apimages.com/metadata/Index/Associated-Press-International-News-China-TIANA-/1015731e49e5da11af9f0014c2589dfb/1/1.

Zeng, Marcella. 2018. "From #MeToo to #RiceBunny: How Social Media Users Are Campaigning in China." *The Conversation*, February 6. https://theconversation.com/from-metoo-to-ricebunny-how-social-media-users-are-campaigning-in-china-90860.

SECTION III

Fan Culture and Digital Activism

7
WAKE UP MR. WEST
Kanye West, the Sunken Place, and the Rhetoric of Black Twitter

Kyesha Jennings

During the first two decades of the twenty-first century, Kanye West morphed into one of the most complex and controversial hip-hop artists, having, arguably, some of the most memorable moments in contemporary pop culture. One example is his interruption of Taylor Swift's acceptance speech at the 2009 VMAs (Video Music Awards) in support of fellow nominee Beyoncé. He also gained notoriety for his political commentary. In the aftermath of 2005's Hurricane Katrina, West championed displaced Black[1] New Orleans natives by blatantly calling out then-president George W. Bush with his infamous statement "George Bush doesn't care about Black people" (Robertson 2005). Then, a decade later, in a controversial political turn, he supported Donald Trump's presidency. Although his public persona has consistently shifted (for better or for worse), his early persona typically positioned him within the context of the intellectual "good guy" or the innovative genius (Samuels 2012; Graves 2014; Morrissey 2014; Houston 2014). This good guy persona was arguably shattered when West argued that slavery was a choice in an interview with TMZ in 2018; this led to Black folks (generally speaking) deciding to cancel[2] West, accusing him of being in the Sunken Place (Parham 2018; Terrell 2018; Coates 2018; Bromwich 2018).[3]

This outlandish comment occurred during a TMZ Live interview while West was defending his right to wear a MAGA hat.[4] West blatantly suggested that chattel slavery was a choice when he stated, "When you hear about slavery for 400 years . . . For 400 years? That sounds like a choice. You were there for 400 years and it's all of y'all. It's like we're mentally imprisoned . . . Do you feel that—I'm being free and that I'm thinking free" ("Kanye West Stirs" 2018). His ahistorical statements immediately caused outrage in the newsroom as TMZ reporter Van Lathan responded directly to West:

> You're entitled to believe whatever you want, but there is fact, and real world, real life consequence behind everything that you just said. While you are making music and being an artist and living the life that you've earned by being a genius, the rest of us in society have to deal with these threats to our lives. We have to deal with the marginalization that has come from the 400 years of slavery that you said for our people was a choice. Frankly I'm disappointed. I'm appalled and brother, I am unbelievably hurt by the fact that you have morphed into something, to me, that's not real. ("Kanye West Stirs" 2018)

Although the exchange was tense, the standoff ended with the two men embracing each other with a hug. West offered an apology for hurting Lathan while Lathan pleaded with him to be "more responsible" ("Kanye West Stirs" 2018). It was Lathan's powerful response that resonated with 2.5 million Instagram viewers, followed by many other compelling public critiques from fellow artists, academics, comedians, actors, and activists.

In a short amount of time, outrage and disappointment circulated within the realm of social media. For example, civil rights activist Deray McKesson (2018) weighed in on Twitter, stating, "Kanye's rhetoric continues to fuel the racist right-wing folks who believe that black people are responsible for their oppression." Contributing to the digital conversation, TV host and Black intellectual Marc Lamont Hill (2018b) added, "There has never been a moment in history when Black people didn't resist slavery . . . Our resistance led to our freedom." Many more people protested West's words using the satirical #IfSlaveryWasAChoice hashtag. This chapter analyzes these public reactions to West's comments by studying a collection of tweets using the hashtag #IfSlaveryWasAChoice. These tweets took on a variety of formats—including wordplay and intertextual referents in the form of memes—and they provide ripe data for critical discourse analysis. These tweeted forms of public commentary allow us to identify how Black Twitter users participate in a larger cultural digital realm that often includes Black humor. More specifically, the tweets mirror the Black oral tradition of signifyin', "a style of verbal play that focuses humorous statements of double meaning on an individual, an event, [or] a situation" (Bailey 2012, 257). Studying this practice on Black Twitter, Keith Gilyard and Adam Banks (2018, 6) define signifyin' as a rhetorical practice that requires "an understanding that communication is subject to intertexual 'play,' shaded levels of critique and/or ritualized dissing." This chapter explores how Black digital participants employed the cultural characteristics of signifyin' to focus on the nonsensical nature and misplaced context of West's statements. This exchange resulted in a larger conversation among the social participants regarding the history of Black folks' perseverance.

In this chapter, I study this Twitter conversation #IfSlaveryWasAChoice to examine how Black Twitter users employ African American Vernacular English (AAVE), creativity, shared in-jokes, and catchphrases through memetic media to offer a viral clap-back[5] that falls within the cultural traditions of signifyin' and which participates in a contemporary form of social activism. To unpack the significance and cultural impact of the digitized satire-driven responses, I establish Black Twitter as a site of cultural performance. I argue that users' investment in celebrity culture is a catalyst for public commentary. Interactions with celebrities through celebratory posts, clap-backs, critiques, or comedic bits are one of the many ways Black Twitter users engage with one another in a culturally influenced performance. I begin this chapter with a brief historical account of Black humor and the cultural importance of oral traditions, as well as its connection to Black Twitter. Next, I outline Ryan M. Milner's (2016) memetic participation theory, which frames my textual analysis of the meme-hashtag mash-up, #IfSlaveryWasAChoice. Finally, I offer a textual analysis of the mediated responses grouped under the hashtag #IfSlaveryWasAChoice via Black Twitter.

Adopting Marc Lamont Hill's (2018a, 287) definition, I define Black Twitter as "a virtual community of twitter users engaged in real-time discourses primarily related to Black American culture and politics." The use of social media sites like Twitter has intensified Black folks' ability to demonstrate creative play, like signifyin', especially through the hashtag function. With 72 million active Twitter users in the United States, Black folks make up 26 percent of Twitter's demographics (Tien 2018). In addition, digital race scholars have found that "Black users are most visible in the 'trending topics'" (Florini 2014, 225). In other words, topics directly associated with Black culture or topics collectively discussed by Black users dominate the list. Beyond dominating a set list, the behaviors or digital customs of Black Twitter users have intrigued scholars. Journalist Farhad Manjoo (2010) explained: "Black people . . . do seem to use Twitter differently from everyone else on the service. They form tighter clusters on the network—they follow one another more readily, they retweet each other more often, and more of their posts are @-replies—posts directed at other users. It's this behavior, intentional or not, that gives Black people . . . the means to dominate the conversation on Twitter." Although Manjoo's investigation of Black users' participation on Twitter was published within the first year of Twitter's existence (2011), his findings still apply today.

There is a wave of scholarship on digital media spaces including Black Twitter. Scholars such as Gilyard and Banks (2018), Hill (2018a), Latoya

A. Lee (2017), Sarah Florini (2014), Sanjay Sharma (2013), and André Brock (2012) have all written about Twitter generally or Black Twitter more specifically, as well as the influence/impact of racial identities and use of the platform. While Brock (2012) approaches Twitter through the lens of critical race and technocultural theory to identify how cultural performances in the online space are understood, Sharma (2013) examines the materialization of online racialized identities by analyzing racialized hashtags. Of particular use for this study, Florini (2014) and Gilyard and Banks (2018) unpack the linguistic practice and cultural tradition of signifyin' to acknowledge the cultural performance of Black Twitter users, and both Lee (2017) and Hill (2018a) view Black Twitter as a tool for political resistance against anti-Blackness. Building on this scholarship on Black Twitter, my study examines the collective resistance displayed by Black folks through humor in digital spaces.

BLACK FOLKS, HUMOR, AND DIGITAL SPACES

Historically, Black people have always relied on humor to navigate difficult or troubling situations. However, it is important to point out that for most, Black humor is more than just a "coping mechanism . . . [Black] humor has been and continues to be both a bountiful source of creativity and pleasure and an energetic mode of social and political critique" (Carpio cited in Bailey 2012, 257). It is signifyin' that ignites a unique form of creativity for Black folks, a form that derives from oral tradition. Florini (2014, 224) explains that within digital spaces like Twitter, "signifyin' serves as an interactional framework that allows Black Twitter users to align themselves with Black oral traditions, to index Black cultural practices, to enact Black subjectivities, and to communicate shared knowledge and experiences." In other words, Twitter is the space where, collectively, Black folks can "be Black." Their behavior is unfiltered, familiar, and rooted in cultural norms. Gilyard and Banks (2018, 84) read the communication practices on Black Twitter as a purposeful refusal to code switch and perform for the white gaze. The unfiltered nature of Black Twitter supports Florini's (2014, 223) view that "Blackness is a practice; it is something you do." Brock (2012, 537) agrees, arguing that "tweet-as-signifyin' . . . can be understood as a discursive, public performance of Black identity." This is not to suggest that Blackness or "Black behavior" is monolithic but more to point out *one* cultural characteristic of Black culture.

In addition, Twitter's hashtag function and open accessibility increase the use of wordplay among its users, thus fostering creativity among Black digital participants. The site's open accessibility is what allows hashtags to trend, public threads to exist, and users to retweet and communicate with folks outside of their network. Sharma (2013, 50) unpacks this further: "Twitter hashtags are unique because rather than merely categorizing content, they enable users to intensify their engagement by 'organizing' content and facilitating participation in conversations . . . [furthermore,] not only are hashtags generative of ad hoc communities, they function as a means of amplifying the significance of a collection of messages." We see this through the hashtag #IfSlaveryWasAChoice, as the hashtag, though lacking a question mark, proposes a question to intentionally foster conversation. For Black Twitter users, the engagement with and use of hashtags is often unique in comparison to that of non-Black Twitter users. According to Sharma (51), "Blacktags are a particular type of hashtag associated with Black Twitter users . . . because the tag itself and/or its associated content appear to connote 'Black' vernacular expression in the form of humor and social commentary." The Blacktag #IfSlaveryWasAChoice expresses both humor and social commentary, mostly through sarcasm and linguistic irony. The call-and-response hashtag pokes fun at the insinuation of slavery being a choice, though the overall sentiment is serious.

THE FUNDAMENTALS OF MEMETIC PARTICIPATION

As anyone who is familiar with internet culture knows, memes are used to poke fun at a wide swath of popular culture. Milner (2016, 1) defines memes as "linguistic, image, audio, and visual text [that is] circulated and transformed by countless cultural participants across vast networks and collectives." Furthermore, he declares that memes are fundamentally multimodal, stating, "a multimodal text is one whose meanings are realized through more than [semiotic code]" (24). This reflects the lived usage of memes in popular culture, as they take myriad (but always multimodal) forms, including mash-ups of images, audio, text, video, and others. In Black digital culture, memes are a useful genre to expand and proliferate public critique. The accessibility and ubiquity of memes make it an ideal genre to analyze the ways Black folks are using this medium. Furthermore, Jannette L. Dates and Mia Moody-Ramirez (2018, 141) argue that "(black people used memes most effectively) to share viewpoints on various topics . . . [and to] contribute to African American humor." They also acknowledge that "Black Twitter is often noted for encouraging clap back culture or giving people a platform to respond to others in a humorous yet stern manner" (129). Black digital participants construct memes that make the content both humorous and culturally relevant by integrating cultural references that are specific to Black culture. Thus, the way memes appear within the setting of Black Twitter align with Gilyard and Bank's (2018, 86) argument that Black Twitter creates a space for "community building happening in real time, opposition to continued forms of racialized oppression, and significantly, an intentional claiming of and holding onto joy as an act of resistance." This is why the hashtag #IfSlaveryWasAChoice resonated so well—the witty images accompanied by comedic hot takes constituted a rhetorical method used for signifyin' within a digital space, using well-known and widespread language practices that spoke to Black Twitter, as well as to internet culture more broadly.

Widespread cultural digital conversations like #IfSlaveryWasAChoice do not occur on a daily basis. There are specific historical moments in Black Twitter history where humorous memes have been employed to equally challenge and disrupt ideas or statements. Soraya Nadia McDonald (2014) points out that people "can observe [Black Twitter's] power and impact in the witty, sharply worded rebukes that haunt public figures when they do or say something stupid, especially if it's racially insensitive." This is not to suggest that activism or general usage of memes does not occur in the larger online Twitter community but that when Black tags/memes trend on Twitter, they permeate Twitter (and sometimes the broader e-discourse space) in ways that are atypical of general internet culture.

To illustrate this phenomenon, consider the following examples. The first image in figure 7.1 features rapper Meek Mill engaging in what appears to be a game of tag with another man. The two men's body language and facial expressions intensify the humor embedded in the caption and hashtag. A historical reference of a field slave in contrast to a house slave is needed, as is access to in-group conversations/debates regarding field slaves versus house slaves. In addition, in order to grasp the humor in the image displayed on the right, it is important to be familiar with Rachel Dolezal, a white woman who problematically performed as Black and served as a chapter president for the National Association for the Advancement of Colored People (NAACP) (Brubaker 2016; Bey and Sakellarides 2016; Millner 2017). The rejection of Dolezal from the identified "Massa" (which is really a collective rejection of her "Blackness") in the meme's caption coupled with Dolezal's facial expression of discontent increases the level of humor this meme offers.

Black Twitter operates on a "for us, by us" ethos (i.e., for Black folks, created by Black folks); therefore, the memes in figure 7.1 and ones like it may not necessarily produce the same amount of laughter from non-Black audiences. The humor is not meant for everyone, and

Figure 7.1. Examples of memes that require cultural context

identical levels of resonance won't occur if an individual is not a part of the discourse community (see #BlackTwitterVerificationQuestions and #BlackTwitterWelcomeManual). As McDonald (2014) suggests, "Understanding the ethos of Black Twitter can be a high bar to clear if you've never socialized significantly with black people." Regardless of a person's presumed familiarity with the cultural references used, as Elaine B. Richardson (2006, 42) explains, "If you don't know how the words [or images] are used within their primary contexts, you cannot read the words and you cannot fully understand . . . the [discourse community]." Therefore, understanding the humor included in #IfSlaveryWasAChoice depends on a shared culture context and an ability to read and understand cultural markers.

RESEARCH PROCESS

In addition to defining memes, Milner (2016, 23) also explored how memes are constructed and propagated, establishing a set of fundamental logics to "further understand the creation, circulation and transformation of memetic media." These logics are multimodality, reappropriation, resonance, collectivism, and spread. Table 7.1 offers a definition of each logic. Milner argues that these fundamental logics "afford individual innovation and variation within a shared criteria" (23). His theory provides the framework for the investigative questions that drive my analysis:

1. How do memes facilitate Black Twitter users in making social critique?
2. How do Black Twitter users leverage memes to enact social justice?
3. How do the various constructions of memes contribute to offering social criticism through humor?

Table 7.1. Milner's fundamental logics

Multimodality	Meaning is constructed through more than one mode of technological representation (e.g., written language, image, audio, video).
Reappropriation	Meaning is constructed through an engagement of use and reuse—mixing the old with the new.
Resonance	Meaning constructed prompts wide circulation.
Collectivism	Meaning constructed prompts wide circulation as a result of engaging collectives such as relational networks, social media sites, or media gatekeepers.
Spread	This is "the pervasive circulation and sharing of resonant media texts" (Milner 2016, 38).

To investigate these questions, I began collecting my data in December 2018. I relied on Twitter's advanced search API, an in-depth Google search of the hashtag, and a number of media articles that archived examples of #IfSlaveryWasAChoice memes. Most of the collected tweets are time-stamped on May 1 or May 2, 2018, though the date of origin is not available for a small percentage of my data. Data collection began approximately six months after the peak of the hashtag, which limited the methods available to retrieve the tweets. For example, affordable plug-ins like NodeXL are only capable of collecting data from up to thirty days prior. Nonetheless, my data consist of a broad range of tweets, primarily posted between May 1 and 2, which reveal the use of culturally specific humor through reappropriation, resonance, and collectivism of memetic media, as well as the role exigence played in the generation of #IfSlaveryWasAChoice.

At the conclusion of the data collection period, I had amassed 100 tweets that accompanied the hashtag #IfSlaveryWasAChoice, which I then analyzed using qualitative content analysis. I first organized the tweets into two main categories: Tweets with Memes and Tweets with Videos. There were 64 tweets that included memes and 36 that integrated video clips, whether in GIF format or in short, recorded clips, though these were not included in the final dataset. However, an analysis of memes with video would be productive for a future study.

My primary interests relied on examining how Black Twitter engaged with, created, and circulated memes to offer public critiques through humor; this orientation to the data provided a guiding principle with which to sort and code the tweets. After determining which meme types (i.e., image vs. video/GIF) would be used in this study, I separated the relevant tweets into two major groups: Themes and Reappropriation. From there, I sorted the memes into subgroups; Themes resulted in

Table 7.2. Categorization of Tweets with Memes

Themes	# of Memes	Reappropriation	# of Memes
Professional setting	31	Black man on phone	3
Rebellious attitude	7	Mock plantation	11
House slave/field slave	4	Squat and squint	6
Black colloquial phrases	10	Jimmy Butler reaction	2
Black popular culture/Black culture	35*	Squidward don't care	2
Refusal	25	Tanisha Thomas fed up	2
Education	6	N/A†	38

* Any image that was reappropriated was counted once.
† Images were not reappropriated.

seven subgroups and Reappropriation resulted in six. As I sorted the memes in relation to specific themes, many of the memes fit into more than one category (see table 7.2).

I recognize the limitations of tracing the exact origin of a meme's creation, as internet meme generation often seems to come from nowhere. However, this limitation is not particular to this study. As Milner (2016, 15) notes, "Like countless memetic texts circulated without signature or citation . . . finding their creator and site origin is largely impossible, and arguably inconsequential when considering how they resonate, [but] both creation and sharing [are] expressive acts [of resistance]." Resistance, in the case of the memes associated with this hashtag, demonstrates the pushback against West's statement, although, notably, the majority of these memes do not directly respond to West.

BLACK TWITTER STRATEGIES IN THE TWEETS

The data collected reveal a strategic rhetorical choice of keeping the subjects in group; that is, the individuals represented in the memes are overwhelmingly Black. In instances where the subject is not Black or at least not visibly Black, the critique toward the subject is far more critical. For instance, as noted earlier, figure 7.1 uses Dolezal, a white woman who received stark criticism for passing as a Black woman despite not having any African ancestry. The meme is particularly interesting not only because of its cultural significance but also because it co-opts and satirizes what Dolezal did while at the same time calling out West.

Outside of the variations of Dolezal memes, my findings do not reveal memes in which white people are centered. What we do find, however,

Figure 7.2. Examples of memes with white folks as extras

are white folks who make cameo-like appearances in the memes. Their presence ultimately contributes to the overall argument and joke. For example, in the first example in figure 7.2, West is the subject of the meme and the joke. In comparison to figure 7.1, where the critique was directed toward Dolezal (and West by default), the critique is not targeted toward record executives Lyor Cohen and Lucian Grainge. The two are arguably comparable to extras in a movie scene. The next example in figure 7.2 is a mediation of a movie scene from the Academy Award–winning film *12 Years a Slave*, an adaptation of Solomon Northup's 1853 slave memoir about how as a northern-born free African American man he was kidnapped, sold into slavery, and put to work in southern plantations. The caption creates a conversational tone between the slave and his new master. The slave and his satirical words are the subject of the meme.

Other memes replaced Black subjects with popular cartoon characters. Although the subjects in figure 7.3 are all cartoons, the cartoon characters' racial identities are not read the same. On the right, Squidward is coded white in the animated kids' show *SpongeBob SquarePants*, but in the meme, it is implied that he is an enslaved Black person. The nonchalant attitude depicted in Squidward's body language and the verbiage attached to the image are what create the comedic vibe. On the left, Peter Griffin is coded as a Black woman in the meme, although he is a white character in the animated series *Family Guy*. More specifically, Peter's added accessory of long acrylic nails is a stereotypical representation of Black women—here he plays the role of a Black female receptionist.[6] The ghetto girl with long nails trope is a staple in Black popular culture, TV, and film. In addition, "per my last email" has been deemed a form of a professional clap-back among Black women circles. Situating

Figure 7.3. Examples of memes whose subjects are not visibly Black

Black women's sass and imagining the autonomy of Black women within that historical context is what makes this particular meme both a critique against West's remarks and comedic. *SpongeBob* and *Family Guy* are fairly popular across demographics, including age and race, and the popularity of these shows helps to further elevate the humor and resonance of these particular images, especially when coupled with racially coded cultural references (i.e., Griffin's hood nails).

An examination of the collected data based on specific themes shows that the creation of fictitious professional settings, references to Black popular culture/Black culture, and responses of blatant refusal dominated the tweets I collected. The fictitious setting of slavery as a workplace critiques West's framing of slavery as a choice. One typically thinks of the professions we enter into or the jobs we hold as having some element of choice. Therefore, the juxtaposition of these workplace settings (e.g., receptionist desk) and corporate phrases (e.g., employee of the month) with references to slavery (e.g., whipping, plantation, masters) reveals the ridiculousness of West's claim. While their social commentary is serious, the visual/verbal play in these memes is comical due to their use of exaggeration, irony, and sarcasm to emphasize the inhumanity embedded in America's painful history. These memes highlight the adverse conditions Blacks experienced, such as the lack of financial compensation, unethical working conditions, and the inability to opt out. As multimodal texts open for interpretation by the consumer, these memes have various layers of critique and meaning. For example, by referencing issues such as professional protection, safety, and options more generally, these memes can also be seen as featuring the resilience of enslaved Africans whose "professional" lives were markedly different.

Figure 7.4. Examples of memes set in a fictitious professional setting

The reappropriation of memes shows how Black digital participants "navigate popular culture [by] engaging in the plurality and creativity or use and reuse" (Milner 2016, 26). Black Twitter users reappropriated viral images to construct an argument refuting West's statement. The first example in figure 7.4 relies on the popularity of Jimmy Butler, an NBA player for the Philadelphia 76ers, whereas the second example relies on recognition of Martin Baker, a former Republican congressional candidate whose image went viral in 2014 and 2017. Milner (14) refers to this as the creation of digital items with "mutual awareness."

The rhetorical choices that contribute to the humor and satire in these memes include the fact that slaves were not allowed to read, the fact that slaves were generally not given time off or other benefits, and the horrific working conditions slaves routinely faced. The captions in the tweets built on the facial expressions and body language of the people included in the images, which further enhanced the shared in-jokes.

In comparison to these examples that used historical information, figure 7.5 shifts the historical accuracy of slavery by depicting Black folks who have refused to work. The first example, though simple, resonated with 21,000 Twitter users because of the popularity of the image used (squat and squint meme) and the understanding that opting out of slavery was impossible. The rhetorical choices of the next example include the capitalization of BOY, the use of AAVE (African American Vernacular English), and the spelling of massa. The fantasy aspect of the memes allows for a remixing of time periods, as the linguistic phrases

Figure 7.5. Examples of memes that depict a refusal to work

are both modern and historical. For example, the terms *massa* and *boy* are outdated. Massa is the slave dialectal spelling of master, and boy was used historically to disregard and emasculate Black men—and there's an important power dynamic present in both terms. This fictional transcription depicted in the meme critically engages with the politics of slavery, but the use of humor disrupts the historical accuracy by using modern slang to rebel (i.e., "This yo problem"). This is situated in the context of a professional setting, as "clocking out" is used to justify the refusal of work. Again, this is all dramatized to reject West's inaccurate statement.

History has a way of negating or simply ignoring the strength and resilience of enslaved people. Harvard professor Henry Louis Gates (2013) argues that "one of the most pernicious allegations made against the African-American people was that our slave ancestors were either exceptionally 'docile' or 'content and loyal,' thus explaining their purported failure to rebel extensively." In understanding the complexity of surviving a slave rebellion or rebelling solo, Black digital participants crafted fictitious scenarios that depict the resistance of slavery in figures 7.6 and 7.7. Similar to the other examples analyzed, each scene is highly dramatized yet culturally familiar and contributes to the collective resistance of West's notion of slavery being a choice. The memes consistently employ AAVE, creativity, and shared in-jokes to not only call out West's ignorance but also to serve as a modern and historical message. Richardson (2006, 4) explains that "AAVE should be understood as [Black] survival culture . . . [The communicative practices visible

Figure 7.6. Examples of rebellious attitudes

through memes on Black Twitter] derive from particular histories, geographies, and social locations. Some of these ways of being were developed during slavery and [were] influenced by two crucial factors: the demand from dominant Whites that all manner of behavior and communications of African people display their compliance with domination and supposed inferiority; and African people's resistance to this demand." Therefore, on the one hand, the resistance reveals the millennial version of "Try Me"[7] mixed with "Knuck if You Buck,"[8] and on the other, it rejects the framing of enslaved people as weak.

The examples in figure 7.6 use repetition in the form of mimicry as a rhetorical strategy to depict the defiant actions of an enslaved person. In AAVE, the use of mimicry as defined by Geneva Smitherman (1977, 94) is "a deliberate imitation of the speech and mannerisms of someone else used for . . . ridicule or rhetorical effect." Richardson (2006, 11) adds that mimicry "has the effect of critique in many cases and is used in signifying . . . to make a point or poke fun." The use of this mode of communication in Black Twitter enables Black digital participants to not only critique West's comments but also to resist and speak freely with no regard to physical consequences. The mocking SpongeBob meme (figure 7.6, left) also functions in a similar manner as the examples in figures 7.3 with non-Black subjects and resonates within the context of the hashtag #IfSlaveryWasAChoice because of its remixing of a popular viral meme, the popularity and familiarity of the show itself, and the aggressive sarcastic diction created in the caption.

The next examples, in figure 7.7, rely on images of two popular Black women—actress and comedian Monique and reality TV star Sheree Whitfield—and the use of colloquial phrases specific to Black culture that exhibit refusal, rebellion, and aggression. Equally important, the

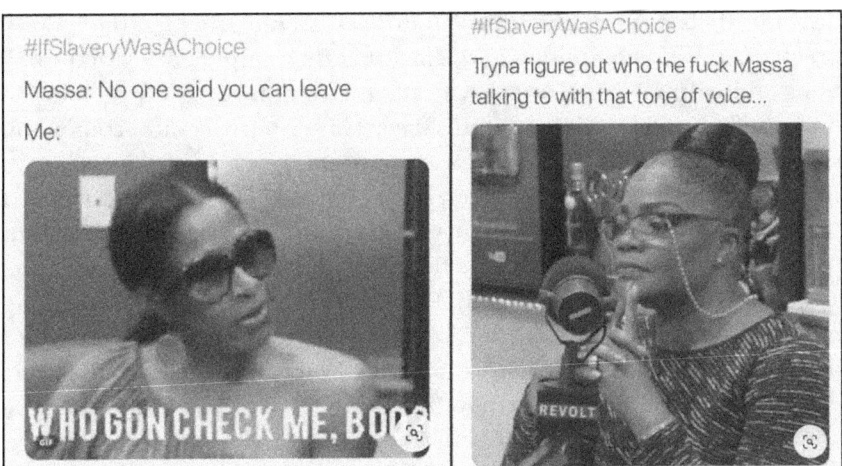

Figure 7.7. More examples of rebellious attitudes

women's facial expressions fit within traditional Black language practices. Richardson (2006, 44) argues that "members of socially and racialized stigmatized groups have devised ways to earn respect and ways to project their value and knowledge, including facial expressions." Both women communicate strength, aggression, and frustration to an intra-communal audience. In both memes, the power dynamic at play between the slave owner and the enslaved woman has shifted, making the fictitious depicted enslaved Black women superior. Whitfield's proposed rhetorical question "Who gon check me, boo?" (figure 7.7, left side) plays on the word *boo*[9] and, more important, the question does not warrant an answer. Within the discourse community, it is understood that the answer is *no one*. Furthermore, the wording in both memes uses semantics of tone: "Tonal semantics refers to the use of voice rhythm and vocal inflection to convey meaning in Black communication . . . the speech rhythms and tonal inflections of [AAVE] are, of course, impossible to capture in print," but the point is to understand that what is being said is equally as important as, if not more important than, *how* it is being said (Smitherman 1997, 134). All of this contributes to the comedic nature of the memes, including the use of contemporary images and phrases in a historical setting.

IMPLICATIONS FOR BLACK RHETORIC

Black Twitter's use of memes checks every single box of Milner's fundamental set of logics; however, despite the fact that Black Twitter's discourse falls right in line with Milner's research on memes, the literacy practices utilized are unique in the fact that they employ Black oral traditions and cultural practices, specifically the notion of signifyin'. In addition, the behavior modeled within Black Twitter mirrors intra-communal practices within Black culture. More important, Black Twitter is indicative of coping mechanisms necessitated by the unique historical experience of Black folks. While other groups may have experienced slavery throughout history, it would be hard to argue that those experiences occurred in the same way or to the same extent. These forms of resistance and coping mechanisms can be traced within Black and African American vernacular discourses. Scholarship has addressed the particular communicative practices of Black folks and how they are markedly different from other discourse groups and their practices (Smitherman 1977; Richardson 2006). Thus, since forever, Black folks have been communicating in ways other people are not necessarily literate about. What marks these practices as new is the available technology (i.e., Twitter) and the mode of use (i.e., memes). In addition, the visibility and modified accessibility of these messages differentiate the discourse in new and interesting ways. While Black folks' discourses might have been obscured and coded in the past (i.e., using hymns to communicate messages among slaves), the public can view and understand what Black Twitter is saying. Still, the meaning made in these spaces is inexorably connected to Black people's historical experiences. Thus, these memes and discourses, while publicly seen and available, are not for all those who can see them. Put another way, just because you can see the BBQ doesn't mean you're invited to join in.

My investigation of the hashtag #IfSlaveryWasAChoice contributes to the growing body of scholarship on Black Twitter, as it reveals how Black Twitter relies on intra-community discourse and the use of colloquialisms to offer valuable critiques. Creativity is a major feature, as the responses are fictitious settings that are designed to satirize historical accuracy. In addition, my research shows that in-group humor and knowledge of Black culture or Black popular culture is necessary. Future research could benefit from an ethnographic approach to studies of Black Twitter, specifically the inclusion of qualitative interviews of Black digital participants to examine closely the collective consciousness and expressions of the discourse community. All in all, Black Twitter is important because of its ability to create a virtual community where Black digital participants can engage in an oral and written tradition specific to Black culture and Black communicative practices. The communal resonance is shown in reflection tweets posted almost a year after the peak popularity of the hashtag (figure 7.8).

Figure 7.8. Black Twitter reminiscing

Based on how Black Twitter talks among itself, where participants reminisce about previous discussions, the dynamic is similar to a family reunion (in this case it would be a virtual cultural reunion). Some users have even informally ranked Black Twitter's "Most funniest Moments," and #IfSlaveryWasAChoice landed in second place following #NiggerNavy.[10] As noted earlier, these specific interactions aren't happening every day; it takes a special intra-communal event to get the discourse going. Furthermore, these public commentaries serve as a method of coping with racism and anti-Blackness, even when the anti-Blackness remarks come from within.

NOTES

1. This chapter uses the term *Black* rather than black or African American. Capitalizing the B distinguishes *Black* as a cultural identifier, which validates the identities of the subjects I am writing about. In addition, *Black* is inclusive of all African descendants.
2. "Canceling" is a popular catchphrase mostly expressed on social media, primarily Twitter and Instagram. It refers to "cancel culture," an understood "digital contract wherein people loosely agree not to support a person (especially economically)" (Garel 2018).
3. The Sunken Place was one of the most lauded elements of the acclaimed film *Get Out*, recognized as a metaphor for the feelings of helplessness and subjugation Black people experience in a society built on systemic, institutional racism ("Sunken Place").
4. MAGA refers to President Trump's 2016 campaign slogan Make America Great Again. The campaign phrase is interpreted by many as racist, xenophobic, and homophobic.
5. Colloquial phrase for rebuttal or refutation.
6. Prior to the Kardashians and *Vogue* magazine gentrifying "hood nails," as Ntianu Obiora (2018) points out, acrylic nails were associated exclusively with Black women. Outside of Black culture they were considered ghetto, unprofessional, and inappropriate.
7. A colloquial phrase that has an aggressive tone and warns against testing the individual.
8. A colloquial phrase adopted from a popular hip-hop song that is considered a national Black anthem. The literal meaning of the aggressive phrase is "knuckle up if you are buck wild"—thus insinuating the need for one to prepare to fight.

9. *Boo* is often a term reserved for a romantic partner, but in Black language practices the term is used sarcastically to communicate where tension has occurred with a person with whom there is no romantic or even platonic connection (this occurs with other words such as honey, sis, friend, and sweetie as well).
10. Yahoo Finance's Twitter account accidentally tweeted a racial slur (as it meant *Bigger* Navy). The aftermath resulted in a series of comical reactions from Black Twitter mocking the typo using a combination of memes and tweets. Popular culture news outlets like Buzzfeed, RollingOut, and VH1 picked up the story.

REFERENCES

Bailey, Constance. 2012. "Fight the Power: African American Humor as a Discourse of Resistance." *Western Journal of Black Studies* 36 (4): 253–263.

Bey, Marquis, and Theodora Sakellarides. 2016. "When We Enter: The Blackness of Rachel Dolezal." *Black Scholar* 46 (4): 33–48.

Brock, André. 2012. "From the Blackhand Side: Twitter as a Cultural Conversation." *Journal of Broadcasting and Electronic Media* 56 (4): 529–549.

Bromwich, Jonah Engel. 2018. "Everyone Is Canceled." *New York Times*, June 28. https://www.nytimes.com/2018/06/28/style/is-it-canceled.html.

Brubaker, Rogers. 2016. "The Dolezal Affair: Race, Gender, and the Micropolitics of Identity." *Ethnic and Racial Studies* 39 (3): 414–448.

Coates, Ta-Nehisi. 2018. "I'm Not Black, I'm Kanye: Kanye West Wants Freedom—White Freedom." *The Atlantic*, May 7. https://www.theatlantic.com/entertainment/archive/2018/05/im-not-black-im-kanye/559763/.

Dates, Jannette L., and Mia Moody-Ramirez. 2018. *Blackface to Black Twitter: Reflections on Black Humor, Race, Politics, and Gender.* New York: Peter Lang.

Florini, Sarah. 2014. "Tweets, Tweeps, and Signifyin'." *Television and New Media* 15 (3): 223–237.

Garel, Connor. 2018. "Logan and Paul and the Myth of Cancel Culture." *Vice*, July 9. https://www.vice.com/en_us/article/8xb9x5/logan-paul-and-the-myth-of-cancel-culture.

Gates, Henry Louis. 2013. "Did African American Slaves Rebel?" PBS. https://www.pbs.org/wnet/african-americans-many-rivers-to-cross/history/did-african-american-slaves-rebel/.

Gilyard, Keith, and Adam Banks. 2018. *On African-American Rhetoric.* New York: Routledge.

Graves, Kirk Walker. 2014. *My Beautiful Dark Twisted Fantasy.* New York: Bloomsbury.

Hill, Marc Lamont. 2018a. "'Thank You, Black Twitter': State Violence, Digital Counterpublics, and Pedagogies of Resistance." *Urban Education* 53 (2): 286–302.

Hill, Marc Lamont (@marclamonthill). 2018b. "There has never been a moment in history when black people didn't resist slavery." Tweet, May 1. https://twitter.com/marclamonthill/status/991500912576421888?lang=en.

Houston, Akil. 2014. "Kanye West: Asterisk Genius?" In *The Cultural Impact of Kanye West*, edited by Julius Bailey, 13–28. New York: Palgrave Macmillan.

"Kanye West Stirs up TMZ Newsroom over Trump, Slavery, and Free Thought." 2018. TMZ, May 1. https://www.tmz.com/2018/05/01/kanye-west-tmz-live-slavery-trump/.

Lee, Latoya A. 2017. "Black Twitter: A Response to Bias in Mainstream Media." *Social Sciences* 6 (1): 1–17.

Manjoo, Farhad. 2010. "How Black People Use Twitter: The Latest Research on Race and Microblogging." *Slate*, August 10. https://slate.com/technology/2010/08/how-black-people-use-twitter.html.

McDonald, Soraya Nadia. 2014. "Black Twitter: A Virtual Community Ready to Hashtag Out a Response to Cultural Issues." *Washington Post*, January 20. https://www.washingtonpost

.com/lifestyle/style/black-twitter-a-virtual-community-ready-to-hashtag-out-a-response-to-cultural-issues/2014/01/20/41ddacf6-7ec5-11e3-9556-4a4bf7bcbd84_story.html?utm_term=.8d79f91ff562.

McKesson, Deray (@Deray). 2018. "Kanye's rhetoric continues to fuel the racist right-wing folks who believe that black people are responsible for their oppression." Tweet, May 1. https://twitter.com/deray/status/991444472138350592?lang=en.

Millner, Denene. 2017. "Why Rachel Dolezal Can Never Be Black." *NPR*, March 13. https://www.npr.org/sections/codeswitch/2017/03/03/518184030/why-rachel-dolezal-can-never-be-black.

Milner, Ryan M. 2016. *The World Made Meme: Public Conversations and Participatory Media*. Cambridge, MA: MIT Press.

Morrissey, Brian. 2014. "Kanye West—Genius or Asshole?" *Irish Times*, June 20. https://www.irishtimes.com/culture/music/kanye-west-genius-or-asshole-1.1850359.

Obiora, Ntianu. 2018. "Vogue Gentrifies 'Hood Nails.'" *Pulse Nigeria*, January 3. www.pulse.ng/lifestyle/beauty-health/cultural-appropriation-vogue-gentrifies-hoodnails/5j1gv4g.

Parham, Jason. 2018. "The Devolution of Kanye West and the Case for Cancel Culture." *Wired*, October 5. https://www.wired.com/story/kanye-west-cancel-culture/.

Richardson, Elaine B. 2006. *Hiphop Literacies*. New York: Routledge.

Robertson, Jessica. 2005. "Kanye West Blasts Bush." *Rolling Stone*, September 5. https://www.rollingstone.com/politics/politics-news/kanye-west-blasts-bush-111113/.

Samuels, David. 2012. "American Mozart." *The Atlantic*, May. https://www.theatlantic.com/magazine/archive/2012/05/american-mozart/308931/.

Sharma, Sanjay. 2013. "Black Twitter? Racial Hashtags, Networks, and Contagion." *New Formations: A Journal of Culture/Theory/Politics* 78: 46–64.

Smitherman, Geneva. 1977. *Talkin and Testifyin: The Language of Black America*. Detroit: Wayne State University Press.

Terrell, Kellee. 2018. "#CancelKanye: Black Twitter Rips the Rapper for His Sunken Place Meeting with Trump." *Hello Beautiful*, October 11. https://hellobeautiful.com/playlist/black-twitter-responds-kanyes-meeting-with-trump-white-house/item/1.

Tien, Shannon. 2018. "Top Twitter Demographics That Matter to Social Media Marketers." *Hootsuite*, June 26. https://blog.hootsuite.com/twitter-demog.

8

LEXA DESERVED BETTER
How One Character's Death Sparked a Revolution and Changed Media Representation for the LGBTQ+ Community

Erin B. Waggoner

The lesbian, gay, bisexual, transgender, and queer (LGBTQ+) community has been highly engaged in both activism and fandom for decades, with the two sometimes colliding. The advent of the internet provided both vehicles for dissent and safe spaces to discuss the issues important to community members. One such issue has been queer representation in popular culture. During the time when virtual bulletin boards were first on the rise, on other screens queer people were finally seeing increased visibility and were no longer relegated to whatever media was willing to give them, which formerly had consisted primarily of subtext and negative tropes. Instead, in the 1990s, television shows like the *Ellen Show* and *Will and Grace* helped normalize positive representations of LGBTQ+ persons, and soon after, websites such as AfterEllen and AfterElton were created to help people find and discuss more issues relating to queer representation.

Decades later, the twenty-first century brought ever expanding social media platforms that provided additional safe spaces and opportunities for LGBTQ+ persons to address contemporary concerns. Social media forums allowed for self-presentation and for individuals to be safely out in digital spaces, even if they did not disclose their sexuality offline. LGBTQ+ persons were able to create separate social media profiles so they could feel comfortable and protected. For example, activist campaigns like It Gets Better, launched by gay activist and journalist Dan Savage in 2010 after a wave of suicides by teenagers who were bullied due to their sexual orientation, found traction thanks to YouTube. The leading video social media site provided a place where people could share their personal stories and spread hope to peers and younger generations.

Social media also provided opportunities for LGBTQ+ community members and allies to demand more from the popular culture products

https://doi.org/10.7330/9781646423187.c008

that can so readily influence cultural sentiments. One such example was when fans of *The 100* were upset when a queer character, Lexa, was killed in a common trope called Bury Your Gays. TV Tropes (2020) defines this trope as "the presentation of deaths of LGBT characters where these characters are nominally able to be viewed as more expendable than their heteronormative counterparts . . . In aggregate, queer characters are more likely to die than straight characters." The plot point of Lexa's death sparked online outrage for better representation through the #LGBTFansDeserveBetter campaign. The #LGBTFansDeserveBetter movement revealed an online community that was connecting and organizing in attempts to affect change in LGBTQ+ representation.

To examine how the LGBTQ+ community engages with hashtag activism, this chapter addresses the history of LGBTQ+ activism, use of mediated spaces, and the way social media has shifted the face of activism to show how this mediated activism has resonated for the LGBTQ+ community. Using a queer theoretical lens, this chapter analyzes the #LGBTFansDeserveBetter campaign, examining how fans used social media to fight for better media representation. As a result, the analysis presents the history of queer media, the fight for better representation, and how this social media campaign finally caused some waves in the media industry. Similar to social media movements like It Gets Better, this investigation notes how one hashtag can make a difference to enact specific changes, such as those shown through LGBTQ+ television representation. Therefore, this chapter focuses not only on the posts surrounding the #LGBTFansDeserveBetter movement on Twitter but also on the subsequent results this movement achieved through activist community-based action. The findings reveal a community focused on creating change for LGBTQ+ television representation, committed to seeing these changes across more than just one media platform, and celebrated for its visible results. This study showcases the ways hashtag activism contributed to a successful campaign that prompted an audience boycott, connected community and encouraged involvement, targeted (and successfully pulled) advertisers from shows, developed successful donation campaigns to LGBTQ+ groups, and changed the representation of LGBTQ+ characters in subsequent television shows and seasons.

HISTORY AND SHIFTS IN LGBTQ+ ACTIVISM

Before I examine hashtag activism, it is important to understand the history of activism as a whole in the LGBTQ+ community and the ways activists gradually integrated media into their social justice efforts.

Activism in the LGBTQ+ community has a history that stretches back to the eighteenth century and is tied to a range of political and sociocultural events that sparked more engagement and visibility. Some of the earliest activism responded to laws that marginalized the LGBTQ+ community. For instance, sodomy laws that criminalized homosexual activity existed from the colonial era until the late twentieth century (Benemann 2006). In this early period of activism, since LGBTQ+ community members were largely fighting against laws that deemed their very existence illegal, many of the early activist groups were considered underground and held private meetings and events to protect the safety of their members. Some prominent examples from the 1950s and 1960s include the Society for Human Rights, the Mattachine Society, and the Daughters of Bilitis (Bullough 2002; Richardson and Seidman 2002). However, the LGBTQ+ community began to become weary of being arrested, blackmailed, and bullied.

Two major events in LGBTQ+ activism history show a shift toward more visibility as protests became more public: the Compton's Cafeteria and Stonewall Inn riots. These two moments in history showcase the LGBTQ+ community forging together to fight for its rights in a time when police raids were common and people were arrested solely for being in a gay bar or dressing in a way that was considered non-gender normative. After these watershed moments in LGBTQ+ activism, the movement's visibility only continued to increase with the launch of the first Pride parade (held during the one-year anniversary of the Stonewall riots) and the first National March on Washington for Lesbian and Gay Rights (which happened only nine years later). Then, in the 1980s, activism in the LGBTQ+ community reached a pivotal battle during the AIDS epidemic as right-wing religious movements warred with LGBTQ+ activist groups, such as ACT UP and Queer Nation, to help the community have access to healthcare (Richardson and Seidman 2002).

As activism increased, so did the means through which such work occurred. Feet on the ground and voices in the street were soon accompanied by creative use of media to continue LGBTQ+ causes. A notable example that predates social media is the explosion of queer zines, which began surfacing in the 1970s but proliferated widely in the 1980s and 1990s (Teixeira 2012). "By blurring stereotypes and fusing identities, this accessible, low-cost medium" created a "counterhegemonic space" that blurred stereotypes, fused identities, transformed the queer body, and "reclaimed silenced narratives of oppressed groups" (Erickson 2013, 1). Many of these zines were a part of the Queercore movement that documented "the lives of queer punk rock artists and activists who sought an alternative to the lesbian and gay movement emerging in the public sphere" (1). With the success of this early multimodal form of activism, it is not a surprise that LGBTQ+ activists were quick to adopt social media for their causes. However, the fact that queer zines rose as a form of counterprotest also previews the ways later hashtag activism would also reveal the complexity of the LGBTQ+ identity and the ways it was represented (or not) in broader civil rights movements. For example, transgender rights and representation were often pushed aside to focus on sexuality instead of gender expression and identity. Data analyzed for this study reveal that this is still true in contemporary LGBTQ+ activism movements, including those that are predominantly online. For example, some users critiqued the hashtag activism focused on in this chapter, arguing that "#LGBTFansDeserveBetter can be a representative movement. It is not yet. But it can be!" While the #LGBTFansDeserveBetter movement appears to be inclusive in its title, the movement focused primarily on sexuality as just one part of the LGBTQ+ spectrum.

SOCIAL MEDIA ACTIVISM AND THE LGBTQ+ COMMUNITY

As LGBTQ+ activism moved more into digital online spaces toward the end of the twentieth century, some benefits were the ways digital spaces allowed activists to organize, share resources, and document their history and culture with more of the world and each other. Instead of waiting on print and news media to disseminate the stories, the LGBTQ+ community now had shared open-access spaces free of outside framing.

Identity and connection have also shifted with the advent of mediated channels. Researchers have noted how cyberspace allows LGBTQ+ youth to express themselves more freely through mediated platforms rife with anonymity and interactivity (Jacobson and Donatone 2009). These spaces provide more fluidity in identity and more visibility for the LGBTQ+ culture. Prior to the World Wide Web, LGBTQ+ persons were still using USENET (an early online sharing system) to post and interact within the community. The first online LGBTQ+ community started in 1983 with net.motss (which stood for members of the same sex) (Wakeford 2002). Since this online community was such an active one, some argue that the LGBTQ+ community helped spur the advent of the World Wide Web in 1991 (2002). While communication styles vary from the older digital platforms to the present, the advocacy remains the same. In earlier spaces, posts were long and in *belles-lettres* style, in contrast to the 280 characters for Twitter or the less aesthetic function of longer Facebook posts available today. However, this continued adoption of evolving digital tools showcases how the LGBTQ+ communities have been using virtual space for advocacy for decades.

BUILDING OFF OF QUEER THEORY: SCHOLARSHIP ON LGBTQ+ HASHTAG ACTIVISM

As a field, queer theory stems from these early activist movements and found its more scholarly origin in the activism of the 1980s, particularly that surrounding the AIDS epidemic. While its origins are more nuanced, some argue that queer theory came into being through Teresa de Lauretis's (1991) seminal article "Queer Theory: Lesbian and Gay Sexualities," which noted that there are three camps working together to challenge heteronormativity. Prior to this, the work of Michel Foucault, Gayle Rubin, and Judith Butler laid the foundation for the field, reconceptualizing and challenging definitions of sexuality, gender, power, and hierarchy (Jagose 1996). However, queer theory examines sexuality and gender with the underlying caveat that both are (often inter)connected to social status, norms, and identity. Thus, building on this accepted premise, this chapter examines media representations of sexuality with the understanding that sexuality and gender are linked regardless of the transparency of that linkage.

As digital platforms proliferate, scholarship focused on how queer persons navigate and use these spaces has been on the rise. For example, research has noted that LGBTQ+ adults who engage with social media for LGBTQ+ issues are more likely to involve themselves in activist movements, boycotts, and buycotts (Becker and Copeland 2016). This means that LGBTQ+ persons who are using social media are seeking out issues that matter to them and collectively pulling together to directly respond to them. As with other communities, another way social media is used by LGBTQ+ members is related to social networking. In one study, LGBTQ+ parents cited using social media to help identify allies and determine disapproval to help them better navigate society (Blackwell et al. 2016). This helped them determine how "out" to be in their social circles at work and their children's schools by examining people's social media accounts for clues to help them determine acceptance versus disapproval. These spaces are used to help identify how people will interact with or respond to certain identities.

As noted earlier, social media spaces have allowed LGBTQ+ youth in particular to explore their identities and interact with others more. Several online resources, such as the previously mentioned It Gets

Better Campaign and the Trevor Project, provide information and interactive digital platforms for LGBTQ+ youth to engage in what are considered safe and supportive environments. Some advocacy groups, such as GLSEN (Gay, Lesbian, and Straight Education Network), have worked offline with schools to become more inclusive to offset the high suicide rates among LGBTQ+ youth (who are five times more likely to attempt suicide than their heterosexual peers) (CDC 2016). Beyond specific organizations and campaigns, popular social media platforms more generally have been found to be beneficial digital resources for LGBTQ+ teens. A study on LGBTQ+ youth and social media use found that those who identify as LGBTQ+ have more friends in online spaces than in real life, especially those who are not out (have not disclosed their identity) to their friends or real-life social and family circles (GLSEN, CiPHR, and CCRC 2013). The most common themes for LGBTQ+ youth to contribute to are those related to sharing their stories with others, such as their difficulties, their coming-out stories, or their stories on how things really do get better (Tropiano 2014). As is evident in the range of engagement available, social media has also allowed older persons in the LGBTQ+ community to serve as support and models for LGBTQ+ youth, which also queers the concept of social media as a space to connect with peers. Instead, social media becomes a place where generations can blend together to help one another build a stronger community and highlight the ways history and modern life can interweave.

Since queer theory, among other aims, is interested in examining the self and society through these sexual/gender lenses, the social media sphere for the LGBTQ+ community offers an online space rife with potential for research. For this purpose, this research uses a qualitative style of observational research known as virtual ethnography to discover how the LGBTQ+ community interacts with social media. Specifically, this research closely examines the #LGBTFansDeserveBetter movement to better understand how social media spaces are used to encourage activism outside the online social sphere, such as donations, community work, and direct-to-producer advocacy.

VIRTUAL ETHNOGRAPHY, CASE ANALYSIS, AND SOCIAL MEDIA OBSERVATION

According to Martyn Hammersley and Paul Atkinson (2019), ethnography is a research method that examines people's routines and daily lives. This methodology allows researchers to become more interactive with their research subjects in what is known as extensive participant observation. Virtual ethnography takes this concept and expands it to include observation of online environments (Hine 2000). Since virtual ethnography does focus on mediated spaces, the researchers do not have to leave their environment and can instead immerse themselves in a virtual community. Similar to ethnography, however, the researcher is asked to become more immersed in the online environment than in engaging in "covert" research (or non-participant observation). The idea that virtual ethnography does allow the researcher to review communities in a more covert manner lends itself to debate in the field on ethical research practices (Ashford 2009; Hine 2004). For this reason, this research does involve a modicum of participation, wherein the researcher does have an online presence within the LGBTQ+ community. However, since this research also utilizes case analysis in conjunction with virtual ethnography, some non-participant methodology is used to gather data for analysis.

Since examining an entire online community would be impossible, case study analysis is used in tandem with virtual ethnography to examine a specific social media activist movement in the LGBTQ+ community. According to Robert K. Yin (2018), researchers use case studies to help explore, explain, or describe particular cultural phenomena—not unlike other research methods. Case studies are in-depth investigations of particular groups or individuals (2018), which researchers use to help guide their other methodologies to provide further insight into their data collection. Instead of examining individuals or the entire LGBTQ+ community, the particular hashtag #LGBTFansDeserveBetter was observed for the purposes of this research. Particular tweets posted between March and July 2016 that utilized this hashtag were examined. As this hashtag began following a particular television event (described more in the next section), early examination of the movement started with #LexaDeservedBetter and various other hashtags (e.g., #Boycott100). However, the bulk of the research and close examination looks at the tweets involved directly with the beginning and development of the #LGBTFansDeserveBetter movement specifically. While the research started with these other hashtags, the #LGBTFansDeserveBetter movement is the only one considered in this chapter, as this is the movement that highlights the clearest direction of social media activism. Numerous posts (approximately 20,000) were coded for their similarities, thus allowing the data to inform the analysis using grounded theory. These posts were mined three times a day (morning, afternoon, and evening) for five months; as a result, posts that had been submitted and deleted between those times were not observed. In addition, retweets were excluded, as were posts written in a language other than English. For insight into the particular case study used, it is important to first understand the event that prompted this social media activism using the #LGBTFansDeserveBetter hashtag.

GONE IN SIXTY-SIX SECONDS: THE SHOT HEARD AROUND THE LGBTQ+ COMMUNITY

Loosely based on Kass Morgan's young adult series, *The 100* (2014–2021) was a television series on the CW network that followed the lives of a group of teenagers who were sent back to Earth to test whether the planet was habitable again after ninety-seven years in space due to a nuclear apocalypse that supposedly destroyed life on Earth. While the show did not obtain a huge viewership or critical acclaim in its first season, it began to pick up traction in its second season, with one reviewer noting, "This is a show about moral choices and the consequences of those choices, and it's been laudably committed to those ideas from Day 1" (Ryan 2015). The show saw a ratings and critical response increase, which some attribute to the introduction of the first-season enemies, the Grounders, as potential allies, which gave further depth to the canonical world created from the first season and further examined the questions of morality and consequences the first season began to explore. People also attribute the increased viewership to the introduction of the Grounders leader, Lexa (played by Alycia Debnam-Carey), who became a potential love interest for the main protagonist, Clarke (played by Eliza Taylor). The introduction of this potential relationship and the cliffhanger at the end of season two that separated them had LGBTQ+ audiences intrigued about what the show would do with this relationship as it entered its third season.

Social media sites, such as Tumblr, and video-sharing sites, such as YouTube, allowed users to become more aware of content related to their community, and *The 100* was no different as Lexa was introduced as a woman-loving-woman character and Clarke as canonically bisexual in the second season of the show. LGBTQ+ characters have historically been invisible in television (Capsuto 2000; Gross 2001); as a result, *The 100* saw an increase in viewership as the LGBTQ+ community became aware of this storyline and its character portrayals. The relationship between Clarke and Lexa led not only to increased viewership of the show but also to an increase in its social media presence. Fans were excited to see how these two characters would mend, if possible, the events from the season finale to come together again. The first six episodes of the third season built up their relationship again until Clarke and Lexa finally consummated their relationship and declared their interest in one another by having sex in the seventh episode, "Thirteen." What happened after this much-awaited relationship milestone, however, had audiences, particularly those from the LGBTQ+ community and their allies, reeling.

At the end of the post-coital scene, the screen fades into the next scene, which shows Clarke's antagonism toward Lexa's main adviser coming to an end. Titus, Lexa's adviser, reveals that he does not trust Clarke and that her relationship with Lexa is ruining the Grounders' way of life and rule. So he tries to frame Clarke and kill her with a gun, which the Grounders see as a weapon of mass destruction. Instead, Lexa rushes into the room to discover what is happening and is shot by a stray bullet meant for Clarke, effectively going from post-coital to near death in the span of sixty-six seconds. Fans responded negatively to this juxtaposition of events and to Lexa's death more generally, as the latter evoked an overly used television storyline/trope called the Bury Your Gays.

As a trope, the Bury Your Gays storyline involves any same-sex couple in which one (or sometimes both) partner must die by the end of the story. This trope began in nineteenth-century literature but became increasingly prevalent in television during the 1970s and beyond. Researchers have noted a direct correlation between the use of this trope and the character's behavior prior to their death, such as a confession of feelings, kissing, or having sex for the first time (Hulan 2017). Lexa's story fits the script: she has sex with Clarke (in whom she had declared her interest in season two) for the first time, and her death is the result of her close relationship with Clarke (which directly challenges the heteronormative advising relationship between Titus and Lexa). However, the problem was not simply that this one character was killed off a fictional show—it was her placement within the ongoing trend. Since its first recorded occurrence in television in 1976, 208 women-loving-women (WLW) characters had been killed off (Riese 2016). With so many WLW characters dying, why did Lexa's death impact so many people in 2016? During the months of January to March 2016, there were 35 WLW characters on scripted television. In the span of those three months, 10 of those 35 characters fell victim to the Bury Your Gays trope, accounting for 29 percent of total WLW characters on television at the time (2016). Lexa's death was just the precursor to restarting the conversation on LGBTQ+ representation. While previous work has examined *The 100* community's response to Lexa's death (Waggoner 2018), this chapter examines the larger social media activist movement that started following Lexa's death: #LGBTFansDeserveBetter.

#LEXADESERVEDBETTER IS TRENDING

After Lexa was killed in the show, there was an uptick of responses on social media from people responding not just to the storyline but also to how it affected them personally. Numerous posts had users disclosing their self-harm and/or suicidal thoughts after seeing Lexa's death. A large portion noted that they had believed Lexa was safe and would not die since producers of *The 100* had responded misleadingly to viewers' concerns that Lexa would fall victim to this trope. This break in viewer trust amplified the situation.

One pattern present in the data was the attempt to connect the community and/or inform others about how they could become involved: "Contact sponsors. Promote the charity. Spread informative articles/sites. Be kind to yourself and others. Stay safe." Some fans even took to social media platforms they normally would not use just to join the movement, such as one who noted, "Honestly. I don't like Twitter. I have it to help #LGBT fans deserve better trends." Early posts were shown bringing the community together for a more organized mode of attack, with later posts including a wider range of strategies to unite people. This organization became a more effective mode of change, as people began to target the arena in which media platforms would feel it the most: the money side.

Fans of the show started a boycott and worked to ensure that #LexaDeservedBetter trended and received more traction than any other social media (e.g., show-/network-specific public relations and hashtags) related to the show. #LGBTFansDeserveBetter was frequently a top trend during the weeks following the episode, with 250,000 or more posts daily. The efforts were successful for several weeks, as was the call to boycott the actual show and companies that advertised during the show on the CW network. In terms of the effectiveness of the call to boycott the show, ratings in the episode following "Thirteen" showed a dramatic drop (0.19 million viewers lost; Porter 2016c) until an eventual 0.21 million viewers were lost by episode eleven in the midst of this movement (decreasing to 1.08 million total viewers; Porter 2016a). Interestingly, another uptick in ratings (increasing to 1.29 million viewers) occurred for the season finale when Lexa made another brief appearance (Porter 2016b). This is an impressive loss of viewership, considering that the show never had a large viewership to begin with.

While losing 0.21 million viewers may not be impressive for larger shows, *The 100* only had 1.39 million viewers going into "Thirteen." Therefore, these drops were a tangible victory for the early stages of the movement. A large portion of the earliest tweets in the movement were devoted to working to have this show (and others) lose viewership.

Users also directly addressed specific companies; and major advertisers, such as Target and Maybelline, did pull ads from the show (though not from the CW completely). Posts shared these accomplishments through the movement. One user posted the letter received directly from Dairy Queen's fan relations managers, which noted, "While DQ commercials have aired on this program in the past, our team had already identified this program as one that does not fit the DQ brand. Commercials will not air again during this program." Similarly, some fans posted on social media platforms about brand loyalty after companies pulled their ads: "I don't buy make up often, but when I do you can be damn sure I'll be buying @Maybelline." Brands that had previously advertised with *The 100* were listening to this community and declared that their commercials had officially been pulled from the show. The episodes after "Thirteen" aired began to show advertisements of other CW network shows or commercials and no longer appeared to include brands that had previously bought advertisement slots for the show.

Media is a business first and foremost, so this was perhaps the biggest hit to producers, who felt they needed to do damage control. However, the damage control that was done did not seem to deter the social movement. As the show's writers and performers began to write open letters and participate in interviews, the online community demanded more; one user tweeted that "no true social movement ever succeeds from lying down [and] accepting false apologies before tangible change was made." Members posted reminders not to fall prey to the spin doctoring being done since no change had yet occurred and no real apology had been given: "The more we get dismissed [and] the more they try to distract [and] misdirect, the more our fight is *not* over." This helped the movement retain traction through the aftermath, as this movement continued to grow and to attempt something larger than a complaint about a single storyline.

What started as a hashtag campaign focused on one show sparked something much larger. Viewers adopted the hashtag to draw attention to other shows that were utilizing the same Bury Your Gays trope after Lexa's death, including several other shows on the CW network. Interestingly, Lexa's death was not the first on a show in the spring 2016 television season to incorporate this trope. The character of Rose on *Jane the Virgin* (also on the CW) was allegedly shot and killed in the February 22 episode ("Chapter Thirty-Four"), which was ten days before *The 100* episode "Thirteen" aired. However, there are two potential reasons why this may not have started a revolution the way Lexa's death did. First, Rose was considered the show's antagonist/villain. Second, Lexa was built up as a warrior-like (i.e., strong, powerful) character on social media, which viewers connected to on a deeper level as positive representation. For this reason, perhaps the #LGBTFansDeserveBetter movement did not start until Lexa because viewers were seeing Lexa as a more positive representation than Rose on *Jane the Virgin*. Once this movement found its niche, more tweets using the hashtag later appeared, sharing and making connections to other LGBTQ+ media representation issues and fan interactions beyond that of Lexa's death. In response to the television show *Person of Interest*, Facebook pages considered it a "barrage of homophobia," as one person tweeted. "It's sad. And gross. It also hurts to know that's how people think of us." People were not only sharing what shows were doing but what others were saying about these shows across various platforms.

What was discovered after Lexa's death was an online community that came together to not just begin an activist movement using social media but also to expand the message of previous activist movements, such as the It Gets Better Project. People were posting on not only the boycott and updates on the growing social movement but also on positive messages to those who were struggling to cope with the death and helpful links to inform others about the issue (Waggoner 2018). Hashtags calling for the show's cancellation eventually reached over 10,000 posts online. Since the show had already been renewed for another season, there was no real chance of getting it canceled. However, people involved online could find ways to affect the future of LGBTQ+ storylines. Thus, the #LexaDeservedBetter movement expanded to be more inclusive and shifted into the #LGBTFansDeserveBetter social activist movement.

#LGBTFANSDESERVEBETTER FOR CHANGE

The campaign may have impacted the future trajectory of *The 100*'s plot, as there was an evident shift in storytelling regarding its LGBTQ+ characters/relationships, particularly those around Clarke Griffin. Instead of having the main character Clarke enter into a relationship with someone else, the show had her engage in a sexual (non-romantic) relationship with another woman while still grieving Lexa. In a fast-paced show like *The 100*, especially one on the CW network, which caters to a younger target audience, deciding not to have the main character become romantically involved was an interesting choice but one that worked for the character's development and provided a chance to show how Lexa's legacy resonated beyond her death. This offsets the trope slightly, as the usual modus operandi of the Bury Your Gays trope is to never again mention the character or the relationship. Instead, Clarke's bisexuality was not buried as had happened in shows in the past, and the impact Lexa's death had on her was not brushed aside.

The ripple effects of this movement are noteworthy. One of the first big wins for the movement was getting the #LGBTFansDeserveBetter hashtag to trend online. There were more than 280,000 posts with #LGBTFansDeserveBetter in a span of a few hours as the next episode of *The 100* aired on television, causing it to become one of the top trending hashtags. The movement expanded internationally, as other countries reported on the movement's traction. Evidence of this was seen in a post that shared an Israeli newspaper article (written in Hebrew) about the #LGBTFansDeserveBetter movement and the Lexa Pledge. Another accomplishment occurred when the episode was aired in other countries; these countries included a trigger warning message at the beginning of the episode to warn of its traumatic events and included information on resources for those who could potentially be affected by watching it.

Also, while the movement started with social media, there was a much larger impact outside of the social media world. The hashtag led an online fundraiser for the Trevor Project, a digital resource for LGBTQ+ teenagers who are struggling and experiencing suicidal thoughts, that raised over $170,000 (Leskru 2019). This fundraiser was started and shared through the #LGBTFansDeserveBetter hashtag, with frequent reports on Twitter of how successful the fundraiser was. Numerous YouTube videos were also created, such as Code 307's project "LGBT Viewers Deserve Better: A Story of Hope and Resilience" that informs the public about the trope and how the movement began (LGBTViewers Deserve Better 2016). Some of the early organizers of the movement created a website (lgbtfansdeservebetter.com) that informed people about the use of tropes in LGBTQ+ representation, addressed the current scope of LGBTQ+ representation, collected news stories on the issue from around the globe, and provided an online platform for people to submit their own stories about how LGBTQ+ representation on television affected them. These articles and websites were also shared using the #LGBTFansDeserveBetter hashtag, making early proponents of the movement's call to action for sharing these resources more tangible.

Another win occurred when the movement directly brought about something called the Lexa Pledge, which challenged current shows to pledge to offset negative tropes and promise better, more nuanced representation. The Canadian hospital drama *Saving Hope* was the first to do this. As a show that frequently dealt with death, the writers and producers created a will and will not guideline for how they would treat LGBTQ+ characters on their show. LGBTQ+ storylines were presented and continued after the pledge was made, and from observation, the team upheld the pledge until the show ended in 2017. Tweets after this first pledge occurred shared the open letter, signed the pledge from the show, and directly (through direct call signs) challenged other shows that included LGBTQ+ characters to do something similar.

Beyond the digital world, there were also expansions from the movement that went offline to bring attention to the issue. While some social media movements stayed in the online world to bring awareness to the issue, #LGBTFansDeserveBetter organizers went beyond the screen and purchased four billboards that were placed in heavily trafficked areas in Los Angeles (Murphy 2016). This campaign raised $15,000 to create a design and purchase the advertising space, and the billboards were in place two months after the start of the movement, reminding entertainment industry personnel about the issue and the fact that viewers would not back down from this movement simply because the 2015–2016 television season was over.

In addition, a new convention was developed on LGBTQ+ representation called Clexacon, which was named after the portmanteau given to Clarke and Lexa's relationship. This fan convention started as an opportunity for fans to get together to continue the conversation in an open, positive environment. What originally started as 100 people who wanted to gather to talk about Lexa as a character eventually expanded due to interest from word of mouth and social media. Eventually, the fan convention was born with the idea that the conversation was much bigger than just Lexa alone and included representation of queer women on television. As the concept developed further, more vendors, sponsors, and performers signed on; and the convention turned into the world's largest multi-fandom event for queer women (Sprayregen 2019). With outcomes like Clexacon, the LGBT Fans Deserve Better movement highlights how important the movement was to the LGBTQ+ community and its continued fight for good televisual representation.

Finally, the biggest victory this movement had was the shift in LGBTQ+ representation during the following television seasons. During the 2015–2016 television season, GLAAD (2015) reported thirty-five

(4%) identified LGBTQ+ characters on primetime programming. Despite the low percentage, this was an increase from the prior year, as the number of LGBT characters on cable increased from sixty-four to eighty-four. This was, however, the same television season that started the #LGBTFansDeserveBetter movement, so ten of those thirty-five characters died using the Bury Your Gays trope. The movement wanted to bring attention to the fact that it was not enough to simply increase the number of characters but that the representation needed to be better. The following years saw a few shifts in LGBTQ+ representation, especially relating to more positive representation and intersectionality (e.g., race). Numbers have continued to increase every year, with a high of ninety-two characters (11.9%) in the 2021–2022 season (GLAAD 2022).

Beyond the increase in representation, LGBTQ+ representation is also now acknowledged in television audience analytics. This could also be associated with the movement. Nielsen, the major US research team, now includes LGBTQ+ households in its reports on viewing habits (Otterson 2018). This falls in line with Nielsen's (2019) mission to provide "the most complete and trusted view available of consumers and markets worldwide." The LGBT Fans Deserve Better movement, which started as a call for people to listen to the LGBTQ+ viewing community and provide better representation, has truly shifted the way people view television but also how television is studied and made.

CONCLUSION

This chapter provides ample evidence that hashtag activism campaigns can have longevity and result in positive outcomes years after their onset. #LGBTFansDeserveBetter demonstrates the ways hashtags can be strategically employed, adapted beyond their original contexts, and moved into offline spaces and global dialogues. With the LGBT Fans Deserve Better movement, activists demanded better representation on television, and they did not back down. They kept the momentum going and shifted television narratives, representation, and research on television viewers. This is but one example of how hashtags can start revolutions for social change by providing information, inspiring action, and building community. Movements like this show the power of an organized online community and the power of hashtag activism to affect real social change. Early LGBTQ+ activists may not have been able to predict the varying ways social justice work would be carried out in the next millennium, but one can imagine that they would be proud to see their continued legacy evolve and play out in so many online and offline spaces.

REFERENCES

Ashford, Chris. 2009. "Queer Theory, Cyber-ethnographies, and Researching Online Sex Environments." *Information and Communications Technology Law* 18 (3): 297–314. doi: 10.1080/13600830903424734.

Becker, Amy B., and Lauren Copeland. 2016. "Networked Publics: How Connective Social Media Use Facilitates Political Consumerism among LGBT Americans." *Journal of Information Technology and Politics* 13 (1): 22–36.

Benemann, William E. 2006. *Male-Male Intimacy in Early America: Beyond Romantic Friendships*. Philadelphia: Haworth.

Blackwell, Lindsay, Jean Hardy, Tawfiq Ammari, Tiffany Veinot, Cliff Lampe, and Sarita Schoenebeck. 2016. "LGBT Parents and Social Media: Advocacy, Privacy, and Disclosure during Shifting Social Movements." In *Proceedings of the 2016 CHI Conference on Human Factors in Computing Systems*, edited by Allison Druin, Juan Pablo Hourcade, Jofish Kaye, Cliff Lampe, and Dan Morris. New York: Association for Computing Machinery, 610–622.

Bullough, Vern L. 2002. *Before Stonewall: Activists for Gay and Lesbian Rights in Historical Context*. Philadelphia: Haworth.

Capsuto, Steven. 2000. *Alternate Channels: The Uncensored Story of Gay and Lesbian Images on Radio and Television*. New York: Ballantine.

CDC (Centers for Disease Control). 2016. "Sexual Identity: Sex of Sexual Contacts, and Health-Risk Behaviors among Students in Grades 9–12, Youth Risk Behavior Surveillance." US Department of Health and Human Services, August 12. https://www.cdc.gov/mmwr/volumes/65/ss/pdfs/ss6509.pdf.

de Lauretis, Teresa. 1991. "Queer Theory: Lesbian and Gay Sexualities, an Introduction." *Differences* 3 (2): iii–xviii.

Erickson, Camille. 2013. "Querying Sex, Gender, and Race through the Queercore Zine Movement: G. B. Jones and Vaginal Davis Protest Conformity." Gateway Prize for Excellent Writing. Paper 4. https://digitalcommons.macalester.edu/cgi/viewcontent.cgi?article=1004&context=studentawards.

GLAAD. 2015. "GLAAD—Where We Are on TV Report, 2015." Glaad.org. https://www.glaad.org/whereweareontv15.

GLAAD. 2022. "Where We Are on TV Report, 2021–2022." Glaad.org. https://www.glaad.org/whereweareontv21.

GLSEN, Center for Innovative Public Health Research, and Crimes against Children Research Center. 2013. "Out Online: The Experiences of Lesbian, Gay, Bisexual, and Transgender Youth on the Internet." GLSEN.org. https://www.glsen.org/sites/default/files/2020-01/Out_Online_Full_Report_2013.pdf.

Gross, Larry. 2001. *Up from Invisibility: Lesbians, Gay Men, and the Media in America*. New York: Columbia University Press.

Hammersley, Martyn, and Paul Atkinson. 2019. *Ethnography: Principles in Practice*. 4th edition. New York: Routledge.

Hine, Christine. 2000. *Virtual Ethnography*. Thousand Oaks, CA: Sage.

Hine, Christine. 2004. "Virtual Ethnography Revisited." Paper presented at the Research Methods Festival, Oxford, England. July.

Hulan, Haley. 2017. "Bury Your Gays: History, Usage, and Context." *McNair Scholars Journal* 21 (1): 17–27.

Jacobson, Brian, and Brooke Donatone. 2009. "Homoflexibles, Omnisexuals, and Genderqueers: Group Work with Queer Youth in Cyberspace and Face-to-Face." *Group* 33 (3): 223–234.

Jagose, Annamarie. 1996. *Queer Theory: An Introduction*. New York: New York University Press.

Leskru. 2019. "LGBT Fans Deserve Better." Trevor Project. https://give.thetrevorproject.org/fundraiser/625415.

LGBTViewers Deserve Better. 2016. "LGBT Viewers Deserve Better: A Story of Hope and Resilience." YouTube, May 22. https://www.youtube.com/watch?v=5NeXYkwEC-M.

Murphy, Shaunna. 2016. "'The 100's Fans Just Took Their Fight against Queer TV Deaths a Giant Step Further." *Revelist*, May 19. https://www.revelist.com/tv/the-100-lexa-bill board/2427.

Nielsen. 2019. "About Us." https://www.nielsen.com/us/en/about-us/.

Otterson, Joe. 2018. "Nielsen Reveals First-Ever LGBTQ Household Ratings (Exclusive)." *Variety*, October 25. https://variety.com/2018/tv/news/nielsen-ratings-lgbtq-house holds-1202992229/.

Porter, Rick. 2016a. "Thursday Final Ratings: The Blacklist Adjusts Up." *TV by the Numbers*, April 15. https://tvbythenumbers.zap2it.com/daily-ratings/thursday-final-ratings-april -14-2016/.

Porter, Rick. 2016b. "Thursday Final Ratings: Bones Adjusts Up, the Catch Finale and Game of Silence Adjust Down." *TV by the Numbers*, May 20. https://tvbythenumbers .zap2it.com/daily-ratings/thursday-final-ratings-may-19-2016/.

Porter, Rick. 2016c. "Thursday Final Ratings: Scandal Adjusts Up, 4 CBS Shows Adjust Down." *TV by the Numbers*, March 11. https://tvbythenumbers.zap2it.com/daily-ratings /thursday-final-ratings-march-10-2016/.

Richardson, Diane, and Steven Seidman. 2002. "Introduction." In *Handbook of Lesbian and Gay Studies*, edited by Diane Richardson and Steven Seidman. 1–12. Thousand Oaks, CA: Sage.

Riese. 2016. "All 208 Dead Lesbian and Bisexual Characters on TV, and How They Died." *Autostraddle*, March 11. http://www.autostraddle.com/all-65-dead-lesbian-and-bisexual -characters-on-tv-and-how-they-died-312315/.

Ryan, Maureen. 2015. "What Happened on the Season Finale of 'The 100?'" *HuffPost*, March 11. https://www.huffpost.com/entry/the-100-season-finale_n_6850268.

Sprayregen, Molly. 2019. "Meet the Directors of the World's Largest Multi-fandom Event for Queer Women." *Forbes*, February 27. https://www.forbes.com/sites/mollysprayregen /2019/02/27/meet-the-founders-of-the-worlds-largest-multi-fandom-event-for-queer -women/#424dff9a246c.

Teixeira, Rob. 2012. "Punk-lad Love, Dyke-core, and the Evolution of Queer Zine Culture in Canada." Brokenpencil.com. https://brokenpencil.com/features/punk-lad-love -dyke-core-and-the-evolution-of-queer-zine-culture-in-canada/.

Tropiano, Stephen. 2014. "'A Safe and Supportive Environment': LGBTQ Youth and Social Media." In *Queer Youth and Media Cultures*, edited by Christopher Pullen. 46–62. London: Palgrave Macmillan.

TV Tropes. 2020. "Bury Your Gays." https://tvtropes.org/pmwiki/pmwiki.php/Main/Bury YourGays.

Waggoner, Erin B. 2018. "Bury Your Gays and Social Media Fan Response: Television, LGBTQ Representation, and Communitarian Ethics." *Journal of Homosexuality* 65 (13): 1877–1891.

Wakeford. Nina. 2002. "New Technologies and 'Cyber-queer' Research." In *Handbook of Lesbian and Gay Studies*, edited by Diane Richardson and Steven Seidman, 115–144. Thousand Oaks, CA: Sage.

Yin, Robert K. 2018. *Case Study Research and Applications: Design and Methods*. 6th ed. Thousand Oaks, CA: Sage.

9
CONSTRUCTING DIGITAL DIASPORIC SPACES AND REFRAMING BLACK MASCULINITY THROUGH *INSECURE*'S #LAWRENCEHIVE

Robert Barry Jr.

The Black male masculinity theme for #InsecureHBO this season had me going "Am I that guy?" every episode lol.

—*Insecure* viewer

ACTIVATING BLACKNESS THROUGH DIASPORIC TELEVISUAL SPACES

On May 31, 2019, the Netflix original mini-series *When They See Us* entered homes and familiarized audiences with the "Central Park Five"—five Black and Brown Harlem teenagers who were arrested in 1989 for the rape and attempted murder of a twenty-eight-year-old female jogger (Gilbert 2019). Directed by the award-winning Ava DuVernay, the four-part series is a story of bias and subjectivity and gives voice and humanity to the now #ExoneratedFive, a luxury that was not afforded to the boys more than thirty years ago.

When They See Us sparked dynamic conversations on social media platforms about the Exonerated Five, about the prison industrial complex, and about how the criminalization of Blackness operates both culturally and politically. Following the release of the trailer, DuVernay released a series of tweets that initiated the project. Raymond Santana, one of the Exonerated Five, tweeted "@AVAETC what's your next film gonna be on?? #thecentralparkfive" (@santanaraymond, April 21, 2015). DuVernay credits this small social media engagement as the beginning of sociocultural vindication for the five wrongly convicted men and the continued vital commentary on criminal justice in marginalized communities. The success of the series and its immediate response is a microcosm of the power of authentic representation, social media awareness, and space making for African descendants.

Through critical conversations using 140-character tweets and clever hashtags, members of Twitter and Black Twitter in particular create awareness through cultural and political discourse on issues of white supremacy, media representation, and more that are underreported by the mainstream media. This chapter uses a particular example of fan activism to argue that Black Twitter functions as a digital African diasporic space for public communion. As by-products of the trans-Atlantic slave trade, African diasporic spaces such as Black Twitter extend Black communities beyond physical locality to construct intricate cultural landscapes for African descendants (Brock 2012, 530). This chapter examines television and social media data through the lens of Linked Fate Theory to explore two questions: first, how does Black Twitter operate as a digital African diasporic space by igniting critical discourse among users? Second, in what way does current Black representation problematize historical representations of Blackness? This chapter contends that Black Twitter, in this instance through its fan activist responses to Black cultural issues on television programming, spreads awareness of social issues such as toxic masculinity. By examining HBO's *Insecure* (2016–2021), I analyze online viewer engagement as it pertains to one male character, Lawrence. Furthermore, I argue that the series features authentic representation of Black males and produces therapeutic exchanges among fans who respond to Lawrence's representation of Black masculinity. This fan activism demonstrates how Black Twitter provides a space for communal reframing of problematic representations of Black masculinity.

THE IMPORTANCE OF *INSECURE*

On October 9, 2016, HBO introduced mainstream culture to Issa Dee, Molly, Lawrence, and a host of other characters on the critically acclaimed comedy-drama series *Insecure*. Created by Issa Rae and Larry Wilmore, the comedy-drama chronicles protagonist Issa Dee (Issa Rae) through her everyday Black millennial experiences in Inglewood, California. Audience members witness Issa's personal and professional conflicts at We Got Y'all, her white nonprofit workplace; her fascinating sisterhood with Molly (Yvonne Orji); and her contentious intimate-partner relationship with Lawrence (Jay Ellis).

The characterization of Lawrence is important in contrast to other contemporary projections of Black maleness on television. In the first episode ("Insecure as Fuck"), Lawrence enters the series with aspirations of breaking through the tech industry with his app "Woot-Woot" after navigating years of unemployment. Lawrence and Issa's relationship is on a downward trajectory that contributes to Issa's infidelity (Rae, Wilmore, and Matsoukas 2016). Resulting in the termination of their relationship, Issa's infidelity taps into cultural narratives surrounding male vulnerability, or lack thereof, as Lawrence journeys to regain a sense of himself, separate from Issa, in seasons two and three.

An analysis of viewer conversations online in response to Lawrence's storyline provides insight into communal engagement within the diaspora related to Black media representation and related cultural issues. Season one provided commentary on gendered expectations and male sensibility, which served as dominant focal points in fan-base discussions. For example, in reaction to a conversation among Issa, Molly, Kelli (Natasha Rothwell), and Tiffany (Amanda Seales) about Molly's reluctant nature to date sexually fluid men (Higgins 2016), one Twitter user expressed displeasure with Molly's homophobic reactions to her partner's same-gender sexual past by asserting that "folks need to be less judgmental of black men & masculinity." This comment illustrates how the show provides a nuanced depiction of Black masculinity that ignites conversation surrounding issues of Black sexuality and gender performance.

Insecure serves as a productive point of entry to engage in millennial conversations surrounding Blackness and maleness. With several nuanced characters, *Insecure* normalizes Blackness on televisual spaces and allows for a particular fan engagement that I investigate in this chapter through a specific focus on Lawrence. The first experience, "Death of a good guy," comes from the season one finale, "Broken as Fuck" (2016), when Lawrence terminates his and Issa's relationship. The next experience, "Bye, Lawrence, Bye," occurs during the off-season following Issa Rae's announcement of Lawrence's onscreen departure. Foregrounding both experiences in theory, I examine the complexities of Black televisual representation and how certain representations help construct space for Black communion. Both experiences portray pivotal moments in Lawrence's character development through his trajectory of pain, anger, accountability, healing, and joy—experiences that are revolutionary for television, central to Black life, and essential in reframing Black masculinity.

An evaluation of the ways *Insecure* sits at the intersection of popular culture, race, gender, and sexuality is imperative to the conversation of Black space making. With a close contextual examination of histories that expound on the construction of Black centered spaces, this chapter begins to unpack the way the viewing of Black bodies and experiences on television supports necessary commentary among Black viewers. I employ Michael Dawson's (1995) Linked Fate Theory to contextualize Black fan engagement as symptomatic of generations of public and private Black degradation. Through online responses on Twitter and Black Twitter in particular, Black fans engage in stories that mirror their lived experiences, critique the projection of the characters (e.g., Lawrence and his toxic maleness), and build community with other folks on digital spaces.

CONSTRUCTING DIASPORA THROUGH DIGITAL SPACES

Scholarship on media representation, spatial and temporal methodologies of space production, Black masculinity, and social activism provides useful ways to explore digital diasporic spaces. First, the concept of diaspora provides us with a framework to consider the significance of space production as a means of survival and community for displaced peoples. The concepts of Blackness in this chapter emerge from the trans-Atlantic slave trade as a preliminary point in the dissemination of Afro-descendants that frames an understanding of Black space making in the context of slavery, survival, and healing. As a result of imperialist white supremacist capitalist patriarchy, the trans-Atlantic slave trade transplanted 12.5 million African inhabitants across the Middle Passage to the New World (Gates 2014). The Middle Passage spatially marks the conception of the African Diaspora. Darker bodies in Brazil, the United States, Cuba, the United Kingdom, Haiti, and Canada are examples of the large-scale displacement of people stolen from their homeland and continued through space and cultural productions.

In contemporary culture, space building continues outside the confines of physical land. In the digital age, the detailing of realities subsists through social media platforms. For example, Farhad Manjoo (2010) explains the inception of Black Twitter: "[Black users] form tighter clusters on the network—they follow one another more readily, they retweet each other more often, and more of their posts are @-replies—posts directed at other users." Black Twitter operates as a subset of the social network that allows a wide range of Black strangers to converse on social issues and experiences that are shared collectively. From #BlackGirlMagic in 2013 to #ICantBreathe in 2014 to #SayHerName and #OscarsSoWhite in 2015 and beyond, Black users leverage social media platforms and construct diasporic spaces to advocate for the safety and liberation of individuals who share ancestral lineages. In this way, Black Twitter is a digital diasporic space for the production and critique of Blackness today.

BLACK AND TOXIC MASCULINITY

An analysis of how Blackness and masculinity are constructed through fictionalized television programming and its fan response allows for an exploration of how Black masculinity situates itself outside universal definitions of masculinity. Black masculinity functions differently in part due to established anti-Blackness within the inner workings of global and domestic institutions (Wallace 2002). Perceptions, expectations, and representations of Black masculinity shape narratives around Blackness and maleness (Jones 2016). Perceptions of Black men are influenced by their embellished representations in film, television, and everyday experiences; and these perceptions morph into expectations that are primarily defined by others (Alexander 2006). Therefore, this chapter discusses Black masculinity as a gendered construct, one established as a "perceptual and cosmological category in flux composed and validated by culturally particular behavioral tendencies that are consonant with personal, social, and communal expectations" (Jackson and Dangerfield 2003, 200). This particular construct interacts and merges with others, such as toxic masculinity.

Toxic masculinity arose as a buzzword to label cultural norms linked with traditional stereotypes of men as emotionally inept, heteronormative, sexual, and physical. The concept is at the center of several feminist social movements calling for the protection of women under the torment of traditional masculinity (e.g., #MasculinitySoFragile in 2013, #WhyIStayed in 2014, and #YouOkSis in 2014). At the same time, attention was drawn to the damage the norms associated with such a limited version of masculinity can do to men. The Good Men Project defines toxic masculinity as "a narrow and repressive description of manhood designating manhood as defined by violence, sex, status and aggression. It's the cultural ideal of manliness, where strength is everything while emotions are a weakness; where sex and brutality are yardsticks by which men are measured, while supposedly 'feminine' traits—which can range from emotional vulnerability to simply not being hypersexual—are the means by which your status as 'man' can be taken away" (O'Malley 2016). In his *New York Times* op-ed "The Boys Are Not All Right," Michael Ian Black (2018) argues that "too many boys are trapped in the same suffocating, outdated model of masculinity . . . Men feel isolated, confused and conflicted upon their natures. Many feel that the very qualities that used to define them—their strength, aggression and competitiveness—are no longer wanted or needed; many others never felt strong or aggressive or competitive to begin with." Aligned with these sentiments, a wave of publications went to press focusing on the so-called crisis of masculinity, such as *Stiffed: The Betrayal of American Men* (Faludi 2011) and *The End of Men: And the Rise of Women* (Rosin 2012). Although these concepts may be relatively new in mainstream dialogue, scholarship on the historical roots of patriarchy reveals its pervasiveness and consequences—especially for Black men.

In *We Real Cool: Black Men and Masculinity* (2004), bell hooks documented historically gendered trepidations that exist within diasporic spaces. hooks's concept of "plantation patriarchy" marks the proselytization of Black male bodies into the world of patriarchal masculinity. For hooks, plantation patriarchy represented the school of thought that evangelizes Black men into gender politics and constructs male-dominated hierarchies: "[Black men] had to be taught to equate their higher status as men with the right to dominate women; they had to be taught patriarchal masculinity . . . and it was this notion of patriarchy that educated Black men coming from slavery into freedom sought to mimic" (3–4). hooks contextualized the plantation as the birthplace of the kind of Black masculinity that is seen through everyday experiences, the kind experienced by characters in *Insecure*. Building on hooks—as well as other scholars who explore the intersections between Black masculinity and slavery/colonialism and its lasting consequences (Richardson 2007; Orelus 2009)—this chapter argues that toxic masculinity is a by-product of patriarchy that factors heavily into how Black men learn how to be men.

BLACK COMMUNAL TELEVISUAL EXPERIENCES

One place where people take up conversations about Black masculinity is on Black Twitter. Whether users are tweeting about the BET Awards or Beyoncé's *Lemonade*, Black Twitter users generate space for themselves and others to converse in a digital diaspora. Furthermore, this digital diaspora has emotional benefits. While not addressing masculinity specifically, Apryl Williams and Vanessa Gonlin (2017) argue that Black Twitter is a constructed space for healing. Users engage in various acts to accomplish this, such as validating shared experiences, showing empathy, and offering suggestions on particular issues. Williams and Gonlin conduct an analysis of televisual representation of Black womanhood and responding fan-viewing practices on Shonda Rhimes's *How to Get Away with Murder* (2014–2020). They find that communal viewing of television shows supports the digital discourse on Black Twitter that navigates the cultural history of Black womanhood and supports the intergenerational transfer of knowledge (985). These ethnic, communal interactions within diasporic spaces illuminate entrenched memories that standardize the experiences of Black people in a world constructed on the deprivation and erasure of African decedents. Herman Gray (1995, 402) also alludes to this notion of collective memories through televisual viewing of Blackness and masculinities when he says "contemporary images of Black masculinity continue to challenge hegemonic constructions of whiteness even as they rewrite and reproduce forms of patriarchal authority." The abovementioned scholarship suggests that imagery of Blackness (re)shapes public perception of ethnic/gendered groups displayed in media and that by responding to these representations, social media users can challenge and even rewrite them.

LINKED FATE THEORY: INTERSECTING ENTERTAINMENT AND FAN ACTIVISM

To examine the connectedness of what the World Bank (2012) calculates as 39 million North American, 113 million Latin American, 13.6 million Caribbean, and 3.5 million European members of the African Diaspora, I employ a theoretical framework that illuminates the interconnected experiences of people of African descent. Linked Fate Theory provides a framework to explore digital diasporic spaces and the ways these spaces amplify communal interactions. Dawson argues that linked fate "represents a stage of identification that starts with a feeling of closeness to others who identify with the group label and involves the acceptance of the belief that individual life chances are inextricably tied to the group as a whole" (quoted in Simien 2005, 529). Scholars have started to consider how specific aspects of identity, such as gender and race, are shaped in this way as individuals take up these shared, collective understandings of their individual lives in relation to the group (2005). Linked Fate Theory therefore reveals how Black lived experiences, notwithstanding geographic limitations, transcend temporality and play out in interesting ways in the contemporary digital landscape.

Digital activism depends on this ability of the communication it creates to transcend time and space. Members of the diaspora have the unrelenting responsibility of being support systems regardless of nation-state heritage. Consider how the American Black liberation movement, #BlackLivesMatter, has echoed globally, inspiring Black folks in Brazil, for example, to initiate #VidasNegrasImportam (Dillon 2016). The philological and political nature of #BlackLivesMatter electrified "digital technology [and] has been a game changer in terms of linking individual experiences to a collective struggle. Social media, such as Facebook, has been boiling over with posts, videos, with conversations that we haven't seen before" (2016). Solidarity work is a direct reflection of linked fate; and in the wake of oppression, space building subsists for personal well-being in conjunction with the well-being of the entire Black racial group.

While locality, language, and other aspects of culture separate the descendants of the enslaved, the intrinsic collectivity is strengthened through the digital diaspora that is furthered through interaction with popular culture. Informed by the concepts of Linked Fate Theory and the digital diaspora, this chapter analyzes examples of Lawrence's Black masculinity and resulting fan tweets. The fan responses show the ways users are not only unpacking the character's issues but are also incorporating their own histories with male vulnerability to spread awareness and improve the conversation surrounding Black and toxic masculinity.

BROKEN AS FUCK AND THE "DEATH OF THE GOOD GUY"

This chapter examines HBO's *Insecure* to illustrate how this show and its fan responses function as a digital diaspora. Viewer tweets from specific junctures within the show were collected through Twitter's Advanced Search function, which allows tweets containing specific hashtags to be collected from a specific date range, such as the live airing of a television episode. This study's first set of collected data stems from *Insecure*'s "Broken as Fuck," which first aired on November 27, 2016, ending a season full of exhilaration showing the complex experiences of young folks of color. The tweets from this episode selected for close analysis focus on the closing scene wherein Issa Dee (Issa Rae) returns home from a weekend vacation with her girlfriends to discover that Lawrence had evacuated their apartment. As Issa discovers Lawrence's departure, a camera cut occurs showcasing Lawrence having sex with Tasha (Dominique Perry), the bank teller he had previously resisted due to his relationship with Issa (Rae and Matsoukas 2016). This led to the inception of a digital support group that defended Lawrence and his behavior. The hashtag adopted by this group stemmed from a single tweet by @JeffJSays (2016): "#LawrenceHive #InsecureHBO." With nine likes and forty-two retweets, this tweet marked the inauguration of #LawrenceHive.

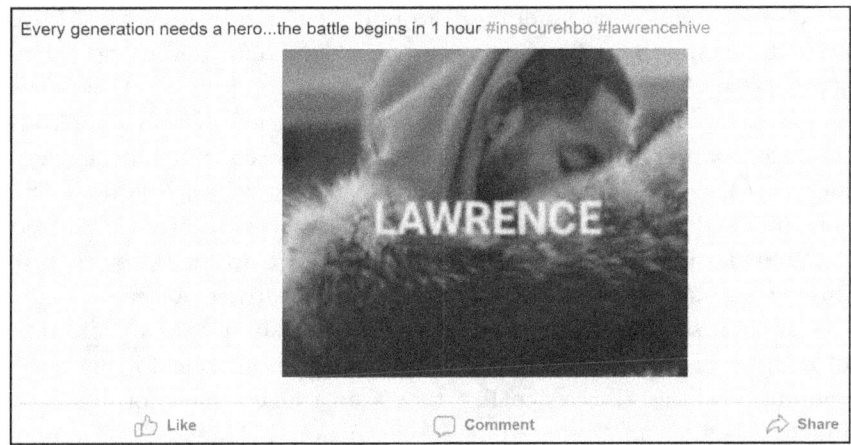

Figure 9.1. A meme in which Lawrence is profiled as Beyoncé's Lemonade *advertisement*

The closing scene of this episode reflects a history of unhealthy tactics that men, and not only Black men, engage in to cope in situations of emotional harm. Lawrence weaponized sex to heal his pain—a tactic scholars find common when discussing toxic practices of masculinity. Devices for reaffirming masculinity have been shown to be maladaptive in nature, with a number of destructive consequences (Smith et al. 2015, 161). While audiences were not yet privy to the disparaging consequences revealed in seasons two and three surrounding Lawrence's sexual escapades, #LawrenceHive united in support of the fictional character moving on so quickly to his next female companion.

The hashtag #LawrenceHive commenced out of collective empathy with the character's situation and exploits, and it materialized through comedic tweets. Given the nature of the television show, one would expect the response to be comedic, like the example shown in figure 9.1 with Lawrence profiled as Beyoncé on her *Lemonade* album advertisement. While many tweets were humorous, other tweets expressed feeling connected Lawrence and rejoiced in his sexual payback. For example, one user defended Lawrence by writing, "Issa dissed his dreams, still sleeping with [the person] she cheated on him with, and dissed him going through mental health issues. Crazy #InsecureHBO #LawrenceHive." At the heart of the tweets, even the comedic ones, is a sense of connectedness and vulnerability that accentuates prevailing gender politics within diasporic spaces. This theme of connectedness and collective empathy showcases the ways the Linked Fate Theory can be used to explain the ways viewers take up these hashtags.

Another theme that emerges is around cheating. In the age of toxic masculinity, men and Black men in particular often look to rid themselves of the historical player archetype (Armstrong 2016). A player is an emotionally inept man who engages in sexual activity with numerous individuals while having a committed partner. Lawrence's character deviates from the player archetype and appears to resonate with viewers. The solidarity in the tweets indicates the ways some male viewers may have also experienced infidelity. Users' reactions validate Lawrence's sexual promiscuity as a symptom of the pain caused by his partner's betrayal. While the tweeted solidarity supports the argument that *Insecure*'s projection of realistic Black characters produces digital communities for diasporic communion, the #LawrenceHive tweets do suggest some problematic practices. Often, male users praised the fictional character's promiscuous behavior without acknowledging the historical pattern of Black men harming themselves in the name of sexual exploration and patriarchy (hooks 2004, 10). The support of #LawrenceHive suggests that levels of vulnerability and complexity are still being learned among the fan base.

The conversation surrounding Lawrence, "death of the good guy," and fan interaction is a peculiar one, where there are many pieces that display users' ability to generate communal support and freedom of expression by discussing the fictional character. Whereas users utilizing the #LawrenceHive hashtag showcase solidarity around Lawrence's toxic male behavior following Issa's infidelity, users using the official #InsecureHBO hashtag show more variance in opinions about Lawrence's behavior. In the tweets in figure 9.2, users demonstrate communal discourse surrounding Lawrence's character and the significance of his behavior in connection with the transgenerational gender performance of Black men.

These tweets support the previous argument in which representations of Blackness facilitate therapeutic discourse surrounding issues within the diasporic community. Viewers name his behavior and their different reactions to further diasporic discourse. Unlike #LawrenceHive users, users outside "the hive" problematize his behavior within the conversation of Black masculinity and a theme of accountability. While Lawrence is suffering, it does not absolve him of his problematic and harmful behavior. Navigating Lawrence's "good guy gone bad" journey, Twitter users demonstrate vulnerability when they connect to the actions of a fictional character as if they were their own. If Linked Fate Theory explains this connectiveness in part, the actions it can prompt are worth considering. This connection is further explored through the scope of fan activism and the televisual experience through "Bye, Lawrence, Bye."

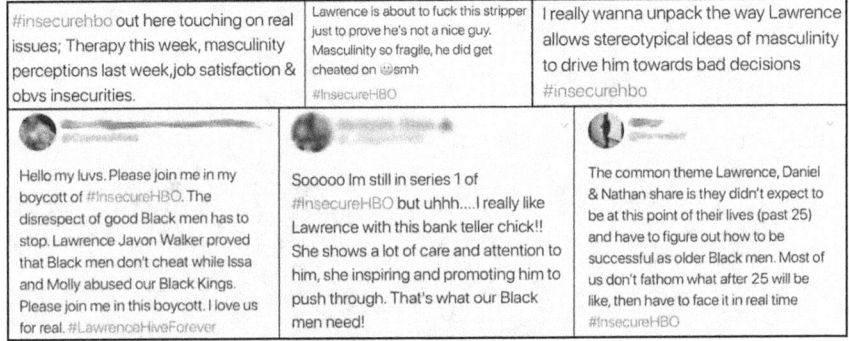

Figure 9.2. Examples of tweets unpacking Black masculinity through Lawrence's performance

BYE, LAWRENCE: FAN ACTIVISM AND #LAWRENCEHIVE

Following two successful seasons, *Insecure* announced that season three would tackle Black masculinity and its impact on Black women (Bennett 2018). Concurrently, an announcement was made that Lawrence Walker would not appear in the 2018 season. Issa Rae explained the decision behind Lawrence's departure in an interview, avowing that "we want to stay as true to life as possible . . . You never see the exes again. And it's okay! You gotta explore life without Lawrence" (quoted in Ferber 2018). Following the announcement, #LawrenceHive members generated a petition to bring their "leader" back to television screens. The petition proclaims, "Over the past two seasons, Jay Ellis has portrayed the conflicted and realistic ways Lawrence has dealt with difficult and rarely explored issues for men such as infidelity, male friendship, depression, and toxic masculinity" (Bennett 2018). With over 10,000 supporters adding their name to the petition, #LawrenceHive mobilized and began to employ tactics of fan activism.

To understand the work of the users operating under #LawrenceHive as activism, one must understand the diverse practices employed in fan activism. Henry Jenkins (2012) defines fan activism thus: "Forms of civic engagement and political participation that emerge from within fan culture itself, often in response to the shared interests of fans, often conducted through the infrastructure of existing fan practices and relationships, and often framed through metaphors drawn from popular and participatory culture." Traditionally, fan activists assemble to save television shows from cancellation, as seen with *Star Trek* in the 1960s with letter writing campaigns (Earl and Kimport 2009, 221). Fan activism works, as seen with #LawrenceHive, in large part due to the connectivity that emerges as fans define their shared interests and shape their public

Figure 9.3. #LawrenceHive members protesting the absence of Lawrence from the season three premiere

status (Jenkins 1992). #LawrenceHive members watched as season three premiered on August 18, 2018, and used their comedic genius to construct memes and tweets as modes of protest for Lawrence's absence. Applying comedy once more, #LawrenceHive members expressed their disdain for the removal of their favorite character by gathering together and dressing in Lawrence's work uniform (see figure 9.3). Such devotion to the character shows how much Lawrence represents and resonates with the fan base.

Lawrence's journey, although complex, roused #LawrenceHive members due in large part to the authenticity of the character. Figure 9.4 shows a range of responses in support of Lawrence and what he represents. The presentation of Lawrence in season one (depressed, jobless, emotionally harmed in his relationship) and his upward trajectory in season two (new employment in the tech field, new apartment, and new exploration of intimate partners) ignited an emotional response and investment from viewers, strengthened by a shared connectivity. The support garnered by *Insecure* viewers in general and #LawrenceHive members in particular shows how marginalized groups reconstruct and safeguard the way they are seen in the world. *Insecure* enthusiasts showed the cultural significance of viewing non-exceptional Black bodies on television for normalizing the everyday humanity of Black people. For example, the depiction of Lawrence projects a regular Black man with

That #LawrenceHive depression with no real job is real...... I've been there befo.... Pride be sooo crushedddd!	i have my issues with the character but i really hope lawrence gets a strong plot that deals with his mental heath in the next season of insecure. i don't feel like i see enough representation for mentally ill black folks.	Good black men always have a struggle, I been thru it, we all have. We good #LawrenceHive
I personally don't want Lawrence back because of his relationship with Issa. I want him back because he's the first time I've seen representation of a black male in the tech industry and I relate to him on a different level. So let's get him a spin-off lol #InsecureHBO	The level of nuance vulnerability, toxic masculinity, and black woman savorship that occurred in this episode is astounding! I'm so happy it ends with Daniel heeding Issa's advice. It also goes to show why he isn't as trash as Lawrence is. #InsecureHBO	Seems as if #LawrenceHive may be wondering when he will have his spinoff. He seemed to be an interesting character that clearly connected to a couch surfing collective who may be on the cusp of getting it together... but that doesn't seem like it will happen.

Figure 9.4. Examples of Black Twitter users supporting Lawrence and unpacking masculinity

dreams and aspirations. Not a basketball player, lawyer, musician, or drug dealer, he was a college graduate who struggled to find himself and a job that supported his dreams. His supporters showed that Lawrence wasn't just a character; he was a representative of Black boys who attend college with dreams of obtaining degrees and careers and are met with the harsh realities of the world following college (Cummings 2018). Furthermore, the complexities of his character allow Black men to learn and unlearn from his behaviors, which represent so many.

Linked Fate Theory provides a useful framework for examining the viewer's response to Lawrence and his absence at the beginning of season three. Linked Fate Theory characterizes a juncture of identification that activates a feeling of closeness to others who identify with the group label and involves the acceptance of the belief that individual life chances are interconnected to a collective (Dawson 1995; Simien 2005). A number of the tweets in figure 9.4 demonstrate users expressing a personal connection to Lawrence through their own lived experiences and aspirations. One user noted that his relation to Lawrence as a Black man in the tech industry was significant to see on television. Users, whether enacting comedy or engaging in serious discourse, recognize the significance of Black representation; the brief removal of Lawrence saw Black men mobilize, emphasizing their desire to be seen, heard, and loved on national television.

CONCLUSION

This chapter contends that *Insecure* and its fan fiction responses on social media created a diasporic space that facilitates strangers creating community with one another. As I have shown, Black Twitter users employ the #LawrenceHive hashtag as a method of constructing diasporic space to engage in conversations surrounding Black representation, particularly about the current state of Black masculinity. The sample tweets suggest that realistic portrayals of characters resonate with viewers and that when there is a threat to that character (e.g., Lawrence's removal from the series), viewers utilize the digital diasporic space to express collective concern.

Employing digital spaces provides the infrastructure for connection with people through shared experiences and interests. Lawrence's portrayal evokes a complexity of emotions for users experiencing similar trials as the fictional character. A level of vulnerability is shown through male participation in digital diasporic spaces as it relates to Lawrence. As emphasized with the use of comedy as a coping mechanism and with the expressions of support, having a space to showcase feelings for men is revolutionary. While some men who navigate the #LawrenceHive tag could benefit from further self-reflection and accountability, many users connect the issues related to Lawrence and fan reactions to toxic practices of masculinity as ways to reframe the problematic representations of Black masculinity.

To consider the broader implications of this work of *Insecure* and Black Twitter users in the realm of activism, researchers should examine how digital diasporic spaces are created in other areas. For example, further research should examine fan activist responses to other Black characters on TV and film across a range of genres. Researchers can study other digital sites as well; beyond Twitter, what other digital communities are holding space for Black men to unlearn their toxic practices of masculinity? Finally, examinations of other media, such as podcasts, would also assist in the exploration of Black cultural space making and how fan activism facilitates the reframing of problematic representations of Black masculinity.

REFERENCES

Alexander, Bryant Keith. 2006. *Performing Black Masculinity: Race, Culture, and Queer Identity.* New York: Rowman and Littlefield.

Armstrong, Olivia. 2016. "Issa Rae on Her Leap to TV, Double Standards and Friendship Goals." HBO. https://www.hbo.com/insecure/season-01/8-broken-as-f-k/issa-rae-on-her-leap-to-tv-double-standards-and-friendship-goals.

Bennett, Jessica. 2018. " 'Insecure' Fans Start Petition to Bring Back Jay Ellis' Character, Lawrence." *Ebony*, July 31. https://www.ebony.com/entertainment/insecure-fans-start-petition-to-bring-back-jay-ellis-character-lawrence/.

Black, Michael Ian. 2018. "The Boys Are Not All Right." *New York Times*, February 21. https://www.nytimes.com/2018/02/21/opinion/boys-violence-shootings-guns.html?auth=login-google.

Brock, André. 2012. "From the Blackhand Side: Twitter as a Cultural Conversation." *Journal of Broadcasting and Electronic Media* 56: 529–549.

Cummings, Jozen. 2018. "Bye Lawrence: Why Insecure Just Doesn't Need Him." *The Root*, August 6. https://verysmartbrothas.theroot.com/bye-lawrence-why-insecure-just-doesnt-need-him-anymor-1828131860.

Dawson, Michael. 1995. *Behind the Mule: Race and Class in African-American Politics*. Princeton, NJ: Princeton University Press.

Dillon, Lessa. 2016. "Brazil's New Black Power Movement." *The Root*, August 8. https://www.theroot.com/brazil-s-new-black-power-movement-1790856322.

Earl, Jennifer, and Katrina Kimport. 2009. "Movement Societies and Digital Protest: Fan Activism and Other Nonpolitical Protest Online." *Sociological Theory* 27 (3): 220–243.

Faludi, Susan. 2011. *Stiffed: The Betrayal of American Men*. New York: HarperCollins.

Ferber, Taylor. 2018. "Issa Rae Confirms Insecure Season 3 Is Taking a Break from Lawrence." *Vulture*, July 23. https://www.vulture.com/2018/07/issa-rae-insecure-season-3-is-taking-a-break-from-lawrence.html.

Gates, Henry L. 2014. "How Many Slaves Landed in the US?" *The Root*, January 6. https://www.theroot.com/how-many-slaves-landed-in-the-us-1790873989.

Gilbert, Sophie. 2019. "Ava DuVernay Does True Crime Differently in When They See Us." *The Atlantic*, May 29. https://www.theatlantic.com/entertainment/archive/.2019/05/when-they-see-us-review-Netflix/590371/.

Gray, Herman. 1995. "Black Masculinity and Visual Culture." *Callaloo* 18 (2): 401–405.

Higgins, Jonathan P. 2016. "Insecure Highlights the Double Standard in Sexual Fluidity." *The Root*, November 16. https://www.theroot.com/insecure-highlights-the-double-standard-of-sexual-fluid-1790857749.

hooks, bell. 2004. *We Real Cool: Black Men and Masculinity*. New York: Routledge.

Jackson, Ronald L., and Celnisha L. Dangerfield. 2003. "Defining Black Masculinity as Cultural Property: An Identity Negotiation Paradigm." In *African American Communication and Identities: Essential Readings*, edited by Ronald L. Jackson, 197–207. Thousand Oaks, CA: Sage.

Jenkins, Henry. 1992. *Textual Poachers: Television Fans and Participatory Culture*. New York: Routledge.

Jenkins, Henry. 2012. "'Cultural Acupuncture': Fan Activism and the Harry Potter Alliance." *Transformative Works and Cultures* 10. https://journal.transformativeworks.org/index.php/twc/article/view/305/259.

Jones, Matthew. 2016. "Defining Black Masculinity: Defining Ourselves by Ourselves." *Odyssey Online*. https://www.theodysseyonline.com/defining-black-masculinity.

Manjoo, Farhad. 2010. "How Black People Use Twitter, The Latest Research on Race and Microblogging." *Slate*, August 10. https://slate.com/technology/2010/08/how-black-people-use-twitter.html.

O'Malley, Harris. 2016. "The Difference between Toxic Masculinity and Being a Man." *Good Men Project*. https://goodmenproject.com/featured-content/the-difference-between-toxic-masculinity-and-being-a-man-dg/.

Orelus, Pierre. 2009. *The Agony of Masculinity: Race, Gender, and Education in the "New" Racism and Patriarchy*. New York: Peter Lang.

Rae, Issa, and Melina Matsoukas. 2016. "Broken as Fuck." In *Insecure*, produced by Issa Rae. Los Angeles: HBO Entertainment.

Rae, Issa, Larry Wilmore, and Melina Matsoukas. 2016. "Insecure as Fuck." In *Insecure*, produced by Issa Rae. Los Angeles: HBO Entertainment.

Richardson, Riché. 2007. *Black Masculinity and the U.S. South: From Uncle Tom to Gangsta*. Athens: University of Georgia Press.

Rosin, Hanna. 2012. *The End of Men: And the Rise of Women*. New York: Riverhead.

Simien, Evelyn. 2005. "Race, Gender, and Linked Fate." *Journal of Black Studies* 35 (5): 529–550.

Smith, Rachel M., Dominic J. Parrott, Kevin M. Swartout, and Adra T. Tharp. 2015. "Deconstructing Hegemonic Masculinity: The Roles of Antifemininity, Subordination to Women, and Sexual Dominance in Men's Perpetration of Sexual Aggression." *Psychology of Men and Masculinity* 16 (2): 160–169.

Wallace, Maurice O. 2002. *Constructing the Black Masculine.* Durham, NC: Duke University Press.

Williams, Apryl, and Vanessa Gonlin. 2017. "I Got All My Sisters with Me (on Black Twitter): Second Screening of How to Get Away with Murder as a Discourse on Black Womanhood." *Information, Communication and Society* 20 (7): 984–1004.

World Bank. 2012. "African Diaspora FAQ." https://siteresources.worldbank.org/INTDIASPORA/Resources/AFR_Diaspora_FAQ.pdf.

SECTION IV

Interruptions and Interpretations of Digital Activism

10

MEME WARFARE AND FAKE HASHTAG ACTIVISM
4chan's Alt-right Trolling Culture

Jeffrey J. Hall

In late October 2016, Donald Trump's presidential campaign appeared to be in serious trouble. A scandalous audiotape of Trump bragging about sexually assaulting women leaked to the media, and polling data indicated that his chances at victory were slipping away. As some mainstream Republican politicians distanced themselves from their party's candidate, a legion of anonymous internet users continued to vigorously fight for the man they referred to as "God Emperor Trump." Many of these users were members of the so-called alt-right. In the final twelve days of the election campaign, they worked together to fabricate and spread images meant to fool people into believing that Hillary Clinton was preparing for war with Russia and wanted to send American women to the battlefields of this war-to-be. Combining the hashtags #DraftOurDaughters and #FightForHer with the legitimate Clinton campaign hashtag #ImWithHer, alt-right netizens successfully made one of their fake Clinton slogans a trending hashtag on Twitter. Although the images were often crude and could easily be debunked through a simple Google search, mainstream news sources such as the *Washington Post* made a point of warning readers that "#DraftOurDaughters is an alt-right meme, not a Clinton campaign initiative," noting that "trending hashtags have a tendency to be noticed and misunderstood, particularly in this campaign season" (Ohlheiser 2016).

In the aftermath of Donald Trump's surprising election victory, there has been increasing attention to the use of Twitter accounts to derail or fabricate hashtag activism. Recent works of scholarship have focused on how automated Twitter accounts ("bots"), with ties to Russian state intelligence agencies, have engaged in hashtag activism (Al-Rawi, Groshek, and Zhang 2018; Badawy, Ferrara, and Lerman 2018; Badawy, Lerman, and Ferrara 2018; Kim et al. 2019). For example, one 2018 paper used data from nearly 3,000 suspected Russian Twitter bot accounts to find patterns of behavior, including the "resetting" of accounts to take on several false identities over time (Zannettou et al. 2018). Another study noted how suspected Russian bot accounts have "promoted discord" with disingenuous messages posted under vaccine-related Twitter hashtags (Broniatowski et al. 2018). Such works, while important, do not address another significant aspect of hashtag trolling and disinformation campaigns: non-state actors on Twitter who proactively create and engage in such activities without direction from foreign governments.

The above-mentioned #DraftOurDaughters hashtag campaign, like many other pro-Trump memes and fake news stories of the 2016 campaign, may have been spread with the help of Russian Twitter bots, but there is no evidence that it originated in a foreign intelligence agency. A recent study has documented the process through which the hashtag originated on the Politically Incorrect (/pol/) forum of the website 4chan (4chan.org) and was rapidly deployed across the internet in a "swarm" of posts on mainstream social media sites including Twitter and Facebook (Wall and Mitew 2018). While it is clear that such activities originate on forums like 4chan, there is a limited understanding of who the anonymous participants are and what motivates their actions.

This chapter, which is based on ethnographic research I conducted between mid-2016 and late 2018, explores how members of 4chan's subculture participated in Twitter trolling and political meme making during and after the election of Donald Trump. Through observation of forum threads and interviews with users of the /pol/ board, I found that users had mixed political motivations for their actions—with some holding conservative or alt-right political views, while others were ambivalent about political ideologies. The only common thread that seemed to tie them together was a shared belief in the humor and entertainment value of the disruption and offense they believed their actions brought about in American society. Such a belief was deeply tied to 4chan's long-standing culture of anti-mainstream trolling that openly embraced virtually all forms of offensive expression, including racist, homophobic, and misogynistic speech. In 2016, 4chan users perceived much of the political left as openly hostile to 4chan's culture of "freedom." Thus, despite mixed political views on other issues, their actions almost exclusively sought to sow chaos within left-leaning hashtag activist movements, something that arguably benefited Donald Trump and the political right. The existence of such users also raises serious questions about the use of Twitter as an organizing tool for political movements.

BACKGROUND: 4CHAN'S TROLLING CULTURE AND PRE-2016 ACTIVISM

The evolution of 4chan's subculture impacted my ethnographic research. Founded in 2003 as a discussion board for Japanese manga and anime, 4chan grew into an extremely popular website for discussions of a wide range of topics, including sports, business, video games, photography, and cuisine. A key feature of 4chan is that it allows users to post without requiring accounts or user names, meaning that almost all posts on the site appear under the shared name "Anonymous." In the years prior to the 2016 election, 4chan's anonymous user base was well-known as a source of non-political memes, such as Lolcats (humorous combinations of cat photos and text) and Rickrolling (the act of tricking people into clicking links to a Rick Astley music video) (Feinberg 2013).

Most pre-2016 research on 4chan focused on the emergence of an anonymous culture in which trickery and trolling were employed for a variety of motivations. One such motivation, noted by Jonathan Bishop (2014), was the maleficent sense of amusement one gets when offending other people ("the lulz"). A notable example of this was "RIP trolling," the act of using fake Facebook accounts to post offensive messages on pages memorializing recently deceased people. In an ethnographic study of internet users who engaged in RIP trolling, Whitney Phillips (2015, 84) argued that although their posts often offended grieving family members, the "vast majority of trolls' RIP energies" were directed at so-called grief tourists, people who "had no real-life connecting to the victim and who, according to trolls, could not possibly be in mourning." In this context, Phillips depicts such trolling as not merely mean-spirited spreading of grief and offense but also as a form of attack on the "fake" mourners who engaged in memorial page "tourism" (84).

The trolls of 4chan have also been depicted as activists fighting against censorship and corporate power. In 2013, Gabriella Coleman (2013, 212) described the 2008 hacktivist campaign against the Church of Scientology as a "political awakening" of 4chan's anonymous users, noting that their culture of "trolling had thus given birth to an earnest activist endeavor, as if Anonymous had emerged from its online sanctuary and set out to improve the world." Based on observations of several 4chan-affiliated hacker groups who fought against Scientology, mainstream media outlets, and corporations, Coleman argued for the existence of "some unifying ideals" and "a moral sensibility" among the anonymous activists, which include "the brazen spirit of lulz and its anti-celebrity ethic, whereby the accumulation of individual public power and prestige is cast in a negative light" (226). Similarly, Lee Knuttila

(2011) argued that the campaign against Scientology "marked the start of many highly organized, collaborative actions and a departure from the early, more childish, lulz." In these kinds of studies, hacker activists who emerged from 4chan were presented as similar to WikiLeaks, "akin to Robin Hood, resisting the powers that be who threaten the desire to keep the Internet free" (Wong and Brown 2013, 1015).

Most pre-2016 works, as well as some more recent studies on 4chan, did not place particular emphasis on something that had existed on the site from its very beginnings: rampant racism, misogyny, and hate. As a site that allows users to post anonymously, there is virtually zero chance that a 4chan user will face any trouble when posting racist, misogynistic, or other speech that is not illegal under US law. The question of whether to take such posts at face value—as a reflection of the true views of users and the overall culture of the site—has proved challenging to researchers. Vyshali Mannivannan (2014, 109), an often cited researcher on early 4chan board culture, argued that many of the offensive posts on the site represented "strategically targeted" trolling of perceived new users based on "exposed identity aspects." This meant that existing 4chan users sought to protect their anti-mainstream subculture by making racist or misogynistic posts that would drive away easily offended newcomers, even if such posts did not necessarily reflect honestly held views of race, gender, or politics. danah boyd (2010), who grew up within a hacker community and believed 4chan had a similar anti-mainstream culture, argued that people should reject certain acts by 4chan users but also "never take the internets too seriously." Ryan M. Milner (2016, 123) noted in detail some of the hateful posts and memes on 4chan but likewise downplayed their importance by stating that "those boards are not the only participatory media collectives antagonizing identities outside of the white, male centrality." As will be shown later in this chapter, this often overlooked and downplayed feature of 4chan's culture was seen as something worth preserving and helped motivate its targeting of left-leaning hashtag activist movements.

4CHAN AND THE ALT-RIGHT

In the years leading up to the 2016 election, significant changes occurred on 4chan that required a reconsideration of whether its racism, misogyny, and hate were serious or worthy of special attention. From the time of 4chan's creation, its Random board (/b/) had been its most popular section, and all of the above-mentioned academic articles accordingly focused on /b/. However, at some point between 2014 and 2016, the

Politically Incorrect board (/pol/) surpassed /b/ and became the site's most active section.[1] According to users of the site, 4chan's administrators created /pol/ in 2011 as a place to "quarantine" excessive hate. Until then, users of various boards had complained about there being too many racist and offensive posts, but due to a policy of preserving a certain degree of free expression, 4chan administrators directed users with extreme viewpoints to a new board instead of completely banning their opinions. The intent may have been to isolate and limit such views, but /pol/ gradually increased in popularity. Due to this popularity and the supremacist ideology expressed in some of its posts, many of its users like to claim that the rest of 4chan's boards are the actual "quarantine" boards, and /pol/ is the true center of 4chan.

Both liberal and conservative media observers of internet activities during the 2016 election came to see 4chan and its /pol/ board as a hub of the alt-right, an internet-based "alternative right" movement that has been characterized as holding deeply racist and misogynistic views of the world (Blades 2016; Bokhari and Yiannopoulos 2016). One notable academic study of this movement, George Hawley's (2017) *Making Sense of the Alt-Right*, focuses on white nationalist propagandists and thought leaders, summarizing the views of those who created the term *alt-right*. Like Hawley, Angela Nagle's *Kill All Normies* (2017, 34, 67), a popular nonfiction book that delves into the online culture wars that have influenced offline politics in the United States, describes alt-right 4chan users as a dangerous subculture of "online racist, foul-mouthed, porn-loving nihilists" who revere anti-moral and anti-liberal transgression. Pointing to examples of offline violence by /pol/ users, Nagle argues that the "anti-PC taboo-breaking culture of 4chan is not just 'for the lulz' " (26). However, the extent to which actual members of this mostly anonymous movement subscribe to such beliefs is unclear. In describing the alt-right's ties to internet trolling culture, Hawley (2017, 74–75) highlights instances in which interviewees "pranked" journalists by intentionally answering queries with "total nonsense."

From the above, it is apparent that a significant gap exists in the understanding of 4chan and its /pol/ board. The anonymous users who post on /pol/ every day do not normally speak to the media or academics; nor do they normally make themselves known offline. Writings on their ideological beliefs, as well as their motivation to participate in hashtag trolling/activism, have been based largely on speculation. My research fills this gap by supplementing online observation with interview data from /pol/ users.

METHODS

My analysis of the beliefs and motivations of 4chan users is based on data collected through online ethnographic fieldwork (netnography) of 4chan's /pol/ board conducted between March 2016 and December 2017, influenced by previous research on 4chan board culture by Asaf Nissenbaum and Limor Shifman (2017), who drew on the work of Robert V. Kozinets (2002). This was combined with data from semi-structured interviews conducted between 2016 and 2018 with fifteen subjects who identified themselves as regular users of 4chan's /pol/ board. The first interview subject, whom I had known since the 2000s and whose social media posts took a decidedly pro-Trump turn in 2016, introduced two of his online friends who were willing to participate in interviews; subsequent interview subjects were found through chain referrals. Chain referrals, also known as snowball sampling, are an imperfect means of gathering interview data, as noted by scholars such as Patrick Biernacki and Dan Waldorf (1981). Nonetheless, given the lack of research data on alt-right internet users and the difficulty in getting any of them to speak to researchers, this limited sample can still offer valuable insights into their subculture and its beliefs. I supplemented the interviews with background observations from a private chat group involving several of the interview subjects as well as a dozen internet users who identified themselves as part of 4chan's /pol/ subculture.[2]

Most of the subjects were extremely reluctant to be interviewed, both because they perceived academia as an untrustworthy left-leaning institution and because they feared the impact of being outed as part of a group viewed by mainstream society as racist extremists. While several potential subjects outright refused to be interviewed, the individuals quoted in this chapter were convinced to participate after being assured that their anonymity would be protected because my research was conducted under ethical guidelines that conformed to the international norm which holds that anonymity should be given to research sites, as well as to the individuals involved in that research (Walford 2005). Accordingly, all research subjects are quoted under pseudonyms and descriptions of them are limited to protect their anonymity.

Eight of the interviews were conducted in person, while the remaining seven were conducted online using Skype. As the alt-right has sometimes been characterized in generational, ethnic, or socioeconomic terms, it may be relevant to state some general data on the research subjects. All subjects were male, with age ranges 20–25 (6), 26–31 (4), 32–36 (3), and 37–42 (2). Nine of the men identified themselves ethnically as "White," while two identified as "East Asian," one as "Mixed White/East Asian," one as "Hispanic," one as "Southeast Asian," and one as "South Asian." Eleven of the men were college graduates, two were college students, and two were high school graduates. Four of the men were married, with children. Only one man, a college graduate in his early twenties, described himself as unemployed.

For the purposes of this volume, analysis will focus on views of and motivations for participation in alt-right hashtag activism. The analysis is divided into two sections—first, the nature of the activism and second, the motivations for participating in or supporting 4chan-based hashtag campaigns.

TROLLING AND SPREADING CHAOS ON TWITTER

Among the 4chan users I interviewed, two men were active in creating and operating fake Twitter profiles, but every research subject participated in /pol/ discussion threads that promoted alt-right attempts to disrupt and derail activist hashtags.

One interview subject, "Brad" (White, Male, 39, High School Graduate), stood out for his active role in Twitter hashtag trolling. His methods involved a remarkable degree of preparation and commitment and were aimed at convincing other Twitter users that his online personas were who they claimed to be. Many of Brad's activities centered on deceiving people discussing the #BlackLivesMatter (BLM) hashtag, whose movement he perceived as defending criminals and promoting "anti-white racism." He would start by monitoring recent posts under the hashtag and identifying accounts he believed represented real African American Twitter users who supported the BLM movement. Next, among those people, he would center on users who included links to public Facebook profiles in their Twitter profiles and seemed to post often about their daily lives. Using the information found in their public tweets and Facebook posts, Brad would craft two or three fake Twitter personas—all of whom claimed to live in the same city and share the ethnic identity of his targets: "You can creep into communities like that if people's Facebook profiles aren't private . . . Then use Google maps [sic] to kind of talk about the area people live [in] and make them trust you more. –Brad." Brad's trolling involved days of preparation, over the course of which he would make the imaginary lives of his fake Twitter personas appear as real as possible. When successful, his targets would begin to treat his fake Twitter accounts as real members of their local community. At this point, Brad would gradually steer his accounts toward discussions of the BLM movement. Using two or more fake Twitter accounts, he would lead his targets to believe an argument was taking place. His fake Twitter personas would post "intentionally stupid" or false arguments and memes, tagging his targets with the aim of drawing them and their followers into the discussion. This included fake anecdotes about his personas' daily encounters with racist white people, fake crime statistics that exaggerated the amount of violent crime committed by white people, fake history (such as the claim that the majority of American slave owners were Jewish), and easily falsifiable conspiracy theories involving the police. In Brad's view, success was achieved when he could sit back and watch his targets retweeting "stupid" ideas that had originated from his troll accounts. Brad did not believe his actions were taking place on a large enough scale to impact the BLM movement, but he enjoyed observing behavior that aligned with his beliefs about the stupidity of its supporters.

Another interview subject, "Stefan" (South Asian, Male, 28, College Graduate), engaged in similar but less time-consuming acts of Twitter hashtag trolling. In late 2016 and early 2017, he created "about a dozen" separate Twitter accounts, all of which presented themselves as left-leaning Americans. To give his accounts an air of being normal and legitimate, he had them follow various sports-related and music-related Twitter accounts. Depending on what controversial news story was popular on a given day, he "mainly just jumped on already popular hashtags and repeated stupid shit I hear liberals say . . . mostly trying to see how absurd and racist I could be and not get banned."

One of Stefan's favorite acts of trolling took place in February 2017, when he created a Twitter account that pretended to be "Shania," an African American woman from Atlanta. He did not know much about Atlanta but picked the location because the Atlanta Falcons were competing in the Super Bowl and he knew of some Atlanta-related sports and music Twitter accounts he could follow to present Shania as a real person. To gain attention for his fake persona, Stefan would follow trending hashtags and attempt to be one of the first people to reply to tweets by famous people: "my tweet would collect retweets/likes/comments early which would make it rise up." Shania was "successful" when it succeeded in "pushing the envelope" and got other liberal users to express agreement with views Stefan considered to be "racist." Stefan wanted to confirm his belief that the political left applauds anti-white racism, and he took great pleasure in seeing how even his most extreme messages of hate against white people would get likes and retweets. Eventually, like all of Stefan's other fake accounts, his Shania personality was banned for posting hateful content.

The activities of these two men had considerable similarities to and differences from the behaviors of Russian Twitter bots described in David A. Broniatowski and his co-researchers' 2018 study of vaccine hashtag trolling. In that particular case, Twitter accounts with ties to Russia sought to polarize online discussions through the introduction of "several distinctive arguments that we did not observe in the general vaccine discourse," including arguments meant to stir up racial divisions (1381). This is similar to Brad's and Stefan's attempts to introduce extreme views to hashtag discussions. However, in the case of the Russian bots, a major difference was observed—the bots gave equal attention to both pro-vaccine and anti-vaccine arguments, sometimes utilizing the same accounts to express contradictory views. It was also observed that Russian bots made fewer spelling or punctuation errors than did general users. Brad and Stefan focused almost all of their efforts on trolling the political left, and they attempted to emulate the non-standard spelling and slang words used by their target audiences.

Users who did not create and use Twitter accounts also played an important role in keeping hashtag campaigns alive. The /pol/ forum, like all other boards on 4chan, automatically deletes discussion threads that are idle for a certain amount of time; if many users do not continually post replies to a thread, it will be "pruned," or removed from the site. All 4chan threads are eventually deleted, and the site maintains no archive. Thus, all memes and topics introduced on /pol/ must "reside first and foremost in participants' brains to survive" and must be replied to and reposted to survive (Nissenbaum and Shifman 2017). All of my interview subjects acknowledged that they regularly posted encouragement and/or constructive criticism in hashtag campaign threads, acts that ensured the survival and visibility of the threads. Six of the interview subjects had created and uploaded meme images that later appeared in Twitter posts by other users. Having one's memes spread over the internet and influence or anger people was considered a brag-worthy example of successful "meme warfare."

POLITICS AND MOTIVATIONS

Despite the fact that these users played a role in hashtag trolling that targeted members of the political left and racial minority groups, my interview data indicated a mix of motivations—some seemingly contradictory—for their actions.

As its name suggests, the alt-right is supposed to be a right-leaning group. Of the fifteen men interviewed, most agreed that they were not "liberal" or "left wing," but there were considerable differences in their political views. Four of the men held views close to the mainstream of the Republican Party, with two having been supporters of Ted Cruz in the presidential primaries. The others, although they did not necessarily identify as conservative, tended to hold very negative views of undocumented immigrants, Islamic migration to Europe, Hillary Clinton, feminism, and left-leaning activists who are often maligned in conservative media as "social justice warriors." Views of ideal government policies, however, varied widely. Two of these men were libertarians who wanted a small government, while four others favored economic and healthcare policy ideas close to those of Bernie Sanders. Views of the Democratic Party were not entirely negative, either: most could agree that Hillary Clinton was a representative of the "regressive" elements of the left, but six of the respondents had generally positive views of President Barack Obama or Vice President Joe Biden. Four men did not seem to care at all about political ideology, did not vote in the 2016 election, and only seemed to care about 4chan's hashtag trolling insofar as it provided them with entertainment.

In contrast to many mass media and academic depictions of the user base of /pol/, it would be hard to describe the views of most of the interview subjects as in sync with individuals who are often portrayed as thought leaders in the alt-right, such as Richard Spencer, Andrew Anglin, Gavin McInnes, Milo Yannopoulos, and Mike Cernovich. In fact, when asked about such figures, only three interview subjects expressed agreement with their views. Stefan (South Asian, Male, 28, College Graduate) described Yannopoulos as "a mong" and Anglin as "a fucking retard."

One respondent, "Cal" (White, Male, 38, High School Graduate), praised Anglin and his neo-Nazi blog, the *Daily Stormer*: "I really respect what Andrew Anglin does. I rarely read his site, but [it] is amazing how a silly blog full of racist jokes has upset the world so much. When his site got kicked off the internet for a long-form fat joke it really helped expose how fragile people are these days. –Cal." Cal described Anglin's beliefs as "basically satire," which cannot be taken seriously. The "long-form fat joke" in this case was an August 2017 blog post in which Anglin mocked Heather Heyer, who was killed when a neo-Nazi plowed his car into people protesting against a white nationalist rally in Charlottesville, Virginia (Mettler and Selk 2017). When asked about white nationalist Richard Spencer, who advocates the creation of a homeland for the white race, Cal stated that he had no "strong feelings for or against him." These views are somewhat incongruous with the fact that Cal had long been married to a woman of another race and was raising mixed-race children.

Although mainstream society would describe the people I interviewed as members of an alt-right community, most of them did not like such a label. They did not see themselves as representative of the way the media defines the alt-right—as white nationalists, neo-Nazis, and fascists. While some shied away from the term altogether, others, such as "Jake" (White, Male, 20, College Student), identified as alt-right but created their own definition for the movement:

> I would say I support the alt-right but really there's no actual group or anything, it's just a bunch of people who don't identify with the typical stereotyped racist skinhead or guy who hates foreigners. The alt-right that I know is really diverse and enjoy [*sic*] mocking one another but aren't [*sic*] serious in wanting to eliminate races and such. However, the main reason people are drawn to the alt right is freedom which is basically what America stands for. There's more freedom in being able to mock people for liking men, being obese and such, than there is in the normalized pc culture that forces you to shut up and not hurt peoples' feelings. –Jake

This young student, who had stumbled on 4chan in late 2016, was convinced that "a lot of the users of 4chan and supporters of the alt-right in general are very diverse." Yet, while believing he was a member of a diverse movement, he still held hostility toward the Black Lives Matter movement, referring to it as a "greedy and corrupt group that just does silly stuff." Jake found it "hilarious" that the "uninformed" supporters of the BLM hashtag were being trolled by 4chan. When a news story broke about one of Facebook's most popular pro-BLM groups being operated by a white Australian man (McGowan 2018), Jake referred to it as a "great success" of trolling, adding, "I bet he used 4chan."

Stefan (South Asian, Male, 28, College Graduate), who, as discussed earlier, used a Twitter account posing as an African American woman to make "absurd and racist" posts, explained his actions in terms of exposing the hypocrisy of the far left. He expressed annoyance at the fact that mainstream society seemed to tolerate "racist and homophobic shit" if the speaker was a member of a "protected" victim group (his two main examples were Muslims and African Americans). As a non-Muslim man of South Asian ethnicity, he felt he was not a part of a "protected" group but could deal with the racism he encountered because he "didn't have thin skin." When asked about the people he was trolling on Twitter, he questioned the intelligence of people who could be offended by his posts: "I still can't believe people take Twitter seriously as a platform for discussion, to be honest."

All of the men I interviewed shared a strong belief that 4chan's numerous posts containing racist, misogynistic, and homophobic language should not be taken seriously and were instead part of a culture of freedom that should be celebrated. As noted earlier, pre-2016 studies of 4chan noted the existence of offensive posts, often portraying them as having more to do with the site's anti-mainstream identity and desire to antagonize newcomers than with serious hate ideologies. In my interviews, subjects often claimed that the political left—especially those who could be labeled as "social justice warriors" or "politically correct"—was in direct opposition to 4chan's culture of free expression. During the 2016 election, Hillary Clinton and her political allies, who made opposition to racism and misogyny a central part of their campaigning, had called out the alt-right as an enemy, helping define 4chan as a center of hate. One interviewee, Joe (East Asian, Male, 29, College Graduate), was the proud owner of an "I am a Deplorable" T-shirt, referencing Clinton's claim that a large portion of Trump supporters were part of a "basket of deplorables." Joe had voted for Obama twice and wished for a Joe Biden presidency, but he believed "Clinton and the radical left" wanted to destroy freedom of expression and replace it with a politically correct America in which jokes, memes, and internet sites would be censored if they offended groups the left believed deserved special protection. Joe, like others I interviewed, claimed to have progressive views regarding race, gender, and sexual orientation but found it ridiculous that people should be offended by 4chan posts and Twitter trolling. After all, he often encountered posts on 4chan that contained anti-Asian racism and saw them as more of a joke than something to "get worked up about." Rather than feel sympathy for those who might feel offended by such posts, Joe and the others interviewed felt contempt for them. There was a shared sense of humor and amusement whenever a "fragile" or "thin-skinned" person reacted negatively after encountering a trollish message or offensive meme. The political left, including pro-Clinton and BLM hashtag activists, were seen as standing against 4chan's culture of freedom, making them a natural target for trolling.

For some, such as those who clearly identified as politically conservative and cared about the implementation of Donald Trump's election campaign promises, hashtag trolling was a legitimate political tactic that aided the former president. Brad, whose elaborate Twitter trolling I described in the previous section, took great pleasure in knowing that he was convincing liberals to adopt and share "stupid" arguments. Another interview subject, "Ted" (Eurasian, Male, 30, College Graduate), voted for Ted Cruz in the primaries but was an enthusiastic supporter of President Trump. He scoffed at the idea that journalists, celebrities, and liberal activists who have great "power in the arena of public opinion" would complain about being attacked by pro-Trump trolls on Twitter: "Receiving messages via an account that you made on an inherently social and public platform, is that harassment? Defining it as harassment is a mistake, in my opinion. –Ted." When asked about the possible harm victims of Twitter harassment faced, Ted, scrolling through his smartphone, showed me a carefully collected folder of screen captures, each of which depicted an example of CNN and other mainstream media reporting that he believed to be inaccurate information about Trump. He argued that the mainstream media's dishonesty and bias against conservatives was something with which people "are bombarded . . . from all angles in their daily lives," making it far worse than whatever harm Twitter trolls might inflict.

Even those who claimed to have no particular political leanings, like Cal, sometimes tried to justify alt-right memes and Twitter trolling as something with a purpose "above mere humor." Cal believed "American politics is a fucking joke" and that 4chan was "showing how the mainstream is retarded and how the emperor is wearing no clothes."

Even entertainment and humor were given as reasons why 4chan was supporting Donald Trump. Throughout and after the election, 4chan discussion threads and the private group chat I observed included users who would laugh at "stupid" things Trump said and did. Stefan, when acknowledging that he had voted for Trump, described humor as a major motivation. He mentioned that a lot of Trump's tweets were "retarded political stunts," adding "but I wouldn't have it any other way, I can only hope Drumpf gets four more years so I can enjoy four more years of pants-on-head retardation." For the foot soldiers of the online meme war, regardless of whether they believed the former president was an idiot, a lot of the enjoyment to be had was apparently in watching "serious" people become offended and angry at Trump's actions. While the former president may not have intended it as such, within the 4chan subculture, users often believed that Trump, like themselves, was intentionally "trolling" people for "the lulz." The societal disruption caused by Trump, both online and offline, was viewed as one of the most entertaining "happenings" in recent history.

This kind of trolling shares significant similarities with the 4chan trolling and online activism observed by scholars in the pre-Trump era. The 4chan trolling of online memorial pages observed by Whitney Phillips (2015) was motivated by a desire to offend and attack "fake" online mourners, and Lee Knuttila (2011) saw Anonymous's anti-Scientology activism as motivated by serious ideology rather than apolitical "lulz." While earlier collective actions by 4chan users were unrelated to party politics, participants justified their actions in terms of attacking stupid or harmful actors in society. My research found that the methods of trolling have perhaps become more sophisticated, but there was still an underlying sense among users that they were fighting against stupid and unjust foes. The 2016 election and the perception among /pol/ users that the political left was fighting for a "politically correct" world motivated them to focus on trolling left-leaning activists. In this sense, it might be fair to say that the only major change in 4chan culture in recent years has been a change of targets. The election of Donald Trump and the increased media attention to 4chan convinced many of my interview subjects that unlike older 4chan trolling activities, their new form of "meme warfare" was offending previously unimaginable numbers of people—something that brought them enormous glee.

CONCLUSION

Although the fifteen 4chan users I interviewed held discordant views on politics, the definition of the alt-right, race, and the motivation behind their actions, those actions nonetheless placed them on one side of a political culture war: the side of Donald Trump. Whether white or non-white, conservative or non-conservative, idealist or nihilist, these users were tied together by a shared idea that the hashtag trolling of the alt-right was deeply entertaining. The fact that the targets of their trolling were part of "politically correct" left-leaning movements made it all the more satisfying for the users of a community that proudly labeled itself as the "Politically Incorrect" board. Few seemed to care about the damage their actions might inflict; most, in fact, welcomed whatever societal chaos might result from 4chan's trolling and Trump's presidency.

It would be fair to say that the post-2016 4chan of /pol/ and the alt-right shares many cultural characteristics that researchers observed in earlier studies of its /b/ board. However, it is now a very different animal. Users might see their actions as playful or just "for the lulz," but those "lulz" are now more deeply tied to impacting the outside world in a manner that many outside of the political right would consider extremely harmful.

The results of this research should be troubling for both participants in hashtag activism and scholars who study Twitter. While it may be possible to use software to detect and screen out crude bot accounts, manually operated troll accounts are a different matter. Highly motivated trolls, some with strong political goals and some that merely want to mess with people, can and do infiltrate serious political discussions with the intent of derailing, damaging, or causing arguments within hashtag activist campaigns. This raises questions about the reliability—as both a platform for activism and a subject of study—of Twitter and similar social media platforms that allow posting under pseudonyms. Therefore, I recommend that future research into such subjects be extremely careful about taking online content at face value. Whenever possible, human research data should be gathered to gain a better understanding of what lies behind content posted on Twitter, Facebook, and online boards such as 4chan.

NOTES

1. Detailed data on the number of posts per day on 4chan can be found at https://4stats.io/. Between late 2014 and mid-2016, the activity on /pol/ increased, from roughly 30,000 to over 140,000 posts per day. However, due to incomplete datasets for /b/, the period when /pol/ became the most active board could not be determined.
2. Members of the invite-only chat group, which was hosted on the application Discord, agreed to allow me to join but did not consent to having any of their words quoted in connection with any particular user. They instead agreed to my proposal that I present data from the chat for general background information on their subculture, without direct quotations.

REFERENCES

Al-Rawi, Ahmed, Jacob Groshek, and Li Zhang. 2018. "What the Fake? Assessing the Extent of Networked Political Spamming and Bots in the Propagation of #fakenews on Twitter." *Online Information Review* 43 (1): 53–71. https://doi.org/10.1108/OIR-02-2018-0065.

Badawy, Adam, Emilio Ferrara, and Kristina Lerman. 2018. "Analyzing the Digital Traces of Political Manipulation: The 2016 Russian Interference Twitter Campaign." In *Proceedings of EEE/ACM International Conference on Advances in Social Networks Analysis and Mining (ASONAM) Spain*, 258–265. https://doi.org/10.1109/ASONAM.2018.8508646.

Badawy, Adam, Kristina Lerman, and Emilio Ferrara. 2018. *Who Falls for Online Political Manipulation?* http://arxiv.org/pdf/1808.03281v1.

Biernacki, Patrick, and Dan Waldorf. 1981. "Snowball Sampling: Problems and Techniques of Chain Referral Sampling." *Sociological Methods and Research* 10 (2): 141–163. https://doi.org/10.1177/004912418101000205.

Bishop, Jonathan. 2014. "Trolling for the Lulz?" In *Transforming Politics and Policy in the Digital Age*, edited by Jonathan Bishop, 155–172. Hershey, PA: Information Science Reference.

Blades, Lincoln. 2016. "Call the 'Alt-right' Movement What It Is: Racist as Hell." *Rolling Stone*, August 26. https://www.rollingstone.com/politics/politics-features/call-the-alt-right-movement-what-it-is-racist-as-hell-251617/.

Bokhari, Allum, and Milo Yiannopoulos. 2016. "An Establishment Conservative's Guide to the Alt-right." *Breitbart*, March 29. https://www.breitbart.com/tech/2016/03/29/an-establishment-conservatives-guide-to-the-alt-right/.

boyd, danah. 2010. "'For the Lolz': 4chan Is Hacking the Attention Economy." Zephoria.org. http://www.zephoria.org/thoughts/archives/2010/06/12/for-the-lolz-4chan-is-hacking-the-attention-economy.html.

Broniatowski, David A., Amelia M. Jamison, Sihua Qi, Lulwah AlKulaib, Tao Chen, Adrian Benton, Sandra C. Quinn, and Mark Dredze. 2018. "Weaponized Health Communication: Twitter Bots and Russian Trolls Amplify the Vaccine Debate." *American Journal of Public Health* 108 (10): 1378–1384. https://doi.org/10.2105/AJPH.2018.304567.

Coleman, Gabriella. 2013. "Anonymous and the Politics of Leaking." In *Beyond WikiLeaks*, edited by Benedetta Brevini, Arne Hintz, and Patrick McCurdy, 209–228. London: Palgrave Macmillan.

Feinberg, Ashley. 2013. "The Best and Worst Things 4chan Gave the World." *Gizmodo*, October 1. https://gizmodo.com/the-best-and-worst-things-4chan-gave-the-world-1436402768.

Hawley, George. 2017. *Making Sense of the Alt-Right*. New York: Columbia University Press.

Kim, Dongwoo, Timothy Graham, Zimin Wan, and Marian-Andrei Rizoiu. 2019. *Tracking the Digital Traces of Russian Trolls: Distinguishing the Roles and Strategy of Trolls on Twitter*. http://arxiv.org/pdf/1901.05228v1.

Knuttila, Lee. 2011. "User Unknown: 4chan, Anonymity and Contingency." *First Monday* 16 (10). https://firstmonday.org/article/view/3665/3055.

Kozinets, Robert V. 2002. "The Field behind the Screen: Using Netnography for Marketing Research in Online Communities." *Journal of Marketing Research* 39 (1): 61–72. https://doi.org/10.1509/jmkr.39.1.61.18935.

Manivannan, Vyshali. 2014. "FCJ-158 Tits or GTFO: The Logics of Misogyny on 4chan's Random—/b/." *Fibreculture Journal* 22: 109–132. http://twentytwo.fibreculturejournal.org/fcj-158-tits-or-gtfo-the-logics-of-misogyny-on-4chans-random-b/.

McGowan, Michael. 2018. "Fake Black Lives Matter Facebook Page Run by Australian Union Official—Report." *The Guardian*, April 10. https://www.theguardian.com/us-news/2018/apr/10/fake-black-lives-matter-facebook-page-run-by-australian-union-official-report.

Mettler, Katie, and Avi Selk. 2017. "GoDaddy—Then Google—Ban Neo-Nazi Site Daily Stormer for Disparaging Charlottesville Victim." *Washington Post*, August 14. https://www.washingtonpost.com/news/morning-mix/wp/2017/08/14/godaddy-bans-neo-nazi-site-daily-stormer-for-disparaging-woman-killed-at-charlottesville-rally/.

Milner, Ryan M. 2016. *The World Made Meme: Public Conversations and Participatory Media*. Cambridge, MA: MIT Press.

Nagle, Angela. 2017. *Kill All Normies: Online Culture Wars from 4chan and Tumblr to Trump and the Alt-right*. Winchester, UK: Zero Books.

Nissenbaum, Asaf, and Limor Shifman. 2017. "Internet Memes as Contested Cultural Capital: The Case of 4chan's /b/ Board." *New Media and Society* 19 (4): 483–501. https://doi.org/10.1177/1461444815609313.

Ohlheiser, Abby. 2016. "What Was Fake on the Internet This Election: #DraftOurDaughters, Trump's Tax Returns." *Washington Post*, October 31. https://www.washingtonpost.com/news/the-intersect/wp/2016/10/31/what-was-fake-on-the-internet-this-election-draftourdaughters-trumps-taxreturns/?utm_term=.fcfd4778704c.

Phillips, Whitney. 2015. *This Is Why We Can't Have Nice Things: Mapping the Relationship between Online Trolling and Mainstream Culture*. Cambridge, MA: MIT Press.

Walford, Geoffrey. 2005. "Research Ethical Guidelines and Anonymity." *International Journal of Research and Method in Education* 28 (1): 83–93. https://doi.org/10.1080/01406720500036786.

Wall, Travis, and Teodor Mitew. 2018. "Swarm Networks and the Design Process of a Distributed Meme Warfare Campaign." *First Monday* 22 (5). https://doi.org/10.5210/fm.v22i5.8290.

Wong, Wendy H., and Peter A. Brown. 2013. "E-bandits in Global Activism: WikiLeaks, Anonymous, and the Politics of No One." *Perspectives on Politics* 11 (4): 1015–1033. https://doi.org/10.1017/S1537592713002806.

Zannettou, Savvas, Tristan Caulfield, Emiliano D. Cristofaro, Michael Sirivianos, Gianluca Stringhini, and Jeremy Blackburn. 2018. "Disinformation Warfare: Understanding State Sponsored Trolls on Twitter and Their Influence on the Web." http://arxiv.org/pdf/1801.09288v1.

11

A RHETORIC OF ZANINESS
Trolling, the Alt-right, and Pepe the Frog

Sean Milligan

On January 20, 2017, the day of Donald Trump's presidential inauguration, white nationalist Richard Spencer was filmed giving an interview on the streets of Washington, DC, while surrounded by protestors. Toward the end of the video, Spencer is asked about the cartoon frog on his lapel pin. Spencer replies, "It's . . . Pepe. He's become kind of a symbol" (ABC News 2017). However, before Spencer can complete his thought, he is punched in the head by a masked protestor. The video went viral in the days following the inauguration, and the image of Spencer getting hit became a relatively popular meme (especially among liberals and leftists looking for a sense of catharsis in the wake of Trump's election). For many, the video raised an ethical question about how far is too far when protesting Trump and the alt-right. That is, the video caused many to focus on the rhetorical practices of the left. Setting aside the ethical question of whether it is okay to punch a Nazi, I believe the video raises other questions about the alt-right's rhetorical strategies and style, specifically Pepe's function as a symbol of the alt-right. Why was Pepe, of all possible images and objects, adopted by the movement? Why does he resonate with this particular group? How does Pepe's rhetorical life help us better understand online social and political movements?

Pepe is undoubtedly a rather odd symbol for any political or social movement, including white nationalism, and any attempt to account for Pepe's rhetorical function must account for this oddness. In perhaps the most appropriate turn of events, as soon as Spencer tries to explain Pepe's significance in the video, he is silenced by the punch from the protestor. Instead of assigning a specific, fixed meaning to Pepe (as Spencer seemed prepared to do), this chapter will describe and analyze Pepe's evolution from comic to meme to hate symbol. By charting Pepe's rhetorical trajectory, we can better understand the values and communication practices of the alt-right. That is, I believe Pepe

https://doi.org/10.7330/9781646423187.c011

has more to tell us about Richard Spencer (and others like him) than Richard Spencer can tell us about Pepe. Specifically, I argue that Pepe characterizes the role zaniness plays in the rhetorical practices of the alt-right. Zaniness is arguably a subset or type of humor; that is, something that might be called zany is funny in (and functions in) its own—often ludicrous or bizarre—way. For Sianne Ngai (2012, 185), zaniness is an aesthetic category that is largely defined by the genre of comedy but "has a stressed-out, even desperate quality that immediately sets it apart from its more lighthearted comedic cousins, the goofy or silly." Ngai argues that zaniness is one of the defining categories of contemporary aesthetic experience, and in what follows, I will argue that zaniness is essential for understanding the rhetorical life of Pepe the Frog and, more generally, online communication in the post-truth era. However, before I proceed in my analysis of some of the key moments in Pepe's rhetorical life, I begin by addressing some methodological concerns and situate this chapter within recent work in the fields of visual rhetoric and media studies.

ZANINESS AND DIGITAL RHETORIC

Laurie E. Gries's (2015) "new materialist approach for visual rhetorics" is perhaps my project's most important methodological influence. A key concept in Gries's work is rhetorical transformation, which she defines as "the process in which things become rhetorical in divergent, unpredictable ways as they circulate, transform, and catalyze change" (27). Gries calls her method for studying rhetorical transformation "iconographic tracking," a process that involves collecting as many variants of an image as possible through "data hoarding" and conducting "a close study of specific collectives to determine how an image intra-acts with humans and various technologies and other entities to materialize, spark change, and produce collective space" (113). Gries chooses a particularly rich case study to demonstrate this method: Obama Hope. She describes how the image was circulated and remixed in ways the image's creator—street artist Shepard Fairey—and the Obama campaign could not have anticipated. Recent work on memetics that argues for memes as a process of production and participation (Shifman 2014; Milner 2016) offers another possible approach for studying Pepe. In particular, the "fundamental logic" of memes described by Ryan M. Milner (2016) (multimodality, reappropriation, resonance, collectivism, and spread) is helpful for describing the process that made Pepe into a meme. In addition, Heather Suzanne Woods and Leslie A. Hahner's (2019) work on how memes function as persuasive tools for the alt-right also offers an important starting point for this project.

While this chapter draws on much of the work cited above, none of these scholars offers a theory or method that fully accounts for why Pepe appealed to the alt-right in the particular way he did. Both iconographic tracking and memetics reduce visual objects to a process of circulation (in the case of iconographic tracking) and participation (in the case of memetics). (For a discussion of ideograph circulation for activist purposes, see chapter 5, this volume.) In the case of iconographic tracking, it does not matter if the object in question is the Mona Lisa or an Obama Hope poster. Attention to the object itself is not as important as the way it travels. Gries's method also treats all iterations of an image as equally important. However, while my project, like Gries's, began with an initial stage of data hording, it became apparent early on that not all Pepe images were equally important in attempting to understand his importance to the alt-right. Woods and Hahner (2019, 90) rightly identify memes as the dominant rhetorical mode of the al-right and explain how Pepe was used by the alt-right to "direct public attention." However, they do not account for what it is about Pepe that caused him to resonate with this particular movement and why he is an appropriate symbol for this group. To understand the particular ways Pepe traveled, we have to begin with an understanding of Pepe's origins as an aesthetic object. Only then can we understand both how and why he circulated online and became a part of the alt-right's rhetorical practices. That is, we must understand not only the zany stylistics of this unusual political icon but also how those stylistics function and play a role in why he rose to the digital presence that he did. For this reason, I find Sianne Ngai's work on zaniness to be a particularly useful starting point for my analysis.

Ngai (2012, 1) claims that zaniness is one of the aesthetic categories "best suited for grasping how aesthetic experience has been transformed by the hypercommodified, information-saturated, performance-driven conditions of late capitalism." Ngai claims that zaniness is "really an aesthetic about work—and about a precariousness created specifically by the capitalist organization of work" (188). A zany character, then, is someone who is in a constant state of action. Yet this action, while often associated with post-Fordist labor, is not necessarily productive. In fact, a zany character's work or activity is often counterproductive. Ngai writes, "On first glance, zaniness seems purely a symptom of the 'perform-or-else' ideology of late capitalism, including its increasingly affective, biopolitical ways of meeting the imperative to endlessly increase productivity. Yet for all its spectacular displays of laborious exertion, the activity of zaniness is more often than not destructive; one might even describe it as the dramatization of an anarchic refusal to be productive" (12). Zaniness "is as much about desperate laboring as playful fun" and its stressed out nature prevents if from being synonymous with goofiness or silliness (3, 185). So, while zaniness is best exemplified through comedy, it is not simply defined by the humorous response it elicits from an audience. Given the destructive labor zany characters so often participate in, zaniness has an unwieldiness that comedy more broadly does not have. For an aesthetic object or a rhetorical appeal to adopt a zany style, it must do more than simply make the audience laugh. Ngai claims that "the experience of zaniness ultimately remains unsettling" because it demonstrates "the easiness with which these positions of safety and precariousness can be reversed" (11). Zaniness is defined by a kind of manic activity that might repel an audience as easily as appeal to it.

As noted earlier, in addition to being an essential concept for understanding contemporary aesthetic experience, I argue that zaniness has come to define a rhetorical style adopted by certain online social and political movements—with the alt-right the most notable example—and is crucial for understanding digital rhetoric in the post-truth era. In what follows, I will describe this rhetoric of zaniness by tracing Pepe from his initial appearance in Matt Furie's webcomic *Boy's Club* (2016) to his appropriation by the alt-right. Ultimately, I will show that zaniness is what caused Pepe to resonate with the alt-right and that Pepe, in turn, has continued to lend the alt-right's rhetorical practices a zany style that distinguishes them from previous right-wing or white nationalist movements.

BOY'S CLUB AND "FEELS GOOD MAN"

The "spectacular displays of laborious exertion" and "anarchic refusal to be productive" that Ngai points to as defining characteristics of zaniness run throughout Furie's *Boy's Club* (2016). *Boy's Club* is a stoner comedy that revolves around four anthropomorphic animals: Brett, Andy, Landwolf, and Pepe. In *Boy's Club*, the characters are constantly engaged in labor, yet this labor is not in the service of biological need; it is also not in the service of political action or social good. Instead, the characters labor in the service of pleasure and self-gratification. They get high, pull pranks, watch TV, and play video games. There is no purpose that the characters' actions seem to fulfill or cause that their actions serve, other than pleasure. Ngai (2012, 23) claims that zaniness is as much about desperate laboring as playful fun. What we find in *Boy's Club* is as much "playful fun" as "desperate laboring." Of course, fun here is not meant in the lighthearted way it is commonly used. As Ngai points out, "Even the word 'fun' is strangely not fun" (297). Ngai traces the etymology of the word, which according to the Oxford English Dictionary (OED) in its original usage meant "cheat or trick; a hoax; a practical joke" (297). Ngai claims that fun "refers here not to one's own feeling of enjoyment or pleasure, but to being the source of somebody else's" (297). This sense of zaniness is present in perhaps the most famous of the comics Furie published, which, though it lacks an official title, I refer to as "Feels Good Man."

In "Feels Good Man," first published on Furie's Myspace page in 2005 and reprinted by Fantagraphics in 2016, Andy sees Pepe peeing with his pants around his ankles. Landwolf later tells Pepe that he "heard you pull yer pants down all the way to go pee," to which Pepe simply replies, "feels good man" (Furie 2016, 42). The comic presents Pepe as the subject of the other characters' fun (in the word's original sense). Even if he is not the target of a practical joke, he is still the source of their amusement. However, rather than being offended or defensive about the way the other characters attempt to humiliate him, Pepe embraces it and relishes the response he receives from them. His gaze directed at what we assume is a video game (Landwolf is holding a controller), Pepe is portrayed with a blank look in his eyes and a quiet, content smile on his face, as if what the other characters think of his behavior is of no consequence to him.

"Feels Good Man" encapsulates the overall ethos of *Boy's Club*, with its emphasis on fun and self-gratification. Pepe's actions and defense of his actions point to a certain disregard for what is deemed socially acceptable or typically adult behavior. Further, he revels in this nonconformity. In "Feels Good Man," Pepe invites the reader to wallow in pleasure. While he may not be intentionally trying to elicit a response from those around him, there is a sense in which the joke is on people who do react. In many ways, Pepe's attitude here mirrors the behavior of the trolls who populate 4chan. It would make sense, then, that this comic would resonate with them and that Pepe would become a symbol of trolling.

By self-publishing the comics digitally, Furie enabled the comics to circulate among other social media sites, including 4chan. The sense of zaniness permeating *Boy's Club* resonated with the trolls on 4chan who first turned Pepe into a meme. In the following section, I will explain Pepe's appeal as it relates to 4chan's communication practices. Specifically, I focus on the act of trolling, itself a kind of zany rhetorical practice that defines the activity on the site.

4CHAN AND TROLLING

4chan is an imageboard founded by Christopher "Moot" Poole in 2003 as a "content overflow site for a Something Awful subforum called 'Anime Death Tentacle Rape Whorehouse'" (Phillips 2015, 57). While the site has boards dedicated to a number of topics, it is perhaps most notable for the /b/ (or "Random") board. In a 2008 *New York Times Magazine* article on 4chan and trolling more generally, Mattathias Schwartz (2008) writes, "Measured in terms of depravity, insularity and traffic-driven turnover, the culture of /b/ has little precedent. /b/ reads like the inside of a high-school bathroom stall, or an obscene telephone party line, or a blog with no posts and all comments filled with slang that you are too old to understand." Due to the fact that almost everything on the site is posted anonymously, the comparison to a bathroom stall is certainly accurate but a bit of an understatement. Since users can post images and videos, the board lends itself not only to the type of scatological and offensive messages one might find in a public restroom but also to revenge porn, hentai, and images of real-life violence. While these kinds of transgressive images and language are no doubt shocking to someone visiting the site for the first time, for the trolls who frequent the site, this is the lingua franca of this particular subculture. That is, the cultural norms of this particular group are rooted in transgression and nihilism.

In her article "The New Man of 4chan," Angela Nagle (2016) discusses the role of transgression on 4chan and the regressive gender politics this type of discourse fosters. She also describes a number of cases where the seemingly ironic messages posted on the site led to real-life violence. Nagle begins by discussing the case of Chris Harper-Mercer, who is thought to have posted a warning to 4chan's+ /r9k/ board the night before he committed a mass shooting at Umpqua Community College in 2015. Harper-Mercer's case is especially interesting because, according to Nagle, his post was accompanied by an image of Pepe. According to Know Your Meme ("Pepe the Frog" 2015), Pepe had been circulating on 4chan since about 2008. Regarding the relationship between Pepe and 4chan, Nagle (2016) writes, "In his original cartoon form, Pepe was a sad sack, prone to bouts of humiliation. But as his froggy visage got meme-ified on 4chan, he took on a distinctly more menacing aspect. Pepe became a favorite icon of last-straw ranters spewing extreme misogyny, racism, and vengefulness." In a sense, Pepe would appear to be both a product and an embodiment of the cultural norms of 4chan and the trolls who inhabit the website.

Of course, posters such as Harper-Mercer who actually act out violently are the minority on 4chan. Typically, offensive images and language are posted to 4chan because the posters find it funny to do so. The purpose of posting offensive or violent language is to get a reaction from other people. That is, the posters are often simply "trolling." The term *trolling* is often used to describe any kind of antagonistic message (regardless of whether it is delivered in an online forum). Given the term's rather inexact popular usage and the important role it plays in the communication practices of forums such as 4chan, it is necessary to provide a more precise definition. According to various dictionaries, to "troll" is to "make a deliberately offensive or provocative online post with the aim of upsetting someone or eliciting an angry response from them" ("Troll" 2021). While this definition adequately describes the activity of trolling, it ignores an important element of the activity, which is the pleasure trolls receive from the "corrective response" they obtain from those being trolled. Trolls commonly refer to this pleasure as "lulz," defined by Whitney Phillips (2015, 57) as "acute amusement in the face of someone else's distress, embarrassment, or rage."

For someone encountering trolling for the first time, the experience can be dizzying. Like the aesthetic experience of zaniness, trolling as a rhetorical practice never allows its audience to gain any sense of sure footing. Unless you are in on the joke, it can be difficult, if not impossible, to determine what is meant ironically and what is meant sincerely. It is due to both the zany sensibility and the transgressive communication practices of 4chan that Pepe became a meme. According to Know Your Meme (2009), "Feels Good Man" was uploaded to Myspace in 2005. Although Furie deleted the page, the comic was uploaded to 4chan's /b/ board by an unidentified user in 2008. Other users then latched on to the cartoon, and the image of Pepe saying "feels good man" was taken out of the context of the original comic and became a popular image macro (see figure 11.1). One can see how this comic and the ethos underlying "Feels Good Man" would resonate with online trolls, who are motivated largely by the pursuit of "lulz."

SAD FROG AND SMUG FROG

Despite Pepe's origins on a social media platform as problematic as 4chan's /b/ board, the earliest Pepe memes did not have the political associations he would take on later in his rhetorical life. Pepe images were often recomposed and shared to express a variety of emotional states. Shortly after "Feels Good Man" began circulating on 4chan, images of Pepe began to be recomposed and shared in other social media platforms. Some of these images closely resembled Pepe's original

A Rhetoric of Zaniness 217

Figure 11.1. "Feels Good Man" image

Figure 11.2. "Feels Bad Man/Sad Frog" image

appearance in *Boy's Club*. For instance, "Sad Frog" (see figure 11.2) simply altered Furie's original drawing so that Pepe is frowning rather than smiling. The text in the speech bubbles is changed from "feels good man" to "Feels bad, man." While "Feels Good Man" and "Sad Frog" reflect opposing emotional states, a sense of zaniness still runs through both images. That is, "Sad Frog" is so exaggerated as to be comical. In "Sad Frog," it is as if Pepe is working desperately to be sad rather than expressing a genuine emotional state.

In 2011, Pepe was transformed again into "Smug Frog" (see figure 11.3). This version of Pepe was noticeably different than both "Feels Good Man" and "Sad Frog." That is, while the others looked distinctly like Furie's original drawings of Pepe in *Boy's Club*, this version did not. While the image is still recognizably Pepe, it is altered so that he is smirking, with his hand held to his chin as if he is thinking. He is also drawn with a rather knowing look on his face, with his eyes directed at the viewer. According to Know Your Meme ("Smug Frog" 2015), the "oldest known" version of the image was posted to 4chan on June 2, 2011. The website claims that the purpose of the image was to "make fun of the style of humor of the television show *The Big Bang Theory*." Although "Feels Good Man" and "Sad Frog" changed Pepe by taking the character out of his original context, "Smug Frog" represents a more drastic departure from the character's original appearance in *Boy's Club*. Both "Smug Frog" and "Feels Good Man" are related to feelings of pleasure. However, there is a sense in which the good-natured tone of "Feels Good Man" is abandoned by "Smug Frog" in favor of something more antagonistic.

"Smug Frog" mocks the viewer in a way "Feels Good Man" and "Sad Frog" do not. After all, smugness is predicated on a sense of superiority over someone else. If in "Smug Frog" Pepe is expressing a feeling of superiority, to whom or what is he feeling superior? While this would

Figure 11.3. "Smug Frog" image

no doubt change depending on the context in which the image was used, Pepe's smugness was often directed at people who were being trolled on social media. For instance, "Smug Frog" would often be inserted into incongruous and often offensive contexts, such as the World Trade Center buildings on 9/11 or dressed as an SS officer in front of the gates of Auschwitz (see figure 11.4). In these cases, Pepe's sense of smugness seems to be directed at the victims of 9/11 and the Holocaust. However, the smugness is also directed at anyone who would be offended by this kind of offensive imagery. While "Smug Frog" is noticeably different from Pepe's original appearance in *Boy's Club*, the zaniness remains, as smugness is predicated on someone having fun at another's expense.

Each of the images discussed above is distinct, both in their depiction of Pepe and in how they were used in social media. However, none of these different versions of the meme is inherently problematic. That is, when Pepe initially became a meme, sharing an image depicting Pepe or having Pepe as your social media avatar may have implied something about your aesthetic sensibility, but it did not necessarily say anything about your politics. However, this changed once Pepe became associated with the more political faction of 4chan, the alt-right. In what follows, I will describe the rhetorical practices of the alt-right, which, I argue, are largely defined by trolling and characterized by a zany sensibility.

THE ALT-RIGHT

Figure 11.4. "Smug Nazi Pepe" image

The alt-right's use of trolling is perhaps best exemplified by an incident involving journalist Olivia Nuzzi and her article "How Pepe the Frog Became a Nazi Trump Supporter and Alt-Right Symbol" (2016), in which she attempts to chart Pepe's evolution from comic character to hate symbol. Nuzzi interviews two white nationalist 4chan users, @JaredTSwift and @PaulTown, who claim to have helped orchestrate Pepe's appropriation. The two men (identified only by their Twitter handles) claim that Pepe's appropriation by the alt-right was "by design" and that there was "an actual campaign to reclaim Pepe from normies." That is, these white nationalists intentionally appropriated the character when celebrities such as Katy Perry and Nikki Minaj began sharing Pepe memes on social media. According to Town, the initial effort to turn Pepe into a white nationalist symbol was undertaken by about ten people who "helped plot it out over drinks in late 2015, before taking to /r9k/," the 4chan board on which the racist Pepe memes initially appeared (2016). When asked why there was such an attachment to Pepe among 4chan users, @JaredTSwift claims "he's a reflection of our souls, to most of us. It's disgusting to see people ('normies,' if you will) use him so trivially. He belongs to us. And we'll make him toxic if we have to" (2016).

If this sounds slightly dramatic and a lot to go through to reclaim a meme, this is because Swift and Town were likely lying to Nuzzi. At least, that is what Jonah Bennett claims in an article published on the conservative website the *Daily Caller* on September 14, 2016. Bennett seeks to undermine Nuzzi's article by claiming it was "a complete troll job." This claim is based on interviews Bennett conducted with the same white supremacists interviewed by Nuzzi. According to Bennett, "The troll consisted of Town and Swift feeding an outrageous narrative to

Nuzzi in the hopes she would scoop it up and feature as many quotes as possible—a fairly common practice among various alt-right groups to gain in-group status." Of course, the fact that Town and Swift provided exaggerated information to Nuzzi is in some ways irrelevant. After all, Pepe was appropriated by and has become a symbol of the alt-right, so there is an association between Pepe and white supremacists that cannot be ignored. The two articles also point to the distinguishing characteristics of the alt-right's rhetoric—their zany aesthetic sensibility and their penchant for trolling.

Political scientist George Hawley (2017) claims that the term *alt-right* describes a particular brand of online right-wing politics. Hawley claims the alt-right is "a white-nationalist movement" that wants "to see the creation of a white ethnostate in North America" (11). However, what sets this movement apart from right-wing and white nationalist movements that preceded it is the central role humor plays in the group's sensibilities. Hawley writes, "The issue of tone is important. Rage and hate were the primary emotions associated with the older white-nationalist movement . . . The Alt-Right offers something more attractive to potential supporters: edginess and fun . . . This is a curious paradox of the Alt-Right; it may ultimately be a greater threat to mainstream politics than these earlier groups precisely because it often comes across as much less threatening" (25). While previous white supremacist movements adopted a symbol such as the swastika sincerely, "The new Alt-Right put swastikas in Pepe's eyes because it was hilarious" (68). This style, this sense of "edginess and fun" associated with the alt-right, is a direct result of the fact that they cohered on the internet, in spaces such as 4chan, where one could share offensive content anonymously without fear of repercussions.

In *Alt-America*, journalist David Neiwert (2017a) places recent right-wing movements in American politics, such as the alt-right and the Trump campaign, into the context of right-wing movements going back to the 1990s. Neiwert sees the development of the internet and the way it enabled anonymous communication as the reason the alt-right movement cohered in the specific way it did. While certain other extreme right-wing political ideologies, such as conspiracy theories and patriot movements, found a forum on the internet during the 1990s, the alt-right, too, came into existence in cyberspace. Therefore, the sensibility of those who associate with this group is more explicitly informed by social media. Like Hawley, Neiwert also sees "irony" and "humor" as what distinguishes the alt-right from other white supremacist movements (256).

What Hawley calls "edginess and fun" and Neiwert calls "irony" and "humor," I call zaniness. The way this zaniness most blatantly manifests itself is through trolling, the group's primary rhetorical mode discussed above. It is important to point out that not all trolls are "alt-right." In fact, many trolls on Twitter come from the political left and use trolling to attack alt-right figures. Nevertheless, trolling is the discourse that created the alt-right and sets it apart from other hate groups and right-wing political groups. Essentially, while the alt-right does not define trolling, trolling defines the alt-right. Of course, if trolling is a rhetorical strategy utilized by the alt-right, this raises the question of who the audience is for the trolling. After all, the recipient of the antagonistic message is not likely to be persuaded by someone openly mocking or insulting them.

Hawley (2017) cites a post on the alt-right blog *The Right Stuff* that describes who trolls should see as their intended audience for trolling. According to the post (which has since been removed but which Hawley quotes at length), "You should assume that you will never manage to convince your ideological enemies of the merit of your position. Rather, the purpose of trolling is to convince people reading your comments of the merit of your position. On many different web forums, lurkers outnumber posters by 10 to 1. The purpose of trolling raids is to convince these anonymous people, not the person you disagree with. As such, you can win hearts and minds even when met with universal opposition" (73). Trolling functions for the alt-right not just as a way to upset the mainstream. It also functions as a recruitment tool, as a way of persuading those with a similar zany sensibility that the social and political leanings of the alt-right are compatible with that sensibility. Again, the audience for trolling is not the people who are the victims of trolling; rather, the intended audience is the anonymous people who might happen upon the trolling. Pepe, with his aesthetic origins in zaniness and his association with smugness, was a perfect symbol of this online political movement prone to what might be considered anti-activism (see chapters 10 and 12, this volume, for more on this). While the two men who were interviewed by Nuzzi might claim that they were trolling her, it is clear that Pepe acted as a symbol for many associated with the group. For some people associated with the alt-right, Pepe became so important to their movement that he became the symbol of a satirical religion and nationality called "Kek."

PEPE, THE CULT OF KEK, AND #FREEKEKISTAN

The term *Kek*, like "lulz," is a derivative of "lol" and started on the fantasy video game *World of Warcraft*. It then became an inside joke on certain online forums, including 4chan. According to Know Your Meme ("Cult of Kek" 2016), a 4chan post from November 27, 2015, claimed there was an Egyptian god named Kuk (also spelled Kek). The deity was considered androgynous, with its female depictions taking the form of a snake and its male depictions taking the form of a frog. The original 4chan post includes a selection from the Wikipedia page on Kuk and an image of the deity's frog form. Although the original poster does not mention Pepe explicitly, a comment on the post makes the connection explicit: "So a meme is 5000 years old. Life is cyclical and humanity never forgets" ("Kekistan" 2017). Not long after this was posted, a satirical religion was started that worshipped "Kek" in the form of Pepe.

In the wake of the initial 4chan post, trolls started multiple blogs and online forums devoted to the religion, including pepethefrogfaith.wordpress.com. The site's home page takes readers to an article titled "The Truth about Pepe the Frog and the Cult of KEK." The site includes entries such as "How 4chan Pays Tribute to Kek (Sacrificial Offerings)" and "Carl Jung Foresaw the Coming of Kek." Another site devoted to the religion is thecultofkek.com. The site's banner image depicts "Smug Frog" along with a collage of Pepe images made to look like a bomb detonating. Other images found on the site include ancient Egyptian gods with Pepe's face and Christian images depicting the Statue of Liberty as Mary, Donald Trump as Christ, and Pepe as Christ's followers. Although the religion is clearly satirical, two important concepts can be applied to it: "meme magic" and "meme warfare." According to Know Your Meme ("Meme Magic" 2016), meme magic is "a slang term used to describe the hypothetical power of sorcery and voodoo supposedly derived from certain internet memes that can transcend the realm of cyberspace and result in real life consequences" ("Meme Magic" 2016). The term *meme warfare*, coined by activist Andrew Boyd in 2002, has a richer conceptual history and is a bit more complex. However, it is similar to meme magic in that it acknowledges that memes are important for disseminating information to create social change. According to Boyd, "A vital movement requires a hot and happening meme" (quoted in Olson 2018). The event trolls attribute most explicitly to Pepe's meme magic is the nomination and election of Donald Trump.

In addition to the "religion," the alt-right trolls also created a fictional country called "Kekistan." According to Know Your Meme ("Kekistan" 2017), the name of the country was coined on Reddit in 2015. However, in 2017, Kekistan gained popularity on Twitter after alt-right YouTube personality Carl Benjamin (aka Sargon of Akkad) claimed in a (since deleted) tweet that "shitposters meet the British govs [*sic*] criteria of an ethnicity" ("Kekistan" 2017). Benjamin's followers then decided that this ethnicity should be called "Kekistani" (2017). A number of Benjamin's followers replied to his tweet with the hashtag #FreeKekistan, and an online (faux) social movement was born.

While many of the original tweets that included the Free Kekistan hashtag were replies to Benjamin, the hashtag took on a life of its own in the days and weeks that followed. Soon, it became something of a rallying cry for the alt-right, with even Richard Spencer tweeting "set our people free! #FreeKekistan." Many (if not most) of the #FreeKekistan tweets included images of Pepe; and a number of these images depict him as a soldier, politician, or diplomat fighting for the Kekistani cause. The alt-right often targets progressive social and political movements in instances of anti-activism meant to disrupt or ridicule. One function of the Free Kekistan hashtag is to mimic and mock other, sincere movements (one hears obvious echoes of the Free Tibet movement). However, like Pepe memes more generally, #FreeKekistan gave the alt-right an object around which they could cohere. By engaging in online activism on behalf of a fictional country, alt-right trolls were voicing their sincere commitment to the zany sensibility of their movement. Trolls created both a national anthem and a flag for Kekistan, and the Kekistan flag has been taken to a number of white supremacist rallies, indicating that the idea of this kind of fictional country—while satirical—is still important to the alt-right. This also reveals the ways memes and hashtags (circulating together and apart) cross over from virtual to physical spaces in important ways.

Despite the offline appearances of these symbols, as with anything associated with the alt-right, the Cult of Kek and the nation of Kekistan constitute a uniquely online phenomenon that exhibits the zany style evident in the rhetorical practices of meme making and trolling. While religious and national identity is often built around certain rhetorical practices, the Cult of Kek and Kekistan are built around the rhetorical practice of trolling. As such, it is unclear how much of the "cult" is sincere and how much is satire. In an article for the Southern Poverty Law Center, David Neiwert (2017b) writes, "In many ways, Kek is the apotheosis of the bizarre alternative reality of the alt-right: at once absurdly juvenile, transgressive, and racist, as well as reflecting a deeper, pseudo-intellectual purpose that lends it an appeal to young ideologues who fancy themselves deep thinkers. It dwells in that murky area they often occupy, between satire, irony, mockery, and serious ideology; Kek can be both a big joke to pull on liberals and a reflection of the alt-right's own self-image as serious agents of chaos in modern society." It is a safe assumption that the trolls who belong to the cult do not believe in a literal deity with the head of a frog. However, the Cult of Keke and Free Kekistan do serve a certain purpose for alt-right trolls. They give their movement something to rally around. They give them a way to communicate their zany sensibility and racist ideology. More than anything, the use of the #FreeKekistan hashtag and the presence of this flag at white supremacist rallies indicate that this fictional nation and its frog deity play a large role in the way this movement has cohered. While those who originally posted about Kek and Kekistan might have been trolling, this trolling has gone beyond the internet and had repercussions in the real world. One has only to look at the images of white supremacists waving Kekistan flags to see that there is something sincere and deeply troubling in this ironic religion and nation.

CONCLUSION

Through his association with the alt-right, Pepe would go on to become associated with Donald Trump's presidential campaign (see figure 11.5). If it had not been for Trump's presidential nomination, Pepe would have likely remained a popular figure in online subcultures but a fairly obscure figure in mainstream culture. However, Pepe's style of zaniness happened to mirror Trump's own zany rhetorical style, and Pepe's image would be shared by a number of figures associated with the Trump campaign (including the candidate himself). As Woods and Hahner (2019, 65) claim, Trump's sharing of a Pepe meme on Twitter was most certainly a "dog whistle to the Alt-right." The fact that sharing a Pepe meme could so safely be interpreted in this way speaks not only to Pepe's function as a symbol of the alt-right but also to the way zaniness has come to define the movement's particular rhetorical style. More generally, this analysis suggests that memes associated with or taken up by particular movements and hashtags function as a visual shorthand for more complicated underlying messages and histories that need to be unpacked through appropriate lenses.

To conclude a project such as this is a difficult task considering that Pepe's story continues to develop in interesting and unexpected ways. For instance, in June 2019, Furie won a $15,000 settlement against conspiracy theorist Alex Jones after Jones tried to sell posters depicting Pepe on his website *Infowars* (Epstein 2019). Although the lawsuit does not help Furie reclaim his creation from the alt-right or erase the character's racist associations, it does prevent others from profiting from those racist associations. In August 2019, Pepe's rhetorical life went in an even more unexpected direction when he was adopted as a symbol by pro-democracy protestors in Hong Kong (Victor 2019). Each of these moments is a significant moment in Pepe's rhetorical life. While

Figure 11.5. "Pepe J Trump" image

space prevents me from adequately dealing with them here, they offer exciting possibilities for the study of digital rhetoric and social movements.

In my analysis of Pepe's rhetorical life, I have focused on those moments that are most important to his emergence as a symbol for the alt-right and have argued that the reason Pepe was adopted by the alt-right is that the movement is distinguished by a particular style of online zaniness. I have also attempted to make an argument about how an object such as Pepe should be studied. To understand how Pepe became a symbol for the alt-right, it is important to account for his aesthetic origins and to take into consideration the sensibility and communication practices of the group that made him (in)famous. While memetics and iconographic tracking may help us generalize about the way visual objects move in digital spaces, they do not help us understand the way objects appeal to particular audiences. While these fields offer concepts and methods for studying how visual objects move in digital spaces, they do not fully provide concepts for describing why certain objects move in the particular ways they do. Zaniness provides scholars with a concept that helps us not only to understand why Pepe resonated with the alt-right but also to describe a significant amount of digital communication in the post-truth era. Future research may delve deeper into what this means for hashtag activism (or anti-activism) in general and the use of memes in such digital movements more specifically.

REFERENCES

ABC News (Australia). 2017. "Far Right Activist Richard Spencer Punched during Interview." *YouTube*, January 22. https://www.youtube.com/watch?v=aFho8JEKDYk.

Bennett, Jonah. 2016. "Here's How Two Twitter Pranksters Convinced the World That Pepe the Frog Meme Is Just a Front for White Nationalism." *Daily Caller*, September 14. https://dailycaller.com/2016/09/14/heres-how-two-twitter-pranksters-convinced-the-world-that-pepe-the-frog-meme-is-just-a-front-for-white-nationalism/.

"Cult of Kek." 2016. Know Your Meme, September 16. https://knowyourmeme.com/memes/cult-of-kek?full=1&page=10273.

Epstein, Kayla. 2019. "Pepe the Frog's Creator Just Won a $15,000 Copyright Settlement against Infowars." *Washington Post*, June 11. https://www.washingtonpost.com/technology/2019/06/11/pepe-frogs-creator-just-won-copyright-settlement-against-infowars/.

"Feels Bad Man/Sad Frog." 2010. Know Your Meme, June 3. https://knowyourmeme.com/memes/feels-bad-man-sad-frog.

"Feels Good Man." 2009. Know Your Meme, April 12. https://knowyourmeme.com/memes/feels-good-man.

Furie, Matt. 2016. *Boy's Club*. Seattle: Fantagraphics Books.

Gries, Laurie E. 2015. *Still Life with Rhetoric: A New Materialist Approach for Visual Rhetorics*. Boulder, CO: Utah State University Press.

Hawley, George. 2017. *Making Sense of the Alt-right*. New York: Columbia University Press.

"Kekistan." 2017. Know Your Meme, February 1. https://knowyourmeme.com/memes/kekistan.

"Meme Magic." 2016. Know Your Meme, February 8. https://knowyourmeme.com/memes/meme-magic.

Milner, Ryan M. 2016. *The World Made Meme: Public Conversations and Participatory Media*. Cambridge, MA: MIT Press.

Nagle, Angela. 2016. "The New Man of 4chan." *Baffler* 30. https://thebaffler.com/salvos/new-man-4chan-nagle.

Neiwert, David. 2017a. *Alt-America: The Rise of the Radical Right in the Age of Trump*. London: Verso.

Neiwert, David. 2017b. "What the Kek: Explaining the Alt-right 'Deity' behind Their 'Meme Magic.'" *Southern Poverty Law Center*, May 9. https://www.splcenter.org/hatewatch/2017/05/08/what-kek-explaining-alt-right-deity-behind-their-meme-magic.

Ngai, Sianne. 2012. *Our Aesthetic Categories: Zany, Cute, Interesting*. Cambridge, MA: Harvard University Press.

Nuzzi, Olivia. 2016. "How Pepe the Frog Became a Nazi Trump Supporter and Alt-right Symbol." *Daily Beast*, May 26. https://www.thedailybeast.com/how-pepe-the-frog-became-a-nazi-trump-supporter-and-alt-right-symbol.

Olson, Deidre. 2018. "How Memes Are Being Weaponized for Political Propaganda." *Salon*, February 24. https://www.salon.com/2018/02/24/how-memes-are-being-weaponized-for-political-propaganda/.

"Pepe the Frog." 2015. Know Your Meme, March 26. http://knowyourmeme.com/memes/pepe-the-frog.Pepe Trump.

Phillips, Whitney. 2015. *This Is Why We Can't Have Nice Things: Mapping the Relationship between Online Trolling and Mainstream Culture*. Cambridge, MA: MIT Press.

RichardBSpencer (@RichardBSpencer). 2017. "Set our people free! #FreeKekistan." Tweet, May 2. https://twitter.com/richardbspencer/status/859511380558458880.

Schwartz, Mattathias. 2008. "The Trolls among Us." *New York Times Magazine*, August 3. https://www.nytimes.com/2008/08/03/magazine/03trolls-t.html.

Shifman, Limor. 2014. *Memes in Digital Culture*. Cambridge, MA: MIT Press.

"Smug Frog." 2015. Know Your Meme, January 7. https://knowyourmeme.com/memes/smug-frog.

"Smug Nazi Pepe." 2014. Know Your Meme, November 7. https://knowyourmeme.com/memes/events/nazi-pepe-controversy.

"Troll." 2021. *Oxford English and Spanish Dictionary and Translator*. https://www.lexico.com/en/definition/troll.

Victor, Daniel. 2019. "Hong Kong Protesters Love Pepe the Frog. No, They're Not Alt-right." *New York Times*, August 19. https://www.nytimes.com/2019/08/19/world/asia/hong-kong-protest-pepe-frog.html.

Woods, Heather Suzanne, and Leslie A. Hahner. 2019. *Make America Meme Again: The Rhetoric of the Alt-right*. New York: Peter Lang.

12
WHO'S THE #FAKEHISTORIAN?
The Rhetoric of #FakeHistory among Conservative (Counter)Publics on Twitter

Anonymous

Much research on hashtag activism focuses on hashtags such as #YesAll Women, #NotYourAsianSidekick, and #SolidarityIsForWhiteWomen (Loza 2014; Dadas 2017). These hashtags challenge the status quo, bringing about positive change by disrupting discriminatory sociocultural systems. Yet this focus raises the question of how hashtags may be used to disrupt less obviously discriminatory systems or to enact injustice. One such hashtag is #FakeHistory. Made prominent by Dinesh D'Souza's ongoing Twitter feud with Kevin M. Kruse, #FakeHistory mobilizes far-right counter-publics against academic institutions in ways that deepen partisan "fault lines," or "sources of discord and tension" (Kruse and Zelizer 2019, 3), around education and perpetuate racist discourse.

A far-right–wing provocateur, Dinesh D'Souza is known for his books, documentaries, and talks criticizing academia as "a cesspool of liberal groupthink" (Pettit 2018). In particular, D'Souza insists that historical evidence showing that Southern Democratic leaders became Republicans in opposition to the Civil Rights movement is wrong. D'Souza leverages this claim as proof that progressive academics, not conservatives, are the real racists. In July 2018, D'Souza picked a Twitter fight with one particular academic: Kevin Kruse, a Princeton University historian specializing in political and civil rights history. On July 2, D'Souza posted a tweet inviting users to name the "racist Dixiecrats who . . . became Republicans." Kruse obliged with a twenty-eight-tweet thread detailing both national- and state-level Southern Democrats who switched parties, yet D'Souza doubled down, continuing to challenge Kruse on Twitter.

#FakeHistory as hashtag activism emerged out of this feud. Though D'Souza used it a few times before July 2018, he posted forty-four tweets hashtagged #FakeHistory between August 2, 2018, and June 10, 2019. At least five of those tweets named Kruse; others used #FakeHistory to

https://doi.org/10.7330/9781646423187.c012

characterize academic discourse broadly as brainwashing students with progressive political ideologies. #FakeHistory even went on tour. From October 2018 through March 2019, during the height of his quarrel with Kruse, D'Souza hosted the "#FakeHistory Debunked" tour. The tour, which promised to "expose . . . [students] to the truth that is left out of their education," amplified and clarified #FakeHistory's activism (New Guard Staff 2019). #FakeHistory emerged from the clash between academic and right-wing discourses to practice a kind of anti-hashtag activism. Drawing persuasive force from preexisting identifications among its right-wing counter-publics, #FakeHistory mobilizes these groups against university systems in ways that promote dehumanizing, racist discourse.

(COUNTER)PUBLICS AS FOSTERING HASHTAG ACTIVISM

In describing how #FakeHistory mobilizes far-right publics against academic institutions, I weave together two lines of research, exploring how hashtag activism generates and enacts counter-discourses as a form of social action. "Hashtag activism" refers to the "harness[ing]" of hashtags "to advocate for causes" on social media networks (Dadas 2017, 19). I focus on Twitter, as its interface ensures a "broad reach" for hashtags to be retweeted across networked communities, relatively unhindered by geographic or social boundaries (19). As a rhetorical tool available to be taken up and re-purposed at the grassroots level, hashtags involve a wide audience in issues often silenced by mainstream society (Loza 2014). Taking hold across multiple networks, hashtags amplify information, capture attention, and, ideally, spark real-world change (2014).

I build on this research in two ways. First, I focus on hashtags deployed primarily by a single, prominent social media user. Hashtags function not only to direct attention but also to collect and organize information, often across multiple locations, making them a kind of digital cataloging device (Potts 2013). Gathering unlimited tweets, along with embedded audiovisual material or hyperlinks, under a single heading, hashtags create fluid, open-access digital texts for audiences to (re)read in ways that enact and motivate social action. The cataloging function of hashtags invites attention to hashtag activism practiced by individual users, particularly those with a substantial follower count. Research on social media rhetoric notes the power of prominent users to shift conversation: in 2014, Donald Trump's tweets about the Ebola crisis forced a more robust Centers for Disease Control (CDC) response, despite the low risk to the American public (Salek and Cole 2019). Similarly, D'Souza, with 2.4 million Twitter followers as of August 2022, has the clout needed to shift the conversation around the perceived biases of academic discourse. In this context, as D'Souza tweets about #FakeHistory, the hashtag collects and recirculates that material among vast conservative networks, guaranteeing that his rhetoric has an impact far exceeding a single tweet or speech.

Second, I argue that the potential of hashtag activism to advocate for issues silenced within the public sphere makes it a powerful resource for counter-publics, including the right-wing counter-publics #FakeHistory addresses. Publics, Michael Warner (2002) writes, are "called into being by address" as listeners resonate with a rhetor's talk. Counter-publics are no different, yet the address that calls them into being centers on questions of power: "A counter-public maintains at some level, conscious or not, an awareness of its subordinate status. The cultural horizon against which it marks itself off is not just a general or wider public, but a dominant one. And the conflict extends not just to ideas or policy questions, but to the speech genres and modes of address that constitute the public" (86). Counter-publics, in other words, are at once subordinate to and defined against larger, socially normative systems, whether the state (Pason, Foust, and Zittlow Rogness 2017) or hegemonic social structures. Defined by their powerlessness within such systems, counter-publics discursively subvert those systems and agitate for oppositional ways of being. As counter-publics have no existential reality outside of discourse, the fact that their discourse "respond[s] to exclusion from dominant spheres" means that counter-publics maintain a provocative, trollish character relative to the hegemonic systems they inhabit (3). In this way, counter-public discourse both enacts and inspires ongoing social action (2017; Salek and Cole 2019).

At first glance, #FakeHistory does not seem to belong to counter-public discourse. After all, D'Souza, a vocal Republican and Trump supporter, deployed the hashtag during a time when both the Republican Party and Trump maintained substantial political strength (2018–2019). Yet as #FakeHistory is deployed, it *frames* conservatives as belonging to a counter-public, one threatened by progressive ideologies in cultural systems; the implicit threat guarantees that #FakeHistory gains traction.[1] As in the tweet in figure 12.1 publicizing D'Souza's talk at Liberty University, #FakeHistory casts its conservative audiences as engaged in a "clash" with the cultural systems they inhabit (Pason, Foust, and Zittlow Rogness 2017, 6).

D'Souza, asked in the embedded video about how to "overcome the movement to silence conservatives," insists that despite conservatives' recent political victories, the "larger battlefield" of culture is "dominated

Figure 12.1. D'Souza tweet urges conservatives to "take back" the culture.

by the Left." Casting the left as an existential threat, this response opens the door for D'Souza to call his audience to engage progressivism on the "battlefield" of culture. Such language, which amplifies the "clash" between the perceptively hegemonic left and the subordinate right, is clearly the language of a counter-public. As D'Souza repeats this language across the #FakeHistory tweets, urging listeners to "fight back" against the left, his discourse calls into being a counter-public eager to act against what it perceives as dominant progressive systems.

In particular, #FakeHistory addresses conservative students who perceive themselves as subordinated to liberal academic systems. Michel Foucault (1972) describes how academic systems maintain a "will to truth" that silences alternative ways of talking and thinking. Because this "will to truth" relies on institutional support, discourse that arises outside of academic institutions or that challenges them is marginalized (218). This exclusion creates conditions ripe for counter-publics to develop, as discourses disenfranchised within powerful academic systems advocate against them. #FakeHistory addresses conservative discourse as among those marginalized by institutions. In figure 12.1, for instance, D'Souza complains that the political left dominates the "cultural megaphone" of higher education and urges viewers, including the conservative students at Liberty University, to counter its powerful discourses, thereby establishing a clash between academic and conservative ways of talking and thinking.

Yet questions of marginalization are complicated, as conservative discourses are not marginalized within the university in precisely the same way as, for instance, discourses associated with People of Color (Flores and Rosa 2015). A majority of university faculty are progressive and likely to have a lower view of evangelicalism than of other religious practices (Tobin and Weinberg 2007). In addition, conservative students receive slightly lower grades during college than do their progressive peers (Woessner, Maranto, and Thompson 2019). Still, Matthew Woessner and his coauthors (2019, 14) insist that "conservative students [are not] under siege," saying there is no clear-cut evidence of ideological bias: "They [conservatives] remain largely satisfied with their college education, and perform nearly as well as, if not better than, their liberal counterparts. While students' political views may play a small role in their overall grades, success in college is more associated with measures of merit, and with demographic variables."

While conservative students may perceive themselves as marginalized within university systems, whatever marginalization exists is limited and dependent on a range of variables, including the institution and area of study. The idea of a systemic conspiracy against conservative students has limited value in explaining how ideas gain traction within academic discourse, especially given the current political power of the right. Yet the #FakeHistory hashtag collapses these complexities into a story about suppressing conservative thought, appealing to counter-publics that resonate with this perception of bias. To resolve these tensions, I place "counter" in parenthesis, using the term (counter)publics to acknowledge that #FakeHistory plays into perceptions of bias and suppression that persist among conservatives—especially in educational contexts—in spite of their current political strength. In the following sections, I analyze how #FakeHistory speaks on behalf of conservative (counter)publics against hegemonic academic institutions. I first analyze how the hashtag identifies with conservative ways of being, including those practiced by evangelical Christians. I then show how D'Souza deploys the hashtag to take a stance against academic discourse as illegitimate and how Kruse responds, rewriting #FakeHistory to expose D'Souza as a fraud. Finally, I discuss how the powerful narratives at stake in #FakeHistory skirt Kruse's criticisms and manifest in racist, dehumanizing discourse.

#FAKEHISTORY AS IDENTIFICATION AMONG (COUNTER)PUBLICS

#FakeHistory generates its power as hashtag anti-activism from purposefully identifying with (counter)publics that perceive themselves marginalized from academic systems, including politically conservative students and evangelical Christians. Kenneth Burke (1969, 55, original emphasis) writes of identification that "you persuade a man only insofar as you can talk his language . . . *identifying* your ways with his." Burke is writing of human rhetors, yet his point holds true for hashtags. Identification is particularly powerful within counter-discourses: since (counter)publics are discursively constructed, counter-rhetoric may easily position audiences "as 'belonging to [its] world'" (Pason, Foust, and Zittlow Rogness 2017, 10). This shared landscape enables the audience to locate itself in the concerns raised by counter-discourses and engage in collective social action as an extension of its own interests. #FakeHistory, drawing out preexisting identifications among its (counter)publics, creates an audience receptive to its warnings against oppressive academic discourse and to its call for social action.

The lines of identification between #FakeHistory and conservative (counter)publics arise from the #FakeHistory Debunked tour. Sponsored by the "conservative youth organization" the Young America Foundation ("Our Mission" 2019), the tour includes ten institutions, from Dartmouth to Liberty University, and centers on D'Souza's claim that university professors are "pushing a leftist message" that "undermine[s] American values" (New Guard Staff 2019). To conservative students, this message establishes the #FakeHistory tour as what Nancy Fraser terms a "parallel discursive arena," where they are free to speak their minds (cited in Pason, Foust, and Zittlow Rogness 2017, 7).

The hashtag #FakeHistory expands this arena to Twitter. Amplifying fears of a liberal bias within university systems, #FakeHistory "exploit[s] circulation systems" to travel swiftly across the vast conservative networks on Twitter (Pason, Foust, and Zittlow Rogness 2017, 13). In doing so, it creates lines of identification with dispersed conservatives who feel marginalized from their own liberal institutions and see the hashtag as speaking truth to power. In tweets such as figure 12.2, audiovisual resources situate #FakeHistory as "belonging to the same world" as students and supporting their interests.

In the picture in figure 12.2, D'Souza stands among "dozens of students," presumably conservative American University students; he appears similarly positioned in tweets hashtagged #FakeHistory posted from Stanford and Michigan State, standing shoulder to shoulder with students and implicitly participating in their cause. Such photographs suggest solidarity between the interests of conservative students and the message of #FakeHistory and invite students at other institutions to "see themselves" in the audience. Notably, in the tweet in figure

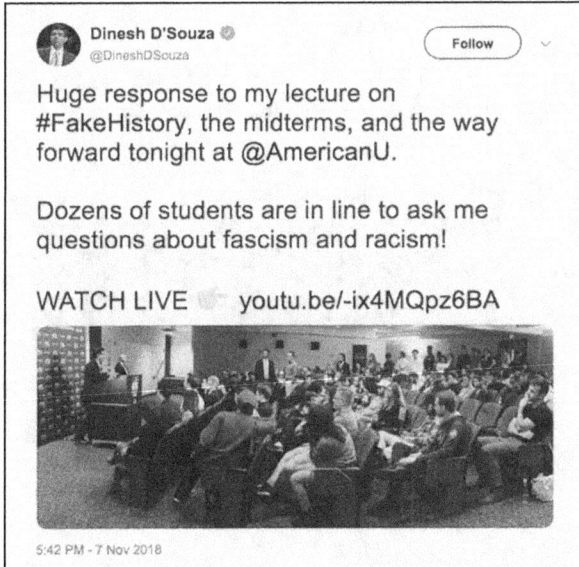

Figure 12.2. D'Souza tweet boasts of his crowd size at American University.

12.2, D'Souza also promises a "way forward" for conservative students, a message of hope and action for students who feel powerless at progressive universities. In this way, #FakeHistory builds a sense of shared interests between its own messages and the (counter)publics it calls into being.

Among those (counter)publics are evangelical Christians, who likewise see #FakeHistory as sharing their interests. D'Souza visits the (in)famous evangelical college Liberty University on his tour, as figure 12.3 indicates; his visit reveals the lines of identification between the hashtag's anti-activism and evangelicalism. Headed by Trump supporter Jerry Falwell Jr., Liberty University's mission statement reflects conservative principles, with references to faith-based learning and a high view of both Western civilization and capitalism ("Mission Statement" 2014). A stark contrast with secular universities, which historically value creating new knowledge, this mission identifies Liberty itself as a "parallel discursive arena," to use Fraser's term (Pason, Foust, and Zittlow Rogness 2017, 7). Aligning itself with the university's ethos, #FakeHistory powerfully advocates for social action against progressive ideologies.

In this tweet, the embedded video positions D'Souza on stage at Liberty University, speaking to evangelical Christians. The video bears Liberty University's watermark (a faint *LU* in the upper left-hand

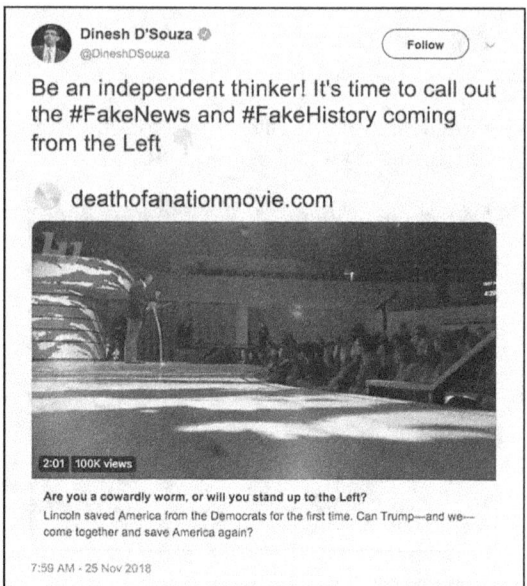

Figure 12.3. Tweet from D'Souza appearance at Liberty University

corner), suggesting institutional endorsement of the #FakeHistory message. In the video, D'Souza repeats his claim that the left seeks to dominate all aspects of culture, from academia to bakeries. Alluding to recent court cases that decided whether Christian bakers are legally obligated to bake a wedding cake for LGBTQ couples, the language of force and control D'Souza uses here stokes evangelical fears of losing their religious liberty. In response, D'Souza urges his audience to "stand up for [their] beliefs" and to "liberate [their] mind[s]." Sharon Crowley (2006) explains that narratives and rhetorics are so ingrained in our belief systems and values that we have a hard time understanding other people's perspectives or seeing a different side of a disagreement. This particularly applies to the narratives of Christianity in US society. Crowley writes that "believers are trained from childhood to defend their version of Christianity" (191), and D'Souza appeals to that belief system. While Liberty University maintains a diverse student body and many in the audience and among evangelicals broadly will reject the inflammatory messages of #FakeHistory, others will recognize its call to stand up for their Christian beliefs, to speak out against academic institutions, to maintain their liberty. Speaking evangelicals' language, #FakeHistory cultivates identifications between Christians' social interests and its own warnings about oppressive academic institutions, lending the hashtag strength.

#FAKEHISTORY AS STANCE TAKING AGAINST ACADEMIC DISCOURSE

The language moves at play in these exchanges demonstrate stance taking. John W. Du Bois (2007, 139) explains that stance taking is a language act that "has the power to assign value to objects of interest, to position social actors with respect to those objects, to calibrate alignment between stancetakers, and to invoke presupposed systems of sociocultural value." Various scholarship exists on the ways stance impacts the production, reproduction, and alteration of social and linguistic ideologies and hierarchies (Jaffe 2009). As of late, there has been increased attention to how this operates in computer-mediated discourse, for example, in subreddit threads (Kiesling et al. 2017), blogs (Myers 2010), and online article comments (Wang 2020). In online interactions, stance taking typically occurs within "the context of a conversational sequence and within the context of a community" (Kiesling et al. 2017, 684). Studies have found that stance taking in digital spaces takes on the form of self-presentation wherein individual positioning is often prioritized over collective and deliberate discussion (Myers 2010). Being that stance taking conveys a socially situated value judgment, it is important to consider how it can serve as a powerful tool in hashtag activism.

Building on the lines of identification between #FakeHistory and conservative, Christian (counter)publics that feel marginalized in higher education, D'Souza deploys the hashtag to take a stance against academic discourse as inaccurate and illegitimate. Yet D'Souza's stance, as a social act, invites a counter-stance: Kevin Kruse responds to D'Souza on Twitter, turning the language of #FakeHistory back to show that D'Souza is the real "fake historian." This double stance taking reveals that while the message of #FakeHistory has no empirical basis, the story it tells about conservatives shaking off an oppressive institution gives it ideological staying power, meaning that Kruse's rebuttals are ultimately insufficient to check the hashtag's anti-activist project.

In stirring up audiences' ire toward academia for allegedly marginalizing conservatives, #FakeHistory takes a stance against both academic discourse and the scholars who practice it as invalid and dangerous, as in the tweet featured in 12.4.

Notably, this tweet singles out a particular academic as a "fake historian": Kevin Kruse. A full professor at one of the most elite universities in the world, Princeton University, Kruse represents academia to the (counter)publics' #FakeHistory addresses. Targeting Kruse's work as "fake," D'Souza takes the stance that not only Kruse's work but the academic discourse it represents are invalid and oppressive or, more accurately,

Figure 12.4. D'Souza tweet claims only "idiots" believe historians such as Kevin Kruse.

invalid *because* they are oppressive. Indeed, this tweet describes historians such as Kruse as "propagating" #FakeHistory. With its obvious association with *propaganda*, the verb casts academic discourse as nothing more than leftist agitprop, a deliberate attempt to dupe the conservative (counter)publics enrolled at universities.

Stance taking "is reflexive," so in standing up to Kruse as a "fake historian," D'Souza asserts that his own work is real, positioning himself as a champion of truth and justice for the conservative (counter)publics he addresses (Du Bois 2007, 141). In video embedded in the tweet in figure 12.4, D'Souza describes his work as "bring[ing] historical research] down to empirical particulars," implying that his way of "doing history" is grounded in facts rather than politics. Among conservatives, who believe that truth is empirically discovered, not socially constructed, this claim to "empirical" discourse establishes D'Souza's reliability contra politically motivated academic historians. Elsewhere, D'Souza doubles down on asserting his reliability: he claims he is ready to "debate up to six opponents at the same time." The claim is ludicrous, of course; as Kruse explains, "real historians" do not "debate each other on a stage." Yet D'Souza's repeated offers of debate, never accepted by academic historians, prove to his audience the manifest strength and truth of conservative narratives.

However, in posting on Twitter, D'Souza is speaking publicly to a world that includes Kruse; because his stance is dialogic, his insistence that Kruse is "fake" invites the historian to respond (Du Bois 2007).

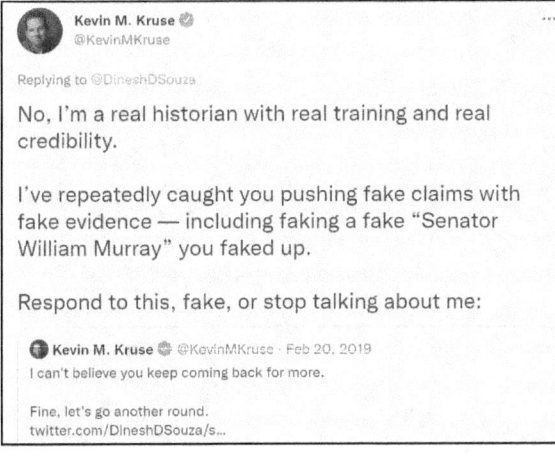

Figure 12.5. Kruse tweet insists he is a "real historian."

Kruse does so, repeatedly. During D'Souza's #FakeHistory Debunked tour, Kruse both replies directly to D'Souza and (more commonly) retweets D'Souza, adding lengthy threads with thorough historical documentation proving him wrong. Because Kruse's response to D'Souza is so robust, a deep dive into how he uses Twitter to undermine disinformation is impossible in this chapter. I focus therefore on a single tweet: Kruse's reply (figure 12.5) to D'Souza's characterization of academic discourse as propaganda (figure 12.4). In responding, Kruse rewrites the #FakeHistory narrative, taking the stance that he himself is the real historian and D'Souza the charlatan (figure 12.5).

In this reply, composed of only forty words total, Kruse repeats some version of the word *fake* six times. While Kruse does not use #FakeHistory, perhaps because in this context the hashtag is irrevocably linked to D'Souza's (counter)discourses, his prolific use of "fake" echoes the hashtag, rewriting its narrative so D'Souza is the real "fake" historian. Notably, Kruse's claim that D'Souza is a "fake" is one he supports with evidence, explaining in two other threads that William Murray was an Oklahoma governor who died a decade prior to the time when D'Souza names him among Democrats resisting the 1960s civil rights legislation. Readers can access this information by clicking on the tweet thread linked at the bottom of Kruse's reply, verifying for themselves that the "empirical particulars" D'Souza takes pride in are false. Because Kruse's rebuttal appears as a reply to D'Souza's tweet about #FakeHistory, it is included in the catalog created by the hashtag. There, within the #FakeHistory oeuvre, Kruse's response stands against its (counter)discourses, identifying D'Souza to his own audiences as a fraud.

Figure 12.6. Kruse tweet rebuts D'Souza's historical terminology.

Implicit in Kruse's stance against D'Souza is an affirmation of the reliability of his own work and of academic discourses broadly. In his reply, Kruse describes himself as a "real historian with real training and real credibility"; the triple "real" stresses the authenticity of his credentials, while the reference to his training—he received his doctorate from Cornell—locates that authenticity at least in part in academic institutions. Accordingly, in debunking D'Souza, Kruse enacts institutional discourse as evidence of his own reliability. In figure 12.6, for instance, Kruse links to a prior thread in which he supports his tweets with particular historical data and documentation.

Contrasting the actual definition of "Dixiecrat" with D'Souza's sloppy use of the term, Kruse marshals specific historical events to support his point. Naming and dating the Southern Manifesto and post–Voting Rights Act realignment, both events unknown to the wider public, Kruse affirms his close familiarity with historical particulars. Uploading relevant historical documentation to Twitter as images, Kruse also encourages readers to verify his claims for themselves. Notably, these are discursive moves that characterize Kruse's interactions with D'Souza; in June 2019, for example, Kruse debunked D'Souza's false claims that no Republicans in 1860 owned slaves by naming specific Republicans, uploading historical documents to Twitter, and retweeting other historians who made similar moves. Ultimately, these moves make Kruse's work more credible to a reading public. Yet they also echo discursive moves that define academic discourse, effectively transferring Kruse's academic ethos to Twitter and locating his credibility within institutional landscapes. Debunking D'Souza with empirical particulars and evidence, Kruse asserts his own reliability on the very terms #FakeHistory rejects.

Kruse's stances, against D'Souza and for the reliability of academic institutions, are productive in inoculating the wider public against historical disinformation. As Kruse himself writes in a tweet that gives his reasons for responding to D'Souza, "push[ing] back with the truth" is important, likening his work to doctors debunking anti-vaccination arguments. Kruse has a substantial following, including celebrities such as Chrissy Teigen; (re)circulating D'Souza's disinformation among them, he effectively shields them and others from falling prey.

Yet D'Souza is speaking more narrowly to conservative (counter)publics; perceiving themselves as marginalized by academic institutions such as the one Kruse inhabits, they are unlikely to buy into the historian's systemic debunking. Indeed, the debunking may further inflame the (counter)discourses of #FakeHistory. As Dana Cloud (2018, 18) writes, "to speak of truth is already to exert power"; as Kruse speaks truth to the anti-activism and disinformation of #FakeHistory, the listening (counter)publics perceive that truth as a power grab, an attempt to further silence conservatives in academic institutions. Relying primarily on empirical data, Kruse's tweets may reach an audience unaffiliated with D'Souza but are unable to touch the (counter)publics that identify with the messages of #FakeHistory. Among them, the powerful narratives attached to #FakeHistory enable it to circulate despite Kruse's criticism, though those narratives also collapse into dehumanizing, racist discourses as a way to enact the hashtag's key themes.

#FAKEHISTORY ACTIVISM AS DEHUMANIZING DISCOURSE

As (counter)discourse, #FakeHistory works not because of its command of historical realities but rather because of its narrative strength, its ability to tell a convincing story that gets at the heart of what its (counter)publics believe. Cloud (2018, 3) writes in *Reality Bites* of the power of such discourse, noting that discourses which "cultivate belief" and use "narrative, myth, embodiment, affect, and spectacle" to involve the reader in stories may resonate powerfully in ways facts cannot. This, ultimately, is how #FakeHistory works. Regardless of its factual inaccuracies, the hashtag is deeply intertwined with its (counter)publics' beliefs about their place in the world and speaks to their values, telling a story about how they may (re)claim a position of security and power.

D'Souza's interactions with audience members exemplify these narratives, enabling #FakeHistory to enact a revolt against the hegemony of higher education in ways that capture its (counter)publics' imaginations. While many audience members are themselves conservatives, a few seem to oppose D'Souza. In taking their questions, D'Souza enacts the anti-activism of #FakeHistory. Given that the hashtag's message takes a dim view of people with different viewpoints or diverse social or political commitments that contrast with conservatives' own, D'Souza's encounters with challengers are highly critical, punching down on less powerful individuals aligned with academic institutions in ways that expose dehumanizing discourses as key to #FakeHistory's anti-activism.[2]

One such encounter, in fact, appears in the tweet in which D'Souza accuses Kruse of producing leftist propaganda (see figure 12.4). While the tweet's text clashes with Kruse, the embedded video clashes with a Dartmouth student, who challenges D'Souza's claims. A young woman who identifies herself as "an immigrant . . . from the same country" as D'Souza (India), she says she is "disappointed because [he is] producing facts that are simply not true" and points to his interactions with Kruse as evidence that D'Souza does not know "how academics works." D'Souza tweets out this exchange in six separate posts over the course of a month (February 19 to March 18, 2019), each time using it to tell the story that makes #FakeHistory work: of conservatives standing up to the harassment and disinformation of progressive academic institutions. Yet crucially, the video tells a different story. The use of the word *battles* in the video title elides the situation's power dynamics. "Battles" positions D'Souza as seeking justice against powerful oppression, but, in fact, D'Souza himself is powerful. He stands behind a podium and has the ability to select the next speaker or to silence the person speaking; the unnamed student, a Woman of Color, lacks power. In "battling" this student as representative of oppressive academic discourse, D'Souza shows how #FakeHistory further marginalizes those who lack power, especially women and People of Color.

The exclusion and marginalization practiced by #FakeHistory are amplified in two additional tweets, including the one in figure 12.7. This tweet, which republishes the exact same video of D'Souza's encounter with his Dartmouth challenger under a different caption, more fully reveals the dehumanizing nature of #FakeHistory's anti-activism.

The tweet characterizes the student as a *heckler*, reducing her to her interaction with D'Souza. Significantly, "heckling" implies irrelevant and disruptive attacks; the student's question about the validity of D'Souza's facts is neither. "Heckler" writes off both her objections and

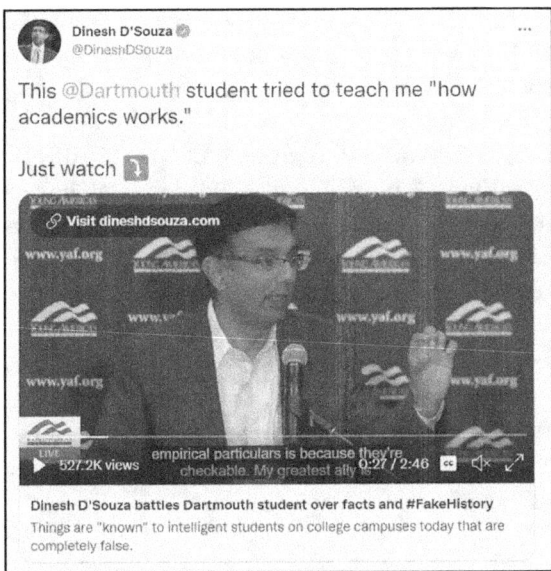

Figure 12.7. D'Souza compares his questioner to an undocumented immigrant.

her personhood as illegitimate, marginalizing her in the name of restoring power to right-wing (counter)publics. Comparing the student to an "illegal" reinforces this dehumanizing. The pejorative "illegal" emphasizes an individual as a threat over and against their humanity; with anti-immigrant rhetoric in the United States at a fever pitch, the term is inflammatory (Mohd Don and Lee 2014). Because the student identifies herself as born outside of the United States, the tweet, in comparing her to an "illegal," casts her and the academic discourses she engages with as foreign to American ways of talking and thinking.[3] As an example of the kind of activism provoked by #FakeHistory, the tweet exposes how a rhetoric of liberating (counter)publics that already inhabit powerful positions hinges on discourses of fear, marginalization, and dehumanization of diverse individuals as a proxy for oppressive systems.

Ultimately, the project of #FakeHistory is not (only) to resist academic discourse or the diverse ideas it circulates, as this final tweet makes clear. Dated February 18, 2019, one of the earliest published tweets in this sequence clearly represents the end game of #FakeHistory hashtag anti-activism: resisting and dehumanizing diverse *people*. D'Souza writes: "Things are 'known' to intelligent students on college campuses today that are completely false. Just look at what this heckler believes." This tweet makes the same moves as other tweets in this sequence: it includes #FakeHistory in the video title, so D'Souza's action exemplifies the "clash" generated by #FakeHistory; it elides the student's personhood with the nominalization "heckler"; and it punches down on a comparatively powerless student in the name of defending conservatives against #FakeHistory. Yet the tweet also invites readers to "just look," an imperative that involves D'Souza's (counter)publics in the action depicted in the tweet/video. Pointing downward, a white hand emoji directs readers' attention to the student. The tweet thus functions as collective action against #FakeHistory in which conservative (counter)publics work to free themselves from academic discourses by participating in D'Souza's oppression and belittling of a fellow student. #FakeHistory, meant to critique perceived power imbalances between progressive academic systems and conservative students, collapses into a tool to exert power over powerless individuals, circulating racist and sexist discourses among its vast (counter)publics. In doing so, #FakeHistory exemplifies the paradox that drives its discourses: its anti-activist work on behalf of a group that already holds substantial social power.

CONCLUSION

Ultimately, drawing persuasive force from identifications with conservative (counter)publics, #FakeHistory engages in anti-activism work meant to paint academic discourse as unreliable, a con job meant to prop up Democratic political power in the United States. By undermining the authority of individuals, both professors and students, who inhabit progressive universities, #FakeHistory enacts discriminatory discourses as it asserts the power of its own conservative audiences. Given that online discourses fan the rise of white nationalism, it's important to take seriously the ways hashtags such as #FakeHistory leverage their circulatory powers to work on behalf of unjust causes. In examining #FakeHistory's anti-activist work on behalf of powerful social groups, this chapter joins a growing body of scholarship on post-truth discourses and demagogic rhetorics. This work is urgent indeed, as rifts in the landscape of civic discourse continue to widen. In identifying how hashtag anti-activism amplifies injustice, this chapter lays the groundwork for further scholarship to probe, define, and respond effectively to rhetorics of injustice.

Key to this work is recognizing the paradox at the heart of such rhetorics: that anti-activist work simultaneously emerges from powerful social groups and asserts the marginalization of those same groups. As #FakeHistory illustrates, this paradox drives the narratives that make (counter)discourse persuasive, over and against empirical realities, and enable it to gain traction in the ideologically divided landscape of public discourse. Rather than making an overt power grab, rhetorics of injustice circulate and persuade by drawing on the fears of particular (counter)publics to masquerade as advocacy discourses, pursuing truth and justice. #FakeHistory reveals this paradox, yet crucial questions remain: How does this paradox take root in more distinctively political or religious spaces than the #FakeHistory tour D'Souza holds? In what way(s) is the paradox adapted for the (counter)publics the speaker aims to reach? Finally, how does the paradox interfere with the practice of civic discourse; and what can be done, in writing pedagogy and in our communities, to effectively respond to paradoxical (counter)discourses? Wrestling with such questions is not only a scholarly but an ethical imperative for rhetoric and writing studies. Addressing questions about how unjust rhetorics proliferate is a crucial step in equipping rhetoricians, writers, teachers, and students with the ability not only to understand but to counter such discourses and to advocate meaningfully for truth and liberation.

NOTES

1. Of course, #FakeHistory is not used solely by people on the political right to resist academic discourses. Unlike hashtags sparked by a specific cultural exigence, #FakeHistory has a range of uses, including mocking President Trump's description, on July 4, 2019, of Revolutionary War soldiers "taking over" the airports. In this chapter, I focus on only one use: the potential for #FakeHistory to resist academic discourse in ways that jeopardize conservative trust in higher education and deepen the partisan fault lines that characterize our national discourse.
2. A discussion of the following tweets, which feature D'Souza's increasingly dehumanizing exchange with the unnamed female Dartmouth student, amplifies D'Souza's hateful speech. I include these posts because as published tweets, they belong to the public record, and it's crucial to talk about them as a way of acknowledging and, it is hoped, disarming racist activism such as #FakeHistory supports. At the same time, to protect the subject of that discourse, I have elected to show the video at a moment when D'Souza, rather than the student, was onscreen.
3. D'Souza's treatment of the Dartmouth student and undocumented immigrants is reprehensible yet also paradoxical: D'Souza is himself an immigrant and a Person of Color. His participation in narratives demeaning such people echoes the way a few people of color, such as Candace Owens, participate in right-wing discourses. Also, demagogic rhetoric such as D'Souza's is defined by an us-versus-them dynamic (Roberts-Miller 2017): given that D'Souza rose to power in a conservative landscape, it is perhaps no longer possible for him to find common ground with any progressive causes or even to recognize the humanity of his fellow immigrants.

REFERENCES

Burke, Kenneth. 1969. *A Rhetoric of Motives*. Berkeley: University of California Press.
Cloud, Dana. 2018. *Reality Bites: Rhetoric and the Circulation of Truth Claims in U.S. Political Culture*. Columbus: The Ohio State University Press.

Crowley, Sharon. 2006. *Toward a Civil Discourse: Rhetoric and Fundamentalism*. Pittsburgh: University of Pittsburgh Press.

Dadas, Caroline. 2017. "Hashtag Activism: The Promise and Risk of 'Attention.'" In *Social Writing/Social Media: Publics, Presentations, and Pedagogies*, edited by Douglas M. Walls and Stephanie Vie, 17–36. Fort Collins: WAC Clearinghouse and University of Colorado Press.

Du Bois, John W. 2007. "The Stance Triangle." In *Stancetaking in Discourse: Subjectivity, Evaluation, Interaction*, edited by Robert Engelbretson, 139–182. Philadelphia: John Benjamins.

Flores, Nelson, and Jonathan Rosa. 2015. "Undoing Appropriateness: Raciolinguistic Ideologies and Language Diversity in Education." *Harvard Educational Review* 85 (2): 149–171.

Foucault, Michel. 1972. *The Archaeology of Knowledge and the Discourse on Language*. London: Tavistock.

Jaffe, Alexandra, ed. 2009. *Stance: Sociolinguistic Perspectives*. Oxford: Oxford Scholarship.

Kiesling, Scott F., Umashanthi Pavalanathan, Jim Fitzpatrick, Ziaochaung Han, and Jacob Eisentein. 2017. "Interactional Stancetaking in Online Forums." *Computational Linguistics* 44 (4): 683–718.

Kruse, Kevin M., and Julian E. Zelizer. 2019. *Fault Lines: A History of the United States since 1974*. New York: W. W. Norton.

Loza, Susana. 2014. "Hashtag Feminism, #SolidarityIsForWhiteWomen, and the Other #FemFuture." *Ada: A Journal of Gender, New Media, and Technology* (5). https://adanewmedia.org/2014/07/issue5-loza/.

"Mission Statement." 2014. Liberty University, March 7. http://www.liberty.edu/index.cfm?PID=6899.

Mohd Don, Zuraidah, and Charity Lee. 2014. "Representing Immigrants as Illegals, Threats and Victims in Malaysia: Elite Voices in the Media." *Discourse and Society* 25: 687–705. doi.org/10.1177/0957926514536837.

Myers, Greg. 2010. "Stance-taking and Public Discussion in Blogs." *Critical Discourse Studies* 7 (4): 263–275.

New Guard Staff. 2019. "Now Is Your Chance to Expose #FakeHistory." Young America's Foundation. https://www.yaf.org/news/debunkfakehistory/.

"Our Mission." 2019. Young America's Foundation. https://www.yaf.org/about/.

Pason, Amy, Christina R. Foust, and Kate Zittlow Rogness. 2017. "Introduction: Rhetoric and the Study of Social Change." In *What Democracy Looks Like: The Rhetoric of Social Movements and Counterpublics*, edited by Christina R. Foust, Amy Pason, and Kate Zittlow Rogness, 1–26. Tuscaloosa: University of Alabama Press.

Pettit, Emma. 2018. "How Kevin Kruse Became History's Attack Dog." *Chronicle of Higher Education*, December 16. https://www.chronicle.com.

Potts, Liza. 2013. *Social Media in Disaster Response: How Experience Architects Can Build for Participation*. New York: Routledge.

Roberts-Miller, Patricia. 2017. *Demagoguery and Democracy*. New York: The Experiment.

Salek, Thomas A., and Andrew W. Cole. 2019. "Donald Trump Tweets the 2014 Ebola Outbreak: The Infectious Nature of Apocalyptic Counterpublic Rhetoric and Constitution of an Exaggerated Health Crisis." *Communication Quarterly* 67 (1): 21–40. doi: 10.1080/01463373.2018.1526812.

Tobin, Gary A., and Aryeh K. Weinberg. 2007. *Profiles of the American University*, vol. II: *Religious Beliefs and Behavior of College Faculty*. San Francisco: Institute for Jewish and Community Research.

Wang, Ping-Hsuan. 2020. "Negotiating Racialized Sexuality through Online Stancetaking in Text-Based Communication." In *Gender, Sexuality, and Race in the Digital Age*, edited by D. Nicole Farris, D'Lane Compton, and Andrea Herrera, 187–203. New York: Springer.

Warner, Michael. 2002. "Publics and Counterpublics." *Public Culture* 14 (1): 49–90. https://muse.jhu.edu/article/26277.
Woessner, Matthew, Robert Maranto, and Amanda Thompson. 2019. "Is Collegiate Political Correctness Fake News? Relationships between Grades and Ideology." University of Arkansas, Department of Education Reform Working Paper Series. http://dx.doi.org/10.2139/ssrn.3383704.

13

DIGITAL MATTERS
Twitter Reacts and Hashtivist Narratives

Gabriel I. Green and Morgan K. Johnson

In our current technological and political moment, popular and scholarly understandings of Twitter are more abundant and important than ever. In addition to statistical and demographic information about Twitter's volume and usage (Cooper 2019; Aslan 2018; Gottfried and Shearer 2017), there is a wealth of scholarship devoted to Twitter's capacity for creating and managing identities, building community, framing events, and facilitating change. Coinciding with the site's ballooning popularity, these functions increasingly amount to a variety of digital activist practices, or hashtivism. In this regard, scholars have theorized about the current and potential uses of Twitter, including but not limited to Twitter as counterspace (Lu and Steele 2019; Graham and Smith 2016; Vats 2015), hashtags as discursive strategies (Hoyt 2018; Clark 2016; Orbe 2015), and the practical and measurable impact of both on social justice/political movements (Ramirez and Metcalfe 2017; De Cock and Pedraza 2018).

Despite this emergence in scholarship, researchers are still learning the many and dynamic ways Twitter is rendered rhetorically effective. That is, given the magnitude of Twitter's opus and a bevy of theoretical and applied knowledges about Twitter and its sociopolitical potentialities, how might we continue to make sense of the plurality of hashtivist conversations and discern what matters—what is rhetorically beautiful—to citizens on and off Twitter? While hashtags help organize digital discourses into trackable and measurable archives that orient users (and others) to particular conversations, the magnitude of some hashtagged discourses is too great to be fully apprehended by users or scholars. Thus, the way discursive threads and even discrete tweets are used to construct narratives from/about larger digital discourses is insightful. We assert that these stories, the narratives assembled from pieces of Twitter's counter-discourses, contribute significantly to the platform's power of persuasion.

https://doi.org/10.7330/9781646423187.c013

This chapter models a way for scholars to analyze such narratives—narratives produced through secondary texts focused on trending hashtags—so they can better understand the creation and (re)circulation of meanings attached to particular events, issues, and movements discussed across and beyond the Twittersphere. To this end, we situate hashtag activism within theoretical conversations about archival magnitude, rhetorical beauty, and the imperative to "[make] things matter" (Farrell 1998, 1). Departing from the practices featured in other chapters, which analyze primary datasets of tweets, in this chapter we examine secondary texts about informally and/or strategically gathered tweets. Here, we study the popular online genre of media content, which we refer to as "Twitter Reacts" (TR) articles, exploring their utility for synthesizing and circulating digital discourses while also producing new narratives. By analyzing TR articles about #BlackLivesMatter and drawing connections to other sociopolitical occurrences such as the rise of #MAGA,[1] we showcase the curatorial function of TR articles specifically and the flow of hashtivist narratives more generally.

A METHOD OF MATTERING

The virality of a hashtag does not fully account for its uptake and reception. With regard to its capacity to persuade, it matters less that #BlackLivesMatter has been tweeted more than 15 million times over the last five years and more that of those 15 million unique tweets, users will only ever encounter a fraction and engage even fewer. Therefore, as Jenny Rice (2017, 38) stated, "a hallmark of big data is not simply the amount of data collected but the way that data is made coherent." For example, she described the use of visualizations to manage archival magnitude and to make sense of raw data. Citing Anthony McCosker and Rowan Wilken (2014), she said that big data visualizations, from simple word clouds to more complex geotag maps, "go beyond merely presenting the data mined in any mass collection"; rather, they "pass over into a *sense* of something coherent, a sense that possibly transcends the individual pieces of datum that are contained within the aesthetic whole" (Rice 2017, 38, original emphasis). In this way, the visualization is "not anything like truth or representation" but a new creation that stands in as a "satisfying" substitute (40). Thomas B. Farrell (1998, 6) also spoke to the significance of coherence, stating, "magnitude can only be said to matter to us, if we are able to take it all in." In fact, for Farrell, this is the very domain of rhetoric: as "the art, the fine and useful art, of making things matter" (1). Both Farrell and Rice note this conception of coherence as "akin to what Aristotle describes as the beauty of proper order," "for beauty depends on magnitude and order" (Rice 2017, 38; Farrell 1998, 6–7). Influenced by these ideas, this chapter asks: with the sheer quantity and unwieldy way meanings travel across and through viral hashtags, how are the movements they relate to understood, framed, and made to matter to those who support and resist their causes?

It is from this shared concern with coherence and Farrell's definition of rhetoric that we locate the value of the "Twitter Reacts" (TR) digital media genre. Our terminology emerges from the relatively common headline refrain "Twitter Reacts to . . ." Increasingly popular as digital news content in the era of clickbait, TR articles appear on almost any topic, from government policy[2] to celebrity drama.[3] TR articles consist of curations of tweets on a particular (often hashtagged) topic. While these curations are not actually representative of the entire discourse, they usually frame narratives and arguments as representative of the greater discourse. That is, when Twitter users discuss a particular event, corresponding TR articles are assumed to provide a reliable peek into the larger conversation/s or at least a larger segment of a conversation.

As a genre, TR articles attempt to provide a specific kind of coherence from the greater archive and, in doing so, they create new narratives and arguments to be read as *beautiful* (Farrell 1998, 7). Under the premise of representing a range of reactions expressed on Twitter, TR articles are highly rhetorical—assembling discourse fragments, framing arguments, and ultimately inventing new narratives that contribute to public discourse surrounding the issues, event, or movement online and offline. In this way, TR as a genre provides valuable insight into the dynamic ways hashtags and their incumbent discourses are framed and understood, engaged and re-purposed, to a variety of audiences and to just as many ends. As Rice argues, the creation and maintaining of archives (in this case, of hashtagged discourses) are rhetorical acts toward persuasive efforts. Thus, similar to the visualizations Rice (2017) identified as aesthetic reproductions, TR articles are rhetorical reproductions of hashtagged discourse, (re)articulating central narratives and arguments to make them both accessible (coherent) and appealing (beautiful) or, we suggest, to make them *matter* to new audiences.

To use a basic and concrete example, consider a bouquet of roses, which can only be appreciated as such when seen and beheld at a certain distance. If one can only see a rose from the microscopic view of a single petal, then the greater coherence of the object is lost. Further, imagine that one's perspective of the bouquet is focused on the prickly thorns that can cause—or perhaps in the past have caused—discomfort; the bouquet is likely to be viewed as dangerous. In this case, not only is one unable to view the full bouquet, but their positionality is such that the encounter is less likely to be beautiful and instead undesirable, threatening, ugly. Mapping this metaphor onto Twitter, consider #GreenNewDeal, a hashtag in reference to the climate-change initiative of the same name. Obviously, goals and plans for the Green New Deal's implementation are far more complex and nuanced than can be captured in one soundbite, let alone a single tweet. However, if a TR article only includes tweets that reference the Green New Deal with regard to the goal of reversing climate change, the potentially astronomical costs of implementation would be erased from this new narrative. Now imagine an (also existing)[4] alternative in which discourse about the Green New Deal is reduced to radical left-wing musings about how cow farts and "attacks on hamburgers" cause global warming, hence suggesting that no proposed legislation could truly solve the problem. In either of these examples, it would not matter that such a presentation would be both insignificant and inaccurate. If that presentation is produced and reproduced as representative of all the initiative is, it would not be far-fetched for one's view of the Green New Deal to be undesirable, threatening, and ugly.

In this way, TRs facilitate coherence through the use of discrete tweets to construct a narrative that is often framed as metonymic of the whole, representative of Twitter reactions writ large. This provides the illusion of a holistic/totalistic perspective (i.e., the full bouquet); however, in relation to the hashtag's corpus, it is really a new configuration of parts, an inventive assemblage of complementary and competing narratives (i.e., a petal or even the tip of a petal). As a result, TR articles prompt readings of and engagements with the specific curation presented as a proxy for the larger discourse, as well as the issue, event, or movement of topic. Rachel Kuo (2016, 497) termed this process "collective action framing . . . an active process of agency and contention at the level of reality construction, which frames an interpreted schemata that actors can locate, perceive, identify, and label within their life space." News outlets and writers participate in this process when they interpret the narratives and arguments in hashtagged discourse and (re)present them by assembling curations of "exemplar" tweets. As interpretive products, TR articles signal to readers what to understand as salient in the discourse. TR articles allow us to consider what, within hashtagged discourse, resonates with particular audiences—what is made to *matter* to them—and is therefore reproduced and recirculated to greater audiences through news media. TR articles ultimately operate as a proverbial <tl;dr>[5] of a larger rhetorical moment, allowing insight into the persuasive techniques that are re-purposed and amplified from Twitter to larger discourse communities (i.e., the readership of a particular website on which a TR article appears) that might not otherwise encounter the social network or contribute to the hashtag. In this way, we understand these articulations of coherence to be significant sites of intervention in issues of rhetorical circulation.

Because TR articles cannot attune to all of the rhetorical nuances of the larger Twitter dialogue they engage with—and, we would argue, they do not necessarily intend to—what is at stake is a construction of reality that re-creates and reinforces aesthetic positionalities and, by extension, difference/identification, angst/conciliation, division/unity, fear/pleasure, and more. In this way, the value of analyzing TRs is not to access the persuasive elements of a hashtagged discourse writ large but rather to grapple with TR articles as sites of invention and means of persuasion. TR articles simultaneously function to index the (re)circulation of hashtagged discourse, as they seek to cohere existing tweets, and to contribute its own invention to broader movement discourses, as they foster particular orientations to the subject matter. This provides insight into the (re)circulation and production of narratives surrounding a given hashtag. To showcase how this plays out, in the next section we analyze TR articles featuring #BlackLivesMatter tweets to demonstrate the ways these articles portray the Twitter dialogue and movement. We attend to common rhetorical moves found in this genre and their potential impact.

EXAMPLE: "TWITTER REACTS" NARRATIVES OF #BLACKLIVESMATTER

#BlackLivesMatter Background

Co-creator Patrisse Khan-Cullors (2018, 66–67) spoke (or rather posted) Black Lives Matter into being on July 13, 2013, as she watched the trial of George Zimmerman for the murder of Trayvon Martin with grief, outrage, bafflement, and fear. With Zimmerman's acquittal, Khan-Cullors understood Martin's death and its sanction by law as exemplary of a larger American culture of Black disposability. Responding to her friend Alicia Garza's Facebook post of shock about and resistance to the legal decision, Khan-Cullors posted simply "#BlackLivesMatter." Immediately, Khan-Cullors, Garza, and friend Opal Tometi began organizing around the hashtag. She recalls, "We [were] determined to take public this basic concept: That our lives mean something. That Black Lives Matter" (Khan-Cullors and bandele 2018, 80). What Khan-Cullors, Garza, and Tometi created is "an ideological and political intervention in a world where Black lives are systematically and intentionally targeted for demise" and one that is purposefully inclusive of Black life across the diaspora experiences and of all genres of identity (Black Lives Matter n.d.).

Since 2013, Black Lives Matter (BLM) has arguably become the most significant social movement of the twenty-first century. When Michael Brown, a Black teenager in Ferguson, Missouri, was shot to death by white police officer Darren Wilson in 2014, BLM organized with local clergy and activists, emphasizing Ferguson "not as an aberration, but in fact, a clear point of reference for what was happening to Black communities everywhere" (Black Lives Matter n.d.). Thanks largely to Twitter, it was in Ferguson that BLM lodged itself firmly into the mainstream consciousness. Now consisting of more than forty chapters across the globe, BLM aims to "create a network where Black People feel empowered to determine our destinies in our communities" (n.d.).

Not only was the movement born as a hashtag, it has since been tweeted more than 30 million times, taking the title of the third most used hashtag in Twitter's first decade of existence (notably, the related hashtag #Ferguson was one of the two that topped it). #BlackLivesMatter has become synonymous with resistance to police abuse, and in 2015, members of the movement collectively made the short list for *Time* magazine's Person of the Year. Use of the hashtag spiked after high-profile police killings, namely those of Eric Garner and Philando Castile.

Rhetorical Utility/Analyses of Twitter Reacts

As one of the most prominent hashtags in Twitter history, much research has attended to #BlackLivesMatter. Many researchers have accounted for the hashtag's volume (Anderson et al. 2018; Freelon, McIlwain, and Clark 2016) and factors of participation (De Choudhury et al. 2016; Freelon, McIlwain, and Clark 2016), identifying how many individuals contribute to the hashtag's conversations and the digital communities with which those individuals associate or belong. Candice Lashara Edrington and Nicole Lee (2018) coded and analyzed all tweets—save retweets and replies—posted by the @BlkLivesMatter account between January 1, 2014 and December 31, 2017. Kate Keib, Itai Himelboim, and Jeong-Yeob Han (2018) examined #BlackLivesMatter tweets over twenty days in February 2015, coding for valences of importance and emotion (i.e., positive, negative, neutral, unclear). An impressively large and frequently cited project is Deen Freelon, Charlton D. McIlwain, and Meredith D. Clark's (2016) study for the Center for Media and Social Impact. Their report, titled "Beyond the Hashtags," involved 40,815,975 tweets purchased from Twitter. In addition to the important insights provided by these studies, we offer analysis of TR as a means of illuminating the appropriation and creation of narratives surrounding hashtags.

Consider the TR article written by Sophie Kleeman (2014) for Mic .com following the grand jury decision not to indict Officer Wilson, titled "15 #BlackLivesMatter Tweets Everyone Needs to See." These tweets "put the [#BlackLivesMatter] campaign into even sharper perspective," Kleeman writes, sanctioning their characteristic nature for readers. These fifteen tweets speak to a number of argumentative themes and rhetorical devices; for example:

Time and history: Nine of the tweets make implicit or explicit reference to a longue durée perspective of anti-Black police violence, indicating variously long histories of Black deaths by police over decades or generations. Explicit references include an illustration of Amadou Diallo, Patrick Dorismond, Timothy Stansburg, and Sean Bell (Reid 2016).

Above their portraits is the question "When Will It Stop?" Listed below their images are their names, the years of their deaths, and the number of bullets police fired into their bodies. An implicit reference to time is found in a tweet that begins, "[It] saddens me that it's 2014 and #BlackLivesMatter is a trending hashtag." Such a perspective functions rhetorically to contextualize this iteration of necropolitics along the time line of the nation and within the broader state regime as well as to emphasize the magnitude of cumulated bodies. The systemic nature of police violence is emphasized in tweets that state "This is bigger than Darren Wilson" and "Everyday I'm reminded this system isn't broke, it was built this way." Tweets that emphasize the issue of magnitude, of ever more *death*, utilize depictions of multiple victims or, as follows, the suggestion that there are simply too many victims to even count.

Listing: Listing is a citation practice and rhetorical tradition that has become strongly associated with the post-Ferguson movement for Black lives, as seemingly daily the name of a Black person becomes a hashtag through death. Four of the tweets feature or reference the listing of names in death. For example, one tweet references the practice, asking "Without looking it up—How many unarmed Black boys/men shot [and] killed by the cops can you name?" Other tweets engage in it, listing the names of Marissa Alexander, Monica Jones, Mike Brown, John Crawford, Tamir Rice, Amadou Diallo, Patrick Dorismond, Timothy

Stansburg, and Sean Bell. Another tweet depicts, but does not name, six apprehended murderers who appear to be white and six victims of police violence, each Black.

Similar practices are found in Celisa Calacal's (2016) TR article for *Think Progress*. Here, the title establishes the representativeness of her curation ahead: "What 3 Years of 'Black Lives Matter' Means, in 11 Powerful Tweets." Reminiscent of Valeriana Colon's (2016) consideration of literacy events in the broader Black Lives Matter social movement, Calacal's (2016) curation centers on the verified Black Lives Matter account's three-year anniversary prompt: "Today, #BlackLivesMatter turns 3. Tell us . . . In a world where Black Lives Matter, what do you imagine?" While the author identifies themes of cultural appropriation, Black children/childhood, and conditions of resistance, there are more rhetorical nuances to the curated narrative. Independently and together, these TR articles represent BLM as historically grounded and currently exigent; as affecting individuals, families, and communities; as a source of hope. They do this by curating existing tweets *and* by contributing this new text to the broader conversation. In doing so, they (re)produce narratives of state violence and suffering, resistance and unity, around both #BLM the hashtag and BLM the movement.

Consider alternatively a TR article written by Megan Maxey of the conservative media outlet *Townhall* following the shooting of three Baton Rouge police officers in June 2016. The article, titled "Five #BlackLivesMatter Tweets Show How 'Nonviolent' the Cause Is," puts the movement into a much different perspective for a different audience. This curation of tweets offers a narrative that presents #BlackLivesMatter as a violent movement through various thematic elements.

Sarcasm: The tweets featured in this TR article (Maxey 2016) rely on sarcasm to counter the claim of #BLM's nonviolent philosophy. For example, one tweet states, "#BlackLivesMatter activist: 'Kill all white babies.' It's a peaceful group though & not racist at all—CNN told me." Above the caption is a video of an African American protester saying the phrase. The sarcastic undertones are also evident in the reference to CNN, which is commonly considered a left-wing news outlet. The sarcastic mention of #BLM and CNN together functions rhetorically to suggest to *Townhall* readers that not only is #BLM a violent organization but that liberal CNN is a complicit enabler of the violent rhetoric #BLM preaches.

Claims of moral apathy: Working in conjunction with sarcastic elements is the narrative presentation of #BLM as a movement of moral apathy. The compiled tweets portray an image of #BLM that juxtaposes the deaths of three police officers with praise, insensitive indifference, or even disappointment that "only three cops were murdered."

Presenting the movement as morally obtuse and violent plays up centuries-old stereotypes around the fear of Black bodies and displays of Black aggression. We assert that this TR, through this extremely small curation,[6] is intended to portray the digital rhetorics of #BLM as frightening and to argue that the aesthetic of the movement is rhetorically ugly. As such, this curation of tweets suggests *Townhall*'s rhetorical audience as either having a distant caution toward BLM at best or perhaps having a predisposed bias against #BLM at worst. This demonstrates the (re)production and (re)circulation of discourse seeking to counter and delegitimize the efforts of BLM—all the while alongside those texts of the same genre that function to do the opposite.

DISCUSSION

Through the abridged analyses of TR articles here, we hope to have demonstrated the analytic utility of this media genre as it both indexes the invention and (re)circulation of topoi in digital movement rhetorics and contributes new narratives to greater movement discourses. While one could surely identify implicit bias in virtually any news coverage, TR articles are unique in that select tweets serve as virtual stand-ins, "empirical" evidence of what a larger discourse contains. For example, these analyses provide insight into the title of Khan-Cullors and bandele's (2018) memoir, *When They Call You a Terrorist*, as a response to a narrative of violence that is recirculated in certain communities (i.e., *Townhall* readership specifically or far-right media more generally). Further, as with Rashawn Ray, Melissa Brown, Neil Fraistat, and Edward Summers's (2016) study and Ryan J. Gallagher Andrew J. Reagan, Christopher M. Danforth, and Peter Sheridan Dodds's (2018) study of counter-movement discourses, we find the TR genre useful for considering the relationship between #BLM and other sociopolitical movements. A comparison of the narratives between positively valanced and negatively valanced TR curations reveals discursive relationships between movements and counter-movements. The significance of TR characterizations is not accuracy but the form's rhetorical *premises of accuracy and representativeness* and therefore heightened persuasive capacity.

Particularly in 2016—with the killing of three Baton Rouge police officers, the viral murders of Alton Sterling and Philando Castile, and the entire fiasco that was the presidential election cycle—such a rhetorical situation was ripe for the picking. While we would stop short of directly attributing the rise of (counter)movements such as #MAGA (Make America Great Again) to negative representations of #BLM, we assert that it is no coincidence that these events overlapped. Ever since he descended the golden escalator in Trump Tower to announce his campaign, the former US president has been able to capitalize on the rhetorical power of #MAGA with undeniable success. Within an increasingly polarized political atmosphere, it is not a far reach to suggest the high level of rhetorical uptake the slogan has enjoyed over the last several years. The former president himself gives a lot of credit to his use of social media as a key part of his campaign's success.

We note attempts of symbolic usurpation of #BlackLivesMatter by #MAGA to further suggest the utility of and possibilities for TR articles as datasets for rhetorical studies of hashtivism. The relationship we posit between these two movements is one characterized not by opposition but by the ways narratives generated by #BlackLivesMatter interacted with and were supplemented (at least in volume) by #MAGA. Both hashtags are responding to the exigence of racial and social anxieties and changes to the sociopolitical landscape that have captured national attention over the last several years. Where #BlackLivesMatter is responding to the history of Black disposability and calls to action to resist—online and offline—systems of white supremacy in an effort to create a more racially equitable public, #MAGA is also, at least in part, a fearful response to anxieties about perceived racial (in)equality and progress. For example, consider the chants of Charlottesville's "Unite the Right" rally in August 2017: "You Will Not Replace Us," "White Lives Matter," "Blood and Soil," "We Will Be Back." The connections between the racialism that implicitly and explicitly constitutes the discourses of #MAGA and the presidency of Donald Trump were strengthened when mainstream news noted his supporters taking to the bleakly allusive chant "Hail Trump" (Cook 2017; Neiwert 2017; Smith 2018). In this light, it behooves scholars to consider the processes through which these movements are *made to matter*. Understanding the invention and (re)circulation of movement narratives between and beyond (counter)publics highlights the texture and motion of movement discourses, and TR as a genre is a manifestation of such in today's digital world.

Because TRs are a rhetorical act of invention, different media outlets can (and do) arrange and order the magnitude of a large archive like #BlackLivesMatter to fit the aesthetic positionality of their respective rhetorical audiences. To return to our rose metaphor, a curation of #BlackLivesMatter tweets that center protests, destruction of property, and the physical embodiment of Black anger as solely representative of

#BlackLivesMatter discourse, while an exercise in coherence, is more the portrayal of a prickly thorn than a bouquet of roses for politically conservative readerships. The same likely rings true for representations of #MAGA as physically hostile campaign rallies, demonstrations for the preservation of Confederate monuments, and calls for a return to the "good ole days" of ambiguous decades passed. As a result of TR representation, #BlackLivesMatter's and #MAGA's relationship dynamic in terms of their online presence is one that is more functionally reciprocal (and perhaps, to some degree, even causal) rather than oppositional.

CONCLUSION

The importance of Twitter is surely made clear throughout this volume. Online communities generally and the platform specifically are largely and loudly credited with Black Lives Matter's cultural prominence and ongoing sustenance. Similar power has been attributed to social media sites with regard to Barack Obama's presidency as well as Donald Trump's. In fact, Donald Trump is so prolific a tweeter that media institutions archive and factcheck his tweets with some regularity, some accusing him of governing from the keyboard (see, for example, Carr 2008; "Trump on Twitter" 2016; Savage 2019). In this light, it is important for scholars to analyze not only tweets but also how tweets *live*: where they go and what they interact with along the way, how they are curated and arranged, and what makes them matter to different audiences and to what ends.

TR articles seek to crystalize exemplary arguments and present consolidated narratives as a form of coherence. In this way, our argument for and demonstration of TR as a resource for rhetorical analysis of hashtagged discourse and interventions in the complications of Twitter's archival magnitude support Rice's (2017, 46) caution that while consideration of "how *megethos* drives our own rhetorics and the archives we build . . . [it] won't unmake our own rhetorics . . . [it] will trouble any comfort we take in the sense of coherence." Twitter Reacts allows us to get at salient arguments and persuasive strategies that become prominent in public discourse as they are (re)circulated by media in an attempt to provide coherence from the diffuse network of tweets. Ultimately, we emphasize that sites of movement and discursive (re)articulation—like TR articles—though they mitigate the complication of magnitude through efforts of coherence, can actually reify the fears and toxic polarity that currently inform the political moment. Thus, regardless of whether TR characterizations are accurate, they are persuasive and important sites to consider when contemplating news media literacy and hashtag activism.

NOTES

1. MAGA or #MAGA stands for "Make America Great Again," the campaign slogan of presidential candidate and forty-fifth US president Donald Trump.
2. For example, see Zhao (2019).
3. For example, see "Twitter Reacts to Jussie Smollett's Dropped Charges" (2019).
4. Consider this tweet posted by Natural Resources GOP (2019).
5. An abbreviation for "too long, didn't read." This notation is commonly used to indicate a brief summary for readers who do not want to read a full text.
6. Three of the tweets selected for this TR stem from a single account.

REFERENCES

Anderson, Monica, Skye Toor, Lee Rainie, and Aaron Smith. 2018. "An Analysis of #BlackLivesMatter and Other Twitter Hashtags Related to Political or Social Issues." Pew Research Center, July 11. http://www.pewinternet.org/2018/07/11/an-analysis-of-blacklivesmatter-and-other-twitter-hashtags-related-to-political-or-social-issues/.

Aslan, Salman. 2018. "Twitter by the Numbers." *OmniCore*. https://www.omnicoreagency.com/twitter-statistics/.

Bennett-Swanson, Meredith. 2017. "Media Coverage of Black Lives Matter." *Critique: A Worldwide Student Journal of Politics* (Spring): 98–130.

Black Lives Matter. n.d. "Herstory." https://blacklivesmatter.com/about/herstory/.

Calacal, Celisa. 2016. "What 3 Years of 'Black Lives Matter' Means, in 11 Powerful Tweets." *Think Progress*, July 14. https://thinkprogress.org/what-3-years-of-black-lives-matter-means-in-11-powerful-tweets-21b30fbeaa49/.

Carr, David. 2008. "How Obama Tapped into Social Networks' Power." *New York Times*, November 10. https://www.nytimes.com/2008/11/10/business/media/10carr.html.

Clark, Rosemary. 2016. "Hope in a Hashtag: The Discursive Activism of #WhyIStayed." *Feminist Media Studies* 16 (5): 788–804.

Colon, Valeriana. 2016. "Citizen Journalist to Activist: The Language behind Black Lives Matter." *Teaching and Learning Publications of the Department of Teaching and Learning at Virginia Commonwealth University*. https://scholarscompass.vcu.edu/cgi/viewcontent.cgi?article=1007&context=tedu_pubs.

Cook, Nancy. 2017. "Trump Fails to Condemn White Supremacists in Statement on Charlottesville Violence." *Politico*, August 8. https://www.politico.com/story/2017/08/12/trump-white-supremacists-charlottesville-violence-241575.

Cooper, Paige. 2019. "28 Twitter Statistics All Marketers Need to Know in 2019." *Hootsuite*. https://blog.hootsuite.com/twitter-statistics/.

De Choudhury, Munmun, Shagun Jhaver, Benjamin Sugar, and Ingmar Weber. 2016. "Social Media Participation in an Activist Movement for Racial Equality." *Proceedings of the International AAAI Conference on Web and Social Media* 10 (1): 92–101. International AAAI Conference on Weblogs and Social Media.

De Cock, Barbara, and Andrea Pizarro Pedraza. 2018. "From Expressing Solidarity to Mocking on Twitter: Pragmatic Functions of Hashtags Starting with #jesuis across Languages." *Language in Society* 47: 197–217.

Edrington, Candice Lashara, and Nicole Lee. 2018. "Tweeting a Social Movement: Black Lives Matter and Its Use of Twitter to Share Information, Build Community, and Promote Action." *Journal of Public Interest Communications* 2 (2): 289–306.

Farrell, Thomas B. 1998. "Sizing Things Up: Colloquial Reflection as Practical Wisdom." *Argumentation* 12: 1–14.

Freelon, Deen, Charlton D. McIlwain, and Meredith D. Clark. 2016. "Beyond the Hashtags: #Ferguson, #Blacklivesmatter, and the Online Struggle for Offline Justice." Center for Media and Social Impact, American University, Washington, DC.

Gallagher, Ryan J., Andrew J. Reagan, Christopher M. Danforth, and Peter Sheridan Dodds. 2018. "Divergent Discourse between Protests and Counter-protests: #BlackLivesMatter and #AllLivesMatter." *Public Library of Science One* 13 (4). https://doi.org/10.1371/journal.pone.0195644.

Gottfried, Jeffrey, and Elisa Shearer. 2017. "News Use across Social Media Platforms." Pew Research Center, September 7. http://www.journalism.org/2017/09/07/news-use-across-social-media-platforms-2017/.

Graham, Roderick, and Shawn Smith. 2016. "The Content of Our #Characters: Black Twitter as Counterpublic." *Sociology of Race and Ethnicity* 2 (4): 433–449.

Hoyt, Kate Drazner. 2018. "#Handsupdontshoot: Connective Images and Ethical Witnessing." *Critical Studies in Media Communication* 36 (2): 103–121.

Keib, Kate, Itai Himelboim, and Jeong-Yeob Han. 2018. "Important Tweets Matter: Predicting Retweets in the #BlackLivesMatter Talk on Twitter." *Computers in Human Behavior* 85: 106–115.

Khan-Cullors, Patrisse, and asha bandele. 2018. *When They Call You a Terrorist: A Black Lives Matter Memoir.* New York: St. Martin's.

Kleeman, Sophie. 2014. "15 #BlackLivesMatter Tweets Everyone Needs to See." *Mic*, November 24. https://mic.com/articles/105002/15-black-lives-matter-tweets-everyone-needs-to-see#.ZWRq4dLOV.

Kuo, Rachel. 2016. "Racial Justice Activist Hashtags: Counterpublics and Discourse Circulation." *New Media and Society* 20 (2): 495–514. doi: 10.1177/1461444816663485.

Lu, Jessica H., and Catherine Knight Steele. 2019. "Joy Is Resistance: Cross-Platform Resilience and (Re)invention of Black Oral Culture Online." *Information, Communication* 22 (6): 823–837.

Maxey, Megan. 2016. "Five #BlackLivesMatter Tweets Show How 'Nonviolent' the Cause Is." *Townhall*, July 18. https://townhall.com/tipsheet/meganmaxey/2016/07/18/social-media-reacts-to-attacks-on-police-n2194192.

McCosker, Anthony, and Rowan Wilken. 2014. "Rethinking 'Big Data' as Visual Knowledge: The Sublime and the Diagrammatic in Data Visualisation." *Visual Studies* 29 (2): 155–164.

Natural Resources GOP (@NatResources). 2019. "Before @AOC and @SenMarkey outlaw our hamburgers because of the Green New Deal, we have to take full advantage of this opportunity." Tweet, February 27. https://twitter.com/NatResources/status/1100877515365715978.

Neiwert, David. 2017. "When White Nationalists Chant Their Weird Slogans, What Do They Mean?" Southern Poverty Law Center, October 10. https://www.splcenter.org/hatewatch/2017/10/10/when-white-nationalists-chant-their-weird-slogans-what-do-they-mean.

Orbe, Mark. 2015. "#AllLivesMatter as Post-racial Rhetorical Strategy." *Journal of Contemporary Rhetoric* 5 (3–4): 90–98.

Ramirez, Gerardo Blanco, and Amy Scott Metcalfe. 2017. "Hashtivism as Public Discourse: Exploring Online Student Activism in Response to State Violence and Forced Disappearances in Mexico." *Research in Education* 97 (1): 56–75.

Ray, Rashawn, Melissa Brown, Neil Fraistat, and Edward Summers. 2016. "Ferguson and the Death of Michael Brown on Twitter: #BlackLivesMatter, #TCOT, and the Evolution of Collective Identities." *Ethnic and Racial Studies* 40 (11): 1787–1813.

Reid, Mikhaela. 2016. "When Will It Stop?" *Mikhaela.net*. http://mikhaela.net.

Rice, Jenny. 2017. "The Rhetorical Aesthetics of More: On Archival Magnitude." *Philosophy and Rhetoric* 50 (1): 26–49. doi: 10.5325/philrhet.50.1.0026.

Savage, Charlie. 2019. "Trump Can't Block Critics from Twitter Account, Appeals Court Rules." *New York Times*, July 9. https://www.nytimes.com/2019/07/09/us/politics/trump-twitter-first-amendment.html.

Smith, David. 2018. "After Charlottesville: How a Slew of Lawsuits Pin Down the Far Right." *The Guardian*, May 29. https://www.theguardian.com/world/2018/may/29/charlottesville-lawsuits-heather-heyer-richard-spencer-alt-right.

"Trump on Twitter: A History of the Man and His Medium." 2016. *BBC News*, December 12. https://www.bbc.com/news/world-us-canada-38245530.

"Twitter Reacts to Jussie Smollett's Dropped Charges." 2019. AOL, March 26. https://www.aol.com/article/entertainment/2019/03/26/twitter-reacts-to-jussie-smolletts-dropped-charges/23700807/?guccounter=1&guce_referrer=aHR0cHM6Ly93d3cuZ29vZ2xlLmNvbS8&guce_referrer_sig=AQAAAC_h_fg6CZgKl_6BUhBJYobZ43nQpIEgZAne3GVdgx7ISU_1oYaKePWCTheHrHC4hyDo1XTCMzC2CMzpjOJ7rE219yhVO9MGZ4ucJfoMa_1kx2usYHknNUDDIe3kpwFPDJtrlEtTz7hAb6l2OWIQxYAP5FdaxemzCoZ2dAzBwEVo.

Vats, Anjali. 2015. "Cooking up Hashtag Activism: #PaulasBestDishes and Counternarratives of Southern Food." *Communication and Critical/Cultural Studies* 12 (2): 209–213.

Zhao, Christina. 2019. "Twitter Reacts to Betsy Devos' Proposed Budget Cuts to Special Olympics: 'More Like Betsy Devoid of Basic Human Empathy.'" *Newsweek*, March 26. https://www.newsweek.com/twitter-reacts-betsy-devos-proposed-budget-cuts-special-olympics-more-betsy-1376326.

Conclusion
CAPTURING A MOVING TARGET
Ethical Research Practices for Hashtag Activism

Elizabeth Buchanan, Rosemary Clark-Parsons,
Stephanie Vie, William I. Wolff, and Kristi McDuffie

SETTING THE STAGE

Kristi: Few issues related to hashtag activism are more pressing and exigent than ethics. While best practices in internet research ethics are ever evolving and have been evolving for decades, studying hashtag activism adds even more opaque challenges for researchers. In this chapter, four scholars who study internet research, from writing in social media to Twitter activism to internet research ethics specifically, answer several questions facing internet researchers today. Specifically, these qualified respondents outline the most pressing issues presently facing hashtag activism scholars, detail their own experiences with this research, provide advice for best practices related to hashtag activism research ethics, and give advice for hashtag activists. Holistically, this chapter provides differing perspectives on ethical issues facing each study in this collection and provides a launching pad for future ethical work on hashtag activism. In addition to reading this conversation, we suggest that you use the references at the end of the chapter as a list of suggested readings for more information on internet research ethics.

Question 1: What are the biggest ethical challenges facing scholars researching hashtag activism?

Rosemary: The biggest ethical challenges facing hashtag activism research stem from two sources. First, those who engage in this form of digital protest are often from marginalized communities, and their tweets often include narratives of personal traumas or struggles. An ethical approach to any scholarship involving vulnerable populations and their personal data, in digital contexts or otherwise, requires researchers to take steps to ensure that their work does not further marginalize their participants. This is a major concern for researchers studying activism, who may seek to align their scholarship with the politics of the community or movement under study. But it's an especially complex issue for researchers studying *hashtag* activism, whose observations are situated within a primarily text-based platform that can feel removed from the actual people using it. This leads to the second source of ethical challenges: developing an ethical research praxis that centers the needs and concerns of a marginalized community becomes difficult when the researcher is not face to face with her participants.

Therefore, the digital environment raises a number of ethical questions for hashtag activism research: what does it look like to treat Twitter data collection and analysis with the same care that we treat more conventional, in-person human subjects research? How do we obtain consent to collect and quote tweets or observe the unfolding of a hashtag campaign when participants can't see us? When we disseminate our findings, does the publication of activists' tweets outside the Twitter platform open them up to any risks or violate their personal sense of privacy? How can we make our findings, especially when published in closed-access academic journals, accessible to the authors of the public tweets that ground our research? Throughout every stage of their projects, scholars studying hashtag activism need to engage in ethical reflection that centers the marginalized people behind the tweets. By engaging in this reflexivity, we can become more aware of and, in turn, more accountable for the ways our research process may reinscribe the same systems of power hashtag activists work to contest.

Stephanie: I agree with Rosemary that some of the biggest ethical challenges around hashtag activism research are connected to acknowledging and respecting the stories that members of marginalized communities are sharing and understanding the potential consequences of circulating other stories or other writing, such as retweeting or recirculating particular hashtags. First, circulation matters: some scholarship can already be found about the implications of circulation (Dieterle, Edwards, and Martin 2019; Edwards 2018; Edwards and Gelms 2018; Gries and Brooke 2018). Brandy Dieterle, Dustin Edwards, and Paul "Dan" Martin (2019, 197) articulated that "sharing preexisting writing—retweeting, forwarding, sharing, reblogging, and so on—assumes and constructs a rhetorical relationship with others and thereby deserves thoughtful contemplation about what such a relationship entails," further arguing for circulation tactics that emphasize "inclusivity, social justice, and mindful contemplation." Second, stories matter; the narratives of those who have experienced structural and systemic violence need to be heard, and hashtag activism can help bring attention to these necessary stories. Finally, *recirculating writing matters* (199, original emphasis).

When considering hashtag activism research in particular, which often incorporates shared lived experiences and stories, it's critical to consider as researchers whether and how to share and recirculate those stories, particularly when they're being shared by individuals from vulnerable populations. I'm thinking specifically about the ethics of retweeting and quote tweeting here as an example of why circulation matters in such research. Both NPR (Johnson 2014) and *The Atlantic* (Jacobs 2012) have spent time discussing the implications of retweeting, particularly retweeting content that is hateful or hostile. I'm thinking here, too, of the careful decision-making around choosing not to recirculate particular hashtags associated with online harassment such as #GamerGate or to strategically use alternative hashtags like #INeedDiverseGames (see Evans and Janish 2015) to counter toxic hashtag campaigns. Strategic circulation of alternative hashtags can thus serve to "draw attention away from the strategic amplification of harassment but also to redirect circulation flows into a [different] discussion" (Dieterle, Edwards, and Martin 2019, 207).

Academics' research on social media—as well as their own social media activity and hashtag circulation—can place them in potential danger, making the choice of whether to (re)circulate or to use a particular hashtag intensely personal. For instance, Shira Chess and Adrienne Shaw (2015) discussed how GamerGaters turned their attention to academics, specifically Digital Games Research Association (DiGRA) conference participants who were collaboratively composing a Google Doc about intersectionality in games research after hosting a fishbowl-style conference conversation at DiGRA. Shaw's DiGRA conference tweets became known to the GamerGaters, and then "tweets from the DiGRA conference led them to the Fishbowl Google Doc . . . Connections and conspiracy theories proliferated following this" (212). They noted further: "The focus on DiGRA and our own work has given us a jarring reminder of how often feminist research and ideology become targets for hate speech, regardless of the specifics or context. As feminist research becomes a more prominent part of other research areas, we realize that the results are often mixed. While our research and the research of other feminist scholars might help create more awareness, it also opens scholars up to the very harassment they are studying" (218). Much as some researchers have called for not naming mass killers when reporting on their crimes, in an effort to prevent their names and notoriety from circulating—and in fact there is a hashtag campaign, #NoNotoriety, regarding this—retweeting hateful content calls into question the implications of further circulating hate and whether further circulation may indicate endorsement of those hateful messages. Even Chess and Shaw's experience shows how participating in academic analysis of digital aggression can potentially place scholars in harm's way, calling into question what our choices might be in responding to online toxicity.

These are complex questions with no easy answers. But given the importance of these conversations, I turn to scholarship that thoughtfully addresses how hashtag activism scholars might think both proactively and reactively about storytelling, circulation, and ethics. One excellent edited collection that grapples with many of these questions is Jessica Reyman and Erika M. Sparby's (2019) *Digital Ethics: Rhetoric and Responsibility in Online Aggression*, which smartly outlines ways participants in online spaces can think carefully about ways to respond to online aggression that move beyond simply staying silent or refusing to engage. Second, I recommend the Association of Internet Researchers' (AoIR) recently updated "Internet Research: Ethical Guidelines 3" document, which provides heuristics for many of the critical ethical questions that emerge in internet research generally and are applicable to hashtag research ethics specifically (franzke et al. 2020). In the previous version, AoIR explained its concerns as follows: "Does the connection between one's online data and his or her physical person enable psychological, economic, or physical harm? One way of evaluating the extent to which these ethical dilemmas may be hidden is to focus on the way that procedures for data collection or analysis extract data from lived experience" (Markham and Buchanan 2012, 7).

In sum, a focus on whose stories are being told, who's circulating them, on what platforms, to what end, and for what purpose(s) is particularly critical for hashtag research. And a consideration of what ethical responsibilities we might have in our various roles—as scholars, as faculty, as platform designers, and as people who use digital technologies—is crucial as well.

Bill: I agree with what Rosemary and Stephanie have written, but I also think it is important to realize that hashtags are often used by individuals who mean to do harm to individuals and societies by, for example, spreading misinformation, hate, and conspiracies; trolling; and undermining democracy. Often these tweets come in the form of bots, but often they are tweeted by humans imitating bot-like activity through complex networks of people who meet in Twitter DM rooms, 4chan,

8chan, Gab, and other spaces where they are provided with orders for what to tweet, when to tweet it, and who to tweet at. I'm thinking about #qanon tweets here, for example. And in still other instances, people spread hate through racist memes and alphabetic content. So I ask: what expectations of privacy do bots, trolls, and racists have?

In the past, we have looked at privacy through a spectrum of public to private with shades of gray in between. We know that people believe they have a semblance of privacy even when their content is public, and most scholarship on the subject, including mine (Wolff 2017), has encouraged researchers to err on the side of caution. We advise not to publish identifying information in our articles, including usernames and even the tweets themselves. But bots, trolls, and racists deliberately want their content spread as far as possible and to be seen by as many as possible. Do those tweets deserve the same privacy expectations? What about accounts that spread disinformation designed to undermine democracy, such as those studied by a group of academics, technologies, and artists who published a report about the #VoterFraud hashtag, where they deliberately released the usernames and avatars of 200 accounts: "The 200 accounts . . . are a sample of a network on Twitter talking about Voter Fraud and amplifying false and/or misleading narratives about election integrity and the democratic process. We discovered that this group of 200 accounts either generated or were mentioned in over 140 million tweets over the last year. This network is not only growing at an accelerating rate but also coordinating with effective tactics that appear to bypass many of the detection methods of existing disinformation research" ("/VoterFraud" 2018).

There was a similar publication of identifiers in the Plain View Project, which exposed racist Facebook posts shared by police officers throughout the county. The identifiers and content were included in the database "because we believe that they could undermine public trust and confidence in our police. In our view, people who are subject to decisions made by law enforcement may fairly question whether these online statements about race, religion, ethnicity and the acceptability of violent policing—among other topics—inform officers' on-the-job behaviors and choices" ("The Plain View Project" 2019). Numerous officers identified in the database faced consequences, including being fired.

Further, as we saw leading up to Brexit and the 2016 US presidential election, fake user accounts targeted specific users in ways designed to change the conversation and spread misinformation. As Amber Buck (2019) discussed in her Computers and Writing talk, the researchers of a #BlackLivesMatter project (Stewart et al. 2017) found out after the publication of their article that 8,500 tweets in their sample of 66,000 were actually from fake accounts created by the Russian Internet Research Agency that "impersonated activists on both sides of the conversation" (Starbird 2018). That led Buck to state pointedly, "We often don't know what we're studying when we study social media" (2019).

Buck's and Starbird's warnings should give researchers pause as we engage in studies of hashtags and hashtag activism and make us question our methods and how we come to conclusions. How, for example, can we ensure that the tweets in our archives were tweeted by real people tweeting authentically? Is that something that could ever be known? Do we accept the fact that some tweets may have been shared by bots or other AI and push on? If not, how do we identify bots and bot-like behavior so we can remove them from our datasets prior to analysis and visualization? Further, we need to consider that there are times when maintaining account privacy is unethical because doing so could continue to undermine the public good. Was it wrong to expose the police officers who shared racist Facebook posts? Or the 200 accounts that spread disinformation about voter fraud? If it was unethical, is it unethical to look to and cite their reports in our research? Questions, as always, lead to more questions.

Elizabeth: Drawing from these pointed comments, it is obvious that no shortage of ethical issues confronts researchers in hashtag activism research. Many of the issues are long-standing in internet research ethics, such as the tensions between public and private spaces, voice and ownership of narrative and representation, and concerns with research harms. A particularly challenging ethical issue in social media spaces, particularly in hashtag activism research, involves the collision of actors in those spaces. Platforms and technologies control and are controlled by varied interests, ideologies, and discourses at play. I feel strongly that researchers need to be active and advocate for rigorous and ethical research in and across social spaces, and they need to combat the misuses and abuses that take place by other non-research actors. Big data and, increasingly, AI-based research have tremendous potential and power to confound actors' identities and their messages. Research integrity itself is under attack, and ethics becomes an even messier domain.

There is a constant interplay between, as Rosemary mentioned, public and private postings and how these posts are used or reused by these various actors. (For examples and extended discussion of this issue, see chapter 13, this volume.) There are the tensions Stephanie described in representing voice and narrative stemming from social media data and re-crafted in other venues. And Bill calls attention to potential bad actors roaming and dominating social media spaces, confounding issues of truth and reality and promoting alternative facts. The ways market researchers, analytics companies, and other third-party actors function vis-à-vis social media spaces is significantly different from academic researchers, predominantly researchers such as those contributing to this volume, who try to fit their work into extant ethical and regulatory models. A question I would ask, then, is this: *is the research playing field fair, and to/for whom?* This question is intentionally broad, as research participants, researchers, and other actors are competing for space and purpose. The ways in which "a fact" can take on completely different meanings on alternate channels is a significant ethical and epistemic issue and a fundamental concern for the integrity of research. Similarly, we must consider the ethics surrounding the ways data can be monetized or misused—subject to algorithmic bias, for example—depending on the platform or technology.

A starting point for researchers, particularly hashtag activism researchers, is a simple question: *why should we (research participant, audience, community, public, and others) believe you, the researcher?* Answering this question first should be prioritized: what if Aleksandr Kogan of Cambridge University (now infamous for his role in creating the app that harvested data from, by some accounts, 87 million Facebook users and that dubiously employed a psychometric profiling technology) had asked that question, prior to his ethics board application? (It is well worth reading the correspondence from the Cambridge Research Ethics Board on its concerns with, and ultimate rejection of, Kogan's research [see Weaver 2018].)

This case is extremely important for us to think about as researchers—not only was the research deemed unethical and substandard in terms of consent and privacy protections, but it shows the ease with which university ethics boards have little standing in industry research. Of course, industry is not governed by the same regulatory regimes, but shouldn't core research ethics apply regardless of setting or actor?

Question 2: What experiences and influences have shaped your views and your work on ethics and hashtag activism?

Rosemary: My research focuses on US feminist movements and their media practices. I draw on ethnographic and interpretive methods, so I often work directly with feminist activists. Their emphasis on personal agency has a significant influence on my approach to internet research ethics. Consent and bodily autonomy are at the core of feminist politics, from campaigns to expand abortion access to movements against sexual violence and harassment to the fight for trans people's rights, and I bring the same values to my research ethics. This means that when I'm studying feminists' digital writing, including hashtags and tweets, I aim to build a methodological approach that respects their agency over their personal information and narratives. This involves taking a contextual approach to privacy. I feel strongly that just because a user consented to publishing a message publicly on Twitter does not necessarily mean they have consented to having that message published in other contexts, such as an academic journal or a news story.

US feminist movements also have a rich history of consciousness raising and public pedagogy. I incorporate these practices into my research process by making my work publicly accessible. This commitment requires additional labor and I am not always successful at making enough time for generating more public-facing writing, but it is especially important for hashtag activism scholarship. Work in this area is grounded in activists' publicly available tweets, so when their scholarship is published, hashtag activism researchers benefit from the labor of the activists who produced the hashtag under study. More often than not, the scholarship we generate benefits us more directly than it does the communities we study. But hashtag activism researchers can correct at least some of this imbalance by making the knowledge they generate out of activists' tweets publicly available and, when possible, accessible to a nonacademic audience.

Finally, as I mentioned earlier, I almost always work with activist communities that are composed of marginalized people. US feminists have long called for political and theoretical frameworks that center the perspectives of those most marginalized (e.g., Collins 2000; Crenshaw 1989; Smith 1990). These approaches also inform my methodological choices.

Stephanie: In my previous role at the University of Central Florida, I worked closely with graduate students. As I've transitioned into a new position at the University of Hawaii at Mānoa, I continue to mentor many of the students from UCF and look forward to supporting new graduate students at this institution. When I mentor students, I often mention how foundational the comprehensive exam and dissertation process can (and in my mind should) be for providing a baseline for research methodologies and ethical stances. Of course, as we grow as scholars and as technologies themselves evolve and change, our methodological approaches, methods, and ethical stances may also change. But I reflect back on the comprehensive exam process I went through when

I was completing my PhD at the University of Arizona, and I chose intentionally to focus one of my lists on feminist and qualitative research. I knew that I was interested in research that listens to people's voices and that works to make a difference in the world, however big or small that influence may be.

Even small steps matter, and some of my previous research attends to the potential influence of supposedly unimportant things like profile pictures, memes, and even hashtags (Vie 2014). So much of my work deals with elements of popular culture, and I try to reclaim their importance, to resist some people's belief that these things don't matter or they have no impact in the world. In the face of critical global climate change and what seems like the steady erosion of democracy in the US (among other pressing issues of our time), it can be difficult to look at something like a hashtag and think it matters. (Or to think that choosing one term versus another matters or that the image one chooses for a presentation matters, and so on.) But I remain convinced that these things do matter. As a scholar of rhetoric, I'm firmly convinced that words, language, imagery, and hashtags matter. These communicative elements are ways we represent our understanding of what happens in the world around us, and I believe strongly that representation matters.

That's a long-winded way to say that my graduate work was foundational in setting the stage for the kind of research I wanted to do, and as I've grown as a scholar—and as the field of rhetoric and composition has grown and evolved, too—my approach to hashtag research and ethics has continued to refine. Some of that refinement has come from attending to work that's coming out of the field about social media, data mining, surveillance, algorithms, and identity from scholars such as Estee N. Beck (2015), Vie and Jennifer deWinter (2016), John Gallagher (2017), Les Hutchinson (2017), Michael Trice, Liza Potts, and Rebekah Small (2019), Colleen A. Reilly (2016), Jessica Reyman and Erika M. Sparby (2019), and others who are pushing us to consider how algorithmic technologies interact with and complicate approaches to internet research that involves human participants. I try to share some of that foundational spark with the students with whom I work, encouraging them to see that choices about methods and methodologies, for example, involve more than just figuring out a theoretical framework on which to hang one's hat. Instead, exploring and understanding methods, methodologies, language, and imagery is all part of understanding the rhetorical nature of communication and as a result is a part of developing one's frameworks for being in the world and being with the world.

Bill: I began studying online writing behaviors after reading Kathleen Blake Yancey's (2004) Conference on College Composition and Communication keynote address in which she called for the field to more thoroughly understand how and why people are writing, unprompted, in spaces outside the classroom. I was at a transitional moment in my scholarship, ready to begin a new project; and I knew that I wanted to focus on Twitter, hashtags, and how people are using both to communicate and, perhaps, create community. I was faced with a choice: I could choose a topic I thought was dry, such as conference hashtags, or something fun that I knew would keep me interested for many years. I chose the latter and, as a result, began my work focusing on the writings of Bruce Springsteen fans (Wolff 2015). Since I was starting to look at fan writings, my initial framework for studying participatory culture came from those in the field of fan studies, most notably at first Camille Bacon-Smith's *Enterprising Women* (1992) and Henry Jenkins's *Textual Poachers* (1992) and *Fans, Bloggers, and Gamers* (2006). Their work on participatory culture opened a whole new world for me, showing just how much work had already been done to address Yancey's questions by scholars in other fields and offering suggestions for how to ethically engage with fans, fan communities, and the work they individually and collaboratively produce. I'll touch on that more in my answer to question 3 below.

Once I decided to focus on Springsteen fans, I had to figure out what kind of study I was going to create. The archiving options at that stage were relatively narrow, and I chose to use yourTwapperKeeper, created by John O'Brien. I was an early adopter of yourTwapperKeeper, archiving class and conference hashtags. But for this study I knew I would need more space and O'Brien was beginning to shift away from hosting everyone's hashtags on his own servers. With his help, in 2012 I set up an instance of yourTwapperKeeper and began archiving. After a year and over 2.5 million tweets in the archive, I had to figure out what to do with all the data: how to narrow them down, how to define my methodology, how to ensure accuracy, and so on. Brian J. McNely's work on hashtags (2010) introduced me to grounded theory, and so I began to read everything I could about the methodology, most notably Kathy Charmaz's (2006) *Constructing Grounded Theory: A Practical Guide through Qualitative Analysis*. Because I was new to it at the time, I repeatedly communicated with Christa Teston and Vincent Rhodes, two scholars who had experience with grounded theory, to ensure that my methods were sound. Once I reached the stage where I was ready to set up the study, I was indebted to Liza Potts, who helped me work through various ethical and practical questions and concerns I had regarding IRB applications, citation and quotation practices, and permissions.

As I reflect on my history with studying hashtags, I realize just how daunting the challenge was to jump into this new world of Twitter archiving and data analysis and how fortunate I was to have a community of peers ready to offer guidance. Those also seem like much more innocent times in studying hashtags and participatory cultures on Twitter. GamerGate and the 2016 election cycle changed all that. It brought home the stark reality that people can and will use participatory spaces not to build community but to manipulate and destroy it. I began to wonder how I could have so enthusiastically bounded into studying hashtags and participatory spaces without fully understanding the potential dangers of these spaces. I began looking back at early texts in the field to see what I might have missed. Were there warnings that I noted but then read past without a second glance because of the potential for these spaces? And there they were, heavily underlined but not fully considered:

> We temporarily have access to a tool that could bring conviviality and understanding into our lives and might help revitalize the public sphere. The same tool, improperly controlled and wielded, could become an instrument of tyranny. (Rheingold 1994)

> People can get lost in virtual worlds. Some are tempted to think of life in cyberspace as insignificant, as escape or meaningless diversion. It is not. Our experiences there are serious play. We belittle them at our risk. We must understand the dynamics of virtual experience both to foresee who might be in danger and to put these experiences to best use. (Turkle 1996)

I now wonder why I chose to look past these warnings. Was it sheer refusal to consider the alternatives to what I wanted the spaces to be? Was my position as a white male clouding my judgment? Was it because I initially read them prior to the advent of Facebook, Twitter, and YouTube? Why did I choose to operate with blinders on, even as I saw harm happening in the Springsteen community I was studying? I'm not sure of the answers to these questions. What I know is that I can no longer see the spaces I am studying as anything other than rife with danger and abuse. I have begun looking beyond our spaces and our scholarship for help with understanding a world where propaganda and disinformation succeed in dehumanizing human beings. I started looking back to the American institution of slavery and the Nazi regime to see how people resisted in those spaces. I have started considering the impact of the Nuremberg Laws on our ethics and whether there are times when maintaining privacy can cause harm to vulnerable people and communities.

I have looked to the words of the leaders of the Civil Rights movement who were working to challenge systems of oppression, misinformation, propaganda, and dehumanization. I have started to wonder how we can leverage our field's knowledge of rhetoric, writing, and participatory culture to partner with community organizations and activists to actively create public-facing (or engaged) scholarship that enters into the digital sphere for the purposes of exposing systems of oppression, communities of hate, and the individuals who perpetrate it. In doing so, I have started looking to the methods of organizations dedicated to combating hate, such as the Southern Poverty Law Center and the Council on American-Islamic Relations.

All of this has led me to wonder what the role of scholar is today. Are we comfortable being object observers of phenomena? Or, because we are members of our local, national, and international communities first and scholars second, do we directly engage? Do we heed the words of civil rights leader and US representative John Lewis, "When you see something that is not right, not fair, not just, you have a moral obligation, to stand up, to say something, to do something, and not be quiet"? What are my moral and ethical obligations as a scholar studying a space overwhelmed by immoral and unethical behavior? That's where I'm at right now. Trying to figure out the answer to that question and the implications that follow.

Elizabeth: I started in the field of internet research ethics in the mid-1990s, after coming out of undergraduate studies with English and philosophy degrees, with an emphasis on critical theory and feminist film theory. I went on for a Master in Information Science degree and a multidisciplinary PhD, where I brought together these various fields. Around the time I was working on my dissertation, the Association of Internet Researchers started work on its first set of ethics guidelines. Shortly thereafter, I put together a volume of papers focused on internet research ethics from scholars working across various disciplines (Buchanan 2004), and looking back, we are still asking some of the same questions and addressing similar concerns as those of early internet research. Some of the problematic areas that emerged in things like health listservs or chat rooms—completely textual spaces—are the same ones we are seeing with hashtag research, such as consent and contextualization.

In subsequent research, I started looking at the role of institutional review boards/ethics review boards and the ways internet research problematized standard notions of respect for persons, justice, and beneficence (Buchanan and Ess 2009). These Belmont principles of ethical research practices are actualized through the informed consent process, the selection and representation of participants, and the maximization of benefits and minimization of harm in research. These principles stem from a biomedical model of research and do not transfer easily to internet research. Early internet research ethics scholars, such as Charles Ess (2002), Annette N. Markham (2006), Susannah Stern (2003), and Amy Bruckman (2006), provided novel frameworks for considering ethics review of internet research. For example, borrowing from feminist theory or Eastern philosophical traditions helped us broaden the ways we thought out research ethics online. And watching the speed with which social media and then big data research exploded pushed all of us to consider and continually reconsider research ethics as process-based and contextual.

I've spent the last twenty-five years or so talking with scholars from all disciplines, which has given me a unique perspective on internet research ethics. It's been fascinating to watch as disciplines such as computer science have moved from a very rigid stand—*this is not human subjects research, it's just simple AB testing; it's just minor manipulation*—to embracing ethics review. Or in literary studies, where it is unclear: *are we studying persons or text?* The biomedical space has also exploded with fascinating conundrums: *how do we control for participant chatter in a clinical trial portal so as not to break the blind in a study?* As data science has become its own discipline, it, too, is struggling with ethics review issues: *are these data sets secondary data? Third-party data? If a Facebook user consented to the terms and conditions of the end user license agreement, under what conditions does that make data de facto public and available for reuse?* And increasingly, concern for researcher safety and well-being in internet research, such as the research undertaken in the massive Vox-Pol project and in any research dealing with political dissidents and social movements or across hashtag research, is a significant issue. Researchers must attend to the protections of their participants and also themselves.

In concluding this question, I think about the ways internet research ethics scholars have influenced regulation, policy, guidelines, and research practices for the better. Despite the increasing complexities, algorithmic manipulation, and its impact on research integrity, research ethics has become a common conversation across disciplines and in public debate. Recent demands for codes of AI ethics and for ethics training for data and computer scientists, as well as a growing concern around the societal implications of our technologies, are all evidence of the success of such work as AoIR's ethical decision-making documents.

Question 3: What suggestions do you have for scholars studying hashtag activism to treat research participants with ethical respect and care?
Rosemary: When it comes to studying hashtag activism, following the feminist approach to ethics I described previously requires a number of specific data collection and analysis practices for preserving hashtag activists' agency and privacy, as well as the validity of their findings.

First and foremost, researchers need to be familiar with the tools they use to collect Twitter data. Most scholarship on hashtag activism uses the Twitter Streaming Application Program Interface (API), which provides access to a sample of all public tweets in real time at no cost and can be queried for tweets that contain particular keywords (such as a hashtag), usernames, or geolocation tags. The API uses a semi-random sampling mechanism that captures approximately 1 percent of all publicly available tweets that match a researcher's query. I use the phrase *semi-random* here because Twitter does not offer public documentation on how the API selects some tweets and not others for inclusion in the API's search output, meaning researchers cannot be certain that the resulting sample is truly random. In fact, through comparative analyses of different Twitter data collection methods, researchers have found that selection biases shape the data returned by most available Twitter data collection tools, including the API (González-Bailón et al. 2014; Morstatter et al. 2013; Tromble, Storz, and Stockmann 2017). Hashtag activism researchers grounding their analyses in Twitter data, then, must be cautious when claiming that their findings are representative of the hashtag campaign under study.

Hashtag activism researchers should also be aware that when they run a query through the API or other sampling mechanisms, authors of sampled tweets are not alerted to the fact that their tweeted messages, usernames, and geolocation data are included in the resulting output. Twitter includes information about its API in the terms of service users must agree to prior to signing up for an account, but research suggests that few people actually take the time to read these lengthy documents filled with legalese in fine print (Obar and Oeldorf-Hirsch 2018). This practice raises red flags about participants' consent and activists' agency over their own narratives.

Depending on the specifics of the project, there are a few strategies hashtag activism researchers can use to navigate this issue. If the researcher plans to quote only a handful of tweets in the writeup of her analysis, she could seek consent from the authors by reaching out to them via Twitter. If authors do not give consent or do not respond, the researcher can move on to other tweets in her dataset. There are, however, cases where obtaining consent is not feasible. In these situations, the researcher can use pseudonyms in place of usernames and make minor alterations to participants' word choices so their tweets retain their original meanings but cannot be traced back to the authors through a search engine. Exceptions might be made in the case of public figures, such as celebrities, politicians, and others with verified Twitter accounts, and in the case of nonprofit organizations and businesses. Alternatively, researchers could avoid the challenges of participant consent and agency by foregoing methodologies that involve large Twitter datasets altogether or by pairing them with methodologies that center the participants rather than their tweets. For example, the researcher could use a large dataset to identify themes or patterns that emerge through a hashtag campaign over time *and* conduct interviews with hashtag campaign participants. Recruiting interviewees for any project is often difficult, but this mixed-methods approach would help the researcher avoid the ethical challenges of working with Twitter data. Following conventional procedures for obtaining consent and checking in with interviewees once the analysis has been drafted, the researcher could quote these hashtag users freely. In all cases, if the researcher is working with a large sample of Twitter data pulled from the API or another source, she should secure the data in a password-protected folder or take similar steps to restrict access to it.

Lastly, an ethical approach to hashtag activism research extends beyond the data collection and analysis stages. Given that much scholarship in this area is grounded in publicly available tweets, hashtag activism researchers should take steps to make their findings publicly accessible. This could involve a range of different practices, including publishing in open-access journals, uploading preprint manuscripts to open-access repositories, or writing up an easily digested version of the project as a blog post. By making public scholarship a priority alongside participants' agency and privacy, researchers move from simply studying hashtag activism to engaging in socially just scholarship, aligned with the values and needs of the communities they study.

Stephanie: Rosemary offers some wonderful and specific suggestions in her response. I would add that researchers should clearly reflect on their own ethical groundings and stances as part of their research process. Start with people and think about a human-centered design approach that can overlay your research approach: who are the people that will be involved—whether explicitly or implicitly—in your research? Are there ways you can involve them in the co-creation of your work? Is there a way to make this a communal project and/or process? So, along with Rosemary's great suggestion to make this scholarship publicly accessible, can you invite participants in as named coauthors when appropriate? Returning to circulation, in academia, often the coin of the realm is authorship, and naming participants as coauthors can in some cases distribute that cultural capital in important ways. It also provides a form of official acknowledgment of authorship and collaboration that many participants find meaningful. I return often to Paul V. Anderson's (1998, 83) *CCC* article in which he reminds us that "in person-based research we are the recipients of gifts": the gifts of their time, expertise, stories, and the like. And he reminds us that we have an obligation to "treat these gifts—and their givers—justly, respectfully, and gratefully." So again, it's a small thing to do, but the acknowledgment of these "simple gifts" through explicit sharing of coauthorship and citation practices can be impactful.

Another means of treating research participants with ethics and care is to ask explicit questions about how they want their stories and their data to be shared and circulated. I remember when I was doing dissertation research on MySpace and Facebook. I was speaking with students and early-career faculty about their experiences and would take the time to talk through some of the implications of sharing user data with my participants. Some of them said, "Oh, I hadn't thought about that" when I discussed things like the potential reach of the dissertation, even unpublished, and whether they would want their names associated with their quotes or whether they would be comfortable with their images being included as screenshots in the dissertation. For each participant, I spent time going through some of those different nuanced options and gauging what their individual comfort level meant they would be okay with me sharing. I tend to do research that deals with smaller numbers of participants and more in-depth qualitative stories (rather than dealing with large corpuses of data and big datasets), so I am able to take this approach while someone who's dealing with large datasets may not. But I think it's important for us as researchers to help guide as much as possible when we're conducting "thick description"–type qualitative research in assisting participants to think through possible issues that could arise when sharing their user data and to reach an understanding collaboratively of how those data will be shared and used. As Elizabeth states below, informed consent itself is not enough, and I agree. And I think Bill gives some wonderfully concrete examples of how to move past simply providing an informed consent document in his response.

Elizabeth: Both Rosemary and Stephanie offer such poignant descriptions of ethics and methods as process, with excellent guidance for protecting participants and for engaging them *in* the research. I really believe in this concept of "ethics as methods" through Annette Markham's (2006, 39–40) work, when she stated: "Online or off, an ethical researcher is one who is prepared, reflexive, flexible, adaptive, and honest. Methods are not simply applied out of habit, but derived through constant, critical reflection on the goals of research and the research questions; sensitively adapted to the specificities of the context." For me, this is a continual reminder for researchers of the ongoing responsibilities we have when we engage in any research, but particularly research with human subjects/participants and now, with their data. As researchers, first and foremost, we must be honest, trustworthy, fair, and just and engage in our work with integrity and rigor. And we have to think about the ways our research today—what it is and how we do it—will set the stage for future researchers. Protecting participants is a moral imperative, but in our current regulatory framework, "informed consent" as the vehicle for protections is not enough. I don't believe it always involves that reflexive and cyclical nature Markham described but instead is a stock document that fulfills a condition, not the moral imperative.

When I advise students or others about research and IRB work, we always start with the consent process. The consent document should always be written first and is written directly to the participant. The job of the consent document is, related to something I said earlier, about belief. Participants must be able to believe and trust you. The words should not be artificially filled with regulatory jingo but must be authentic: "We will keep your data confidential to the extent of the law." "If you have questions or concerns about your rights as a research participant, contact THE IRB ADMINISTRATOR." Are these statements that imbue warm feelings of trust?

In the 2018 Common Rule, a new requirement was added that consent documents must be written so that a "reasonable person" would be able to understand the research and would want to participate. And consent documents must begin with a "concise summary," with key information. IRBs are still working on exactly what this means and how to implement the new requirements, but there is opportunity for enlightening empirical research on participant expectations in light of these new requirements. I haven't seen a thorough study that allows participants to describe in detail what *they* want in the consent process in internet/social media research. There may be simple, practical reasons for this: most internet-based research is either exempt and therefore does not require consent, or IRBs are not seeing this as research at all, relying on notions of "not human subjects" or "does not meet the definition of research." Either way, we aren't hearing from our participants about consent, which is the only mechanism we have in place to protect them.

In the 2012 AoIR guidelines, Annette Markham and I talked about the fact that the greater the vulnerability, the greater the responsibility the researcher has to protect. When we think of hashtag activism and the potential for high-profile visibility and vulnerability, the imperative is even stronger. This means researchers in these spaces must be absolutely prepared and equipped with a strong method and ethic from which to move forward. I've recently commented (Samuel and Buchanan 2020) about how we—the research enterprise—need to rethink the way we teach research methods across disciplines and ensure more attention to how both participant and researcher protections are enacted.

Bill: Rosemary, Stephanie, and Elizabeth have covered so many vital ways to treat research participants with ethical respect and care that I can only add a few additional thoughts, specifically about four reflexive practices I have employed for building trust among researchers and participants: transparency, consultation, integration, and acknowledgment. These methods are adapted from those of Henry Jenkins (1992, 7), who saw research subjects "as active participants in the research process." Jenkins's primary concern was building a trusting, respectful relationship with his study participants because he knew the communities he was studying had been disrespected in "the popular press or in academic articles [and] many remained distrustful of how their culture might look under scholarly scrutiny" (6). Jenkins was only able to build trust by being transparent with his work and inviting his participants into the process. Though these methods may not apply to all communities that can be studied, I believe these goals of building trust and respect can be adapted to any research situation.

By transparency, I mean being completely clear about who you are, your study goals and methods, and your publication goals. Post this information in as many spaces as necessary, such as social media bios or a pinned tweet. In the past, I have built websites dedicated to my studies that contain an overview of the study, a bio, a page with links to all study documents (such as IRB documents, including revisions), and a contact form. I have also created a blog dedicated to the study that contained updates I thought the community would be interested in. By creating a dedicated space where participants (and other interested parties) can learn about me, the study, the study's intentions, and how to contact me with questions or feedback, I am prioritizing ethics and participant care.

I have found consulting with community members to be vitally important as well, especially when words and phrases in a corpus might require additional explanation for me to fully understand the community's discourse. Reaching out to community members can be daunting, but I have found if you are open and honest with your objectives and have been transparent throughout the process, people are generally polite. Maintaining open communication with community members can also be a boon when seeking permissions to use their content in your publications—and it is essential to respect their wishes when they do not give permission, even if that content is integral to your arguments. Further, I have found it invaluable to share drafts of complete articles and/or relevant sections with members of the community to ensure that I am accurately representing the community and its discourse practices. On more than one occasion, participant feedback has transformed my understanding of what I was seeing in the corpus.

Then, once you have received their feedback, the next step is overtly integrating that feedback into final versions of your publication. I have asked community members how they would like to be cited—real name, username, or anonymous—and have honored all wishes. Finally, acknowledging their contributions is important, both in the publication itself and by contacting them when the publication appears with a final thanks and a link to where they can see it. These practices can go a long way toward building relationships and ensure that participants feel as though they are being treated with respect and care.

Question 4: What suggestions do you have for users engaging in hashtag activism?

Rosemary: The ethical questions facing hashtag activism researchers parallel the challenges activists often encounter when they engage in this mode of digital protest. Like researchers working within the digital environment, activists using social media to advance their cause must also take questions of privacy into account. Of course, all internet users should be aware of what happens to their personal data once they share it with a corporately owned social media platform like Twitter, Facebook, or Instagram. Hashtag activism, however, often raises a unique set of privacy and safety concerns. For example, in my own work, I have studied how feminist activists in the United States have used hashtag activism to ignite national and even international discussions on sexual assault and harassment and intimate partner violence. But while campaigns such as #MeToo, #WhyIStayed, and #YesAllWomen are powerful platforms for survivors and their allies, these activist hashtags ask people to share deeply personal stories of trauma on the globally networked stage of social media, which can have negative consequences. In my case study of #MeToo (Clark-Parsons 2019), I found that survivors who chose to share their stories under the hashtag often faced harassment from internet trolls, backlash from friends and family, and re-traumatization from recounting the details of their assault with a public audience. Hashtag campaign organizers and participants should be aware of the privacy concerns that extend beyond data security and take steps to protect and uplift those who share personal experiences online. #MeToo participants modeled some strategies for performing this online care labor: they assured survivors that they did not need to share their stories if they did not feel comfortable doing so; they intervened on trolling and harassment; and they offered survivors support and resources (2019). Almost all forms of protest involve risking one's personal safety. While the digital environment presents new challenges and pitfalls, there are strategies hashtag activists can practice to protect themselves and one another, starting with learning from the strengths and shortcomings of previous campaigns.

Stephanie: My discussion here aligns with some of the things I mentioned in my response to the previous question, but I think it's important to consider some of the worst-case scenarios that might occur when sharing information on social media and then considering one's personal comfort level from there. Both activists and researchers should think through preemptively how to prevent doxxing or other forms of online harassment—I hate to say it, but it's always a possibility, and as Rosemary states above, there are often risks to one's personal safety. The previously mentioned edited collection *Digital Ethics: Rhetoric and Responsibility in Online Aggression*, co-edited by Jessica Reyman and Erika M. Sparby (2019), is a helpful resource. In particular, James E. Porter's foreword to the collection discusses the different levels of response to harmful and uncivil discourse in digital spaces—when to ignore, when to turn the other cheek, when to denounce and exclude. And as Porter (2019, xix) reminds readers, "We can leap to the defense of those who are under attack . . . so that they are not receiving the attack alone, as individuals." For users engaging in hashtag activism, then, reaching out to their networks when needed for support—and being able to expect that support will be provided—is important.

Finally, thinking about utilizing different technologies that can be helpful if one wants to be more, rather than less, anonymous and secure online is also useful. You can clear out old tweets with technologies like TweetDelete, add two-factor authentication to your social media accounts, adjust your privacy settings and perform regular privacy check-ins (sites make changes and do not always notify users), remove your personal data listings from sites like Spokeo and Intelius, and use unique email addresses for social media that are not tied to any other activities you do online. These are only some of the actions that can help make one more secure against doxxing, and searching online will provide many more that can be tailored to one's own individual needs. Each user will have to balance the time and effort these elements take versus their anticipated benefits; there is a significant tension between sharing information in personally and publicly recognizable ways and the possibility of digital harassment and doxxing.

Elizabeth: Hashtag activism is one of many areas in internet and social media research that causes us to rethink research protections for both participants and the researchers who are studying them. We discussed the concept of beneficence earlier, and each response above provides excellent strategies and approaches to protect users/participants as well as to maximize benefits, such as coauthorship, community support, and resources.

CLOSING REMARKS

Kristi: Rosemary, Stephanie, Bill, and Elizabeth have made thoughtful and informed suggestions for scholars engaging in the research represented in this collection on hashtag activism and beyond. While we hope the best practices and other issues discussed will be useful for many readers, we know this conversation can only capture a moment in time during an ever-evolving research landscape. We look forward to seeing how many of you continue this conversation in your own work moving forward.

REFERENCES

Anderson, Paul V. 1998. "Simple Gifts: Ethical Issues in Person-Based Composition Research." *College Composition and Communication* 49: 63–89.

Bacon-Smith, Camille. 1992. *Enterprising Women: Television Fandom and the Creation of Popular Myth.* Philadelphia: University of Pennsylvania Press.

Beck, Estee N. 2015. "The Invisible Digital Identity: Assemblages in Digital Networks." *Computers and Composition* 35: 125–140.

Bruckman, Amy. 2006. "Teaching Students to Study Online Communities Ethically." *Journal of Information Ethics* 15 (2): 82–98.

Buchanan, Elizabeth A., ed. 2004. *Readings in Virtual Research Ethics.* Hershey, PA: Information Science Publishing.

Buchanan, Elizabeth A., and Charles M. Ess. 2009. "Internet Research Ethics and the Institutional Review Board." *Computers and Society* 39 (3): 43–49.

Buck, Amber. 2019. "Disruptive Experiences: Changing Approaches to What Matters Now." Paper presented at Computers and Writing, East Lansing, MI. June 20–22.

Charmaz, Kathy. 2006. *Constructing Grounded Theory: A Practical Guide through Qualitative Analysis.* New York: Sage.

Chess, Shira, and Adrienne Shaw. 2015. "A Conspiracy of Fishes, or, How We Learned to Stop Worrying about #GamerGate and Embrace Hegemonic Masculinity." *Journal of Broadcasting and Electronic Media* 59 (1): 208–220.

Clark-Parsons, Rosemary. 2019. "'I SEE YOU, I BELIEVE YOU, I STAND WITH YOU': #MeToo and the Performance of Networked Feminist Visibility." *Feminist Media Studies* 21 (3): 362–380.

Collins, Patricia Hill. 2000. *Black Feminist Thought: Knowledge, Consciousness, and the Politics of Empowerment.* New York: Routledge.

Crenshaw, Kimberlé. 1989. "Demarginalizing the Intersection of Race and Sex: A Black Feminist Critique of Antidiscrimination Doctrine, Feminist Theory, and Antiracist Politics." *University of Chicago Legal Forum* 1989 (1): 139–167.

Dieterle, Brandy, Dustin Edwards, and Paul "Dan" Martin. 2019. "Confronting Digital Aggression with an Ethics of Circulation." In *Digital Ethics: Rhetoric and Responsibility in Online Aggression, Hate Speech, and Harassment*, edited by Jessica Reyman and Erika M. Sparby, 197–213. New York: Routledge.

Edwards, Dustin W. 2018. "Circulation Gatekeepers: Unbundling the Platform Politics of YouTube's Content ID." *Computers and Composition* 47: 61–74.

Edwards, Dustin W., and Bridget Gelms. 2018. "The Rhetorics of Platforms: Definitions, Approaches, Futures." *Present Tense* 6 (3). http://www.presenttensejournal.org/editorial/vol-6-3-special-issue-on-the-rhetoric-of-platforms/.

Ess, Charles, and the AoIR Working Committee. 2002. *Ethical Decision-making and Internet Research: Recommendations from the AoIR Ethics Working Committee.* Chicago: Association of Internet Researchers.

Evans, Sarah Beth, and Elyse Janish. 2015. "#INeedDiverseGames: How the Queer Backlash to GamerGate Enables Nonbinary Coalition." *QED: A Journal in GLBTQ Worldmaking* 2, (2): 125–150.

franzke, aline shakti, Anja Bechmann, Michael Zimmer, Charles Ess, and the Association of Internet Researchers. 2020. "Internet Research: Ethical Guidelines 3.0." *AoIR*, October 6. https://aoir.org/reports/ethics3.pdf.

Gallagher, John. 2017. "Writing for Algorithmic Audiences." *Computers and Composition* 45: 25–35.

González-Bailón, Sandra, Ning Wang, Alejandro Rivero, Javier Borge-Holthoefer, and Yamir Moreno. 2014. "Assessing the Bias in Samples of Large Online Networks." *Social Networks* 38: 16–27.

Gries, Laurie E., and Collin Gifford Brooke. 2018. *Circulation, Writing, and Rhetoric.* Louisville, CO: Utah State University Press.

Hutchinson, Les. 2017. "Writing to Have No Face: The Queer Orientation of Anonymity in Twitter." In *Social Writing/Social Media: Pedagogy, Presentation, and Publics*, edited by Douglas M. Walls and Stephanie Vie, 179–207. Boulder: University Press of Colorado. https://wac.colostate.edu/books/perspectives/social/.

Jacobs, Alan. 2012. "Why You Shouldn't Retweet the Haters." *The Atlantic*, March 12. https://www.theatlantic.com/technology/archive/2012/03/why-you-shouldnt-retweet-the-haters/254300/.

Jenkins, Henry. 1992. *Textual Poachers: Television Fans and Participatory Culture.* New York: Routledge.

Jenkins, Henry. 2006. *Fans, Bloggers, and Gamers: Exploring Participatory Culture.* New York: New York University Press.

Johnson, Anne. 2014. "The Ethics of Retweeting and Whether It Amounts to Endorsement." *NPR Public Editor*, July 31. https://www.npr.org/sections/publiceditor/2014/07/31/336921115/the-ethics-of-retweeting-and-whether-it-amounts-to-endorsement.

Markham, Annette N. 2006. "Method as Ethic, Ethic as Method." *Journal of Information Ethics* 15 (2): 37–55.

Markham, Annette N., and Elizabeth Buchanan. 2012. "Ethical Decision-making and Internet Research: Recommendations from the AoIR Ethics Working Committee (Version 2.0)." *AoIR*, December. http://www.aoir.org/reports/ethics2.pdf.

McNely, Brian J. 2010. "Exploring a Sustainable and Public Information Ecology." In *Proceedings of the 28th ACM International Conference on Design of Communication*, 103–108. https://doi.org/10.1145/1878450.1878468.

Morstatter, Fred, Jurgen Pfeffer, Huan Liu, and Kathleen M. Carley. 2013. "Is the Sample Good Enough? Comparing Data from Twitter's Streaming API with Twitter's Firehose." In *Proceedings of the Seventh International AAAI Conference on Weblogs and Social Media*, 400–408. AAAI Press, Cambridge, MA.

Obar, Jonathan A., and Anne Oeldorf-Hirsch. 2018. "The Biggest Lie on the Internet: Ignoring the Privacy Policies and Terms of Service Policies of Social Networking Services." *Information, Communication and Society* 23 (1): 128–147.

"The Plain View Project." 2019. https://www.plainviewproject.org/.

Porter, James E. 2019. "Foreword: Interacting with Friends, Enemies, and Strangers." In *Digital Ethics: Rhetoric and Responsibility in Online Aggression, Hate Speech, and Harassment*, edited by Jessica Reyman and Erika M. Sparby, xv–xxii. New York: Routledge.

Reilly, Colleen A. 2016. "Coming to Terms: Critical Approaches to Ubiquitous Digital Surveillance." *Kairos: A Journal of Rhetoric, Technology, and Pedagogy* 20 (2). http://kairos.technorhetoric.net/20.2/topoi/beck-et-al/reilly.html.

Reyman, Jessica, and Erika M. Sparby, eds. 2019. *Digital Ethics: Rhetoric and Responsibility in Online Aggression*. New York: Routledge.

Rheingold, Howard. 1994. *The Virtual Community: Homesteading on the Electronic Frontier*. New York: HarperCollins. http://www.rheingold.com/vc/book/intro.html.

Samuel, Gabrielle, and Elizabeth Buchanan. 2020. "Guest Editorial: Ethical Issues in Social Media Research." *Journal of Empirical Research on Human Research Ethics* 15 (1–2): 3–11.

Smith, Dorothy E. 1990. *The Conceptual Practices of Power: A Feminist Sociology of Knowledge*. Toronto: University of Toronto Press.

Starbird, Kate. 2018. "The Surprising Nuance behind the Russian Troll Strategy." *Medium*, October 20. https://medium.com/s/story/the-trolls-within-how-russian-information-operations-infiltrated-online-communities-691fb969b9e4.

Stern, Susannah. 2003. "Encountering Distressing Information in Online Research: A Consideration of Legal and Ethical Responsibilities." *New Media and Society* 5 (2): 249–266.

Stewart, Leo G., Ahmer Arif, A. Conrad Nied, Emma S. Spiro, and Kate Starbird. 2017. "Drawing the Lines of Contention: Networked Frame Contests within #BlackLivesMatter Discourse." *PACM on Human-Computer Interaction* 1 (CSCW 96): 2–23. https://doi.org/10.1145/3134920.

Trice, Michael, Liza Potts, and Rebekah Small. 2019. "Values versus Rules in Social Media Communities: How Platforms Generate Amorality on Reddit and Facebook." In *Digital Ethics: Rhetoric and Responsibility in Online Aggression, Hate Speech, and Harassment*, edited by Jessica Reyman and Erika M. Sparby, 62–79. New York: Routledge.

Tromble, Rebekah, Andreas Storz, and Daniela Stockmann. 2017. "We Don't Know What We Don't Know: When and How the Use of Twitter's Public APIs Biases Scientific Inference." *SSRN*, November. https://ssrn.com/abstract=3079927.

Turkle, Sherry. 1996. "Who Am We?" *Wired*, January 1. https://www.wired.com/1996/01/turkle-2/.

Vie, Stephanie. 2014. "In Defense of 'Slacktivism': The Human Rights Campaign Facebook Logo as Digital Activism." *First Monday* 19 (7). https://firstmonday.org/article/view/4961/3868.

Vie, Stephanie, and Jennifer deWinter. 2016. "How Are We Tracked Once We Press Play? Surveillance and Video Games." *Kairos: A Journal of Rhetoric, Technology, and Pedagogy* 20 (2). http://kairos.technorhetoric.net/20.2/topoi/beck-et-al/vie_dewin.html.

"/VoterFraud." 2018. https://www.iwr.ai/voterfraud/index.html#s2.

Weaver, Matthew. 2018. "Cambridge University Rejected Facebook Study over 'Deceptive' Privacy Standards." *The Guardian*, April 24. https://www.theguardian.com/technology/2018/apr/24/cambridge-university-rejected-facebook-study-over-deceptive-privacy-standards.

Wolff, William I. 2015. "Springsteen Fans, #bruceleeds, and the Tweeting of Locality." *Transformative Works and Cultures* 19. http://journal.transformativeworks.org/index.php/twc/article/view/589/478.

Wolff, William I. 2017. "Twitter Archives: A Discussion of Systems, Methods, Visualizations, and Ethics." *Kairos: A Journal of Rhetoric, Technology, and Pedagogy PraxisWiki*. http://praxis.technorhetoric.net/tiki-index.php?page=PraxisWiki%3A_%3ATwitter+Archives.

Yancey, Kathleen Blake. 2004. "Made Not Only in Words: Composition in a New Key." *College Composition and Communication* 56 (2): 297–328.

INDEX

Actor Network Theory, 25; agentive network, 28, 34, 35
activism: digital, 5, 8–9, 11–14, 21–24, 33–35, 38, 40, 53–54, 61, 69, 77, 83, 96, 120, 126, 133, 181; definition of, 5; feminist, 77, 266, 278; LGBTQ+, 6, 8, 13, 158–173; online, 8, 23, 39, 205, 223. *See also* hashtag activism; hashtag feminism; social media activism
affect, 4, 7–9, 11–12, 38–45, 48–49, 53–70, 101–102, 125, 133, 239; affective community, 42–44, 48, 57, 64; affective publics, 40, 48; circulation of, 11, 38, 41–42, 66; collective, 43, 60, 64–65, 70, 183; power, 102; theory, 7, vicarious, 61–63, 68
African American vernacular (AAVE), 13, 141, 150–154
agency, 21–22, 24–27, 33–35, 127, 194, 249, 266–267, 273–274; agentive, 22, 24, 27–30, 34–35; rhetorical, 24, 34. *See also* Actor Network Theory
Ahmed, Sara, 7, 11, 38, 40–44, 46, 48–49
#AllLivesMatter, 9
alt-right, 13–14, 193–194, 197–199, 201–206, 210–213, 218–225; definition of, 197; trolling, 219–221
#AmplifyWomen, 7
Anderson, Benedict, 70n3, 119, 121. *See also* community: imagined
anti-activism, 4, 8–9, 13, 15, 221, 223, 225, 231, 233, 239–242
anti-Blackness, 142, 153, 155, 179
appropriation, 4, 106, 109, 213, 219, 252; cultural appropriation, 121, 253; reappropriation, 145–147, 150, 211
Arab Spring, 23, 119
Aristotle, 24, 103, 248
Association of Internet Researchers (AoIR), 10, 43, 263, 271–272, 277. *See also* ethics: Internet research

/b/ board. *See* Random Board
Ballard, Tom, 101, 104, 111–112
Banks, Adam, 140–142, 144
Benjamin, Carl, 222–223

Beyoncé, 62, 139, 180, 183
Biden, Joe, 202, 204
big data, 15, 247, 265, 272, 275
Bizzell, Patricia, 24–25
Black masculinity. *See* masculinity
Black Twitter, 5, 8, 10, 13, 140–146, 150, 152–155, 176, 178–181, 187–188; definition of, 141, 178
Black womanhood, 8, 180–181
#BlackGirlMagic, 70, 178
#BlackLivesMatter, 3, 6, 9, 14, 49, 53, 69, 100–101, 104, 182, 199–200, 203–204, 247, 250–256, 264; movement, 3, 52, 203, 250–251, 253, 256; #VidasNegrasImportam, 182
Blacktags, 7, 143
BLM. *See* #BlackLivesMatter
boyd, danah, 102, 196
#BooksNotBullets, 69
#BringBackOurGirls, 40, 77
brevity, 12, 100–115
Brock, André, 5, 142, 176
Brown, Michael, 6, 77, 251. *See also* #Ferguson
Bruckman, Amy, 15, 70n4, 272
#BostonHelp, 11, 21–35
Boston Marathon bombing, 11, 22
boundary work, 11, 21–23, 27–33
Boy's Club (webcomic), 213–214, 217–218. *See also* Furie, Matt; Pepe the Frog
Buchanan, Elizabeth, 43, 52, 260, 263, 271, 277
Burke, Kenneth, 24, 243. *See also* identification
Bury Your Gays trope, 8, 13, 159, 166, 168, 170, 172
Bush, George W., 139
#BystanderIntervention, 8

Castile, Philando, 251, 254
censorship, 6, 125, 195
Central Park Five. *See* #ExoneratedFive
Civil Rights movement, 6, 14, 161, 227, 271; civil rights legislation, 237
Chaudhuri, Supriya, 122
Chatterjee, Rimi B., 130

Chess, Shira, 262–263
#ChildAbuse, 46, 114; #HowToStopChildAbuse, 46; #StopChildAbuse, 48
Clark, Rosemary. *See* Clark-Parsons, Rosemary
Clark-Parsons, Rosemary, 5, 77, 83
climate change, 52, 249, 268
Clinton, Hillary, 64, 193, 202, 204
Cloud, Dana, 239
coding (qualitative data analysis), 27, 33–34, 42, 55, 82–84, 93, 251. *See also* grounded theory
collective: action, 6, 97, 151, 182, 206, 232, 242, 249; affect (*see* affect); empathy, 183; identity, 9, 55, 146, 154; movement, 5, 23, 53, 142
community, 5, 8, 9, 32–33, 41, 44–45, 47, 48–50, 57, 64, 83, 91, 106, 114, 121, 141, 144–145, 153–154, 163, 168, 178, 187, 196, 199, 203, 206, 247, 261, 266, 269–271, 277–278, 280; affective (*see* affect); diasporic, 184; imagined, 10, 64, 66–68, 121; LGBTQ+, 158–161, 163–167, 171–172; virtual/online, 164, 168–169, 172
counter-publics/(counter)publics, 14, 40, 102, 229–233, 235–236, 239, 241–243, 255
COVID-19 pandemic, 3, 9
#CripTheVote, 6
Croeser, Sky, 7, 23, 53–54
Cult of Kek. *See* Kek
cultural capital, 130, 132–133, 275
cultural endoxa, 79–83, 89–93

D'Souza, Dinesh, 14, 227–243
Dadas, Caroline, 40–41, 47–49, 61, 103
Dawson, Michael, 178, 181, 187. *See also* Linked Fate Theory
dedications, 53, 58, 61, 65–66
Dedoose, 55
diaspora, 177–178, 181; African Diaspora, 178, 181; digital diaspora, 180, 182
Diallo, Amadou, 252
digital: activism (*see* activism); network, 9, 46, 48–49; publics, 7, 38, 40, 42, 102 (*see also* networked publics); rhetoric (*see* rhetoric)
discourse analysis. *See* qualitative research
disinformation, 194, 237, 239–240, 264–265, 270; misinformation, 263, 270–271
Dixiecrat, 227, 238
Dixon, Kitsy, 5, 54
Dolezal, Rachel, 144, 147–148
doxxing, 15, 279–280
#DraftOurDaughters, 193–194

double consciousness, 7
DuVernay, Ava, 175. *See also When They See Us*

Ellis, Jay, 176, 185. *See also Insecure*
emotionality, 11, 38, 40, 49
enthymeme, 79, 81–82; naturalistic, 76, 79; visual, 82, 88–89, 91
ethics, 10, 261, 265–266, 270, 272–273, 275–277; Internet research ethics, 4, 14–15, 70n4, 260, 262–263, 265, 267–268, 271–272
ethnography. *See* qualitative research
ethos, 9, 93, 121, 131, 133, 144, 145, 214, 216, 233, 239, 256
#EveryDaySexism, 70
#Exonerated Five, 175

Facebook, 10, 76, 78, 81, 122, 124–126, 130, 162, 169, 182, 194–195, 199, 203, 207, 250, 264–166, 270, 272, 275, 278
#FakeHistory, 14, 227–243; definition of, 228; #FakeHistory Debunked tour, 228
Family Guy television series, 148–149
far-right, 227–228, 254
Farrell, Thomas B., 247–248
fan activism, 8, 176, 184–185, 188
feminism, 64, 67, 77, 112, 202; feminist, 5, 8, 45, 54–55, 64, 65, 67, 112, 262, 267–268, 271–273; feminist theory, 4, 272. *See also* hashtag feminism
#Ferguson, 77; Ferguson, Missouri, 77. *See also* Brown, Michael
#FightForHer, 193
Florini, Sarah, 141–142
Floyd, George, 3, 53
Foley, Megan, 103–104, 109
4chan, 9, 13–14, 194–207, 214–222, 263. *See also* Politically Incorrect Board; Random Board
Foucault, Michel, 162, 230
Fraser, Nancy, 232–233
#FreeKekistan. *See* Kek
Furie, Matt, 213–214, 216–217, 224. *See also Boys Club*; Pepe the Frog

#GamerGate, 262, 279
Garza, Alicia, 250–251. *See also* #BlackLivesMatter
Get Out (film), 155n3. *See also* Sunken Place
Gilyard, Keith, 140–142, 144
Gladwell, Malcolm, 22–24, 33
Gong, Rachel, 7, 54
Gonlin, Vanessa, 8, 180
Google search, 87, 146, 193; Google Doc, 30–31, 33, 262; Google Images search,

12, 75–80, 94–95; Google Maps, 199; Google People Finder, 26, 28
#GreenNewDeal, 249
Gries, Laurie E., 49, 111, 211–212
Gross, Nora, 5–7
grounded theory, 27, 55, 164, 269. *See also* coding
gun control, 52, 56–58, 60, 65, 67–69; gun violence, 53, 57, 60–61, 65, 67–68. *See also* #MarchForOurLives; shooting

#HandsOffJU, 12, 119–120, 127, 129–130
hashtag, definition of, 5, 228
hashtag activism, 3–15, 39, 41, 43, 46–48, 50, 52–55, 59–61, 63, 66, 69–70, 77, 84–86, 93, 96–97, 100–102, 104–105, 113, 115, 122–124, 133, 159, 161, 172, 193, 199, 206, 225, 227, 228–229, 235, 247, 257, 260–263, 265–267, 273–274, 278–280; definition of, 4, 228; hashtivism, 246–247, 255. *See also* activism; hashtag feminism
hashtag feminism, 5, 10, 53–54, 56, 69, 77–78, 84; definition of, 5; feminist causes/movements, 61–62, 179, 266–267
Hawley, George, 197, 220–221
#HBOInsecure. *See Insecure*
#HeForShe, 70
Highfield, Tim, 7, 23, 53–54
Hirst, Russel, 104, 115
#Hokkolorob, 12, 119, 122, 125, 133
hooks, bell, 180, 184

#IAmGay, 6
#ICantBreathe, 178
identification, 54, 129, 181, 187, 228, 232–235, 242, 250. *See also* Burke, Kenneth
ideograph, 101, 111–112
#IdleNoMore, 6
#IfSlaveryWasAChoice, 13, 140–141, 143–146, 152, 154–155
#IfTheyGunnedMeDown, 5–6
#iLookLikeAnEngineer, 7, 12, 75–97
imagined community. *See* community
Indigenous: campaigns, 6; Lakota, 25; *los indigados*, 23; voices, 6
#INeedDiverseGames, 262
informed consent, 15, 207n2, 261, 266, 267, 271–277
Insecure (television series), 13, 176–177, 180, 182–188; #InsecureHBO, 175, 182–184; #LawrenceHive, 13, 182–188
Instagram, 140, 278
institutional review board (IRB), 271. *See also* informed consent

Internet research ethics. *See* ethics
intersectionality, 6, 10, 14, 48, 77–78, 110, 132, 172, 177, 180, 262; intersectional feminism, 77
It Gets Better campaign, 158–159, 169

Jane the Virgin (television series), 169
Jenkins, Henry, 185–186, 277
#JusticeforZainab, 11, 38–40, 42–50

Kek, 221–222; Cult of Kek, 221–223, 225; #FreeKekistan, 223; Kekistan, 222. *See also* Pepe the Frog
Kerl, Simon, 103
Khan-Cullors, Patrisse, 250–251, 254. *See also* #BlackLivesMatter
Khoja-Moolji, Shenila, 45, 77
Kleeman, Sophie, 252
#Kony2012, 40
Knutila, Lee, 195, 205
Kress, Gunther, 76, 79, 82, 85–86, 100. *See also* grounded theory
Kruse, Kevin, 14, 228, 235–236
Kuo, Rachel, 249, 100–102

Lathan, Van, 139–140
Lakota. *See* indigenous
Lamont Hill, Marc, 140–141
#LawrenceHive. *See Insecure*
#LexaDeservedBetter. *See* #LGBTFansDeserveBetter
#LGBTFansDeserveBetter, 13, 159, 161, 163–165, 167, 169–172; #LexaDeservedBetter, 13, 164, 167, 169; Lexa Pledge, 170–171
LGBTQ+: activism (*see* activism); couples, 234. *See also* #LGBTFansDeserveBetter
Linked Fate Theory, 176, 178, 181–184, 187
Longinus, 100, 105
lulz, 195–197, 205–206, 216, 221

Make America Great Again (MAGA), 112–113; hat, 112–113
Malik, Aqdas, 7, 82–83, 93
Manjoo, Farhad, 141, 178. *See also* Black Twitter
Mann, Benjamin W., 6
#MarchForOurLives, 10, 53, 55–58, 60–65, 67–69; March For Our Lives, 11, 52–54, 58–60, 64–65, 68–69
Marjory Stoneman Douglas High School. *See* #Parkland
Markham, Annette N., 43, 263, 272, 276–277
masculinity, 13, 128, 177–180, 183; Black masculinity, 13, 175–182, 184–185, 188;

INDEX

toxic masculinity 9, 176, 179–180, 182, 184–185
McDonald, Soraya Nadia, 144–145
McGee, Michael Calvin, 101, 111. *See also* ideograph
meme, 10, 12–14, 28, 119–120, 125, 140, 153–156, 200, 204, 210, 264, 268; analysis of, 122–123, 125–133, 144–156, 183, 186, 221–223; alt-right/Trump, 14, 193–194, 200–201, 205, 212; definition of, 143; #IfSlaveryWereAChoice, 144–153; meme warfare, 13–14, 201, 206, 222; memetic media, 145–146; memetic participation, 141, 143; memetics, 211–212, 225; Pepe the Frog, 210–211, 214–219, 221–225; theory about, 143–145, 147, 195–196, 211
meme warfare. *See* meme
memetic participation. *See* meme
#MeToo, 5, 39, 45–46, 48, 100–101, 109, 125, 278–279. *See also* #RiceBunny
Milner, Ryan M., 141, 143, 145–147, 150, 153–154, 196, 211
multimodality, 12, 100–101, 104–106, 111–112, 115, 125, 143, 149, 161
Murray, Joddy, 105, 111
#MSDstrong, 69
Myspace, 214, 216, 275

Nazi, 210, 219, 270; neo-Nazi, 202–203
Nagle, Angela, 197, 215
Neiwert, David, 220, 223, 255
neo-Nazi. *See* Nazi
networked publics, 40, 102. *See also* digital networks
#NeverAgain, 69. *See also* #MarchForOurLives
new materialist, 25, 211
Ngai, Sianne, 211–214. *See also* zaniness
#NiggerNavy, 155
NodeXL, 55, 146
#NoNotoriety, 263
#NotAllMen, 9
#NotYourAsianSidekick, 227
Nuzzi, Olivia, 219–221

Obama, 111, 202, 204; Obama Hope image, 111
Occupy movement, 7, 23, 53–54, 120; Occupy Oakland (#oo), 7, 53
The 100 (television series), 13, 159, 165–170
#OperationGridlock, 9
oppression, 41, 45, 77, 182, 240, 242, 271; racialized oppression, 140, 144; systemic oppression, 12
#OscarsSoWhite, 178

Papacharissi, Zizi, 7, 40, 102
#Parkland, 61, 69; Marjory Stoneman Douglas High School, 11, 53. *See also* #MarchForOurLives
Paasonen, Susanna, 7, 61–62
patriarchy, 7, 48, 59, 129, 178, 180, 184
Pepe the Frog, 210–225; as alt-right icon, 212–213, 219–221, 224; in *Boys Club*, 213–214; on 4chan, 215, 219; in the Kek movement, 222–223; as a meme, 216–219, 224; as Trump imagery, 224
Phillips, Whitney, 195, 205, 215–216
Plain View Project, 264
Performance/performativity, 5–6, 26, 128, 212; cultural, 141–142; gender, 177, 184–185
personal narrative, 5–6, 10–12, 53–58, 65, 69–70
police, 21, 28, 30, 200, 253–254, 264; policing, 27, 30–35, 264; violence, 3, 5, 126, 160, 251–253
/pol/, *See* Politically Incorrect board
Politically Incorrect board (/pol/) (4chan), 13, 194, 197–199, 201–202, 206
postmodern, 24–25
Potts, Liza, 23, 34, 38, 102, 228, 268–269
pride (emotion), 38, 41–43, 46, 62
Pride (LGBTQ+), 6, 160
propaganda, 45, 197, 237, 240, 270–271
pronouns, 53, 55, 57–58, 60
Pulse nightclub, 58. *See also* #MarchForOurLives
pussyhat, 59, 107–114; Pussyhat Project, 12, 100–101, 105–109, 111, 113–115; #Pussyhat, 101, 108–109, 113–114. *See also* Women's March

qualitative research, 15, 268–269, 275; analysis, 11, 21, 24, 27, 53, 146; discourse analysis, 121, 140; ethics (*see* ethics); ethnography, 14–15, 163–164, 194–195; interviews, 14, 154; rhetorical analysis, 13, 256. *See also* coding; grounded theory
queer theory, 13, 159, 162–163

Rae, Issa, 176–177. 182, 185. *See also Insecure*
Random board (/b/) (4chan) 9, 196–197, 206, 215–216
reappropriation. *See* appropriation
Rentschler, Carrie A., 8
Reyman, Jessica, 263, 268, 279
retweet(s), 33, 46, 61, 83–84, 89, 102, 228, 261; in data sets, 91, 93, 164, 182, 237–238, 251; as a rhetorical tool, 102, 104, 141, 143, 178, 200, 261–163

Index   289

rhetoric/rhetorical: agency (*see* agency); analysis (*see* qualitative research); beauty, 247; circulation, 250; digital, 4, 10, 12, 15, 40–41, 55, 213, 225, 254; practice, 120, 140, 210–214, 216, 218, 223; situation, 15, 254; strategy, 5, 7, 10–12, 53, 55, 57–59, 61, 65–66, 69–70, 100, 115, 152, 210–211, 221; velocity, 103, 114; visual, 4, 6–7, 12, 65
Rice, Jenny, 247–248, 256
#RiceBunny, 125. *See also* #MeToo
Richardson, Elaine B., 145, 151–154
right-wing, 14, 140, 160, 213, 220–221, 227–228, 229, 241. *See also* alt-right
#RiseUp, 69

Sandy Hook, 67
#SaveJNU, 12, 119, 131
Saving Hope (television series), 171
#SayHerName, 178. *See also* #BlackLivesMatter
signifyin', 13, 140–142, 144, 154
Scientology, Church of, 195–196; anti-Scientology, 205
sexual assault, 39, 56, 109, 278
Sharma, Sanjay, 7, 142–143
Shaw, Adrienne, 262–263
shooting, 6, 60, 77, 253; mass, 58, 60–61, 215; school, 11, 53, 65, 67, 69. *See also* gun control
slacktivism, 22–23. *See also* Gladwell, Malcolm
slavery, 13, 139–140, 143, 148–152, 154, 178, 180, 270
Smitherman, Geneva, 152–154
social justice, 3–6, 8, 10–11, 13–15, 45, 50, 52–53, 66, 69, 96, 145, 159, 172, 246, 261; movement, 3–4, 10, 13, 15, 45, 52–53; warriors, 202, 204
social media: activism, 34–35, 49, 120, 161, 164–165; campaign, 12, 76, 159; movement, 124, 159, 171
#SolidarityIsForWhiteWomen, 227
South Asia, 38–39, 48–49, 199–200
Sparby, Erika, 9, 263, 268, 279
Spencer, Richard, 202, 210–211, 223
Spongebob Squarepants (television series), 148–149, 152; Squidward, 147–148
Springsteen, Bruce, 269–270
#StayAtHome, 9
stance taking, 235–236
Star Trek (television series), 185
stickiness/sticky, 11, 39, 41–46, 48–50
Suh, Krista, 106, 108–110
Sunken Place (the), 13, 139, 155*n*3

#TakeAKnee, 69
Taylor, Breonna, 4, 52
#ThisIsWhatDemocracyLooksLike, 69
Tiananmen Square, 122–123, 133
toxic masculinity. *See* masculinity
Tometi, Opal, 250–251. *See also* #BlackLivesMatter
Trevor Project, 163, 170
troll. *See* trolling
trolling, 4, 13, 15, 194–197, 199–201, 203–206, 214–216, 218–224, 229, 263–264, 279; definition of, 216; trolls, 9, 195, 200, 205–206, 214–216, 219, 221–223, 264, 279
Trump, Donald, 11, 52, 101, 139, 193–194, 204–206, 211, 222, 224, 228, 255–256
Tumblr, 8, 165
12 Years a Slave (film), 148
Twitter bot, 194, 201, 263, 265
Twitter Reacts, 14, 246–251, 256
Twitter Application Program Interface (API), 83, 273
#2A, 58, 69. *See also* #MarchForOurLives

Unite the Right rally, 255. *See also* alt-right
us-versus-them binary, 57, 127
USENET, 161

van Leeuwen, Theo, 76, 79, 82, 85–86. *See also* grounded theory
velocity. *See* rhetorical: velocity
vicarious affect. *See* affect
victim blaming, 9, 47–49
#VoterFraud, 264

Weibo, 6, 125
Wells, Karen, 66
Wenger, Isis Anchalee, 75–76, 80–84, 95. *See also* #iLookLikeAnEngineer
West, Kanye, 13, 139–140, 147–149, 151–152
When They See Us (mini-series). *See* DuVernay, Ava
white nationalism. *See* whiteness
white supremacy. *See* whiteness
whiteness, 7, 85, 181; feminism, 77; gaze, 142; nationalism, 197, 202–203, 210, 213, 219–220, 242; supremacy, 176, 178, 219–220, 223–224, 255
Whitfield, Sheree, 152–153
#WhyIMarch, 53–56, 58–63, 67–70
#WhyIStayed, 5, 70, 83, 179, 278
Williams, Apryl, 7, 180
#WomensMarch, 54, 56, 62–63, 114; Women's March, 11–12, 52–60, 63–69, 101, 109–110, 114–115
World of Warcraft (video game), 221

Yancey, Kathleen Blake, 269
Yang, Guobin, 84, 104
#YesAllWomen, 9, 40, 70, 278
#YouOkSis, 8, 179
yourTwapperKeeper, 269
YouTube, 158, 165, 170, 222

zaniness, 14, 211–218, 220–221, 224–202; definition of, 211–212. *See also* Ngai, Sianne; Pepe the Frog
Zweiman, Jayna, 106, 108–110, 112. *See also* Pussyhat

ABOUT THE AUTHORS

Melissa Ames is the director of English education and professor of English and women's, gender, and sexuality studies at Eastern Illinois University. She specializes in media studies, television scholarship, internet studies, popular culture, and pedagogy. Her most recent publications include her books *Small Screen, Big Feels: Television and Cultural Anxiety in the Twenty-first Century* (University Press of Kentucky, 2020), *How Pop Culture Shapes the Stages of a Woman's Life* (Palgrave, 2016), *Time in Television Narrative* (University of Mississippi Press, 2012), *Women and Language* (McFarland, 2011); chapters in *Grace under Pressure: Grey's Anatomy Uncovered* (2008), *Writing the Digital Generation* (2010), *Bitten by Twilight* (2010), *Manufacturing Phobias* (2016), *Adventures in Shondaland* (2018), *Young Adult Literature in the Composition Classroom* (2018), and *Computers and Writing Proceedings* (2018); and articles in the *Journal of Dracula Studies* (2011), *The Women and Popular Culture Encyclopedia* (2012), *High School Journal* (2013), *Journal of Popular Culture* (2014), *Feminist Media Studies* (2017), *Pedagogy* (2017), and *First Monday* (2021).

Robert Barry Jr. is a PhD candidate in the Department of Comparative Studies at The Ohio State University. Through his research interest in performance, media, and Black gender studies, Rob employs counter-storytelling, autoethnography, and Black visual culture to interrogate historical processes of Black un/gendering in the afterlife of slavery. Specifically, he is concerned with the ways performances of Black masculinities are affective remnants of chattel slavery that animate, a/temporally, through diasporic spaces.

André Brock is associate professor of media studies at Georgia Tech. His scholarship examines racial representations in social media, video games, Black women and weblogs, whiteness, and technoculture, including innovative and groundbreaking research on Black Twitter. His book *Distributed Blackness: African American Cybercultures* (New York University Press, 2020) offers insights into understanding Black everyday lives mediated by networked technologies.

Elizabeth Buchanan, PhD, is director of the Office of Research Support Services and senior research scientist at the Marshfield Clinic Research Institute. For more than twenty years, Elizabeth's scholarship has focused on research ethics, compliance, and regulations, specifically around internet, social media, and big data research. In these areas, she has written guidelines for IRBs/REBs, contributed to the Secretary's Advisory Committee to the Office of Human Research Protections (SACHRP) in 2013, and coauthored the 2012 Association of Internet Researchers Ethics Guidelines. Elizabeth serves as faculty at Fordham University's Research Ethics Training Institute (RETI), associate editor of the *Journal of Empirical Research on Human Research Ethics*, and board member and secretary, Open Door Free Clinic, a community resource in Chippewa Falls, Wisconsin. Prior to joining the Marshfield Clinic Research Institute, she was endowed chair in ethics at the University of Wisconsin–Stout.

Rosemary Clark-Parsons is a postdoctoral research fellow at the Annenberg School for Communication at the University of Pennsylvania, where she also serves as associate director of the Center on Digital Culture and Society. She received her PhD in communication from

Penn State University. Her research revolves around the relationship between digital media and gender justice projects, with a specific focus on feminist social movements in the United States. Drawing on ethnographic and interpretive methods, Clark-Parsons studies the ways feminist digital media users are reconfiguring the shape and reach of feminist activism.

Gabriel I. Green is assistant professor of African American literature at Xavier University of Louisiana. He researches African American rhetorical traditions within art and culture.

Neha Gupta is a doctoral researcher at the Department of Humanities and Social Sciences, National Institutes of Technology Silchar. Her writings focus on the intersection of digitality and visual cultures. Her doctoral thesis looks at the performative and affective possibilities of the digital. Her research appears in journals such as *Convergence* and *Journal of Creative Communications*, among others.

Jeffrey J. Hall is a special lecturer in Japanese studies at Kanda University of International Studies in Chiba, Japan. His research focuses on conservative activism in Japan and the United States, as well as the relationship between popular culture and militarism in modern Japan. He is the author of *Japan's Nationalist Right in the Internet Age* (2021).

Kyesha Jennings is content director for the North Carolina Arts Council where, as a part of the marketing and communications team, she curates, produces, and develops content that highlights the diversity and vitality of the arts in the state. An award-winning hip-hop scholar, Kyesha is a fourth-year PhD candidate at Indiana University of Pennsylvania, where her research focuses primarily on Black women writers, hip-hop feminism, and popular culture.

Morgan K. Johnson is assistant professor of communication studies at Colorado State University. Johnson researches discourses of racial in/justice in the United States, with much of her work focusing on police violence. Her current projects examine rhetorics of personhood and citizenship in policing oversight initiatives that followed the 2014 Ferguson unrest, including crowdsourced and media databases, federal task forces, civilian review boards, nonprofit organizations, and Mothers of the Movement.

Salma Kalim is a PhD student in the Department of English at Miami University, Ohio. Her research interests include digital public rhetorics, feminist rhetorics, and affect theories. She is experienced in working with second-language learners and writers across the curriculum.

Kristi McDuffie is director of the Rhetoric Program at the University of Illinois at Urbana-Champaign, where she manages a first-year writing program that serves around 4,000 students per year taught by more than sixty-five instructors. In this role as writing program administrator, she edited, produced, and composed a large portion of an in-house textbook, *I Write: A Writing Guide for the Undergraduate Rhetoric Program at the University of Illinois*. She teaches composition theory and pedagogy, digital rhetoric, and first-year writing. Her research interests center on the intersections of digital writing, rhetorical theory, and social justice; her recent projects and publications investigate hashtag feminism, citizenship rhetorics, and internet research methods. She is also a section editor of PraxisWiki at *Kairos: A Journal of Rhetoric, Technology, and Pedagogy*, where she has worked with authors to develop, edit, and publish dozens of pieces of digital scholarship over the past six years. She was the recipient of the 2021 University of Illinois Chancellor's Academic Professional Award.

Megan McIntyre is assistant professor and director of the Program in Rhetoric and Composition at the University of Arkansas. Megan's research focuses on anti-racist writing programs, postpedagogy, and social media. You can find some of her recent work in the *Journal of Multimodal Rhetorics, Peitho, Academic Labor, Present Tense,* and *WPA: Writing Program Administration*'s special issue on Black Lives Matter and anti-racist projects in writing program administration.

Sean Milligan received his PhD in English from Wayne State University and is a lecturer in the Department of Liberal Arts at Kettering University. He researches visual rhetoric and digital culture. He has presented his work at Rhetoric Society of America, the Cultural Rhetorics Conference, and the Watson Conference.

Avishek Ray teaches at the National Institutes of Technology Silchar. He is the author of *The Vagabond in the South Asian Imagination: Representation, Agency and Resilience* (Routledge, 2022) and co-editor of *Nation, Nationalism, and the Public Sphere: Religious Politics in India* (SAGE, 2020). His research appears in *South Asia: Journal of South Asian Studies, Contemporary South Asia, Journal of Literary Studies, Inter-Asia Cultural Studies, Multicultural Education Review,* and *Continuum: Journal of Media and Cultural Studies,* among others. He has held research fellowships at the University of Edinburgh (UK), Purdue University Library (USA), Centre for Advanced Study, Sofia (Bulgaria), Mahidol University (Thailand), and Pavia University (Italy).

Sarah Riddick is assistant professor of professional communication at Worcester Polytechnic Institute, where she teaches courses on social media communication and visual rhetoric. Her research examines digital rhetoric and writing, online audiences, social media, and rhetorical methods. Some of her recent work can be found in *Computers and Composition, Journal of Multimodal Rhetorics,* and *Rhetoric Review.*

Stephanie Vie is associate dean of the Outreach College and professor of English at the University of Hawaii at Mānoa. She is co-editor of *Social Writing/Social Media: Publics, Presentations, and Pedagogies;* and her scholarship has been published in numerous journals such as *Computers and Composition, Technical Communication Quarterly, Kairos,* and *First Monday.* She is the 2016 recipient of the Charles Moran Award for Distinguished Contributions to the Field and the 2018 winner of the 7C Committee Technology Innovator Award. She tweets at @digirhet.

Erin B. Waggoner (PhD, University of Connecticut) is assistant professor of communication studies at Longwood University, where she teaches various media, communication, and digital editing courses. Her academic interests include the intersections of media, representation, and identity. She identifies as a media scholar who often flirts with interpersonal communication studies. Her work can be found in *Journal of Homosexuality, Continuum,* and *Popular Culture Studies Journal.*

Holly M. Wells is associate professor of English at East Stroudsburg University. Her research focuses on visual rhetoric and gender in digital media. Recent publications include *Reclaiming the Tomboy: The Body, Representation, and Identity* (coeditor), as well as works in *Journal of Excellence in College Teaching, Comic Connections: Building Character and Theme,* and *Learning, Design, and Technology.*

William I. Wolff is associate professor of the Department of Communication and Digital Media at Saint Joseph's University, where he teaches courses on social media analytics, participatory culture, and digital storytelling. His work has appeared in *Computers and Composition, Kairos: A Journal of Rhetoric, Technology, and Pedagogy, Technical Communication Quarterly,* and *Transformative Works and Cultures.*

www.ingramcontent.com/pod-product-compliance
Lightning Source LLC
Chambersburg PA
CBHW071230070526
44583CB00017B/2123